SOCIAL THEORY OF THE
SCOTTISH ENLIGHTENMENT

Social Theory of the Scottish Enlightenment

Christopher J. Berry

Edinburgh University Press

Dedication
To all those Politics Honours students at Glasgow
who opted for the Scottish Enlightenment

© Christopher J. Berry, 1997

Reprinted 2001

Edinburgh University Press
22 George Square, Edinburgh

Transferred to digital print 2008

Typeset in Monotype Ehrhardt
by Carnegie Publishing, 18 Maynard St, Preston and
printed and bound in Great Britain by
CPI Antony Rowe, Eastbourne

A CIP record for this book is available from the British Library

ISBN 0-7486-0864-8

Contents

Preface

When asked the standard academics' question, '... and what are you working on?'
I replied, 'I'm writing a "new Bryson"'. I was alluding to Gladys Bryson's *Man
and Society: the Scottish Inquiry of the Eighteenth Century*. This book was published
in 1945 and has remained the only general book on the social thought of the
Scottish Enlightenment. But this is not because the topic has remained moribund.
On the contrary, interest has burgeoned and at an increasing rate of productivity.
While Bryson's book is still not redundant, this increased interest, coupled with
the fact that inevitably foci shift and scholarship accumulates, makes another
overview opportune. This book attempts that task.

As an 'overview' it is designedly a synoptic volume rather than a detailed
monograph on some particular theme. Any synopsis presumes judgements as to
what is important but, consistent with that presumption and thus also with my
offering a reading of my own, I am consciously taking stock. While I hope that
specialists will find something of value, my main target audience is the less specialist
reader – students as well as academics. In line with this, I've thought it appropriate
to confine my exposition to printed sources and not quarry the rich seams of
unpublished material. (I break this rule on a couple of occasions in some notes
where the material is particularly perspicuous and where it has already been quoted
in academic commentary.)

A Preface justifies its existence by enabling the author to set out his or her stall
and attempt (often in vain) to forestall some predicted criticisms. Nothing if not
conventional I want to use it similarly. The best place to begin is the beginning.
My title comes in two parts and each requires a gloss. By 'Scottish Enlightenment'
I do not mean to be making any substantial point. There has been considerable
debate as to what the term signifies – which I touch on in Chapter 8 – but I have
decided that to make that an 'issue' would ill serve my purposes. In the broadest
of senses I am using the term to refer to the intellectual literature written in
Scotland between approximately 1740 (the date of the third volume of Hume's
Treatise of Human Nature) and 1790 (the date of the sixth and final edition of
Smith's *Theory of Moral Sentiments*) with the third quarter of the century repre-
senting its core. Of course there is an element of arbitrariness about my parameters,
and I do discuss works written before 1740, but since there is no agreed definition
then it would court unnecessary controversy to insist on a hard and fast definition
of my own.

The phrase 'social theory' in my title is indicative rather than definitive. I can
best outline its scope by stating what I take it to exclude as well as include. I am
(relatively speaking) excluding *philosophical* issues in the narrow sense. What this
means in practice is that, with the exception of his treatment of causality (see

Chapter 3 (Biii)), Hume's arguments in *Treatise* Books I and II will not be covered. This also means that Reid and the 'Common Sense' reaction to Hume will not be discussed. I also exclude *scientific* topics. I do not examine the theories or experimental work of eminent figures like Black, Cullen, Hunter or Maclaurin. However, I do discuss the importance of 'science' in shaping the outlook and agenda of the Scots' social thought (see especially Chapter 3). Somewhat similarly though I discuss their artistic and literary theorising (Chapter 7 (C)), I do not examine the poetry penned, the plays performed, the pictures painted or the buildings built. Also excluded is any extensive treatment of the social, economic, political and cultural setting. I do provide an initial 'scene-setting' discussion of these factors (Chapter 1 (B)). This book, therefore, does not seek to emulate Anand Chitnis' valuable *The Scottish Enlightenment* (1976), which he explicitly sub-titles 'A Social History'. Rather, it deals almost exclusively with 'intellectual' matters as the phrase 'social theory' suggests.

What the book includes under the label 'social' is the historical theorising, the political and economic writings, the moral philosophy and the more generally pervasive concern of the Scots with 'cultural' issues. These hang together in their thought, and my aim in Chapters 2 to 7 is to explore this coherence. Some additional comments on this exploration are in order.

The book is organised thematically but these themes do not exist in hermetical isolation one from another, and there is, therefore, considerable cross-referencing. The very rationale of the book supposes the appropriateness of talking of 'Scottish' theory rather than only of Hume's or Smith's or ... (It is worth adding parenthetically that just as my treatment of Hume's *Treatise* is selective so, too, do I not claim to supply a comprehensive examination of the other great book of this time and place, Smith's *Wealth of Nations*, I focus on the early chapters of Book 1, and Books 3 and 5.) Given that it is the theory of the Scots in general that is under consideration, then it is a matter of some moment to identify and demonstrate where particular arguments are echoed, and, on these occasions, this requires the provision of more than one citation or quotation – duplication is itself the point.

While the generalising term 'the Scots' can justifiably be used, they are, of course, not homogeneous; there are particular differences. Some of these are chronological (when Hutcheson died in 1746, Millar was only eleven years old), some are institutional (the Aberdeen Enlightenment is not full square with that of Edinburgh) and some intellectual (Monboddo and most of the rest). In acknowledgement of this, but in line with the book's thematic identity, I do cite differences where appropriate.

As I explore these themes, I focus on the primary sources themselves. The notes indicate relevant secondary literature, but I do not engage (save by implication from what I choose to emphasise or downplay) in the scholarly debates. I have, however, thought it worth while to canvass the various interpretations given, and reasons why the Scots' social theory has been valued, in a separate concluding chapter. Questions of methodology in the history of ideas have taken on a life of their own in recent years but I have quite deliberately side-stepped them in order to avoid becoming embroiled in disputes which are peripheral to my concerns. To speak boldly, the guiding aim in my exploration is to attend to the issues that the Scots themselves can be seen as addressing in their writings. These writings, by and large, tackled 'big' themes and ideas ('the history of mankind'; 'the wealth of nations'; the nature of 'civilisation') and were presented as contributions to debates of a general and wide-ranging character and not as engagements in parochial affairs. I have largely followed that presentational bias.

Prefaces also serve a dues-paying function. I first began work in this area at the London School of Economics in the heady days of the late sixties under the supervision of Donald MacRae and (initially) Ken Minogue. This gives me an opportunity to record publicly an appreciation of their supportive steerage. I kept the interest in the Scots alive in the congenial atmosphere of Glasgow by teaching an Honours course on the Scottish Enlightenment. The shape and emphases of this book derive so much from the experience of teaching that course that I dedicate it to all those students who took it (and opted to do so on the graveyard shift of Friday afternoons). As I produced drafts of the various chapters, I sent them off to Roger Emerson, whose full and speedy comments demonstrated not only his great expertise but also the highest standards of academic co-operation. My debt to him defies repayment. For some helpful observations I am also grateful to Colin Kidd, who read at a later stage a draft of the whole.

Christopher J. Berry
Glasgow

Abbreviations

By author, the following abbreviations of frequently cited works (and editions used) are inserted in parentheses in the text.

BLAIR
LRB   *Lectures on Rhetoric and Belles Lettres* (1783), in one volume 1838.
DUNBAR
EHM   *Essays on the History of Mankind in Rude and Cultivated Ages*, 2nd edn, 1781.

FERGUSON
ECS   *An Essay on the History of Civil Society* (1767), ed. D. Forbes, 1966.
IMP   *Institutes of Moral Philosophy* (1769), 3rd edn, 1785.
PMPS   *Principles of Moral and Political Science* (1792), 2 vols. repr. New York, 1973
Rom   *The History of the Progress and Termination of the Roman Republic* (1783), 5 vols.

GREGORY
CV   *A Comparative View of the State and Faculties of Man with those of the Animal World* (1765), in *Works* vol. 2, 1788.

HUME
Abs   *An Abstract of a Treatise of Human Nature* (1740), ed. C. Hendel, 1955.
DNR   *Dialogues concerning Natural Religion* (1779), in *Hume on Religion*, ed. R. Wollheim, 1963.
E   *Essays: Moral, Political and Literary* (1779), ed. E. Miller, 1987.
AS   Of the Rise and Progress of the Arts and Sciences (1742).
CL   Of Civil Liberty (1741: original title, Of Liberty and Despotism).
Com   Of Commerce (1752).
FPG   Of the First Principles of Government (1741).
IPC   Idea of a Perfect Commonwealth (1752).
LP   Of the Liberty of the Press (1741).
Mon   Of Money (1752).
NC   Of National Characters (1748).
OC   Of the Original Contract (1748).
OG   Of the Origin of Government (1774: publ. 1777).
PAN   Of the Populousness of Ancient Nations (1752).
PC   Of Public Credit (1754).
PD   Of Polygamy and Divorces (1742).
PG   Of Parties in General (1741).
PrS   Of the Protestant Succession (1752).
RA   Of Refinement in the Arts (1752: original title, Of Luxury).
SE   Of Superstition and Enthusiasm (1741).

ST	Of the Standard of Taste (1757).
Sui	Of Suicide (publ. 1777).
EPM	*An Enquiry concerning the Principles of Morals* (1751), eds. L. Selby-Bigge & P. Nidditch, 1975.
EHU	*An Enquiry concerning Human Understanding* (1748), eds. L. Selby-Bigge & P. Nidditch, 1975.
HE	*The History of England* (1786), 3 vols., 1894.
Letts	*The Letters of David Hume*, ed. J. Greig, 2 vols., 1932.
NHR	*The Natural History of Religion* (1757), in *Hume on Religion*, ed. R. Wollheim, 1963.
THN	*A Treatise of Human Nature* (1739/40), ed. L. Selby-Bigge, 1888.

HUTCHESON

SIMP	*A Short Introduction to Moral Philosophy* (1747), repr. Hildesheim, 1969.
PWD	*Philosophical Writings*, ed. R. Downie, 1994.

KAMES

EC	*The Elements of Criticism* (1762), 9th edn, 2 vols., 1817.
ELS	*Elucidations respecting the Common and Statute Law of Scotland* 1778.
HLT	*Historical Law Tracts* (1758), 3rd edn, 1776.
PMNR	*Essays on the Principles of Morality and Natural Religion* (1751), 3rd edn (corrected and improved), 1779.
SHM	*Sketches of the History of Man* (1774), 3rd edn, 2 vols., 1779.

MILLAR

HV	*An Historical View of the English Government* (1803), 4 vols., 1812.
HV(L)	*Ibid.* (extracts) repr. in *John Millar of Glasgow*, W. Lehmann, 1960.
OR	*The Origin of the Distinction of Ranks* (1779), 3rd edn, repr. in *John Millar of Glasgow*, W. Lehmann, 1960.

MONBODDO

OPL	*Of the Origin and Progress of Language*, 6 vols., 1773–92.
AM	*Antient Metaphysics*, 6 vols., 1779–99.

MONTESQUIEU

SL	*The Spirit of the Laws* (1748), tr. A. Cohler et al., 1989.

REID

AP	*Essays on the Active Powers of the Human Mind* (1788), in *Works*, ed. W. Hamilton, in one volume, 1846.
IP	*Essays on the Intellectual Powers of Man* (1785), in *Works*, ed. W. Hamilton, in one volume, 1846.

ROBERTSON

HAm	*History of America* (1777), in *Works*, ed. D. Stewart, in one volume, 1840.
HSc	*History of Scotland* (1759), in *Works*, ed. D. Stewart, in one volume, 1840.
India	*An Historical Disquisition concerning Ancient India* (1791), in *Works*, ed. D. Stewart, in one volume, 1840.
VPE	*A View of the Progress of Society in Europe* (1769), in *Works*, ed. D. Stewart, in one volume, 1840.

SMITH

Corr	*Correspondence of Adam Smith*, eds. E. Mossner and I. Ross, 1987.

EPS   *Essays on Philosophical Subjects* (1795), ed. W. Wightman, 1982.
LRBL   *Lectures on Rhetoric and Belles Lettres*, ed. J. Bryce, 1985.
LJ   *Lectures on Jurisprudence*, eds. R. Meek, D. Raphael and P. Stein, 1982.
TMS   *The Theory of Moral Sentiments* (1759, 1st edn), eds. A. Macfie and
         D. Raphael, 1982.
WN   *An Inquiry into the Nature and Causes of the Wealth of Nations* (1776), ed.
         R. Campbell and A. Skinner, 1981.

STEUART
PPE   *An Inquiry into the Principles of Political Oeconomy* (1767), 2 vols. ed.
         A. Skinner, 1966.

STUART
Diss   *Historical Dissertation concerning the Antiquity of the English Constitution*,
         1768.
PLS   *Observations concerning the Public Law and the Constitutional History of
         Scotland*, 1779.
VSE   *A View of Society in Europe in its Progress from Rudeness to Refinement*
         (1792), 2nd edn, repr. Bristol, 1995.

ALSO
SB   *British Moralists* (1897), ed. L. Selby-Bigge, 2 vols. in one, 1964.

The Enlightenment and Scotland

This opening chapter performs the customary task of introduction. A lot of ground is traversed quickly but the necessary speed is only achieved by treading lightly. In section A, I outline the general intellectual context by providing an overview of the broad movement known as the 'Enlightenment' while in section B I outline some salient aspects of the Scottish environment. These outlines are modest in both design and execution. They provide some information to help fill in the background to the Scots' social theory. Of course, this provision is not neutral; any process of selection necessarily draws attention to some aspects rather than others. Nevertheless, the information is (so to speak) passive. In so far as it is possible I am avoiding the thicket of problems that are involved not only in relating social circumstances to ideas but ideas to ideas.

A: The Enlightenment

The term 'Enlightenment' is a convenient piece of intellectual short-hand that serves to summarise a set of ideas. Like all summaries there is room for dispute as to what is the core, and therefore has to be included, and what peripheral, and therefore excludable. It follows from this that the stability of the core cannot be taken for granted. Nevertheless, there has to be the possibility of a 'core', else the term itself is purely fictional – there needs to be some minimal identity. Peter Gay (1967: 4) uses the analogy of the family to this end. A family is a recognisable entity (both internally and externally), but along with its ties and bonds go squabbles and differences. The attractiveness of the analogy is that it enables the Scots to be linked to the wider movement while allowing them to be differentiated. One justified criticism of Gay's account is that it over-emphasises the French experience (cf. e.g. Ford 1968, Darnton 1971, Leith 1971). This is but another way of saying that his 'core' marginalises what others think to be central elements and vice versa. Certainly if the Enlightenment is too closely identified with an 'anti-establishment' posture then much about the Scottish branch of the family can look only distantly related.

Gay openly admits that the familial analogy is not his own but was one used by contemporaries. This itself is a good indicator of a core ingredient. The Enlightenment was a self-conscious movement. The participants – referred to variously as *philosophes*, the *Aufklärer* and the literati – were by definition members of the educated stratum of society. In Scotland as elsewhere, many were professionals, especially lawyers, doctors and university professors, although for the last of these the nearest equivalent, in England, were teachers in Dissenting Academies. In France, with one or two exceptions, they were either professional men of letters or of independent means. As participants they came from the full extent of the western world – from Aberdeen in the north to Naples in the south, from St Petersburg in the east to Philadelphia in the west (cf. Venturi 1971: Ch. 5, Gusdorf 1971: Pt. I; Porter & Teich 1981).

They were genuine participants in that they saw themselves as engaged in the same debates. Moreover, this engagement was not a parochial affair but spread across the world of letters. Two Scottish examples of this phenomenon are the impact of Rousseau's *Discourse on Inequality* on Smith or Monboddo or Dunbar and Kant's admission that it was reading Hume that awoke him from his dogmatic slumber. Kant's case bears out the further fact that writings were quickly translated and disseminated. Although the *Wealth of Nations* (1776) was clearly an exceptional work it was translated into Danish, French (twice) and German (twice) all before Smith's death in 1790 (Campbell & Skinner, 1985: 168). There were also personal and institutional links. Hume befriended Rousseau and brought him to Britain and Robertson was a member of the Royal Academy of Madrid. A striking non-Scottish example is the French philosopher and mathematician D'Alembert, who was a member of the Royal Academy of Science of Prussia, the Royal Society of London, the Royal Literary Academy of Sweden and the Institute of Bologna (Cranston 1991: 128).

If we turn to the core concerns of these self-conscious intellectuals then their imagery of 'light' provides the best guide. They thought of themselves as living in and promoting *un siècle des lumières* (cf. Gusdorf 1971: Pt. 3 Ch. 1). This implied that earlier times were comparatively benighted. In less metaphorical terms this contrast between light and dark is the contrast between knowledge, reason or science and ignorance, prejudice and superstition. Hence any institutions such as slavery, torture, witchcraft or religious persecution that still existed were to be opposed as relics, as creatures of the night. The radiance of reason and the appliance of science would likewise clear away the light-blocking debris of poverty, disease and crime (Beccaria's *On Crimes and Punishments* (1764), for example, was an international best-seller with its passionate attack on the death-penalty).

In a short essay 'What is Enlightenment?' (1784) Kant answers his own question by saying that it is 'dare to know!' The motto of Enlightenment is 'have the courage to use your own reason' (1963: 3). Kant stresses that 'enlightenment' is an escape from the direction or control of another and that it requires determination or resolution to take control of one's destiny. To fail to make this escape is to remain in the dark. However, the escape is not a private individual task but a public one that requires freedom. What is crucial to the attainment of enlightenment is 'the public use of one's reason' and that 'must always be free' (5). And, as Kant makes clear, this extends to religion; it cannot be exempted from the operation of this freedom, the light of reason must shine forth there, too.

While Kant is perhaps the most austerely intellectual of all the Enlightenment thinkers it was a central plank in his philosophy that theory and practice be wedded not divorced. (He wrote an essay on this very theme arguing that this separation causes great damage (1949: 414).) Nowhere is this unity better exemplified than in the *Encyclopedia or Rational Dictionary of Sciences, Arts and Professions*. This is one of the key products of the Enlightenment. Under the general editorship of Diderot, seventeen large volumes were published between 1751 and 1765 and four more between 1776 and 1780, accompanying these were twelve volumes of plates (cf. Lough 1971).

A revealing insight into this emblematic project can be gained from the *Preliminary Discourse* (1751) written by D'Alembert. This discourse has been called the best resumé of the spirit of the eighteenth century (Schwab's Introduction 1963: xi). Somewhat like Kant was later to argue, D'Alembert too, but in a blunter fashion, emphasises the link between enlightenment and liberty while decrying the ignorance and superstition of earlier ages (in Schwab (ed.) 1963: 62). He admits that, as a consequence, there is a tendency to belittle earlier thinkers and counsels that this should not be carried to excess. In the second part of his *Preliminary Discourse* he identifies four significant predecessors, who 'prepared from afar the light which gradually by imperceptible degrees would illuminate the world' (74). His choice of the quartet is instructive and we shall benefit from it, but it is also strategic. There are some key omissions. The most notable of these is Pierre Bayle, whose own *Historical and Critical Dictionary* (1697) was a significant precursor of the *Encyclopedia* itself.[1]

Francis Bacon is the first of D'Alembert's quartet. Continuing the dominant metaphor he describes Bacon as 'born in the depths of the most profound night' (74). Bacon's major advance was to regard philosophy as knowledge that should contribute to improving the human lot. This practical, utilitarian bent is a key feature of the Enlightenment (Chapter 3 will deal with its presence in the Scots). D'Alembert also points out Bacon's hostility to arid intellectual systems, with late medieval Scholasticism, which clung to an Aristotelian framework, the particular target. Bacon's own alternative schema had a direct influence on the organisation of the *Encyclopedia* itself in its acceptance of the three-fold division of history, philosophy and poetry corresponding respectively to the three faculties of memory, reason and imagination. (D'Alembert did, however, take pains to point out differences – see his *Observations on Bacon's Division of the Sciences* (in D'Alembert/ Schwab: 159–64).)

Second in line is Descartes, who 'opened the way for us' (78). His critical method showed how to 'throw off the yoke of scholasticism, of opinion, of authority' (80). He himself received no benefit, but posterity has; even though, as D'Alembert admits, one consequence of his legacy was for his heirs to assail much of his own positive philosophy. (That the Enlightenment was in fact deeply Cartesian is argued by a number of scholars (e.g. Vartanian 1952, Frankel 1948, Crocker 1963).) In the vanguard of this assault were the two remaining members of the quartet – the English philosophers Newton and Locke.

Newton is *the* hero of the Enlightenment. According to D'Alembert he gave to science the 'form which it is apparently to keep' (81). This accolade was repeatedly bestowed throughout the world of letters. To speak generally, Newton's achievement was to encompass within one comprehensive schema an explanation, derived from a few simple principles (laws of motion plus gravity), of the range of natural phenomena, from the orbit of the planets to apples falling from trees. Scots were at the forefront in adopting Newton's framework. The acceptance of his 'system' was slower elsewhere, and in France, despite Voltaire's endorsements, there was considerable debate as to whether Newton's or Descartes' 'celestial mechanics' was correct. Newton won out, and an important factor in his success was that he was proved right. One such proof, and this captures much of the spirit of the Enlightenment, was an expedition in 1735 to Lapland led by the Frenchman Maupertuis but sponsored by the Berlin Academy (cf. Hankins 1985: 38–9). According to Newton the earth was not, contrary to Descartes, elongated at the poles and flat at the equator but flatter around the poles (was a turnip not a lemon cf. Hall 1970: 319). Maupertuis' expedition took measurements and these vindicated Newton.[2]

Newton also made a fateful methodological prediction. In the Preface to his *Optics* (1704) he declared that the method of natural philosophy or science would when perfected enlarge the bounds of moral philosophy (that is, of social science). This inspired many attempts to apply Newton to the moral world (human nature and society). As we shall later discuss in some detail (Chapter 3), this was especially true of the Scottish Enlightenment. One hallmark of Newton's status is that to liken someone's work to his was to pay it the highest possible compliment. For example, John Millar declared Smith to be the 'Newton of political economy' because he had discovered the principles of commerce (*HV*: II 429–30n./*HVL*: 363n.). Other examples include Kant calling Rousseau the 'Newton' of the moral world due to the central unifying role given to the 'will', while Rousseau's musicological competitor Rameau's work on the principles of harmony resulted in him being likened to Newton.

Of John Locke, the final member of his quartet, D'Alembert said 'he created metaphysics almost as Newton had created physics' (83). By 'metaphysics' here D'Alembert means 'the experimental physics of the soul' (84). This is what it ought to be, not the grand schemes and systems of medieval philosophy or of moderns like Spinoza, Malebranche or even Descartes. D'Alembert, following Condillac (cf. Knight 1968: 60), distinguished between the *esprit de système* and the *esprit systématique* (D'Alembert/Schwab: 22–3). The former 'flatter(s) the imagination' (94) while the latter corresponds rather to a Newtonian synthesis – the reduction of complexity to a few simple principles.

Locke's key work is his *Essay concerning Human Understanding* (1689). In his 'Epistle to the Reader' prefaced to the book, Locke called himself an 'underlabourer' (1854: II 118). There were two reasons why. First, he realised he was not a 'master-builder', like the 'incomparable' Newton or Huyghens or Boyle (121). That is to say, he was aware not only that he was unable to practise 'science' (the mathematics was beyond him) but also that, at that time, it represented the 'cutting-edge' of intellectual progress. His second reason was to draw something positive from this. His task, as he saw it, was to remove 'some of the rubbish that lies in the way of knowledge' (121).

Central to this 'rubbish' was the doctrine of innate ideas or the argument that the mind contained within it certain universal truths or primary ideas. Locke denied that this was the case. Rather the infant's mind was a 'white paper' (205) or 'empty cabinet' (142). If we now ask, where do our ideas come from? Locke answers 'from experience, in that all knowledge is founded, from that it ultimately derives itself' (205). This bold and apparently uncomplicated assertion of empiricism establishes the parameters for the bulk of Enlightenment thinking. There are two notable exceptions. Kant towards the end of the century is forced to re-think epistemology in order to salvage knowledge from scepticism and Reid, in the mid-century, is forced to attack the Lockean 'way of ideas' in the name of 'common sense'. Both Kant and Reid were galvanised into action by Hume.

Hume, while exceptional in his thoroughness, was typical of the generation after Locke as it set to work to tidy up his account. A particularly potent development was to emphasise that if all knowledge comes from experience, then it means all knowledge is gained by means of the senses. All mental 'actions' like judgements and reflections, which Locke had distinguished from sensation, were in fact only transformations of sensation. Condillac used the example of a statue to dramatise the issue. The statue was given each of the five senses in turn and at the completion of this task it was declared to possess the full range of human mental ability (see *A Treatise on Sensation* [1749]). To much the same end, if from a Cartesian rather than Lockean starting-point and more iconoclastic agenda, La Mettrie wrote a book entitled *Man a Machine* (1748).

The established authorities quickly saw the dangers in this 'sensationalism'; it left no room for the soul. Strictly there should be no threat since the soul, being 'immaterial', could not be 'disproved' by material facts about the 'body'. Yet medical theory (La Mettrie was a doctor) increasingly occupied itself with the relation between the two (cf. McManners 1985: 150–1) – as we will see in Chapter 4 this spilt over into the debate on 'climatic' influence. Beyond these confines the worry was more 'political'. An attack on the soul was an attack on the social order, that is, an attack on the systems of control (the threat of eternity in hell) and on the role of the clergy, as 'doctors of the soul', in upholding that order. There was general agreement that a belief in an after-life was a useful prop in that way;[3] it was the privileged place of the priesthood that was objectionable. Here is the setting for a basic core element in the Enlightenment – the battle between the philosopher and the cleric. This is not the same as non-believers against believers. With a few exceptions, the common Enlightenment view was Deist. That is, the very orderliness of the Newtonian cosmos made the attribution of Design, and thence of a Designer, reasonable (and for Newton himself indispensable[4]). Although most strident in France, it was a general characteristic of the Enlightenment that it saw itself as waging war against unreasonable religion or superstition. This self-perception is captured in Voltaire's battle-cry *'écrasez l'infâme'*. Here, even if in softer tones, the Scots were at one with Voltaire (see Chapter 7 (B)).

Superstitions were the product of credulous ignorance, flourishing like mushrooms in dark places away from light. Since the social power of priests rested on keeping the bulk of the population in the dark, they had an interest in blocking out the light of reason. However, if the 'white paper' was inscribed by agents of reason not unreason then enlightenment was possible. In this way Lockean epistemology laid the foundations for an essentially optimistic philosophy. To mould experience is to mould human character. False ideas (like superstitions) are the product of faulty experience (like the fraudulent teachings of priests), but sound ideas can be produced by sound experience. As Bacon had said, knowledge of causes is power (see Chapter 3). Informed by the findings of science it becomes possible to set humans on the right track. The more rational society becomes then the more rational will be the experience that it passes on to the next generation.

Given in this way the pivotal role played by the right transmission of knowledge then 'education' is clearly vital. Helvetius put the case simply and starkly, 'education makes us what we are' (*On Man* [1773] tr. II, 405). Once again Locke had set the scene with his tract *Some Thoughts concerning Education* (1693). Much of the popularity of discourses on education in the form of handbooks – a genre in which some Scots participated [5] – is doubtless due to practical and cultural 'needs'. The *Encyclopedia* itself is symptomatic of this as are other numerous enterprises like Chambers' *Cyclopedia* (identified by Diderot himself as a precursor of his own endeavour). But beyond this practical aspect is a theoretical dimension. The power that education, in a broad sense, possesses (the 'malleability of man' as Passmore (1971) called it) was a crucial premise in the belief in progress (cf. Vereker (1967), Frankel (1948), Sampson (1956)).

The most poignant of the accounts of 'progress' was Condorcet's. Condorcet was a brilliant mathematician (his 'paradox' of circulating majorities is still cited in studies of electoral systems). More than a theorist he was also an important independent voice in the Revolution. But his independence proved his downfall. Under sentence of death and in hiding before committing suicide, he wrote his tract *Sketch of the Progress of the Human Mind* (1795) (cf. Manuel 1962, Baker 1975). In this work he divided history into ten epochs – nine lay in the past and all bore the stigmata of ignorance and the superstitious connivance of priests. There was, however, one redeeming feature – the growth of knowledge, with Newton again being heaped with praise. The tenth epoch of the future will, he believes, see the abolition of inequality between nations, the progress of equality within nations (including that between the sexes) and, with the extirpation of vice and ignorance, the true perfection of mankind. In short, 'the time will therefore come when the sun will shine only on free men who know no other master but their reason' (tr. 179).

The very simplicity of Condorcet's scheme makes it atypical but there were others of recognisably the same stamp (Condorcet himself identifies Turgot, Price and Priestley as precursors). Rousseau famously made his name by denying that progress had improved the lot of mankind (see his *First* (1750) and *Second Discourses* (1755)). Of course what made Rousseau famous was precisely the fact that he was going against the flow. The Scots, for their part, are believers in progress. This belief required a theory of history and much of the Scots' social theory was in this way historical (see Chapters 3 and 5). In this they were part of the Enlightenment mainstream. The Enlightenment's attitude to the past has come in for heavy criticism, for being in effect 'unhistorical'. (Collingwood (1946) is a classic statement but see also, for example, Stromberg (1951), White (1973).) Others have been more sympathetic, seeing in this period a new conception of history as universalist, including all of humanity and all facets of humanity in its scope (cf. e.g. Dilthey (1927), Barraclough (1962), Trevor-Roper (1963)).

In the Scots this twin-track universalism was captured in the idea of 'civilisation'. While they do maintain that it has advanced across a wide front and that the growth of knowledge is indeed a crucial ingredient in this advance, they are less confident than the French, or Englishmen like Priestley, that it is automatic and necessarily always an improvement. An important factor accounting for this less than whole-hearted approach is that the Scots attach less weight to reason (cf. Forbes 1954). As we will see one of the persistent strains in their social theory is an awareness of the recalcitrance, the 'stickiness', of institutions and the fact, as they see it, that habit and custom are more decisive in shaping behaviour than reason.

In heeding the role of custom the Scots are demonstrating their debt to Montesquieu. Montesquieu's *Spirit of the Laws* (1748) has been called the most influential book in the eighteenth century (Gay 1970: 325) and the Scots are fulsome in their praise. Ferguson goes so far as to proclaim, 'when I recollect what the President Montesquieu has written I am at a loss to tell why I should treat of human affairs' (*ECS*: 65). The *Spirit of the Laws* is a large rambling book but its key theme is announced in the Preface, where he declares that amid the great variety of political systems there are some basic explanatory principles (*SL*: xliii). Montesquieu shows an acute awareness of the diversity of social systems, and he brings forward a range of factors to explain this divergence – including climate, which, as we will discuss in Chapter 4, is one area where the Scots disagreed with him. Montesquieu himself thinks these factors come together to constitute a 'general spirit' (310). In Section B, I attempt something along the same lines for eighteenth-century Scotland, but before that a further aspect of Montesquieu's work is worth developing.

It is possible to detect inside the ramshackle structure of the *Spirit of the Laws* the presence of (at least) two sets of vocabulary. He speaks the language of natural law and gives voice to the idiom of republicanism. Speaking generally, the former stems ultimately from the systems of Roman jurisprudence. In governing the empire there was a need to systematise and codify the various local laws. This legalism penetrated the Church and then entered either directly or indirectly the newly established university curricula. The decisive developments in jurisprudential thinking came in early modern Europe. The causes of these developments are manifold but include the post-Reformation collapse of Christendom and the discovery and colonisation of the 'New World'. The effect of these causes was the formulation of principles of law to encompass the new realities of (frequently warring) sovereign states. Among the most notable of these formulations were those of Grotius (*On the Law of War and Peace* [1625]) and Pufendorf (*On the*

Law of Nature and Nations [1672]). The latter was especially influential, obtaining a central place in University curricula; Scotland not excepted. Against this backdrop when Enlightenment thinkers criticised institutions they frequently did so invoking the claims of 'justice' (see e.g. Diderot (1992)). The very fact that Montesquieu entitled his book the 'Spirit of the *Laws*' is itself testament to the importance of this legal framework (see *SL*: Bk I).⁶

But for all its obvious importance, 'social' thinking was never entirely encompassed within talk of law and rights. An equally venerable vocabulary, with its roots in Aristotle, spoke of virtue and the political or civic life as the authentic expression of human nature. While the language of law suited empires, these latter terms accommodated themselves more easily to republican self-rule. This is of course a sweeping generalisation but the highpoints of republican rhetoric coincided with the flowering of independent city-states in Renaissance Italy, the commonwealth of seventeenth-century England and in the Enlightenment itself in the new American republic. In each of these cases the model was again Rome. But Rome as a republic and before it was 'corrupted' (a key term of art) and succumbed to imperial rule. What gave this tradition an added edge in the eighteenth century was its sensitivity to commerce, which, because of its preoccupation with private gain, it tended to regard as subversive of the commitment to the 'public weal'. That is to say it had in its lexicon the terminology and concepts to respond to the economic changes being experienced as the eighteenth century progressed. The *Spirit of the Laws* within its pages contained such a lexicon along with a treasure trove of examples of the relationship between political forms and economic practices (see *SL*: Bks 20–2).⁷

Montesquieu is not alone in enveloping these two vocabularies. Rousseau, for example, is both a contractarian (a central jurisprudential concept) and an ardent republican. It is accordingly no special attribute of the social theory of the Scottish Enlightenment that it, too, can be seen as engaging with both the language of law and of virtue. Nonetheless it is possible to see in its theory an especially well-articulated account of that engagement (see Chapter 8). That articulacy itself is an expression of the 'general spirit' of enlightened Scotland – at once a cause and an effect.

B: Eighteenth-century Scotland

As I will present it, this general spirit has five inter-related components: political and legal arrangements; economic changes; the role played by two key institutions – the Church and the universities; and, finally suffusing the whole, the 'culture' or, in a phrase Hume himself used, the 'spirit of the age' (*E–RA*: 271). Of necessity this presentation can consist only of generalisations and derivative summaries; nuance and qualification will be lost. To attempt something less gross-grained would be beyond the scope of this book. I repeat the earlier point that the aim of this section is to provide general background information to help 'situate' the Scots in time and place.

i) Politics

On the death of Anne in 1714 the throne of England and Scotland passed to George of Hanover. Anne herself had been a daughter of the last Stuart king, James II (and VII), who had effectively been deposed in the Glorious Revolution of 1688. The agent of that deposition was the English Parliament and one consequence of the Revolution was to give Parliament a heightened sense of its own powers. The Scottish Parliament had a similar good opinion of itself. However, circumstances were unpropitious. A succession of bad harvests and the ruinous collapse of the Parliament's chief initiative – the attempt to establish Scotland as a colonial power (the Darien scheme) – together with a trading dispute with the English supplied a backcloth to the Union of the Parliaments in 1707. Whether the Union was necessary, was an act of betrayal by some leading Scots, was the product of English chicanery or just a 'way-out' of immediate pressing difficulties is still a matter of dispute. At the time there was an extensive pamphlet war, which, especially in the contribution of Andrew Fletcher, has been seen by G. E. Davie (1981), for example, as a significant factor in shaping the character of the Enlightenment.

According to the Treaty of Union, Scotland was to send sixteen nobles to the Lords and forty-five (out of a total of 568) to the Commons. This arrangement clearly gave the Scots as Scots little direct political power, but the Treaty very significantly allowed them to retain their own legal system and their own form of church administration and doctrine. This was no mere sop since it kept what was of most immediate concern to most people in local hands. We will examine the Church later but the lawyers can best be treated in this section because it was they who played a key role in administering Scotland throughout the eighteenth century.

Eighteenth-century British politics is the era of patronage par excellence and Scotland was an integral part of the process. After some toing and froing in the years following the Union a fixed pattern emerged (cf. Simpson 1970). The Argyll faction, in exchange for keeping the Scottish peers and MPs on the government's side, was given, subject to circumstances, a free hand to 'govern' Scotland. The form this governance assumed in the shape of patronage over the Church and universities will be covered below. The actual administration was overseen by a 'sub-minister' based in Edinburgh. This role was played by law-lords. The two most conspicuous being Andrew Milton (Lord Justice-Clerk between 1734 and 1748 and then Keeper of the Signet (Murdoch 1980: 12, Shaw 1983: 62)) and Henry Dundas (Lord Advocate and Keeper of the Signet) in the last quarter of the century (see Dwyer & Murdoch 1983).

The salience of lawyers generally was abetted by the fact that the Union had in a perverse way strengthened their role (along with the Kirk) as the embodiment of a distinctively Scottish way of doing things. Unlike English law, Scots law had always had closer links with European/Roman systems; indeed until the eighteenth century its lawyers were educated abroad, especially at the great Dutch universities of Leiden and Utrecht. While, as we noted earlier, the most renowned developers of systematic jurisprudence were continental, the Scots also participated, and some scholars (e.g. MacCormick 1982) have considered Lord Stair's *The Institutes of the Laws of Scotland* (1681) as setting the scene for the Enlightenment. Certainly a legal background is prominent in several of the social theorists – Kames was a law-lord as was Monboddo; Millar was a Professor of Law; Smith and Ferguson lectured on 'law'; and Hume had some legal training.

To pick up the political thread, the members of the Scottish Enlightenment were Hanoverians. This meant more than supporting the current system because that very support signified their opposition to Jacobitism. The Jacobites were the supporters of the Stuart line, and in the first half of the eighteenth century there were regular flare-ups against the new dynasty. The regularity of these suggests that the Hanoverian succession was far from bedded down. The two most significant rebellions were the '15 and the '45. The former had widespread support, tapping into a well of general dissatisfaction with the perceived lack of benefits flowing from the Union. For example, the staff of the two Aberdeen universities (Kings and Marischal Colleges) had to be purged due to their support for the uprising. Although the '45 initially posed a great threat to the British state (the Young Pretender's army penetrated as far south as Derby), it was, within Scotland, poorly supported outside a few Highland clans. This time the Aberdeen universities were loyal, indeed some members took up arms against the rebels (Emerson 1992: 12), while St Andrews elected Cumberland, the victor ('the butcher') of Culloden, as its Chancellor.

After the battle of Culloden, which crushed the rebellion, it was deliberate policy to destroy the political separateness of the Highlands (Youngson 1972: 26). This destruction was the work of several Acts of Parliament. The Annexation Act of 1752 confiscated Jacobite estates and, under the aegis of the Board of Annexed Estates, run by Milton and of which Kames was a member, their rents were used quite deliberately to assimilate Highlanders into Lowland culture.[8] Another consequential measure was the passing of an Act abolishing 'heritable jurisdictions'. These jurisdictions, which gave local clan chiefs rights to administer justice (including the power to punish by death), had been explicitly preserved by the Treaty of Union but were nonetheless overturned on the grounds that it had given these chiefs the power to raise an 'army' from their vassals (Shaw 1983: 169). Adam Smith refers to one of these chiefs (Cameron of Locheil) in the *Wealth of Nations* (*WN*: 416) in the context of an explanation of the emergence of a commercial society. The Scots identified their own (i.e. urban Lowland plus Aberdeen) society as 'commercial'. This apparent sensitivity to the definitive quality of the economy is both a hallmark of their social theory and testimony to the economic changes taking place.

ii) The Economy

One of the motives behind the Union was the need for Scots to gain unrestricted access to English markets. Eventually by about mid-century the Union began to have an economic pay-off and rapid change took place (cf. Devine 1985). The scale and rapidity of this change can be conveyed by reciting a few statistics. Between 1751 and 1801 the population grew by over a quarter. That increase, however, was not evenly distributed; the process is better described as urbanisation since Glasgow's population in that period grew from (roughly) 27,500 to 77,400 and Edinburgh's from 52,250 to 82,500, while Dundee's doubled and Aberdeen's increased by 80 per cent (Lenman 1981: 3). Excluding agriculture, the production of textiles, especially linen, was the chief industry. Here, too, expansion was dramatic with a seven-fold increase in output between the early 1730s and late 1790s (Durie 1979: 158). A similar growth took place in the tobacco trade with the Scottish share of the British trade rising from 10 per cent in 1738 to 52 per cent in 1769 (Smout 1969: 244). This signalled the beginning of the rise of the Glasgow 'tobacco lords' whose mark is left in present-day Glasgow in the guise of street names such as Ingram and Glassford (as well as Virginia).

The development of 'heavier' industry like mining, chemicals and smelting did not take off until the last quarter of the century. These developments required the urbanisation and textile production to have burgeoned sufficiently to generate a demand for their products. War, as ever, was a further stimulus, especially to iron-works like Carron, which was founded in 1765 at the time of the Seven Years War. A supportive infrastructure, both physical and financial, was also needed. Transportation was by horse and boat. While there was a reasonably efficient coach service between Edinburgh and London, cross-country travel was arduous. The biggest fillip to road-building came from military rather economic considerations. In fact because the roads were built to facilitate the movement of troops they did not always follow the routes most favourable to trade (Hamilton 1963: 231). The only way to transport in bulk was by boat and to get from Glasgow to Edinburgh that meant a long and hazardous voyage via the Pentland Firth. A canal linking the Forth and Clyde was started in 1768 and completed in 1790. This was a considerable engineering achievement but clearly took extensive capital funding. Like many such projects (think of the Channel Tunnel) financing was precarious and a lifeline had to be provided in 1784 by funds drawn from the Annexed Estates (Hamilton 1963: 237).

The concomitant of this capital investment was the develoment of a banking system.[9] The Bank of Scotland predated the Union, but the Royal Bank was established in 1727 and the British Linen Company (Bank) in 1746 (another institution in which Milton had a hand (Durie 1979: 115)). There were a host of smaller banks, not all of them viable. One of the problems faced by the shareholders in the Forth–Clyde Canal was the depression in confidence caused by the crash of the Ayr Bank in 1772. So bad was that collapse that a contemporary report (in London) declared that 'all buildings and agriculture improvements' have stopped (quoted in Smout 1969: 247).

'Improvement' is a key term. A society grandly entitled 'The Honourable Society of Improvers' was founded in 1723. This society was established with the practical aim of reforming agricultural practices (Campbell 1982: 11). The 'improving' practices included introducing the 'English Method' (Ramsay 1888: II, 227) via new crops like clover, rotation and fertilising as well as the introduction of new tools and the re-organisation of tenure. Particular landlords set about these tasks systematically. Kames, for example, upon taking control of his wife's estate at Blair Drummond, was one such, and as a good member of the Enlightenment also wrote a handbook with the splendidly evocative title, *The Gentleman Farmer: Being an attempt to improve Agriculture, by subjecting it to the Test of Rational Principles* (1776). (Ramsay remarked that he did a great deal of good though not as much as he meant (II, 229).) The 'Society of Improvers' also aided the development of the linen industry in as much as key members were involved in the foundation of the Board of Trustees for Fisheries and Manufactures (1727). There were in fact many such societies, of which the most prestigious was the 'Select Society' of Edinburgh, which included many of the literati (as they were known) among its membership (cf. Emerson 1973).

As this involvement by the literati suggests, the pace and character of these economic changes was not something that happened 'behind their backs'. A number of commentators (see Chapter 8) have indeed seen in their awareness one of the distinctive features of the Scottish Enlightenment. Certainly their social theory does associate societal differences with different forms of subsistence (see Chapter 5) and the contrast between the Highlands and Lowlands seems almost ready-made for that purpose. We have already noted that Smith cites the case of Cameron of Locheil and elsewhere in the *Wealth of Nations* he uses the Highlands to illustrate the underdevelopment of the division of labour (*WN*: 31). On broadly similar lines the proposal to 'civilise' the Highlands fitted the conception of the uncivilised savage or barbarian. For example, Pennant's description in 1769 of the Highlanders as 'idle and lazy except when employed in the chace . . . and will not exert themselves farther than to get what they deem necessaries' (*Tour* 1774 edn: 117 cf. 193) is echoed by Robertson's description of the Amerinds as 'languid' and setting no value on anything that is 'not the object of some immediate want' (*HAm*: 819).[10] This exploitation of their 'economic' environment should not be oversold. The contrast between Highlands and Lowlands can only play that role if it is asked to do so in the first place. Imputed self-evidence is always a shaky historical assumption. The Scots are *not* primarily 'merely' theorising their own society. It is true that a serious attempt was made to elicit contemporary 'facts' by means of the *Statistical Account* (1790) undertaken on the initiative of Sir John Sinclair. Every parish minister was to supply for their parish the answers to a questionnaire of some 165 items (Mitchison 1962: 124; for an interpretation of the *Account* that sees it as *the* distinctive product of the Scottish Enlightenment, see Withrington 1987). Notwithstanding this endeavour (the 'positivism' of which should not be stressed) the Scots' social theory never left the confines of moral and evaluative enquiry. If nothing else their roots in the Kirk and the universities would have made such an enquiry central.

iii) The Church

After much struggle and bloodshed, and after the accession of William and Mary, the 1690 Settlement established Presbyterianism as the officially sanctioned form of Church government and subscription to the tenets of the Westminster Confession was made the test of orthodoxy (Cameron 1982: 116). (See Chapter 7 (Biii).) Six years later this was put into fateful effect with the execution of a nineteen-year-old student Thomas Aikenhead for blasphemy (even after he had recanted of his alleged view that theology was 'a rapsidie of faigned and ill invented Nonsense' (quoted in Hunter 1992: 224; Hunter discusses the affair in general)). Here, on the face of it, is an event that represents all that the Enlightenment was fighting against. It is, therefore, all the more remarkable that a leading figure of the Scottish Enlightenment like William Robertson should not merely have been a cleric but also Moderator of the General Assembly of the Church of Scotland. Nor was he exceptional. Alexander Gerard was also Moderator and Ferguson, Reid and Campbell were all ordained ministers. What brought about this change?

The Union itself should have confirmed the Church's position since the retention of Presbyterianism was one of the articles of the Treaty. Beyond this the Union can be thought to have enhanced that position because with the loss of a Parliament the nearest equivalent to a national debating forum became the General Assembly (Clark 1970: 202). Arguably, however, this enhanced position made it the focus of political attention and this helped eventually the Scottish Church (or elements of it) and the Scottish Enlightenment to come to some sort of rapprochement.

There are two strands to this: doctrinal and organisational. Gradually as the new century advanced the rigours of Calvinist theology lessened, not that it ever had been accepted universally or always construed narrowly. The Toleration Act of 1712 proscribed lay magistrates from enforcing Kirk judgements, thus obliging the Church to maintain its own discipline. A crucial marker of the changes was the acquittal of heresy of John Simson, Professor of Divinity at Glasgow, in 1717 and again in 1727. From the 1730s onwards there was a divergence between those who held fast to what they regarded as authoritative Calvinist doctrine and those who took a more 'rational' or less scriptural approach and who emphasised social obligations at least as much as personal salvation (Cameron 1967: 1944). Thomas Halyburton, who had penned a vindication of the execution of the hapless Aikenhead, gave an early indication of this divergence when he lamented, 'that a rational sort of religion is coming in among us: I mean by it a religion that consists in bare attendance on outward duties and ordinances without the power of godliness' (quoted in Cameron 1982: 121). The perceived weakening of orthodoxy did not happen without resistance. Inside the Church itself there remained a faction (the 'High-Flyers') committed to an evangelical approach and there were secessions, though even here there is evidence of increased emphasis upon manners and civility (cf. Landsman 1991). Doctrinal disputes were not the only cause of dissent. Equally important were organisational factors.

The initially telling blow was the Patronage Act of 1712. This reasserted the right of lay patrons to apppoint ministers. In the royal burghs this right was held by the town council but in the remaining 90 per cent of livings it was held by the nobility either directly or indirectly where the Crown was the official patron (Sher

1985: 47). Such patronage ran contrary to the entire ethos of Presbyterianism where the minister was supposed to be the appointee of the local Kirk itself. When some lairds tried to exercise their right it did not go down well. Some presbyteries resisted. The fact that the Assembly was less than forthright in supporting the lairds' rights resulted in the emergence of a group known as the Moderates.[11] These individuals, all on the 'rational' wing of the Kirk doctrinally, wished to re-establish for their own reasons the Assembly's authority (see 'Reasons of Dissent' [1752] excerpted in Rendall (1978): 213–14). Prominent in this group were literati like Robertson and Hugh Blair, who through astute manoeuvrings managed to make themselves the dominant 'party' in the Assembly. It was not that the Moderates were puppets pulled by political strings but that they were eking out pragmatically a mutually beneficial accommodation. As Clark says, acquiescence in patronage was the 'price' which the Church had to pay to continue to occupy a 'central place in the national life' (1970: 207). Keeping the Assembly 'sweet' helped in the 'management' of Scotland (Shaw 1983: 100). While the Assembly upheld and enforced the (legal) exercise of the power of patronage it, in return, was left free from direct 'interference'. In this way candidates sympathetic to improvement and to 'enlightenment' could be more easily placed.

This does not mean the Moderates' religious beliefs were insincere. Hellfire sermonising may have given way to an emphasis on social duties (Christian neighbourliness) but a shift in emphasis is not apostasy (cf. Emerson 1989: 79). Indeed both this concern with the 'social' and its continuing links with the theological heritage has been claimed by some commentators (e.g. Chitnis 1976, Sher 1985, Allan 1993) to be a significant contributory factor to the Scots' social theory. Be that as it may – and the level of generality makes it difficult to give definitive substance to the claim – what is evident is that the Moderates were the 'Enlightenment' party. This, together with their institutional centrality, makes the Enlightenment in Scotland very different from that typically associated with the French situation. This difference is reinforced by the close relationships between the Moderate clergy and other members of the Enlightenment, even including the notorious infidel – David Hume. There was a further institutional dimension to these relationships. Robertson, Blair, Gerard, Ferguson and Reid were also university professors.

iv) Universities

For a country of Scotland's size and population the presence of five universities – St Andrews; Glasgow and Kings College Aberdeen, which predate the Reformation; and Edinburgh and Marischal College Aberdeen, which were Reformation foundations – is striking. The traditional task of these universities was to turn out ministers of religion, and this continued throughout the century (Cant 1982: 44). This helps explain why law had to be studied abroad and why the provision of a medical education was moribund. As with law, the Dutch universities taught many Scots their medicine (Alexander Monro, who in 1722 was the first Professor of Anatomy in Edinburgh, had studied at Leiden). The eighteenth century saw a marked change. In general terms there was a shift away from the heavenly to the earthly city. Hence medical schools were officially recognised in Edinburgh (1740) and Glasgow (1760), and Edinburgh established four law chairs between 1707 and 1722 (Chitnis 1976: 135).

Two organisational changes marked this move to the mundane. Lecturing in Latin was gradually abandoned. Here an important pioneer was Francis Hutcheson, Professor of Moral Philosophy at Glasgow, whose personal impact (he was Smith's teacher) as well as his writings (see Chapter 7) have led to him being called the 'father of the Scottish Enlightenment'. The second change was in the system of teaching. The tradition of regents was gradually abandoned (only Kings College retained it). By this system one teacher took the same class for all its subjects throughout its four years of study. It was replaced by the professorial system of specialist teachers and classes. It is, therefore, no coincidence that Edinburgh, which led the way in abolishing regents in 1708, made those appointments in the teaching of law.

The practical aspect of learning was clearly important. Aside from the development of vocational classes in law and medicine, there was expansion in subjects like chemistry and botany, which had obvious uses in agricultural improvement and 'industry'. For example, Cullen at Glasgow corresponded with Kames on the chemistry of fertilisers and gave special lectures on the principles of agriculture – he had a farm of his own where he put his own principles into practice (cf. Donovan 1982: 100). Cullen also researched into the application of chemistry to linen-bleaching (Guthrie 1950: 62). But the universities were also open to intellectual developments (in which Cullen also made his mark). Curricula were changed, and especially notable was the speed with which Newton's system was adopted and professed (Newton himself gave Colin McLaurin – already a professor at Marischal College – a testimonial for his appointment at Edinburgh in 1725 (Chitnis 1976: 129)). Over against these high-powered intellectual developments the realities of the classroom need to be borne in mind. Students generally entered university in their mid-teens.[12] The admittedly precocious McLaurin graduated from Glasgow at the age of fifteen and took up his Aberdeen post when only seventeen, while at the other end of the century Dugald Stewart was teaching at Edinburgh when he was nineteen (Chitnis 1976: 139).

Student numbers increased as did the staff. Among the latter there was considerable mobility. We have already noted McLaurin's itinerary and other notable transfers included Reid from Kings College to Glasgow and both Cullen and Black – the two outstanding chemists – from Glasgow to Edinburgh. Inside the universities professors moved chairs. Smith at Glasgow switched from being Professor of Logic to Professor of Moral Philosophy and Ferguson at Edinburgh from Natural Philosophy to Pneumatics and Moral Philosophy.

Such manoeuvrings smack of university politics, and in the eighteenth-century context university appointments were, not surprisingly, another arm of the patronage system. The apparently simple fact that the theorists of the Scottish Enlightenment were overwhelmingly university professors is prima facie evidence that in this system 'talent' counted. By and large dullards would not be appointed since not only would they not attract students to pay their fees (a Scottish practice that Smith compared favourably to Oxford, where he had also been a student (see *WN*: 761)) but also that itself would depress the 'market' to the detriment of their colleagues (Emerson 1992: 7). For example, Kames, in writing to Milton to get Cullen his Edinburgh chair, remarked that Cullen will help raise the reputation of the college and draw strangers in abundance (letter reprinted in Rendall 1978: 59). Beyond the immediate concerns of revenue and prestige there was generally an 'interest' in appointing those favourable to 'improvement' (Emerson 1993: 188). This meant in practice appointing those committed to the established order. In that same letter to Milton, Kames also notes that Cullen is a 'fast adherent to the Duke of Argyll' (Rendall 1978: 59). It is no great surprise therefore to discover that Moderates like Robertson and Blair were appointed (respectively) to the Principalship and Professorship of Rhetoric at Edinburgh in 1762 and 1760. They were appointed by Lord Bute, who had inherited the Argyll political machine. Bute was also responsible for placing John Millar in the Regius Chair of Civil Law at Glasgow (Millar was another protégé of Kames). Indeed in 1764 seven of the nineteen posts at Edinburgh and five of the thirteen at Glasgow had been filled with Bute's support (Emerson 1988c: 159–60).

Of course the universities were not altogether shining exemplars of meritocracy. Nepotism remained. Gilbert Gerard, for example, followed his father Alexander at Kings College (Kings was the most inbred of the Scottish universities – see the table in Emerson 1992: 147) but he was not alone – Dugald Stewart also followed his father at Edinburgh. Even if 'quality' was being recognised in these cases, it was not guaranteed. By all accounts Millar's successor at Glasgow, Robert Davidson, the son of the Principal, was not up to the job (cf. Cairns 1995: 151–2). And there were countervailing pressures. For all Hume's recognised intellectual abilities his reputation for religious heterodoxy was sufficient to bar him from chairs at both Glasgow and Edinburgh. Hume was not sufficiently beyond the pale that he obtained a plum 'establishment' post of Keeper of the Advocates' Library in 1752. Indeed so much a member of the leading coterie of the Enlightenment was he that others gave him their writings to vet for stylistic impurities. This preoccupation with writing well was a striking feature of the Scots' self-consciousness; their awareness that they were both different and special in the context of Great Britain.

v) 'Spirit of the Age'

One of the chief reasons for giving Hume a sight of their writings was a fear of 'Scotticisms'. (Of Hume himself it was said by Monboddo that he died confessing not his sins but his Scotticisms (cf. Mossner 1980: 606).) The anxiety was that they would appear to be different (suspiciously so) from the norms of Hanoverian England. Alexander Carlyle, one of the founders of the Moderate movement, remarked in his *Autobiography*:

To every man bred in Scotland the English language was in some respects a foreign tongue, the precise value and force of whose words and phrases he did not understand and therefore was continually endeavouring to word his expressions by additional epithets or circumlocutions which made his writings appear both stiff and redundant. (1910: 543) [13]

There is plenty of supporting evidence for this self-consciousness. That a concern with language and style was widespread is borne out by James Beattie, Hume's bitterest Scottish opponent (the antipathy was mutual [14]), publishing a brief pamphlet, *Scotticisms arranged in Alphabetical Order, designed to correct Improprieties of Speech and Writing* (1787). The explicit aim of this pamphlet was to put young writers 'on their guard against some of the Scotch idioms which in this country are likely to be mistaken for English' (2). As Beattie's sub-title indicates the spoken as well as the written word was a topic of concern. The Select Society (mentioned already) spawned, in 1761, an off-spring – the society for 'Promoting the Reading and Speaking of the English Language in Scotland' (McElroy 1969: 58). In the same year it invited the Irishman Thomas Sheridan (father of the playwright) to Edinburgh to lecture on elocution. These lectures were attended not only by students but also, as a contemporary put it, by 'ladies and gentlemen of the highest position' because the study of elocution had become a 'rage' (Somerville 1861: 56).

A further, and related, symptom of this self-consciousness was the vogue enjoyed by English periodicals. The *Tatler* and the *Spectator* were reprinted quickly in Edinburgh and widely circulated (cf. Phillipson 1987: 235, 1981). What was attractive in these publications was the attention paid to politeness and 'manners'. In the words of another contemporary they 'descanted in a strain of wit and irony peculiar to themselves on those lesser duties of life which former divines and moralists had left almost untouched' (Ramsay 1888: I,6). Such a concern with social propriety was the corollary of the burgeoning urban culture so that indeed 'urbanity' (and the related 'civility') became positively valued traits of character and behaviour.

This attentiveness to politeness and civility also manifested itself in the proliferation of clubs and debating societies. Some of these we have already referred to and among the many others was an especially productive 'philosophical' society (the 'Wise Club') in Aberdeen (cf. Ulman 1990). These various societies were an important part of the institutional fabric (cf. Phillipson 1973a, 1973b). They formed a point of convergence for the universities, the law, the Church and the 'improving' gentry. This interweaving establishes one of the crucial 'sociological' facts about the Scottish Enlightenment. Though academies were widespread throughout the Enlightenment as foci of debate and the dissemination of ideas, the relative proximity of the Scots to each other allowed close and strong, yet diverse, interests to cohere (cf. Ross 1972: 67). This almost corporate identity built on deep institutional foundations and personal ties also helps to distinguish the Scots of the Enlightenment from their predecessors, like Pitcairne or Sibbald or Stair, who, though eminent scholars, had shallower institutional support and, as predominantly episcopalian, were more at odds with the ambient culture.

The Scots, however, were not purely passive in the face of the English. They tried to emulate the periodical literature by developing their own such as the *Scots Magazine*, started in 1739 (Murdoch & Sher 1989: 133). (This journal published in 1760 Hume's list of Scotticisms which had first appeared in his 1752 *Political Discourses* but had been omitted from later editions – see Basker 1991, who reprints the list.) More ambitious and intellectually serious – too much so since the readership was insufficient to give it financial viability – was the publication in 1755 by the literati (including Smith and Robertson) of the *Edinburgh Review*. In the Preface to the first volume the editors refer to themselves as living in 'North Britain' (quoted in Rendall 1978: 223). This reference is significant because it reveals both their touchiness about being called 'Scottish' ten years after the '45 and their desire to be seen as part of the wider society, to be distinguished by latitude not culture.

The Scots seemingly wanted to be simultaneously of a province but not provincial – an aspect of what Daiches (1964) called the 'paradox' of Scottish culture. This fear of being thought to be, in a deprecatory sense, 'provincial' (Clive & Bailyn 1954), while it produced this concern to assimilate themselves to the 'metropolitan' or English culture, nonetheless coexisted with the Scots possessing a 'guid conceit' of themselves; they were not in point of fact inferior to the English. This coincided with the fact that they did not necessarily take their bearings from London. Their European, especially Dutch, connections made them 'cosmopolitan' just as much as 'provincial', as Chisick remarks of Hume his 'experience was European rather than narrowly Scottish and British' (1989: 23 cf. Emerson 1995). This might be all very well in matters of business or questions of intellect, but political realities ever obtruded. A sore case in point was the raising of a Scots' militia. Here the real issue was less 'Should the Scots have their own militia?' than 'Are the Scots to be trusted?' Various but unsuccessful campaigns were waged to get a militia. To that end, a society (of course) was established. Prominent among the membership of this Club – the so-called Poker Club (see Robertson 1985) – were Ferguson and Carlyle. Smith was also a member, but, as we shall see in Chapter 6, this shared membership did not prevent Smith and Ferguson disagreeing as to the relative merits of a militia vis-à-vis a standing army. Although the British Parliament would not grant the Scots their militia, it had no compunction in raising Scottish regiments to promote and sustain the Empire (Colley 1992: 132).

Whenever the Scots ventured into London they were made aware of their status. Hume, whose correspondence is particularly revealing, remarked that 'some hate me because I am not a Tory, some because I am not a Whig, some because I am not a Christian and all because I am Scotsman' (*Letts*: I, 470). English 'Scotto-phobia' (what Hume called in another of his letters the 'general rage against the Scots' *Letts*: I, 383) was not mere hysteria since as Colley argues there was some factual basis for the view that the Scots were 'taking over' (1992: 122). In politics the most palpable evidence was the premiership of Bute, who was the main butt of the popular agitation stirred up by and around Wilkes. However, it was in intellectual matters that the Scots' take-over seemed most assured and which gave them the justified high opinion of their own achievements. Hume again neatly sums up this ambivalence as a characteristic of the 'spirit of the age' in one of his letters:

> Is it not strange that, at a time when we have lost our Princes, our Parliaments, our independent Government, even the Presence of our chief Nobility, are unhappy, in our Accent & Pronunciation, speak a very corrupt Dialect of the Tongue which we make use of; is it not strange, I say, that, in these Circumstances we shou'd really be the People most distinguish'd for Literature in Europe? (*Letts*: I, 255)

Central to that distinction was their social theory. Before expounding that theory, this opening chapter can best be concluded by briefly addressing the question, *who* were the social theorists of the Scottish Enlightenment? Though there will be some twenty or so performers, eight key actors will be on stage in what follows. In order of seniority here are some programme notes on these central *dramatis personae*.

Henry Home (Lord Kames) (1696–1782)

The son of the laird of Kames in the Scottish borders, he was educated at home and qualified in Edinburgh as an advocate. He was appointed a Lord Ordinary of the Court of Session (taking the title Kames) and later a Commissioner of Justiciary. He was a member of the Board of Trustees for Fisheries, Manufactures and Improvements and was a Commissioner for the Forfeited Estates. He is the subject of two lengthy modern biographies (Lehmann 1971, Ross 1972).

David Hume (1711–1776)

A (distant) cousin of Kames, he was the son of the laird of Ninewells in Berwickshire – his father was also a practising lawyer. He was educated at Edinburgh University and his main source of income was his own writing but he was also appointed Judge Advocate, Keeper of the Advocates' Library and Embassy Secretary in Paris. He is the subject of an important biography by Mossner (1980, 2nd edn).

William Robertson (1721–1793)

The son of an Edinburgh minister, he was educated at Edinburgh University and was appointed minister of Gladsmuir near Edinburgh. He later became a minister in Edinburgh itself, progressing to become one of His Majesty's Chaplains before his appointment as Principal of Edinburgh University in 1762 and in 1764 the Historiographer-Royal of Scotland. There is no modern 'life' but there is a lengthy relevant discussion in Sher (1985), Camic (1983) has a fanciful psychological profile and Dugald Stewart wrote a substantial 'memoir'.

Adam Ferguson (1723–1816)

The only member of the literati born in the Highlands, at Logierait in Perthshire, where his father was minister of the parish. He attended St Andrews University intending to follow in his father's footsteps. He served with the newly-formed Black Watch regiment as a chaplain. He did not in fact succeed his father and left the ministry. After a break he succeeded Hume at the Advocates' Library before becoming a professor at Edinburgh in 1759. There is a nineteenth-century 'life' by John Small and an intellectual biography by Kettler (1965). The edition of his *Correspondence* contains the most authoritative biography by Fagg (1995).

Adam Smith (1723–1790)

The son of a customs official he was born in Kirkcaldy and was educated at Glasgow University and later at Oxford on a Glasgow scholarship. After some freelance lecturing he was appointed a professor in Glasgow in 1750. He resigned in 1764 to take up the better-paid post of tutor to the Duke of Buccleuch, although the death of his charge in 1766 made it a short-lived appointment. In 1778 he was made Commissioner of Customs. There is a brief biography by Campbell and Skinner (1985) and an important 'memoir' by Dugald Stewart as well as a 'classic' nineteenth-century biography by Rae (1895 repr. 1965) but Ross (1995a) has now produced a full scale definitive life.

John Millar (1735–1801)

Another son of the manse, he was born in Kirk O'Shotts and educated at Glasgow University (where he was taught by Smith). At the age of twenty-six he became Professor of Civil Law at Glasgow, where he remained for the next forty years until his death. Outside the classroom he undertook occasional law cases, principally on behalf of poor defendants. He had the reputation of being a radical Whig; he dedicated the *Historical View* to Fox. His son-in-law, John Craig, wrote a long memoir (included in a reprint of the *Ranks* (1990)) and Lehmann (1960) prefaced his edition of the *Ranks* with a biography.

James Dunbar (1742–1796)

The only member of our octet from Aberdeen, he was a son of the minor laird of Boath (near Nairn). He was educated at Kings College before becoming a regent there in 1765. He remained at Kings until his retirement caused by ill-health in 1794. What little biographical information there is is contained in Berry (1974b).

Gilbert Stuart (1743–1786)

Although the son of an Edinburgh professor, he was something of an 'outsider'. He was educated at his father's university and made several attempts to obtain a post there. He made his living as a reviewer and pamphleteer in London while writing works of history that contested Robertson's views (he put his failure to get a university job at Edinburgh down to Robertson's opposition). He is the subject of a biography by Zachs (1992).

Notes

1. In fact a passage on Bayle written by Diderot was dropped before publication (see Wilson 1972: 743). A brief account of Bayle is given in Labrousse (1983): she is the leading Bayle scholar. All accounts of the Enlightenment pay attention to his impact (e.g. Cassirer (1955), Brumfitt (1972)). Bayle is part of a general strand of French free-thinkers (other members include La Rochefoucauld, Saint-Evremond) who, via Mandeville, also had an impact in Britain. It is Bayle's links with this tradition, as well as his reputation as an extreme sceptic, that made it politic not to celebrate him in the *Preliminary Discourse*. The battle with censorship was a live one; several members of the French Enlightenment, including Diderot, were imprisoned.

2. There was a complementary expedition, led by LaCondamine in 1735 but only reporting back a decade later, to the Amazon to confirm that the earth bulged. Another successful experimental coup for Newton was the return of Halley's comet as predicted (Hankins 1985: 39, 40). Voltaire wrote poems to celebrate Newton's triumph (Aldridge 1975: 96).

3. Cf. Payne (1976: 190–1), 'In a rare display of virtual unanimity, the writers of the *Encyclopedia* agreed that all societies need a god and specifically one who rewards good and punishes evil.'

4. Not only did Newton think that the 'beautiful system of the sun, planets and comets could only proceed from the counsel and dominion of an intelligent and powerful Being' (*Principia Mathematica* Bk 3 (in 1953: 42)) but also implied that God had to 'reform' the system periodically (*Optics* Q. 31 (1953: 177)). This last point was picked up by Leibniz, who said it implied God had insufficient foresight and had to wind up his watch from time to time. Newton was defended by S. Clarke in a well-known correspondence with Leibniz (see Alexander, 1956).

5. Cf. G. Turnbull, *Observations upon Liberal Education* (1742); D. Fordyce, *Dialogues concerning Education* (1753); Kames, *Loose Hints upon Education* (1781).

6. From the legion of books on the theme of this paragraph a classic is Gierke (tr. 1934) and of the modern works those of Tuck (1979, 1993) are illuminating. For Montesquieu's participation see, for example, Mason (1975).

7. The modern classic that outlines this tradition – known as civic humanism or classical republicanism – is Pocock (1975). Though the lexicon may be found in Montesquieu, the dominant scholarly view is that Montesquieu himself was more a supporter of 'modern liberty' than 'ancient virtue'. For an expression of the 'minority view' see Keohane (1980: Ch. 4) and Shklar (1987) is a brief overview. More particularly, for a discussion of Montesquieu and the Scots that focuses on the relationship between commerce and virtue, see Sher (1994).

8. The Board was to act 'for the Purpose of civilizing the Inhabitants ... and promoting amongst them the Protestant Religion, good Government, Industry and Manufactures and the Principles of Duty and Loyalty to his Majesty his Heirs and Successors' (quoted in Youngson 1972: 27). The learning of English was emphasised and the traditional 'dress' was proscribed.

9. Thomas Somerville in his Memoir (c. 1814) reports on the inconvenience caused by the absence of banks and mentions the case of the Duke of Roxburghe having in 1720 to receive a £100 a month by wagon. Somerville also comments how the absence of banks also contributed to the importance (and opulence) of lawyers as money-lenders (1861: 353).

10. The Highlanders were also depicted as especially prone to superstitions – those hall-marks of a vulgar, unenlightened mind. Ramsay of Ochertyre's manuscripts contain a long chapter on Highland superstitions (1888: II, 417–74) and Pennant in his *Tour* remarks upon the precautions to preserve cattle against witchcraft by placing boughs of mountain ash in cow sheds (1774: 141). Superstitions were not the prerogative of

Highlanders alone. Somerville in his Memoir of his 'life and times' in the borders, also gives examples of belief in witchcraft (1861: 366).

11. The nineteenth-century historian of the secessionist Relief Church commented that they 'were called Moderates because of their moderation as to doctrine and discipline, were openly hostile to the doctrines of grace ... [and] flattered human nature as to its ability to obey the moral law' (Struthers 1848: 188). The leader of the secession, Thomas Gillespie, was removed from his post by Robertson, who, according to Struthers, 'preached on Christian character and practice, overlooking in a great measure those evangelical principles from which all holy practice must proceed' (209).

12. A survey of the social background of Glasgow students claims that the percentage classified as coming from the 'Industrial and Commercial' sector (as indicated by father's occupation) rose from 26 per cent to 50 per cent between the 1740s and the the 1790s. By contrast the percentage from noble and landed families declined from 39 per cent to 13 per cent over the same period. An analysis of the Industrial and Commercial category indicates that in the 1740s it comprised 96 per cent 'middle-class' students while by the 1790s that has halved with an equal percentage originating from the 'working class' (Mathews 1966: 78–80). As the author of the survey remarks the fees 'could scarcely have been lower' (93).

13. From the perspective of the late twentieth century this does often seem a fair description of Ferguson's *ECS*. Carlyle, for his part, thought the *Essay* possessed a 'species of eloquence peculiar' to the author (1910: 299) while the *Wealth of Nations* was 'tedious' (295).

14. Ramsay of Ochtertyre giving further testimony to Hume's 'establishment' credentials remarks how the 'junto at Edinburgh' took a condescending view of Beattie's anti-Humean *Essay on Truth* (1888: I, 508).

2

Sociality and the Critique of Individualism

Since this is a book on the *social* theory of the Scottish Enlightenment then the best place to begin is the idea of human sociality. This might be thought to be an unpromising place to start because who could ever doubt that humans are social beings. But this is too hasty. Once further questions are asked – in what sense are humans social? Does sociality rest on instinct or choice or what? – then the issue looks less cut and dried. Aside from picking up on these questions the Scots pursued another line of enquiry. In this they confronted an important factor in their intellectual legacy. The (natural) jurisprudential approach to social relations hypothesised as one of its key ingredients a non-'social' circumstance (the State of Nature). What we also find, therefore, in the Scots' discussions of sociality is a critique of that hypothesis and its associated ideas. Indeed one of the historically important factors that make the Scots worth studying is that aspects of this critique prefigure Burke's well-known assault, without it, in their case, requiring them to revoke their membership of the Enlightenment family.

A: The Evidence

The title of the opening chapter of Ferguson's *History of Civil Society* is 'Of the Question relating to the State of Nature'. Ferguson's aim is to criticise the assumptions and methods of those theorists who talk of a State of Nature. The theorists he has in mind, although they are not named, are Jean-Jacques Rousseau and Thomas Hobbes. They differ in their accounts but, more significantly for Ferguson, they share the same fatal weakness. They have each erected a 'system' based upon selecting 'one or few particulars on which to establish a theory' (*ECS*: 2). In adopting this approach Ferguson says they have deviated from the practice of the 'natural historian', who thinks the 'facts' should be collected and general tenets should be derived from 'observations and experiments'. By contrast Hobbes and Rousseau resort to 'hypothesis' or 'conjecture' or 'imagination' or 'poetry'. To these Ferguson juxtaposes respectively 'reality', 'facts', 'reason' and 'science', and it is the latter list that 'must be admitted as the foundation of all our reasoning relative to man' (2). We must, in other words, turn to evidence. The evidence uniformly returns the same verdict: 'both the earliest and latest accounts collected from every quarter of the earth represent mankind as assembled in troops and companies' (3 cf. 16, *IMP*: 21).

All the Scots endorse this verdict, although the militaristic echoes in this particular formulation by Ferguson reflect his own emphases and preoccupations.

By 'earliest' accounts Ferguson means those of the ancient historians (the staples of their educational diet). The favourite authors were Herodotus, Xenophon and Thucydides especially among the Greeks and Livy, Caesar and Tacitus especially among the Romans.[1] By the 'latest' he means the reports and journals of various travellers and missionaries, pre-eminent among which were the accounts of the various tribes of North America supplied by many authors but by Lafitau and Charlevoix especially.[2] The assumptions at work in assimilating these two sources will be discussed in Chapter 3. To rely (not uncritically) on such sources is to accept that experience provides the evidence.

The Scots are in a straightforward sense empiricists. Hume worked up the doctrine to the height of philosophical sophistication and in so doing generated in response a distinctively Scottish counter in the work of Reid and the so-called Common Sense School (cf. Grave 1960). At a less elevated level the acceptance of empiricism meant taking facts or evidence, not fantasy or conjecture, as the baseline. On this basis we have 'no record' of a time when humans were not social (Ferguson *ECS*: 6). But what about a 'wild man' caught in the woods or a feral child, a number of whom were *causes célèbres* in the eighteenth century (cf. Malson 1972)? These were individuals who appeared to have had no contact with other humans. However, these specimens were not regarded as authentic counter-evidence. As Reid remarked, we cannot 'build conclusions upon them with great certainty' (*AP*: 548), though, typically, that did not inhibit Monboddo, who uses the muteness of such beings as evidence to support his own argument that language is not natural to humans (*OPL*: I, 174). Ferguson is clear that every 'experiment' should be made with 'entire societies not with single men' (*ECS*: 4).

This is partly a recognition of the principle of induction – the practice of the 'natural historian' as mentioned earlier in the critique of Hobbes and Rousseau. There is another well-established source of evidence. My own experience is relevant. If I read myself correctly then I am, as Hobbes said in the Introduction to *Leviathan* (1651), also reading mankind. This underlies Dunbar's observation that the history of the world will be mysterious if the philosopher makes 'no serious appeal to his own constitution' (*EHM*: 159 cf. Hutcheson *On Human Nature*: 139). Kames argues that human sociality 'will be vouched by the concurring testimony of all men, each vouching for himself' (*SHM*: I, 386). This appeal to introspection was frequently made when the joys and sorrows of social life were being discussed; each and everyone of us knows the anguish of loneliness and the pleasures of companionship (cf. Ferguson *ECS*: 3, 17, 19; Hume *THN*: 353, 363, 421; Smith *TMS*: 38, 85, 116). What validates introspection as a source of evidence is the belief that human nature is uniform or constant across time and space: what I feel in my breast I may truly infer to be present in yours no matter where, no matter when. (This fundamental belief will be examined at some length in Chapter 3.)

B: Explanations of Sociality

Although presented with a panoply of empirical credentials, the Scots' position that humans are social is no novelty. From at least Plato and Aristotle onwards this has not been seriously disputed. There is, however, room for controversy and divergence when it comes to furnishing the correct explanation of this fact. The Scots discuss four explanations – the first three of which are examined in this section, leaving the fourth for a separate section.

i) Instinct

A common explanation of human sociality was that it was instinctive or appetitive.[3] Kames declares that 'there is in man an appetite for society never was called in question' (SHM: I, 376 cf. PMNR: 79, 136, 139 etc.) and similar assertions are made by, for example, Ferguson (ECS: 11, PMPS: I, 32), Gregory (CV: 114), Turnbull (The Principles of Moral Philosophy: 175) and Dunbar (EHM: 24). Within this consensus there was still room for debate. One central issue was the extent to which human instinctive sociality was similar to that of other animals. Nobody denied that there were limits to this but there was disagreement over its extent. This uncertainty can even be detected within a single text. In his Essay Ferguson declares at one point that, notwithstanding his mental activities, man is 'an animal in the full extent of that description' while having earlier announced that 'we can learn nothing of man's nature from the analogy of other animals' (ECS: 46, 6).

In a general treatment of this issue John Gregory is clear that this analogy is of limited validity. While he identifies an important role for instincts in humans and regards reason as a weak principle, nonetheless it is, in line with both received wisdom and modern science,[4] the human possession of the latter that differentiates them from animals (CV: 10ff.). In the more particular case of the social instinct Kames is the most systematic. He reasoned that since many animals are social then it was probable that 'the social laws by which animals are governed might open views into the social nature of man' (SHM: I, 377). His approach was taxonomic. In one group he placed animals which are not sociable, basically predators, and in another he put sociable herding animals; these have an 'appetite for society' for either defence or food (I, 380). While this two-fold classification was also adopted by Ferguson (IMP: 23-4; PMPS: I, 20-1) Kames had a third. Some animals (his example is horses) are social without need for defence or subsistence, and Kames held that their sociality was 'derived from pleasure from living in society' (I, 380). However, this third class is an 'imperfect kind' (I, 381) and when humans are examined Kames puts them into the second class – it is 'evident ... that to no animal is society more necessary than to man for food or for subsistence' (I, 387; my emphasis).

Dunbar produced an interesting commentary on this line of argument. He has a distinctive account of sociality and as part of his argument he wished to criticise not the existence of an instinct but the 'message' it conveys. He admitted that animals crowd together in danger but he doesn't think such herding significant since they derive 'no security from mutual aid' (*EHM*: 8). This differentiates humans for 'man alone becomes considerable by the combination of his species' (*Ibid.*). With an implicit reference to Kames' argument, Dunbar remarks that 'I am not ignorant that [animals] are gregarious from *necessity* ... and require joint labour for their subsistence or accommodation' (9; my emphasis) but he questions the necessitarian character of instinct. He maintains that through anthropomorphism the role of a social instinct in animals has been misinterpreted so that a 'concourse of animals', however fortuitous, is magnified into the product of a 'social principle'. And in the case of humans they are 'impelled by no necessity' but rather by 'generous passions'.

The significance of these passions for Dunbar will be picked up later but in the course of his argument he says a lot about language. He was not alone in this; speculation on the nature and character of language was widespread. Two questions in particular were asked. First, why do humans speak and animals do not? Second, as posed by Rousseau, which is the most necessary: society for language or language for society? (*Second Discourse*: tr. p. 179) Both merit an excursion.

Most Enlightenment thinkers adopted a naturalistic approach to language; its origin lies in human nature. From that assumption they were able to conjecture how language developed alongside man's own development and, simultaneously, to search for that special capacity that differentiated humans from brutes. This latter issue was the leitmotif for Monboddo's multi-volume *Of the Origin and Progress of Language*. Monboddo's thesis was that language was not natural to man and that in consequence, and quite explicitly, the answer to Rousseau's question was that society came first (*OPL*: I, 197). What gave his argument its notoriety was that he cited the behaviour of the Orang Outang as proof of its validity. According to Monboddo, the Orang was really a species of Homo sapiens, since, although devoid of language, it nevertheless practised such other human traits as living communally, building homes, possessing a sense of decorum, using weapons, desiring human females and so on (see *OPL*: vol. I, Bk 1, Ch. 14; I, 2–8, 9 cf. *AM*: vol. 3, Bk 2, Ch. 1). Dunbar (*EHM*: 67) and Kames (*SHM*: I, 44n.) comment on the fact that Orangs and humans both possess vocal chords. Kames simply thinks that possession not crucial while Dunbar refers to the work of Camper, which he interprets as demonstrating that the Orang is organically incapable of speech (203).[5]

For Dunbar the origin of language is to be found in natural exclamations or cries, what the nineteenth-century philologist Müller called the 'bow-wow theory' (1875: II, 93). Dunbar identifies interjections as survivals of this origin, they have retained speech's 'primeval character' (71 cf. Blair *RBL*: 67, Monboddo *OPL*: II, 181 – for extended discussion see Berry [1973]). The second step in the development of language is imitation (*EHM*: 78 cf. Blair *LRB* 65, Monboddo *OPL*: I, 191, Beattie *Dissertations*: 237 also, more generally, Gregory *CV*: 129). After the imitative faculty Dunbar posits another – the analogical (*EHM*: 79). This marks a decisive move because it is here that the 'instinct borrows aid from the imagination' so that it forms 'perhaps' the 'boundary of art and nature' and explains 'the law of silence ... in the animal world'.[6] There is a social counterpart to this because 'every effort beyond what is merely animal has reference to a community' (5). If for humans language and society are co-eval (cf. Kames *SHM*: I, 44n.) then there is no need to answer Rousseau's question by giving one or the other priority.

Two consequences follow from this linkage. The explanation of language is no more mysterious than the explanation of sociality. This makes redundant the need for a specifically 'theological' account of language's origin, as was still put forward by Beattie (*Dissertations*: 304) and Blair (*LRB*: 64). It also means, given that language is to be 'attributed to some succeeding effort of the human mind' (Dunbar *EHM*: 63), that society is a similar 'effort'. Both language and society develop from simple to complex and from the concrete to the abstract. The 'societal' aspect of this is a major element in the Scots' social theory (see Chapter 5). The linguistic aspect focused on explaining the evolution of the parts of speech (see especially Smith's *Considerations concerning the First Formation of Languages*).[7] In each case there is no need to resort to extraordinary individuals to explain the developments (see section Ciii below).

ii) Family

That families are little societies had long achieved the status of cliché. Similarly well-worn was the view that societies are the growth of families, whether from the original source in Adam and Eve or as the product of pacts between fathers. It is no surprise therefore to discover Ferguson remarking that families 'may be considered as the elementary form of society' (*PMPS*: I, 27). However, in Ferguson this explanation is closely linked to the operation of instinct since he immediately continues that families are 'indispensably necessary to the existence and preservation of the kind'. Their initial bond is 'the mutual inclination of the sexes', supplemented by 'natural affection' (parental concern for their offspring) (I, 31; cf. Dunbar *EHM*: 18, also Hutcheson *Essay on the Passions*: 52). Hume, who made no reference to a social instinct, did attribute the origin of society to the 'natural appetite betwixt the sexes' and their natural affection to their children (*THN*: 486).

Despite this instinctive component it is with the family that the human/animal difference becomes more evident. Even so the family as a distinctive explanation of sociality does not loom large. This minor role stems from the very circumstances of human family relationships. The crucial circumstance is, in Dunbar's words, that 'the period of pregnancy ... were by far too short to dispense in the human case with parental cares' (*EHM*: 18). Locke had said as much (*Second Treatise*: §§79–80) and Dunbar, as part of his own distinctive argument and probably following Rousseau's *Discourse on Inequality* to which he was greatly indebted, subjects this fact to further analysis. Since Dunbar wants to argue that society originates in 'generous passions' or unrestricted fellow feeling (*EHM*: 7, 16, 17) he has to reject the familial principle as too restrictive. He claims that just as the paternal instinct is generally regarded as precarious so the maternal instinct 'at an aera further back' may also have been 'fluctuating and temporary' (23). Dunbar historicises the family. We should not, he affirms, generally transfer current practices and assumptions into 'all preceding times' (6).

Dunbar also makes a more conventional observation. The fact that humans at birth are totally dependent on nurture means that the parent–child bond is more durable than in animals (18). Ferguson fastens upon this to account for the family's minor role as an explanation of sociality (*PMPS*: I, 27). This durability results in family ties extending beyond mere instinct. The affection that children have for their parents does not disappear once physical independence has been reached; rather, it grows closer 'as it becomes mixed with esteem and the memory of its early effects' (I,16). While memory is not perhaps the prerogative of humans, the capacity for esteem is. What is important here is less the positive presence of this capacity than what its operation denies. Children do not esteem their parents as a contractual obligation in return for having been nurtured by them. As we shall see, this is integral to a general critique of all such rationalistic or instrumentalist explanations. In this same context Ferguson refers to a principle that plays a central role in the Scots' social theory. He states, as a further consequence of the durability of the child–parent relation, that the instinctive attachments 'grow into habit'. Habit expands the family tie so that it encompasses not only siblings but also a third generation and collaterals. This, for Ferguson, explains how consanguinity is regarded as a 'bond of connection' (*PMPS*: I, 30).

iii) Friendship and Loyalty

For Ferguson there was more to human sociality than either 'parental affection' or a 'propensity ... to mix with the herd' (*ECS*: 16). Once some durability has been established then the independent principles of friendship and loyalty come into play. In each case they represent a sphere of human conduct that is not reducible either to animal instinct or to self-interested rational calculation. Ferguson indeed declares that the bonds formed by these principles are the strongest of all and this is precisely because they transcend the self-centred quality of the other two. They are for that reason the most genuinely *social*. As supporting evidence he offers the observation that 'men are so far from valuing society on account of its mere external conveniencies that they are commonly most attached where those conveniencies are least frequent' (19).

Friends are those who cling to each other 'in every season of peril' (18). But that is *not* because they derive some quid pro quo benefit; that would be in Hutcheson's forthright terms to ascribe to it 'a mean and despicable original' (*SIMP*: 83).[8] Rather, it is an expression of the intrinsic non-instrumental quality of their relationship. The quality of friendship is one of 'resolute ardour' (Ferguson *ECS*: 17). Friends differ from kin because they are selected (*Ibid.*, *PMPS*: I, 32). Selection implies discrimination, hence the important distinction between friends and others. But Ferguson does not see this consequence as anti-social, on the contrary he places great emphasis on the fact that this discrimination is a crucial component in the bond of friendship (see further Dii below).

This mutually reinforcing duality of friend/other is extendable into the more general relationship of loyalty. For Ferguson 'our attachment to one division, or to one sect, seems often to derive much of its force from an animosity conceived to an opposite one' (*ECS*: 16). We can now appreciate part of the force of Ferguson's references to men always being found in 'troops and companies'. The commitment or loyalty to one's own group explains the sentiment of patriotism (19). The evidence here is overwhelming and unequivocal. Time after time, instance after instance, it has been seen that humans are willing to risk their lives for the sake of their *patria*. This can only be explained by the human capacity to bond on principles that go beyond both the instinct for self-preservation and judicious calculation of self-interest. To lay down one's life for one's friend or country is not some mental aberration (as Hobbes would have it) but is the very stuff of humans as social beings. As we shall see in Chapter 6, Ferguson's thoughts on this issue are closely connected to his worries about the tendency of contemporary commercial societies to increase the prevalence of calculative behaviour.

That humans have both friends and foes is scarcely an original insight on Ferguson's part. That we possess anti-social as well as social passions was commonly upheld (e.g. Hutcheson *System of Moral Philosophy*: Bk I, Ch. 1; Smith *TMS*: Bk I, Pt. 1 Chs. 3–5, and see Dii below). Kames continues to use the analogy of animals to support this commonplace. His researches reveal to him that no animal has an appetite to associate with the whole species (*SHM*: I, 381) and humans are no exception (388). Not only does this mean that a 'great empire is ill-suited to human nature' (*Ibid.*) but that humans possess 'dis-social' as well as social passions (403).

It was the deliberate intention of Dunbar to refute this theory. His argument was genetic in the sense that he wished to claim that partial affections (both in the strict sense of being non-universal as well as being biased) were not part of original human nature but generated by society itself. According to Dunbar after a pre-linguistic phase, humans developed a genuinely social stage before thirdly and imperceptibly moving to an era of civil government (*EHM*: 2–3). The crux of this second stage is that a 'delight in their kind, congenial with all natures' constitutes the fundamental principle of association (7). Humans have a fellow feeling with and for each other (16). This means that the principles of union, which as we saw, antedate familial relationships, are prior to the principles of hostility. There must be some social concourse before humans begin to discriminate between relatives, friends and strangers, and it is the very dynamics of this concourse – and here Dunbar's debt to Rousseau is particularly clear – that produce such discrimination and hostilities.

The fourth explanation offered for sociality is that it is rational. The Scots reject this explanation but so important is this rejection in their overall theory that it merits an extended treatment. The next two sections are devoted to that task.

C: The Critique of Individualism

The Scots do not deny that humans are rational but it is not their reason that explains their sociality. As Dunbar crisply put it, humans are sociable long before they are rational (*EHM*: 16). What is at stake here is the adequacy of a particular model of rationality. On this model I use my reason to calculate the best (i.e. most efficient) means to realise an objective. For the Scots when sociality is the issue this model is found wanting. Its inadequacy was intimately bound up with one particular theory, namely, the original or social contract. Since this theory was central to an important strain in jurisprudentialist thinking then a critique of contract necessarily had wide repercussions. The hallmark of Contractarianism is that it makes civil society the outcome of individual rational decision. In this section the focus is on the individualism, the next will concentrate on the rationalism.

i) State of Nature and Social Contract

The twin devices of the State of Nature and Social Contract were developed in the sixteenth and seventeenth centuries (though they continued into the eighteenth). It is important to stress that they were developed in the admittedly broad context of *political* thinking; this is why the reference is to *civil* society. To generalise, the central problem of post-Reformation Europe was legitimacy. What gave *that* individual, or group, the right or authority to command others? This is only a 'problem' once it is denied that rulers possess some natural, or super-natural (divine), entitlement to govern the ruled. If these abstract points are made concrete by referring to Protestants and Catholics (as either ruler or ruled) then the seriousness of the problem, as well as the breadth of the context, can be appreciated.

Once the principle of natural rulership is abandoned then, politically, individuals are on a par. Equality is the natural condition. This same conclusion can be expressed by saying humans are equal in the State of Nature. Since the equality also entails freedom (there are no 'natural' slaves or subjects just as there are no 'natural' rulers) then each individual has the right in the State of Nature (the natural right) to enjoy this freedom. The normative natural equality is thus that of 'rights' and this is perfectly consistent with inequalities in physical or mental capacities. The 'inconveniences' (to use Locke's terminology) attendant on the exercise of these rights resulted in the inhabitants of the State of Nature deciding to create their own artificial political/civil condition. This creation was the product of a contract. Typically the terms of this contract were that I would agree to lay aside my natural right to govern myself and obey your rule, *provided* you protected me and did not interfere with my other natural rights. The powerful prescription in this theory was that it equally provided grounds or criteria for disobedience – if you renege on your part of the contract then I am absolved from my obligation to obey.

The self-interested individualist dimension to this theory needs underlining. In any contract the assumption is that the parties must perceive some mutual benefit –

I have cheese and want ham, you have ham and want cheese, we can therefore contract (agree) to swap. We are each of us treating the other as a means to the realisation of our separate ends. This transaction not only starts with self-interest it also finishes with it. Once I have ham and you cheese then we have no further interest in each other. On this model, therefore, civil society subserves the pre-determined ends of its members.

We saw earlier that the Scots dismiss the State of Nature as fantastical, as empirically unwarranted. But it now appears that this dismissal is misplaced. The State of Nature is central to a normative or prescriptive theory (the criteria of legitimacy) and it is not overturned by descriptive considerations. At one level this is undeniably true but at the same time it obscures some significant further aspects. We can identify three.

First, the above account of Contractarian thought imposes a misleading simplicity and clarity upon it. On the one hand the Contractarians can admit, as Pufendorf did, that the State of Nature 'never actually existed' (*On the Law of Nature and Nations*: Bk 2 Ch. 2 Para. 4) and, on the other, cite supporting evidence. There was, for example, much talk of American Indians. Hence, since the Contractarians themselves did not make any sharp distinction between prescriptive and descriptive elements[9] then the Scots have some justification for reading them as putting forward a factual account as to what happened. The second aspect is that even if Contractarian theory is prescriptive, the Scots' critique can still have an impact on the grounds that any prescriptive theory requires some foothold in experience. The central point here is often expressed as 'ought implies can'. If the circumstances in which the transaction of an Original Contract is theoretically held to have occurred are so far removed from any relevant experience then the theory itself is seriously undermined. Instead of being a practically pertinent argument (when to obey/disobey government) it becomes a species of imaginative literature. This sort of writing might open closed minds but it will not be able to do the work required here. Certainly the Contractarians themselves did not think they were writing satires. It is however the third aspect that is most instructive. The Scots' descriptive rejection of the State of Nature is itself a prescriptive theory. In their own account of sociality they are also putting forward an alternative normative account of the authority of government.

In the opening chapter of the *Essay*, Ferguson comments that 'all situations are equally natural'. This means, as he goes on to illustrate, that 'the State of Nature' is 'here and it matters not whether we are understood to speak in the island of Great Britain, at the Cape of Good Hope, or the Straits of Magellan' (*ECS*: 8). It equally follows that it matters not whether it is eighteenth- or eighth-century Britain and so on. Since the 'natural condition' of humans is life in society then the premise from which norms are generated must also be social. It is, therefore, illicit to generate those norms from some extra-social or extra-temporal perspective. We cannot meaningfully assess the legitimacy of a government by invoking such a perspective, by, so to speak, stepping outside our social selves. The legitimacy has to be found within society. It is still possible to talk of 'natural rights', as

Ferguson and other Scots do, but given natural sociality these rights are not divorced conceptually or normatively from actual social existence. As we shall discuss in Chapter 4 the Scots do not adopt a form of moral relativism – all societies may be assessed by the extent to which they adhere to certain basic moral practices. Similarly the focus on the social context of legitimacy does not compromise for most Scots some ultimately theological underpinning precisely because the 'naturalness' of human social existence, especially its appetitive source, was typically seen as part of a Providential order (see later).

Before exploring the Scots' own positive explanation of legitimacy we need to say some more about their critique. Just as Ferguson undermined the idea of a State of Nature by declaring all situations to be equally natural so he undermined the case for a Social Contract by observing in Baconian fashion that 'art itself is natural to man' (6). There is no meaningful contrast between the 'natural condition of mankind' (the State of Nature) and their artificial (made by a Contract) civil or political existence. The most celebrated critique of Contractarian thought is Hume's.[10] He explicitly develops a two-pronged attack – historical and philosophical.

The historical critique is straightforward: that government originated in a contract is 'not justified by history or experience in any age or country of the world' (*E–OC*: 471). (Quite what Hume does believe is justified will be considered shortly.) If the Contractarian account of origins is empirically invalid, it is even less tenable when it claims the legitimacy of current government rests on consent (469), since if 'these reasoners' were to examine actual practice and belief they 'would meet with nothing that in the least corresponds to their ideas' (470). Neither rulers nor subjects believe their relationship is the effect of some prior pact. This is a damaging line of argument. The very core of Contractarian doctrine is that it is some 'act of mind' (giving consent) that constitutes legitimacy so that its absence (an act Hume declares to be 'unknown to all of them') is fatal to the theory's cogency. As we will note shortly, the contemporary political situation (the stability of the House of Hanover) was a more than incidental backdrop to this line of argument.

Hume reinforces the argument by also pointing out the implausibility of any notion of 'tacit consent'. Locke, who was Hume's acknowledged target (487),[11] for example, held that those who enjoy the protection of the laws (even by only travelling on the highway) were tacitly giving their consent (*Second Treatise*: §119) and it is a signal of withdrawal of consent if they leave the jurisdiction (§121). Hume pours scorn on this notion. He asks rhetorically how serious is any account that claims a 'poor peasant or artisan' who knows no foreign language and has no capital has a 'free choice to leave his country' (475). This is analogous, he claims, to remaining aboard ship and freely consenting to the captain's rule even though one was carried aboard asleep and the only alternative is leaping overboard and drowning.

Hume's historical/empirical refutation was widely followed. Smith explicitly cites his attacks on tacit consent even to the extent of repeating the analogue

(*LJ*: 317). Millar adopts a similar line. Merely obtaining some form of protection does not warrant the conclusion that some 'tacit promise of submission' has been given (*HV*: IV, 303/*HVL*: 354). Ferguson regards the idea of men assembling together as equals and as deciding their mode of government as 'visionary and unknown in nature' (*PMPS*: I, 262). Stuart thinks there is no evidence and 'it absurd to suppose that the original contract ever happened' (*Diss*: 151n.). As a final illustration, Steuart maintains that the 'rights of kings' are not founded 'upon the supposition of tacit contracts between them and their people'; their foundation is to be 'sought for in history' (*PPE*: I, 209). In addition to following Hume on tacit consent Smith also follows him by arguing that contemporary obligation cannot stem from consent not only because it is unknown but also because no contract can bind its successors (*LJ*: 316). Smith also picks up the parochiality of an apparently universalist argument (premised on the natural condition of *mankind*) by pointing out that it appears to be confined to Britain (*Ibid.*).

Hume's explicitly philosophical rejection turns on a distinction in moral duties (*E–OC*: 479–80). One category of duties emanates directly from a 'natural instinct or immediate propensity' and operates independently of any ideas of obligation or utility. His examples are love of children, gratitude to benefactors and pity to the unfortunate. When humans reflect on the social advantages of these propensities they 'pay them the just tribute of moral approbation and esteem'. The duties in the other category do not emanate immediately from instinct, they operate only after reflection upon their necessity for social intercourse. His examples here are justice, fidelity and, crucially for the present argument, allegiance.[12] Hume now proceeds to argue that the Contractarian claim to base the duty of allegiance on the duty of fidelity (promise-keeping) is a conceptual redundancy. We keep our promises and also obey our rulers because both are necessary for social life. That necessity is sufficient explanation – in either case 'we gain nothing by resolving one into the other' (481). Though this argument is very much Hume's own, Millar indicates that he accepts its force when he observes, in passing, that referring to a promise 'adds but little' to the obligation to obey (*HV*: IV, 301/*HVL*: 353).

ii) Time, Habit and Legitimacy

Having in their own lights rubbished the Contract account of legitimacy for its empirical inadequacy, what do the Scots put in its place? Their own positive account pretends to be true to the evidence. I shall discuss the Scots' account of the institution of government in Chapter 5, in this section I wish to concentrate on how this alternative is part and parcel of their commitment to sociality and the critique of individualism.

Locke had claimed that in order to understand the 'true, extent and end' of civil power it was necessary to identify its origins (cf. *Second Treatise*: §1). This typical claim in fact goes a long way to explaining why the dominant reference is to an 'original' contract. Hume argues that the actual origins do not correspond to a Lockean-type story of free, equal individuals contracting with each other. He does allow that the effective equality of individuals means that an element of consent was involved in the establishment of government. However, he denies that in practice this amounted to any more than irregular, temporary and ad hoc arrangements; it is clear, he maintains, that there was 'no compact or agreement . . . expressly formed for general submission'. (For reasons that will be brought out in Chapter 5, Hume observes that any such agreement is an 'idea far beyond the comprehension of savages' (*E–OC*: 468).) Moreover, even if some element of consent is present it was never the sole principle (474).

For Hume all the evidence points to the fact that all existing governments were originally founded on usurpation or conquest (471); that is, 'in plain terms, force by dissolving the ancient government is the origin of all the new ones which ever were established in the world' (474). It was to side-step these considerations that the Contractarians had sought the touchstone of legitimacy in an original contract, and both Hutcheson (*SIMP*: 285) and Reid (*Practical Ethics*: 15) followed this reasoning. But, as we saw in the last section, Hume recognised that this touchstone was not true to the facts; contemporary governments were believed by their subjects to be legitimate regardless of their origins. This recognition sets the agenda for his own positive argument. That is to say he is committed to demonstrating how illegitimate origins (force) can produce legitimate allegiance; how might can change into right. When we recall the circumstances of 1688 and the Hanoverian succession of 1714 then the practical purchase of this entire line of enquiry is not going to be far away (see *E–PrS*).

Although Hume's demonstration is perhaps the most articulate the general principles upon which he draws were shared by his compatriots. The key principle we have already met. The explanation of the facts of obligation has to be sought in social life and not by invoking an extra-societal notion of a state of nature. Hume's account of how might becomes right pivots on the effect of time. But time is effective because it enables habits to be formed. As we have already hinted, the role played by habit is one of the crucial components in the Scots' social theory.

For Hume all governments (even despotic ones) rest on 'opinion' (*E–FPG*: 32). He also claimed more specifically, that 'antiquity always begets the opinion of right' (33 cf. *E–IPC*: 512). ('Opinion' here refers to what we have called 'belief'; the fact that allegiance reposes on a disposition in the minds of those who obey, see Chapter 5 for further discussion.) This claim echoes the argument that Hume had recently put forward in Book III of the *Treatise*. In that work he had noted already that the 'first origin of every nation' is scarcely ever anything other than usurpation and rebellion and had observed that it is 'time alone' that 'gives solidity' to the right of rulers to govern (*THN*: 556). A few pages later he repeated the observation with a significant refinement, 'time *and custom* give authority to all forms of government and all successions of princes; and that power which at first was founded only on injury and violence becomes in time legal and obligatory' (566; my emphasis).

Hume is here exploiting the established principle of prescription. This principle is a standard component in the jurisprudential account of property. That Hume should exploit it reveals his close linkage, especially in the *Treatise*, with that whole body of theory (cf. Buckle 1991). In the *Treatise* in his discussion of property Hume had defined prescription or long possession as conveying title 'to any object' (*THN*: 508). Given this context it should come as no surprise to discover Smith in his jurisprudence lectures echoing Hume's argument with his remark that 'everything by custom appears to be right' (*LJ*: 322). To gloss this: I might not be able to explain how this clock came originally to be associated with my family but the fact that it has been in my family's possession for generations means that it is just as rightfully mine as if I had purchased it this morning. A contentious concrete example would be: even though the British contest the basis of the Argentines' contractual title to the Malvinas Islands, they maintain independently that they own the Falkland Islands because they have had jurisdiction of the islands for over a century and a half and the inhabitants consider (believe, opine) themselves British.

The principle of prescription thus provided Hume with an established means to show how what matters is current belief (right) not any set of facts about what happened in the past, 'originally' (might). Support for this interpretation is found in the essay on the original contract. He there uses this same terminology when he observes that subjects from originally obeying a ruler out of 'fear and necessity' come to consent willingly 'because they think that from long possession he has acquired a title' (*E–OC*: 475).[13] Note how Hume here has reversed the order of normative cause and effect. People consent *because* they think their rulers are entitled to their obedience; they do not think that entitlement is the effect of an act of consent on their part (cf. 478).

Like the prescriptive title to a piece of property so the ruler's title is the product of time. But, for Hume, since time produces nothing 'real' then to talk of property, or title, as the effect of time can only mean it is the 'offspring of the sentiments on which time alone is found to have any influence' (*THN*: 509).[14] How does time influence sentiments? Time is the medium, so to speak, through which custom, or habit, operates and 'nothing causes any sentiment to have greater influence upon us than custom' (556). As we shall see in Chapter 4, Hume attributes to custom a decisive role in establishing the coherence of experience; it is indeed the 'cement of the universe' through its indispensable presence in identifying causal relations. At this point it is more useful to concentrate on custom's assumptions and preconditions.

A custom is necessarily a creature of time. It is meaningless to talk of acquiring a habit overnight. Walking to work through the park is only a habit if I have done it many times. A corollary of this is that an ineliminable gradualness is built into the process – on each occasion that I take that walk I become more accustomed to that routine. Hume implies this when he states that 'time by degrees ... accustoms the nation' to regard as lawful princes who were initially thought usurpers (*E–OC*: 474–5). We shall come across this gradualness again.

In order that a routine can be established there has to be some fixity or constancy in the experience – I have had that job in that location and lived at my current address for some time. Habits are repeated responses to a stable set of circumstances. This repetitiveness leaves its mark. In a common but revealing phrase, habits become 'second nature'. As such they share some of the key features of 'first nature', or instinct. Reid quite explicitly linked them. Both are 'mechanical principles' that 'operate without will or intention' (*AP*: 550). They can both in this way also be contrasted with rational action. In a straightforward sense rationality can be associated with maturity, whereas a baby's behaviour is largely instinctive (Reid prominently includes breathing, sucking and swallowing in his examples of instincts and these are for him clear testament to a Providential scheme (545)). Habits, too, are especially potent in childhood (cf. Hume *THN*: 486). The Scots implicitly attach a lot of importance to this point. The very fact that humans are social creatures means that they are exposed to the formative force of habit, they are, as Ferguson put it, 'withal in a very high degree susceptible of habits' (*ECS*: 11 cf. *PMPS*: I, 209). We noted earlier how Ferguson saw the duration (the constancy) of familial relationships growing into habit. By stressing habit formation in childhood (what Turnbull calls 'early accustomance' (*Principles*: 99)) the Scots are emphasising the importance of socialisation.

A good example of this process in operation is provided by Hume in his account of legitimation or the temporalisation of value. He argues if human generations (like silkworms) replaced themselves totally at one moment then that might give credence to the Contractarian theory. (As Annette Baier happily puts it 'contractarianism is for the butterflies' (1991: 264).) But the facts are different. Human societies comprise continually changing populations, so that to achieve any stability it is necessary that 'the new brood should conform themselves to the established constitution and nearly follow the path which their fathers, treading in the footsteps of theirs, had marked out to them' (*E–OC*: 476–7). The 'brood' conforms not as a consequence of any deliberate (read, adult) decision but because there is a pre-existent path. This path they follow because they neither know no other route nor even consider the possibility of there being one; they have been socialised into it. As Hume puts it in another related essay, 'habit soon consolidates what other principles of human nature had imperfectly founded and men once accustomed to obedience never think of departing from that path in which they and their ancestors have constantly trod' (*E–OG*: 39). Custom and habit 'operating on the tender minds of the children' thus 'fashion them by degrees' for social life (*THN*: 486).

As Hume's use of the verb 'fashion' suggests, habits or customary ways of behaving not only stabilise they constrain. Ferguson remarks that they 'fix the manners of men' (like instinct fixes the behaviour of animals) (*PMPS*: I, 232). Echoing Hume's argument about stability, Ferguson goes on to observe that without that fixity 'human life would be a scene of inextricable confusion and uncertainty' (*Ibid.*). This fixity constrains by circumscribing the range of effective or discernible options. This delimiting of options applies to institutions as well as to individuals. Governments, for example, are restricted as to what policies they can effectively implement. Dunbar thinks it 'seldom in the power of government to mend the morals of a people' (*EHM*: 51). Likewise Robertson, referring to trial by combat, thinks that no custom 'how absurd soever it be' was 'ever abolished by the bare promulgation of laws and statutes' (*VPE*: 325). Since customs are creatures of time then time, that is gradual alterations in the sentiments of people, is what changes them. Trial by combat thus fell into disuse with the development of 'science' and 'civility'.

This example has another message. While the Scots clearly appreciate the conservative power of custom, they also recognise that customs can be bad as well as good, though in either case they are capable of enduring for a considerable period (see Ferguson *PMPS*: I, 208). Kames' 'improving' essay on *The Gentleman Farmer* (1776) provides some good examples. He criticises his countrymen because in their agricultural practices they have been 'led entirely by custom not reflection' (361). Custom is so powerful that 'execrable husbandry' continues to be carried on even when remedies are at hand (262). In the true enlightened spirit of Bacon (see Chapter 3) Kames advocated setting up a Board (like that established to deal with manufacture and fisheries – see Chapter 1 (Bii)) which will issue informed instruction for improvement (369–71). For all Kames' conviction that bad customs can yield to 'rational principles' he is under no illusions that this is an easy task (elsewhere he remarked that it is 'a sort of Herculean labour to eradicate notions that from infancy have been held fundamental' *Loose Hints upon Education* (1781): 282). Certainly he lacks the optimism of a Frenchman like Helvetius that habit and prejudice cannot withstand what Priestley called 'the empire of reason'.[15]

The social, anti-individualist, aspect to this recognition of habit, or custom, was widely shared. It expressed itself in a variety of contexts. The critique of Great Legislators is a revealing case in point.

iii) The Critique of Legislators

While the use of Contractarian language was widespread it had no monopoly. There was an older tradition that offered an explanation of why particular societies adopted the particular political forms, or constitutions, that they did. Here the focus was on some especially gifted individual who gave or shaped the constitution. This individual was the Legislator, or Law-giver. Like the Contractarian theory this tradition also emphasised origins. While it had a long pedigree in Scotland as elsewhere (see Kidd 1993: 81) it had not died out in the eighteenth century. Brumfitt claims it was prevalent among the Encyclopedists (1958: 101) while Rousseau, for example, quite explicitly incorporates the Legislator *within* his Contractarian theory. And Lafitau in his comparison of Amerindian and 'ancient' institutions constantly refers to Legislators (see e.g. *Moeurs*: I, 457). The individualism implicit in this tradition was criticised by many of the Scots, with Ferguson and Millar being particularly prominent.

Who were these Legislators? Millar refers to Brama, Solon, Alfred and Lycurgus and Ferguson to Romulus and Lycurgus. (Lycurgus – the giver of laws to Sparta, as portrayed by Plutarch – is also used by Steuart as a model (*PPE*: I, 218ff.).) The general thrust of Millar's and Ferguson's account is similar. It has two aspects; they explain why in accounts of constitutions these 'persons' are cited and also give an alternative non-individualist account.

In their alternative the force of custom is decisive. Millar comments that before any Legislator could have the requisite authority 'he must probably have been educated and brought up in the knowledge of those natural manners and customs which for ages perhaps have prevailed among his countrymen' (OR: 177). Ferguson argues that if today in an age of 'extensive reflection' we 'cannot break loose from the trammels of custom' then it is very unlikely that in the times of the Legislators, when 'knowledge was less', individuals were more inclined to 'shake off the impressions of habit' (ECS: 123). Along somewhat similar lines Stuart criticises historians for resorting to Legislators 'before legislators could exist', that is, these historians suppose that in an era of the 'greatest ignorance' the 'most difficult' of the sciences is presumed to have approached perfection (Diss: 222–3).

The consequence of this 'entrammelling' is that, according to Millar, the Legislators will 'be disposed to prefer the system already established'. From the effects of this socialisation it follows that it is 'extremely probable' that they will have been 'at great pains to accommodate their regulations to the spirit of the people' and 'confined themselves to moderate improvements' rather than 'violent reformation'. Millar thinks the case of Lycurgus bears this out, because his regulations appear 'agreeable to the primitive manners of the Spartans' (OR: 178). Alfred, too, fits this picture. Voltaire regarded Alfred as 'the English Lycurgus' (see Forbes 1954: 663) and Millar notes how his interpositions have been identified as 'the engine' to explain the origin of various English institutions (HV: I, 271). To this Millar responds that juries, for example, rose from the 'general situation of the Gothic nations' (Ibid.) and the military institutions were not the product of some 'political projector' (I, 181) but stemmed 'imperceptibly' from 'the rude state of the country' (I,179). Hume's treatment of Alfred had been similar. While he does indeed praise Alfred fulsomely (he deserved the appellation 'the Great') he also remarked that the general similarity of his institutions to those found elsewhere at that time precludes him from being 'the sole author of this plan of government'; rather, 'like a wise man he contented himself with reforming, extending and executing the institutions which he found previously established' (HE: I, 50, 53).[16]

Ferguson argues that the supposed Legislator in fact 'only acted a superior part among numbers who were disposed to the same institutions' (ECS: 124; Stuart cites this argument and closely follows Ferguson's terminology (Diss: 248)). For Ferguson the 'rise' of Roman and Spartan governments came not from 'the projects of single men' but from 'the situation and genius of the people' (Ibid.). Millar adopted the same line, 'the greater part of the political system' derived from the 'combined influence of the whole people' (OR: 177). While both Millar and Ferguson point to a 'sociological' rather than individualist explanation they also both go beyond it. What – and this is the first of the two aspects mentioned above – they also do is explain why the individualist argument has been so popular.

From Millar and Ferguson's perspective individualist theory of this sort is myopic, it can only see what is in front of its face. As a result only part of the picture is seen, the part that is easiest to see. Millar allows that some *peculiar* institutions will *sometimes* take their origin from the *casual* interpositions of *particular* persons who *happen to be* placed at the head of a community' (*OR*: 177; my emphases). However, this contingent fact has been exaggerated by individualism into a general explanation. The exaggeration itself is attributable to the 'admiration of distant posterity', which necessarily relates to events and persons that are irredeemably obscure so that they are often 'only recorded by uncertain tradition' (178). Like Millar, Ferguson too believes there is a strong element of the fabulous in these traditions (see *Rom*: I, 3).

That aside, Ferguson's chief observation is that this whole individualist approach cannot provide institutional explanations. When confronted with a particular institution or social practice the 'simplest' explanation (the one most obvious to the myopic) is to attribute it to some 'previous design', that is, to attribute it to some individual's will or purpose as the cause of the institution as an effect.[17] Stuart observes that 'it is easy' to talk of the deep projects of princes, it is 'more difficult to mark the slow operation of events' (*PLS*: 108). Kames gives this a psychological twist when he judges that 'a busy mind ... cannot rest til it find or imagine a beginning to every art'. As examples of this 'busy-ness' he gives Bacchus (inventor of wine) and the various (female) inventors in different 'cultures' of spinning (*SHM*: I, 92). Without the psychological trappings, Dunbar similarly thinks the connection of events with an individual is a 'more popular idea' than seeing them as arising 'necessarily out of the system of man'. This popularity is put down to a natural human trait to celebrate 'founders' and 'inventors'. Of course, like Millar, Dunbar allows, there have been such individuals but institutions are 'more justly reputed the slow result of situations than of regular design' (*EHM*: 61). His account of language (see section Bi above) regards it as a 'fundamental error' to refer to 'great projectors' in order to explain the development of the different parts of speech (93).

Individualistic explanations are thus simplistic and because of that are misleading. They remove individuals from their social context, and since humans are naturally social then this removal is a distortion. From the perspective of the history of social theory this is an important conclusion: social institutions – like pre-eminently but not solely the mode of government – are to be explained by social causes. Stuart neatly summarises this point when he remarks that the disorders between the king and the nobles which affected the whole of Europe in the high Middle Ages are 'not to be referred entirely to the rapacity and the administration of princes. There *must be a cause more comprehensive and general* to which they [the disorders] are chiefly to be ascribed' (*VSE*: 71; my emphasis). From the earlier discussion we can identify these general causes as 'situation and genius' (Ferguson, who also refers to the 'humour and disposition' of the age (*ECS*: 177)) or prevalent 'manners and customs' (Millar) or the 'slow result of situations' (Dunbar) or 'slow operation of events' (Stuart).

D: Unintended Consequences and the Demotion of Purposive Rationality

We have already seen how a number of the Scots give a role to instinct or appetite in their accounts of sociality. The certainty and fixity of instinct (usually indicative

– as in Reid or Kames – of some Providential superintendence) was contrasted with the weakness of reason, that 'feeble and fluctuating principle', as John Gregory called it (*CV*: 19). The critique of Contractarianism was also directed in part against its overestimation of reason's role in guiding action. The more general implication was that *social* institutions were not adequately accounted for by the purposive, or deliberate, acts of individuals. That implication needs explicating.

i) Social Complexity

As we saw in section Ciii, Ferguson thought recourse to Great Men could not provide an adequate explanation of social institutions; the supposed link between intention and institution is missing. Ferguson obviously does not deny that humans are purposive (recall his views on the limitations of the human/animal analogy). Indeed, as we shall see in Chapter 6, he wants to retain a significant element of deliberate action in political life. Nonetheless, he believes that individual purposive action falls short of explanatory power when it comes to institutions.

In perhaps his best-known expression of the point he writes 'nations stumble upon establishments which are indeed the result of human action, but not the execution of any human design' (*ECS*: 122).[18] His use of the verb 'stumble' here is not inadvertent. He wants to suggest the role of 'accident'. This is reinforced by the contrast drawn between 'action' and 'design'. Hence, in this context, forms of government are not simply 'givens' but are the product of human life ('action'). To live in a monarchy, for example, is not the same as living where it snows in winter. But it does not follow from this that monarchy was a 'design', a deliberate outcome of action. Hume provides a good example of this very point. He points out that the first leader was an effective military leader and that in due course (through time and custom) this ad hoc position solidified into a monarchical form of government (*E–OG*: 39–40). Hume comments on this process (see Chapter 5 for details) that though it 'may appear certain and inevitable' in fact government commenced casually because it 'cannot be expected that men should beforehand be able to discover them [principles of government and allegiance] or foresee their operation' (39).

There are two reason for this. First, humans are predominantly engaged in what is most immediately pressing. According to Ferguson, they follow 'the present state of their minds', they strive to 'remove inconveniences'[19] and aim to gain 'apparent and contiguous advantages' (*ECS*: 122). Millar argues similarly. He rejects the view that Anglo–Saxon government was the result of 'deep-laid schemes of policy', rather it was the product of what occurred successively to the people 'for the supply of their immediate wants and removal of accidental inconveniences' (*HV*: I, 375 cf. II, 261). What he has in mind here is how Parliamentary procedure arose merely from the nature of the business under consideration and was not 'the fruit of any pre-conceived system of policy'. In the same vein Stuart thinks that feudal institutions 'were not the effect of a plan or the creation of a projector' but 'unfolded themselves under the influence of human passions and human conduct in a certain condition of society' (*PLS*: 4).

Feudalism, Parliamentary procedure and the like are clearly the product of human action but they are not the fruit of design. To deal deliberately with pressing, immediate or urgent matters produces outcomes that were not part of the original intention. This dissonance between intention and outcome is the second of the two reasons mentioned above. Through pursuing their immediate goals humans arrive 'at ends which even their imagination could not anticipate' (Ferguson *ECS*: 122). Ferguson illustrates this process by utilising (unacknowledged) an image from Rousseau: 'He who first said "I will appropriate this field: I will leave it to my heirs" did not perceive that he was laying the foundation of civil laws and political establishments' (*Ibid.* cf. Rousseau *Disc. Inequality* tr. p. 192). This lack of perception is not, like the inability to digest granite, something that comes simply with the territory of being human but is also the effect of sociality. *Because* individuals are social it means even their most deliberate actions ramify.

The current significance of this ramification is picked up most clearly by Ferguson. As part of his argument to puncture the superiority that 'polished nations' like to parade, he observes that their institutions arose not from their superior wisdom but 'from successive improvements that were made, without any sense of their general effect; and they bring human affairs into a state of complication, which the greatest reach of capacity with which human nature was ever adorned, could not have projected'. Indeed so extensive is this complication that it cannot be 'comprehended in its full extent' (*ECS*: 182). This failure in comprehension means that the process of ramifying complication has produced outcomes far removed from any individual's intentional design.

This can cover two general types of case. The first is when a series of discrete purposive decisions by separate individuals produces an overall outcome that none of them individually intended. This case fits 'market', or 'economic', behaviour, and we shall examine Smith's version shortly. But although this behaviour may be self-interested that is not a necessary feature of this first case. Hutcheson, in fact, supplies an example of the general principle where the process operates the other way round. As part of his argument for a moral sense (see Chapter 7) he remarks that while 'we are only intending the good of others, we undesignedly promote our own greatest private good' (*Inquiry* in *PWD*: 75/*SB*: I, 83).

The second type is when a particular intended policy sets in train a series of events that eventually produce results the opposite of that originally planned. Millar, for example, points out that the benefits of the grand jury in curbing abuses of discretionary power is the opposite of its original intent, which was to facilitate an increase in prosecutions (*HV*: II, 311). Nor is this reversal unique. He regards Magna Carta in the same light. It was intended to establish the 'privileges of a few individuals' not the 'freedom of the common people' yet it was the latter that came about (*HV*: II, 80–1/*HVL*: 360–1).

The argument for ramifying complexity thus reinforces that of section Ciii and the critique of Legislators. The freedom of the English was not the intention or purpose behind the actions of the barons at Runnymede although getting Magna Carta 'signed' was. English freedom is for Millar to be put down to 'the general progress of society' (*HV*: II, 340, 81 etc.), but although that 'progress' consists of an almost infinite series of individual actions it itself was not designed. To reduce the course of history and the subject-matter of history to the purposively rational actions of individuals is a misleading reductionism. This is not the same as saying that individuals are merely carried along by the flow of history. It is one of the hallmarks of the Scottish Enlightenment that (to use later terminology) it recognises both structure and agency.

ii) Ferguson and 'conflict'

One aspect of Ferguson's thought that has been subsequently highlighted is his awareness of the social function of conflict. This emphasis is usually laid by those who want to underwrite his credentials as a pioneer sociologist (see Chapter 8). Like many such recruitments this runs the risk of wrenching an argument out of its original context. Here I want to associate what Ferguson says about conflict with the more general issue of 'unintended consequences'. In this context two passages in the *Essay* stand out.

In the first of these Ferguson is in fact evoking a well-worn traditional argument and not saying anything novel at all. The tradition is civic humanism (see Chapter 1) and one of its leading characteristics is that political tranquillity can be dangerous to liberty. (We will consider this argument in some depth in Chapter 6.) In this vein Ferguson writes that liberty is maintained by 'continued differences and opposition of numbers' and that 'in free states' the 'wisest laws' emanate from the compromise 'which contending parties have forced one another to adopt' (128). It is through each party striving to uphold their own particular concerns that the general interest is fostered. Although Ferguson does not here say so openly, his 'model' is the conflict between patricians and plebeians in Rome.[20] This is part of a familiar story (also told by, for example, Montesquieu (*SL*: Bk 11, *Considerations on the Causes of Roman Greatness and Decadence*, Ch. 8)). The internal struggle was deflected into conquest and territorial expansion but this, in turn, corrupted Rome through the importation of what Kames typically calls 'Asiatic luxury' (*SHM*: I, 473) and an increase in the power possessed by generals; a sequence of events that culminated in Caesar, civil war and the end of the republic (cf. Ferguson *ECS*: 231). The whole of this conventional story of the decline of Rome was a ready-made illustration of the power of unintended consequences. There was also a ready-made vocabulary. The Roman themselves, and their Renaissance heirs, especially Machiavelli, evoked the goddess Fortuna to dramatise how human actions and intentions were blown off course to produce outcomes far removed from those envisaged. Sallust, for example, attributes the decline of Rome after the defeat of Carthage to Fortune turning capriciously against her (*Catiline*: Pref. §10 tr. p. 181) and Machiavelli's *Prince* is pervaded by an interplay between *virtu* and *fortuna* (see especially Ch. 25). This same language is used by the Scots. Dunbar, for example, states simply 'Fortune governs events' (*EHM*: 175). However, this idiom is also typically intermingled with the more overtly Christian vocabulary of Providence.

This vocabulary is a significant presence in Ferguson's second passage. In Chapter 4 of Book I of the *Essay*, entitled 'Of the Principles of War and Dissension', he states that 'mankind ... appear to have in their minds the seeds of animosity' (20). It is because mankind also possesses principles of union or sociality that this otherwise unremarkable statement attains some significance. It is not simply either a comment on human imperfection (sin) or a recognition, as in Contractarian theory, of the need to identify a motivation to quit the state of nature and establish civil society.[21] Ferguson detaches the motivations from the natural jurisprudential preoccupation with government. It is this detachment that provides the best grounds for Ferguson-as-sociologist.

In support of his claim for natural animosity Ferguson cites the evidence. Everywhere, regardless of geographical or physical circumstance, humans have fallen into 'cantons and affected a distinction of name and community' and these distinctions prompt loyalty to one's own (see above) and hatred of the 'other' (21). Hence the 'perpetual hostilities' among rude tribes and separate clans. Ferguson does not attribute these hostilities to an 'economic' conflict over resources, rather 'we are fond of distinctions, we place ourselves in opposition and quarrel under the denomination of faction and party without any material subject of controversy' (*Ibid.*). The 'nations of North America' engage in 'almost perpetual wars' even though they have 'no herds to preserve, nor settlements to defend' (22). In addition, this natural disposition to oppose is reflected in sports and amusements; these are 'frequently an image of war' and, indeed, often fatal. These 'facts' are significant for two linked reasons. Not only do they support 'natural' as opposed to socially-induced animosity but also, as a consequence, they severely damage a 'materialist' interpretation of history (see Chapter 5).

Although this natural animosity might seem to 'arraign our species', Ferguson is now able to itemise a number of positive social consequences. These occur on both the societal and individual level. On the latter, Ferguson believes, that conflict can manifest the 'best qualities' (20) or 'greatest abilities' (24) of men. He cites generosity, self-denial, candour and resolution as examples. The social principles of loyalty and patriotism that we discussed earlier can now be seen to be the by-product of natural animosity. In the light of this Ferguson claims that the apparently 'amicable intention' of disarming envy and jealousy and replacing them with humanity and justice is a waste of effort (25). If we want amicable virtues or principles of union then we have also to buy their apparent opposites, we can't pick and choose.

Since these principles of union go beyond the individual then this same conclusion has to be drawn at the societal level. Hence, it is that external threat is 'frequently useful to nations' since it cultivates solidarity and unity (22). Ferguson goes further than this trite observation. He claims that 'without the rivalship of nations and the practice of war, civil society itself would scarcely have found an object or a form' (24); with no 'emulation' from abroad 'we should probably break or weaken the bonds of society' (25). The unintended consequence of aggression is thus to strengthen your opponent and make the success of your assault less likely.

Ferguson's version of the principle of 'asocial sociability'[22] is thus part of the wider recognition that the explanation of social institutions and practices is not reducible to outcomes that emanate from deliberate human purposes. It is also part of a theodicy – the problem of evil, or the reconciliation of human wickedness with God's goodness. The presence of this aspect is evident in the concluding paragraph to this chapter of the *Essay*. Ferguson, in summation, observes that these reflections 'tend to reconcile us to the conduct of Providence' (25). I shall return to this issue at the end of the chapter.

iii) Smith and the 'Invisible Hand'

Smith only uses the phrase 'invisible hand' three times but the phenomenon that this image captures pervades the whole of his work, especially the *Wealth of Nations*. While its presence in that work is its best-known appearance, its occurrence in the *Moral Sentiments* is well worth a close scrutiny. For completion's sake the third reference is a passing literary flourish in the posthumous *History of Astronomy*.[23]

In the *Moral Sentiments* the phrase crops up in the course of a complex argument. In a sense this is fitting because one of the strands of that argument is that humans delight in complexity and contrivance even though strictly these are purely functional 'means' to some desired 'end'. This 'delight' Smith believes is a 'secret motive of the most serious and important pursuits of both private and public life' (181). The 'pursuit' he considers in most detail is industry or the motivation to attain imagined benefits. The fact that these benefits are 'imagined' is crucial. Smith presents a contrast between the 'real satisfaction' afforded by the palaces of the rich and the 'pleasures of wealth and greatness' that 'strike the imagination as something grand, beautiful and noble' (183). It is the latter, which although a 'deception', nevertheless 'raises and keeps in continual motion the industry of mankind'. The fact that Smith a little later contrasts 'real happiness' – understood as 'ease of body and peace of mind', a condition that can be possessed by all ranks, even beggars (185) – with the 'baubles and trinkets' with which the rich surround themselves suggests a classically Stoic perspective. Many commentators have duly interpreted Smith in that way[24] but in the current context this interpretation would miss the thrust of Smith's argument.

Smith commends the deception. It is through toil and industry that the earth has been transformed, cities founded, population increased and provided for and 'all the sciences and arts which ennoble and embellish human life' have been invented (183). The implication is that if Stoic precepts had been adhered to, that is, had mankind confined themselves to 'real' satisfactions, then human life would have been crude and impoverished. (As we shall see in Chapter 6, Smith sees nothing ennobling or redemptive about poverty.) Indeed Smith later calls the cultivation of land, the advancement of manufactures and increase of commerce 'real improvements' through which 'mankind are benefited' and 'human nature ennobled' (229). If nothing else this last passage when juxtaposed to the earlier one should alert us to the dangers of building an interpretation on the foundation of Smith's use of the word 'real'.

It might seem we have strayed from our theme but the reference to 'deception' is a pointer to the implicit presence of 'unintended consequences'. This ennoblement was achieved as a result of individuals desiring to obtain benefits for themselves. The fact that Smith refers to these desires in unflattering terms (they are 'vain and insatiable' and embody 'natural selfishness and rapacity' (184)) and denigrates their objects as baubles is closely related to Mandeville's dictum of 'private vice, public benefit'. It should come as no surprise that this dictum has itself been seen as an expression of 'unintended consequences' (see Hayek 1967). In Smith the link with unintended consequences comes to the surface in the person of the 'proud and unfeeling landlord'. It is in telling his tale that the 'invisible hand' becomes visible as a phrase. This landlord (or generically the rich) cannot literally consume any more than his meanest peasant (or the poor); the human stomach can only hold just so much food (see *WN*: 81). The consequence is:

> They are led by an invisible hand to make nearly the same distribution of the necessaries of life which would have been made had the earth been divided into equal portions among all its inhabitants and thus without intending it, without knowing it, advance the interest of society and afford means to the multiplication of the species. (*TMS*: 184–5)

Two further points are worth making about this passage. To illustrate the principle Smith refers also to the desires of the rich to 'fit up the palace'. To realise that desire means employing many people. Not only does this mean that the 'luxury and caprice' of the rich has provided employment but also that it has provided more employment than would have been forthcoming from 'humanity and justice' (184). This juxtaposition will figure prominently in the *Wealth of Nations*, and I will take it up in Chapter 6. The second point is that immediately after the long sentence containing the phrase 'invisible hand' Smith continues, 'When Providence divided the earth ...' This vocabulary was, as we have already noted, common in this context but before discussing it the reference to the 'invisible hand' in the *Wealth of Nations* has to be addressed, not least because that vocabulary is there absent.

Compared to the reference in the *Moral Sentiments* the context in the *Wealth of Nations* is more straightforward. Each individual (with capital) seeks to employ it to his own advantage and, in practice, this means preferring domestic over foreign industry. Through pursuing this preference he also promotes the public interest. The latter, however, was 'no part of his intention'; he was led to promote it 'by an invisible hand' (*WN*: 456). Three comments on this are in order.

First, this is polemical. Since the public interest is furthered in this manner then for someone to attempt to achieve that end through design is superfluous. Indeed the attempt is unwarranted since should a 'statesman' take that role upon himself then it would be to 'assume an authority' which cannot even be safely entrusted to a 'council or senate'. This is indicative not only of Smith's critique of mercantilism but also of his positive commitment to the 'system of natural liberty'. That commitment will be examined in Chapter 6, where the *political* dimension of the invisible hand will be brought out.

Second, Smith does not put forward this process without reservation. What he does say is that, 'nor is it always the worse for the society that it [the public interest] was no part of it [his intention]. By pursuing his own interest he frequently promotes that of society more effectually than when he really intends to promote it.' Although the general drift of this passage is clear, it does allow for exceptions. Smith has left room for intervention, he is consistently able to license departure from laissez-faire. This licence he duly utilises.[25]

The final comment is that Smith himself remarks of this process that it applies in 'many other cases'. This reinforces the earlier remark that though the phrase 'invisible hand' might be rare, the phenomenon it captures is not. We will come across a number of these 'other cases' as we proceed but one of them is worth mentioning now. Smith is fearful of the consequences of public debt. However, this indebtedness is the unintended consequence of the stability that commercial societies enjoy. Those with money feel confident enough to extend credit to the government, whereupon government dispenses with saving and relies on tax to repay. In due course the government has to borrow in order merely to pay back the interest on money lent with the consequence that the capital debt continues to grow. The consequence is the probable ruin in the long run of 'all the great nations of Europe' (*WN*: 911). This is a case (here heavily abbreviated, see Chapter 6 for a fuller discussion) where the outcome of individual actions is not benign. This suggests that for Smith, at least, unintended consequences are not simply to be subsumed under some ultimately benevolent Providential plan. This point we can briefly pursue in a concluding subsection.

iv) Providence and Complacency

A number of bold claims have been made for the articulation of the idea of 'unintended consequences' by the Scots. Duncan Forbes thought that their recognition of what he calls (after Wundt) the 'law of the heterogeneity of ends' was the 'deepest insight into the historical process that the rationalist eighteenth century ever attained' (1954: 651). Ronald Hamowy judged the development of the 'theory of spontaneously generated orders' the 'single most significant sociological contribution of the Scottish Enlightenment (1987: 3). In apparent contrast other scholars have argued that in context the passages reveal the continuing presence of a tradition in Scottish Presbyterianism that God uses people for divine purposes that remain unknown to them (Sher 1985: 180) or that the 'doctrine of unintention' was part of a still potent Calvinist legacy (Allan 1993: 207–17).

Certainly Providence is frequently invoked, but the crucial issue is what interpretative weight to put on this. As a generalisation the thinkers of the Scottish Enlightenment operate within a theologically underwritten conception of cosmic order and regularity (see Chapter 7). This applies both to individual actions and interactions, both to the possession of a social appetite and to the presence of enduring social practices and institutions. Within this generalisation there is room for nuance. There is little reason to doubt that for professional clerics like Reid, Blair, Robertson (and a former one like Ferguson[26]) or committed theists like

Kames evocations of Providence were no mere rhetorical flourish. The relative insignificance of the individual when set against the solidity and utility of human institutions suggested a 'gap' that only some deep-seated superintendence could 'fill'. Yet as Hume bears out this is not necessary despite the fact that all the key ingredients seem to be present in his thought. He is clearly committed to the idea of the uniformity of nature; he attributes the coherence of society to habitual expectation (cf. Berry 1982); and he also accounts for the emergence of key social institutions through a piecemeal accretion of short-term decisions (cf. Haakonssen 1981: 19–20[27]). While for others these ingredients are evidence of Providential Design, Hume is notorious for his religious scepticism (see Chapter 7).

Smith is, in many ways, a test case. MacFie (1967: 107), for example, interprets the doctrine that underlies the 'invisible hand' as grounded ultimately in faith while Campbell (1971: 73,70 cf. Forbes 1954: 653) thinks the phrase 'unfortunate' and that it operates in a supplementary fashion 'to cap a causal explanation with a teleological one'. (Hume dispenses with the cap.) Clearly there is room for debate but Campbell's position seems to me to be about right. Smith does subscribe to the underwritten conception of order and regularity but his actual explanations proceed without that backcloth becoming an actor on the stage. And the example of the national debt is a salutary reminder that the process is not invariably benign.

Providentialism is also easily allied to complacency. If all's well that ends well and if that is so thanks to God rather than man, then present hardships and inequities may be accepted. An alliance, however, is not the same as an identity. Doubtless the sentiment that all is well with the world when the rich man is in his castle and the beggar is at his gate was not unknown to the Scottish Enlightenment and doubtless, too, the sentiment could be pressed into ideological service.[28] But that does not mean that the Scots were mindless supporters of the status quo. As later chapters will demonstrate, all the Scots who belong to the Enlightenment, in differing respects and to differing degrees were critical of their society.

E: Conclusion

The Scots take human sociality seriously. This seriousness is evident in two important ways. First, sociality is not taken for granted as an axiomatic first principle. There is a conscious attempt to establish it on an evidential footing. While this may not have been philosophically very sophisticated, the exploitation of the classical literature of their upbringing and the ransacking of the various ethnographic reports now readily available reveal a commitment to actual human experience as the touchstone of true knowledge.

Having established empirically that humans are social beings, the Scots – and this is the second expression of their seriousness – proceeded to address the consequences that followed. Since humans are social then any acceptable account of human society must start there. It was because much of the prevailing social theory did not appear to do that that the Scots criticised it so wholeheartedly. Individuals we certainly are and rational we certainly are but an individualistic rationalism is inadequate as a *social* theory. The recognition of that inadequacy is what helps to make the Scots historically important.

Hobbes, to take the clearest if therefore also the least typical case, deliberately decomposed 'society' into its constituent individual components and then pared individuals down to their basic motivations. Having done that, he believed he knew how society operates and that he could prescribe how it should be organised so that it would operate effectively. For the Scots this represents a false reductionism. Society and its institutions cannot be accurately understood in this manner. If these institutions are thought of as something in need of explanation then the principle of explanation must be commensurate. Social institutions require social explanations. What counts as an explanation was a question the Scots asked. How they asked it and what answers they came up with it is the subject-matter of the next chapter.

Notes

1. Hume thought that the first page of Thucydides was 'the commencement of real history' (*E–PAN*: 422) and Smith believed that no author has 'more distinctly explained the causes of events than Thucydides' (*LRBL*: 95); Smith thought Livy the best of the Latin historians (108). See Chapter 3 for the importance of the reference to 'causes'.
2. J. Lafitau *Moeurs des sauvages ameriquains* (1724); P. Charlevoix *Journal historique d'un voyage de l'Amérique* (1744). Millar, for example, in his *Ranks* cites each author 6 times (Caesar's *De Bello Gallico* and Tacitus' *Germania* were cited 10 and 8 times respectively); Ferguson cites Charlevoix 13 times and Lafitau 5 times in the *Essay*.
3. Reid (*AP*: 545) distinguishes these where an instinct equals a 'mechanical principle' and an appetite equals an 'animal principle' but also admits that this is a distinction for distinction's sake.
4. He draws support from Buffon's comprehensive and vastly influential *Natural History* (1749 onwards) and cites his judgement that there is an 'infinite distance' between human faculties and those of the 'most perfect animal' (*CV*: 10). Buffon himself in his *Natural History of Man*, which was part of the multi-volumed *Natural History*, still differentiated humans by the traditional criteria of reason, language and the possession of a soul (III, sect. 1). Gregory, who was a doctor, also cites (7) the work of Stahl and while criticising the presentation of his argument states his approval of Stahl's opposition to mechanism and its superiority to (by implication) La Mettrie (see Chapter 1). Gregory is here tip-toeing around the edge of a lively debate. Stahl's ideas were criticised by Cullen but had been picked up, though still critically, by Whytt, Cullen's predecessor at Edinburgh (cf. Hankins 1985: 124; Wright 1990 is especially informative). Gregory's book was translated into French by Robinet and his view of instinct criticised by Diderot (cf. Hastings 1936: 136n.).
5. Dunbar also thinks standardly that the Orangs need an enlargement of ideas but believes that the ideas of animals are fixed. For Monboddo it is the capacity of acquiring higher faculties not their actual possession that differentiates human nature (see letter to Harris in Knight 1900: 73, cf. Cloyd 1972: 64). He thinks the Orang and large monkeys stand to humans as the ass does to the horse (letter to Pringle in Knight 1900: 85), and because they cannot speak is not sufficient reason to deny them 'the appellation of men' (*OPL*: I, 176n.). For discussion of the debates raised by the Orang see Wokler (1976, 1988).
6. Although he does not cite Dunbar's work this passage gives a perfect exemplification of Aarsleff's (1974: 104–5) thesis that the point behind the search for the origins of

language was an attempt to get down to basic principles in order to distinguish what was owing to nature and what to art. For a detailed discussion of Dunbar on 'analogy' and its links with associationist psychology, see Berry 1987.

7. For example, substantive nouns predate adjectives, impersonal verbs predate personal and prepositions and pronouns 'expressing so very abstract and metaphysical idea would not easily or readily occur to the first formers of language' (*Considerations* in *LRBL*: 219 cf. 214, 213 etc.). (For discussion of Smith's argument, see Land (1977) and for a comparative analysis, see Berry (1974a)). Smith's argument was closely followed by Dunbar (to the extent of using the same example – cf. *EHM*: 83 *Consids*: 216) and drawn upon by Blair (*LRB*: 101) and even by Monboddo despite basic disagreements (*OPL*: II, 45).

8. Hutcheson's account is close to Aristotle's account of *philia* since he stresses its basis in moral excellence and defines friendship as 'the affectionate union of minds resembling each other in virtuous manners' (*SIMP*: 84).

9. There is extensive secondary commentary on this point. For example that Locke's account of the State of Nature in the *Second Treatise* contained a historical as well as a normative component is argued by several commentators, for example Ashcraft (1968) and reiterated with discussion of other interpretations in Ashcraft (1987).

10. There is a large body of commentary. For contextual discussions see especially Buckle & Castiglione (1991) and Thompson (1977); less historical and more analytical are Gauthier (1979) and Brownsey (1978). A good general exposition is to be found in Miller (1981). That Hume's account is pivotal in the history of Contractarian thought is upheld by Lessnoff (1986).

11. Why Locke should have been thus singled out is largely explained by the role that he was seen as playing in early eighteenth-century British political debate (cf. Thompson 1976, Kenyon 1977, Dickinson 1977). Locke's route into the Scottish Enlightenment is not straightforward but it would seem that Carmichael's commentary on Pufendorf (much praised by Hutcheson, see *SIMP* Preface) is an important conduit (see Moore & Silverthorne 1983, 1984).

12. In the *Treatise* justice (and the others) are called 'artificial' virtues. In part this earlier term reflects Hume's closer adherence to the Contractarian/jurisprudential approach and its omission in the later *Essay* is a deliberate ploy by Hume to avoid interpretative confusion (the idea that justice was 'artificial' was criticised by many of his contemporaries – most notably and reflectively by Reid (*AP*: 5, 1) but also by Kames *PMNR*: 65ff., 129ff.). Even Smith thought Hume had overstated utility (*TMS*: 87ff.). In the *Treatise* Hume had declared that 'artificial' was not to be contrasted with 'natural' in the sense of 'inseparable from the species' (*THN*: 484); justice is a necessary invention and when any invention is absolutely necessary it can be said to be as 'natural' as 'anything that proceeds immediately from original principles'. Vlachos (1955: 38) sees Hume's thought in the *Treatise* as steering (like Pufendorf's) a middle course between Hobbes and Locke. See Chapter 6 for an extended discussion of justice.

13. Hume also uses the phrase in the politically charged context of the Hanoverian succession – 'long possession ... must ere this time, in the apprehension of a great part of the nation, have begotten a title ... independent of their present possession' (*E–PrS*: 511).

14. Cf. Smith *LJ*: 32, 37. Kames had included a treatment of prescription in his *Essays upon Several Subjects in Law* (1732) – and reiterated in *ELS* (Art. 33) – where he criticised the standard natural law account and linked property rights to the psychological feelings of ownership (see Ross (1972): 36). This would seem to have had some impact upon Smith and arguably also paved the way for Hume's exploitation.

15. Priestley, Letter to Burke (1791) in *Writings* (1965: 255 cf. 198). Cf. Passmore 1970: esp. Chs. 9 and 10.

16. Forbes regards Hume's views on Legislators as one of the areas where he differs from

the other Scots (1975a: 308). In support he cites (316) Hume's reference to 'Legislators and founders of states who transmit a system of laws and institutions' (*E–PG*: 54). Despite this, Forbes is also quick to point out Hume's awareness of the gradual process whereby laws are slowly developed. Indeed in another essay this gradualism makes Hume undermine the case for a Legislator: 'To balance a large state or society, whether monarchical or republican, on general laws, is a work of so great difficulty that no human genius, however comprehensive, is able, by the mere dint of reason and reflection to effect it. The judgments of many must unite in this work ...' (*E–AS*: 124). Since the sentiments here jell so well with Hume's general argument (as exemplified in his view of Alfred) Forbes may be judged to have overdrawn Hume's distinctiveness.

17. In his history of the Roman republic he is more even-handed. Referring to those institutions that the Romans themselves ascribe to Romulus and Numa, he remarks that whether they were the 'suggestions of a particular occasion' or the 'invention of ingenious men directed by deep premeditation' does not detract from their existence (*Rom*: I, 11). Kames too at one point implies that he accepts that Lycurgus was a real person (*SHM*: I, 487). On 'Euhemerism' (the doctrine that mythical personages were in fact historical) generally, see Manuel 1959: 85ff.

18. This phrase is frequently cited by Hayek, see Chapter 8.

19. This term probably deliberately echoes Locke (see *Second Treatise*: §13), though Hume, too, had used it in the same context (*THN*: 485), also Kames *HLT*: 20.

20. Ferguson details the struggle in *Rom*: I, Chs. 2 and 3. Although he points out defects he also comments that the Romans 'enjoyed the most envied distinction of nations, continual prosperity and almost uninterrupted succession of statesmen and warriors elsewhere unequalled in the history of mankind' (90).

21. Hobbes, with his depiction of 'natural' life as nasty and brutish may have given an unacceptably dramatic version of this motivation (*Leviathan*: Ch. 13) but Locke refers to the 'corruption and vitiousness of degenerate men' (*Second Treatise*: §128) and Pufendorf to man being 'at all times malicious, petulant, and easily irritated, as well as quick and powerful to do injury' (*On the Law of Nature and Nations*: 2–3–15). Neither Locke nor Pufendorf regard this as the whole truth about the natural condition but both require some such traits to provide a reason to contract out of the State of Nature and establish civil government.

22. This particular term (*ungesellig Geselligkeit*) is Kantian (*Idea for a Universal History* [1784] tr. 1963: 15). Ferguson's work was popular in Germany (the *Essay* was translated into German in 1768) – see Oz-Salzburger, 1995 – although the notion captured by that term is hardly his alone; for a brief survey (that does not include the Scots) see Wood (1972).

23. Smith writes, '... heavy bodies descend and lighter substances fly upwards by the necessity of their own nature; nor was the invisible hand of Jupiter ever apprehended to be employed in those matters' (*EPS*: 49). The context is the polytheism of savages and heathen antiquity. The presence of the phrase here appears to have been noticed first by MacFie (1971).

24. Cf. inter alia MacFie (1967), Dwyer (1987), MacIntyre (1985), Sher (1985) and (the most developed) Brown (1994). But Stoicism is a philosophical language with many idioms. For a fuller discussion doubting the active role of Stoicism in Smith, see Berry (1994).

25. Scholars have identified these departures. For a good survey, see Skinner (1974a). In Chapter 6 we will see a significant illustration of this in his view of education as an antidote to some of the consequences of the division of labour.

26. Ferguson does not always invoke Providence. Commenting on the wide distribution of power, he says that this favourable result was the work of 'a species of chance' rather than anything 'human wisdom could ever calmly devise' (*ECS*: 237).

27. Haakonssen calls Hume's account of justice as the unintended consequence of individual

human actions 'one of the boldest moves in the history of the philosophy of law' (1981: 20).

28. Sher thinks the Providentialism that enwrapped the notion of 'unintended consequences' was part of a 'profoundly conservative doctrine' that was central to the ideological role played in Scottish society by the Moderate clergy (1985: 327, 53–4, 205, 240, 189 etc.). On 'ideology' see Chapter 8.

3

Science, Explanation and History

For the Enlightenment 'science' was a powerful weapon to hurl against the forces of darkness. Nowhere was this potency more evident than in the achievements of natural science. In a celebrated snatch of verse Alexander Pope captured the impact of the greatest scientist:

> Nature and Nature's laws lay hid in night:
> God said, Let Newton be! and all was light.

For thinkers of the Enlightenment, with Scotland at the forefront, Newton's achievement was both a model and a challenge. He had shown what could be done and how to do it. The challenge was to emulate his work; to achieve for the moral or social sciences what he had done for natural science. Newton himself speculated on precisely these lines. In his *Optics* he remarked that if, through pursuit of his method, natural philosophy becomes perfected, so, in like fashion, 'the bounds of Moral Philosophy will be also enlarged' (Qn. 31 (1953: 179)). Clear proof that this remark did not go unheeded is provided by its presence on the title-page of George Turnbull's *The Principles of Moral Philosophy* (1740). (Turnbull even worked it into his *Treatise on Ancient Painting* (1740): 134.)

Turnbull was not alone in following Newton's agenda. What this shared aspiration reveals is that the social *theorists* of the Scottish Enlightenment should not be identified as a breed apart from social *scientists*. For the Enlightenment as a whole any sharp such division would have seemed perverse. Of course some discrimination can be made. There is a difference between the laboratory-based experimental science of Cullen or the mathematical investigations of McLaurin and the work of Turnbull. Nevertheless it is important to appreciate that the Scottish social theorists were engaged in a scientific enterprise as they understood it. The assumptions and character of that enterprise are the subject of this chapter.

A: Baconianism

The Enlightenment was the heir of the 'scientific revolution' of the seventeenth century. In Scotland this legacy can be plotted via the changes in university curricula. For example, in Aberdeen between 1660 and 1670 Aristotle was replaced with Descartes and Cartesianism was in turn superseded by Newton between 1690 and 1710 (Wood 1993: 6–7). The story is much the same in the other Scottish universities (cf. Shepherd 1982). Newton was not alone; Locke and Bacon also made an impact. The importance of these changes in university curricula is that, as we sketched in Chapter 1, they helped to sow the seeds that bore fruit as the Scottish Enlightenment.

If we leave to one side the actual discoveries and achievements of Newton, Boyle, Huyghens and others, we can best sum up the general pervading 'scientific' spirit in the label 'Baconianism'. Bacon himself was not a scientist but, rather, was a propagandist on science's behalf; as Hume put it, he 'pointed out at a distance the road to true philosophy' (*HE*: II, 112) (cf. Walton 1990 for a detailed comparison of Bacon and Hume). He campaigned for old practices to be swept away. Included in this campaign were not only medieval scholasticism but also two other trends in early modern thought: the alchemical tradition, with its reliance on individual practitioners of natural magic, and scepticism, with its philosophy that all was uncertain or doubtable. But arguably more important than this negative element were Bacon's positive proposals. He redrew the map of knowledge in order to advance learning. The new cartography was based on the three faculties of Memory, Imagination and Reason, to which corresponded the three divisions of human learning – history, poetry and philosophy (*Advancement of Learning*: Bk 2, Ch. 1 (1853: 77–8)). The basis of this advance was 'genuine induction' (*New Organon*: Bk 1, sect. xiv (1853: 386)).

One mark of Bacon's impact is terminology. He divided history into natural and civil. The latter deals with human affairs whereas the former (a 'new kind' *AL*: Introd. [17]) encompassed not only the history of animals and plants but also the 'history of arts'. Bacon was critical of those who separated nature from artifice; the history of arts is the history of 'nature wrought' or 'in constraint' (*AL*: Bk 2, Ch. 2, 79). This understanding of the history of arts (or 'mechanical history' (*Ibid.*: 82) narrows the distance between natural and civil history and it is possible to see the Scots' universalistic conception of history (see Cii below) as effectively assimilating them.[1]

The purpose behind natural history was not mere data collection but also, and this is of especial significance as we shall see, 'to afford light to the discovery of causes' and provide thereby 'a foundation to [natural] philosophy' (*AL*: Introd. 16–17). Philosophy itself encompassed God, nature and man (*AL*: Bk 3, Ch. 1, 116). This ambit proved to have two useful effects. First, it helped deflect charges of atheism that were levelled against some forms of 'new learning' (see Webster 1975: 515). Second, by lumping nature and man together under the label 'philosophy', the foundations for Newton's conviction that natural and moral science might methodologically advance together had been laid. Bacon himself explained that his division of the sciences was only a convenience and was without prejudice to their unity (*AL*: Bk 4, Ch. 1, 151).

There is another element in Bacon's legacy. His whole project had a resolutely utilitarian bent. The discoveries of philosophy are not for their own sake since the 'real and legitimate goal of the sciences is the endowment of human life with new inventions and riches' (*NO*: Bk 1, sect. lxxxi, 416). This goal was institutionalised by the setting up of the Royal Society (Webster 1975: 99) and more generally it jelled with the ethos of 'improvement'. The 'improvers' were centrally concerned to apply 'science' in order to make land increase its yield (agriculture, for Bacon, was an example of 'nature wrought'). John Gregory crisply summarises what is involved in Baconianism when he observes, 'the civil and natural history of Mankind becomes a study not merely fitted to amuse and gratify curiosity, but a study subservient to the noblest views, to the cultivation and improvement of the Human Species' (*CV*: 19). And Bacon himself laid down the governing principle of this joint aim in perhaps his best-known proposition, 'knowledge and human power are synonymous, since the ignorance of the cause frustrates the effect' (*NO*: 1, iii, 383 cf. *AL*: Introd. 20).[2] If we couple that proposition with the aspiration to emulate Newton then we have a succinct characterisation of the Scots' approach and ambition.

B: Causal Explanation

Thanks to Newton we now know why the orbit of the planets is what it is and, moreover, we also know that the explanation of that celestial motion is of a piece with the explanation of terrestrial motion (why the apple when detached from its branch falls to the ground). But why is it that the Amerinds worship many gods? Why is it that the status of women was higher in the feudal era than in earlier times? Why is political power at its most unbridled among the nomadic tribes of Asia? Why do we now treat our prisoners-of-war with more humanity than in the past? Questions such as these require an answer. And not only that, we also need to know if the answers given to one question have any bearing on the answers to the other questions. The way to provide these answers was to see these various social practices as 'effects' to which appropriate 'causes' can be identified. The social theory of the Scottish Enlightenment was a search for such causes and for the connecting links between the causes. Later chapters will cover the actual answers they came up with, here we are interested in their procedure or methodology in arriving at those answers.

i) Narrative Links

In the Preface to the *Historical Law Tracts* Kames laments that law has not been treated or studied effectively. The standard practice is to treat it like geography – 'as if it were a collection of facts merely' (*HLT*: iii). What is needed, instead, is a historical approach. Only upon the adoption of that method will law become a 'rational study'. Nor is law exceptional. In this same context Kames also refers to 'manners' and 'arts' and, a little later, adds 'the constitution of a state' and 'its government' (iv).

These are all examples of basic social institutions. What makes them 'basic' is their permanency. But the permanent is not the immutable. There is change but that itself presupposes something enduring. I, Chris Berry, have changed physically and emotionally since I was eighteen but thirty years on I am still Chris Berry: the personal pronoun refers to an enduring subject (identity). The fact that identity can be lost is not here relevant. What matters is, first, that personal identity has a temporal or narrative structure and, second and as a consequence, that the way to understand me today is to retell the story of my life. The upshot of all this is that to understand basic social institutions means to tell the story, to write history. This is important. The Scots' social theory is to a large extent and for this reason presented as history.

Hume said in an oft-quoted letter that he believed 'this is the historical Age and this the historical Nation' (*Letts*: II, 230). In part this belief reflected the popularity of historical works and, in his own case, on the fact that this popularity could bring considerable financial rewards.[3] There are however different ways of writing history and different reasons for writing it. What best characterises history-as-social theory is the scientific endeavour to explain. For Kames, law is a 'rational science' (*HLT*: xiv cf. Stuart *VSE*: vi) when 'reason is exercised in discovering causes and tracing effects through a long chain of dependencies' (v).[4] By this means an overall structure or order can be discerned. What he calls 'events and subordinate incidents' are 'linked together and connected in a regular chain of causes and effects' (iii). In his later *Sketches* Kames repeats the point with emphasis: 'The perfection of historical composition ... is a relation of interesting facts connected with their motives and consequences. A history of that kind is truly a chain of causes and effects' (*SHM*: I, 148).

These repeated references to 'causes' betray the presence of the pervasive Baconianism. It also reflects a long-standing definition of history as 'philosophy teaching by examples'.[5] This combination of the Baconian stress on causes and history as instruction can be seen in Smith's rhetoric lectures. He is reported to have professed that

> The design of historicall writing is not merely to entertain ... besides that it has in view the instruction of the reader. It sets before us the more interesting and important events of human life, points out the causes by which those events were brought about and by this means points out to us by what manner and method we may produce similar good effects or avoid similar bad ones. (*LRBL*: 90)

In the following lecture Smith, like Kames, identifies the connection between cause and effect as the one in which 'we are so interested'. It is the key to historical narration since 'we are not satisfied' with just having 'a fact told us which we are at a loss to conceive what it was that brought it about' (98). It is because in Smith's judgement it is Thucydides who has 'more distinctly explained the causes of events' than any other author that he is pre-eminent among historians (95 cf. 106). Hume, too, thinks very highly of Thucydides (*E–PAN*: 422) and Kames explicitly commends him for his recourse to causal explanation, though he reverses Smith's order of merit by regarding Tacitus as his superior in that regard (*SHM*: I, 148).

ii) Chance and Regularity

In addition to his disparagement of 'geographers' in the *Preface*, Kames also denigrates the sort of history 'much relished by the vulgar' (*HLT*: iv). What the vulgar like are histories of war and conquest, not histories of institutions such as law. More significant is why they prefer the former. A war is 'a singular event' and, like all such events, because of 'the prevalence of chance or fortune', it 'excites wonder' (we will meet this terminology again). The important contrast here is between rational history, which traces causal chains, and writing which catalogues 'facts'. A 'bare recital of facts' is 'uninteresting' (Gregory *CV*: 221) and, to the scientific historian, was the prerogative of chroniclers or annalists.[6] Though not without some merit, the special fault of annalists was that they detached their facts from their antecedents. Why a particular event happened when it did is not explained or, what is the same thing, it is put down to chance.

Hume is instructive on this point. In the opening paragraphs of his essay 'Rise and Progress of the Arts and Sciences' he comments generally on the need to distinguish chance and cause (*E–AS*: 111). If an event is put down to chance then it precludes all further enquiry. This leaves everybody (including the enquirer) in a 'state of ignorance'. However, when an event is 'supposed to proceed from certain and stable causes' then this advances the enquiry and, by means of this advance, it uncovers 'what escapes the vulgar and the ignorant'.

Hume does not deny there is a distinction between chance and cause ('certain and stable') but it is not a distinction in kind. He illustrates it with the performance of a biased die. In a few throws the bias will not reveal itself but it 'will certainly prevail in a great number' (112). Millar uses a very similar example. He supposes that in one or two throws of a die very different numbers will be produced but 'in a multitude of dice thrown together at random the result will be nearly equal' (*OR*: 177). Millar uses this example to underline the difference between 'the character and genius of a nation' and that of an individual. In the former, 'fixed causes' can be identified. The context is the attack on the explanatory utility of Legislators that was discussed in Chapter 2. The significance of that attack (we recall) was to undermine purposive *individual* design as the explanation of *social* institutions. Hume's use of the die was in this way a means of pointing up the difference between the multitude and particular individuals. The latter may by chance escape 'common affection' and 'be ruled by passions peculiar to themselves' but the former will be 'governed' by that affection 'in all their actions' (112).

Despite this difference Hume's use here of two similar verbs ('ruled' and 'governed') indicates why the distinction is one of degree and not kind. This is made explicit when in this same essay he twice refers to 'chance, or secret and unknown causes' (112, 114. In the *Treatise* he had referred to 'what the vulgar call chance' as 'nothing but a secret and conceal'd cause' (*THN*: 130). Cf. Kames *PMNR*: 195). If chance really did operate then it would be impossible to talk of passions 'ruling' even in a particular case, for 'rule' presupposes some traceable linkage between a passion and an outcome: I hit you *because* I was enraged by your behaviour and not coincidentally as a result of my arm lifting. More generally it would reduce events to sheer chaotic randomness. The work of science, however, is to discover cosmos in chaos. The way it has done that, as Newton has recently and triumphantly demonstrated, is by eliciting general rules that themselves represent stable causal relations. It was a major element in Hume's philosophical programme – and the element upon which much of his current renown as a philosopher rests – to analyse exactly what constitutes a causal relation.

iii) Hume on Causation

Hume's analysis of cause has produced a veritable library of commentary.[7] My aim here is modest. The briefest outline of his argument will be enough. The guiding principle is how Hume's analysis fits into his broader programme. For all Hume's heightened philosophical acumen (only Reid is a serious rival) this programme was widely shared among his fellow social theorists. For example, Gregory, who is one of Hume's critics, nevertheless affirms that there are 'laws of the mental constitution' (just as there are of the physical system) which operate in a 'fixt and invariable manner' (CV: 5).

Hume accepts Locke's argument that the principle of innate ideas is false (THN: 160), and its consequence that 'knowledge' must come from experience. Experience comes in the form of 'perceptions', which Hume divides into 'impressions' and 'ideas' (1). The former precede the latter, all our simple ideas proceed from some impression (5); a principle that Hume identifies as the first he has established in 'the science of human nature' (7). These simple ideas can be separated and reunified and made complex by the imagination. We can in this way obtain the idea of a unicorn without, of course, ever perceiving such a thing. However, the imagination is not fickle in its operations, for Hume believes that it is guided by 'some universal principles which render it, in some measure, uniform with itself in all times and places'. There is a 'gentle force', an 'associating quality', whereby simple ideas regularly fall into complex ones (10). There are three principles of association – resemblance, contiguity of time and place, and cause and effect (11).

While strictly a priori (i.e. outside experience) 'anything may be the cause of anything' (249), the world appears in experience as orderly and not capricious, it exhibits regularity as one set of causes is consistently and persistently followed by one set of effects. Accordingly it is to experience that this order and regularity must be traced. In summary:

> All those objects, of which we call the one cause and the other effect consider'd in themselves are as distinct and separate from each other as any two things in nature, nor can we ever, by the most accurate survey of them, infer the existence of one from that of the other. 'Tis only from experience and observation of their constant union that we are able to form this inference; and even after all, the inference is nothing but the effects of custom on the imagination. (405 cf. 103)

Hume's most famous example is the impact of a moving billiard ball upon a stationary one (Abs: 186–7). Upon impact the latter ball moves and this seems an obvious case of causation. But since only a sequence of movements of balls is perceived why is it 'obvious' that this is indeed a causal sequence? Hume analyses the process and identifies three elements – contiguity (the first ball hits the second), priority (the second was static until hit by the first and then it moved) and constant conjunction. There is nothing else. There is no other source of knowledge about causation available to us; in particular we can know nothing of any supposed causal power or force (193 cf. *EHU*: 63). Hume's denial of the knowable existence of some such power was where his contemporaries took philosophical issue with his analysis (see Reid *IP*: Essay 6, Ch. 6; Kames *PMNR*: Pt. 2, Ch. 5). Of the three elements Hume identifies the third is crucial. It is only because every time we have perceived a collision of balls the same sequence occurred that we can properly say the movement of the second ball has been *caused* by the impact of the first. The first two elements alone are insufficient – I might open my desk drawer and the filament in my desk light burns out. As a discrete, one-off sequence this is akin to the billiard balls; it is, however, not causal because each time I open my drawer my light does not fail, there is no constancy in the conjunction.

What this means for Hume is that we attribute causal relations because we habitually associate phenomena. We are 'determined by custom' (*Abs*: 189) to expect or believe that the second ball's movement was caused by the impact upon it of the first ball. We expect, that is to say, that 'like objects placed in like circumstances will always produce like effects' (*THN*: 105). On the basis of this we can predict that the second static ball *will* move when hit by the first ball in motion. The Baconian dimension to this is now evident. If we know, or can predict, that a set of effects will follow from a certain set of causes then we can act accordingly – that building will collapse unless the foundations are of a certain depth ('knowledge of causes is power'). The prediction is the product of our belief that 'nature will continue uniformly the same' (*Abs*: 188). Here ultimately lies the order we experience; an order that is 'nothing but the effects of custom on imagination'. So it is that Hume can claim that custom is the 'guide of human life' and 'the cement of the universe' (189, 198). We can now see that the role that habit plays in Hume's thought, which we discussed in Chapter 2 and which we will meet again, is underpinned by his basic epistemology.

These principles of causation apply universally. They are not restricted to 'natural' phenomena like ballistics, they also apply to the workings of the mind and to the interactions of social life. This extension is indeed Hume's basic purpose in the *Treatise*. In the Introduction, using a striking military metaphor, he states that his aim is 'instead of taking now and then a castle or village on the frontier to march up directly to the capital or centre of these sciences, to human nature itself'. His conviction is that an explanation of the 'principles of human nature', or the formulation of 'the science of man', is the 'only solid foundation' for a 'compleat system of the sciences' (*THN*: xx). As Turnbull's exactly contemporary work demonstrates, Hume was not alone in this ambition and later Ferguson, for example, is equally forthright, 'The history of man's nature is the foundation of every science relating to him' (*IMP*: 15).

For Hume, as the sub-title of the *Treatise* announces, victory will come from the 'experimental method of reasoning'. This method will be employed upon 'moral subjects' in the way it has been upon 'natural', that is, by considering only experience and 'explaining all the effects from the simplest and fewest causes'

(*THN*: xx–xxi). Though Newton is not here mentioned he is undeniably the inspiration.[8] The absence of an explicit reference is due to Hume's concern to distance himself from the directly Providentialist use made of Newton by Turnbull and many others.[9] Although Newton's impact is marked, he was not the only inspiration; Boyle, for example, is another likely candidate (cf. Barfoot 1990).

Perhaps the most important consequence of Hume's commitment to a 'science of man' is the conviction that causal analysis must apply to 'moral subjects'. This application is, indeed, the hallmark of 'science'; it takes the study of mankind and society beyond the range of the vulgar. Hume makes a number of bold claims in this respect. For example, it is equally certain that 'two flat pieces of marble will unite together' as it is that 'two young savages of different sexes will copulate' (*THN*: 402). The essence of Hume's position can be best captured in one of his examples (one he uses on two separate occasions, which strongly suggests that he himself thought it telling). The example is a case where 'natural and moral evidence cement together' such that they are 'of the same nature and deriv'd from the same principles' (*THN*: 406, *EHU*: 90). He presents the predicament of a prisoner in jail. The individual has 'neither money nor interest' and thus escape is impossible due as equally to the 'obstinacy of the gaoler' as it is to the 'walls and bars with which he is surrounded'. Experience has taught that human physical strength cannot destroy stone walls (natural evidence) and that deprived of the means to bribe jailers the latters' interests are bound to their custodial role (moral evidence). In both cases a series of constant conjunctions prevails.[10]

It is the presence of this constancy that enables Hume to believe that 'moral subjects' are amenable to causal explanation and it is this explanation that the 'science of man' is primed to provide. Among the significant consequences of this position is a commitment to 'determinism'. What this commitment involves will be spelt out in Chapter 4, but we can say here that it is this commitment that explains why 'chance' is truly a matter of 'secret causes'. Just as there is no chance randomness or uncaused event in the natural world (*EHU*: 95), neither is there in the interpersonal social world or intrapersonal world of motives and character. This does not mean there is no variation. The theme of Chapter 4 will be how the Scots generally, Hume included, explain diversity. The crux is that causal regularity underpins this diversity and serves to explain it. Hence, although Hume allows that there are 'characters peculiar to different nations and particular persons' yet the knowledge of these characters stems from the necessary uniformity of the actions that flow from them (*THN*: 403). The differences in national character and their explanation are 'experiments in the science of man'. Hume affirms that these must be gleaned from a 'cautious observation of human life'. Provided these experiments are 'judiciously collected and compared', then this science will possess the Baconian hallmarks of certainty and utility (*THN*: xxiii).

iv) Smith and the History of Science

Among Smith's unpublished manuscripts were a series of essays on the history of science. Of these the longest deals with the history of astronomy and this is of interest not only intrinsically (see Skinner (1974b), Longuet-Higgins (1992), Raphael (1985: 107ff.)) but also, more especially, because it serves to link together a number of the themes that we have already covered. This extrinsic interest can be gauged from its full title (also shared by the other essays on Ancient Physics and Ancient Logics) – *The Principles which lead and direct Philosophic Enquiries; illustrated by the History of Astronomy*. Smith is here using 'philosophy' to mean (as he says in the essay) 'the science of the connecting principles of nature' (*EPS*: 45 cf. 119 [*Logics*]). His aim is to explain 'philosophical systems' as attempts 'to order chaos' by allaying the 'tumult of the imagination' (45–6 cf. 105, 107 [*Physics*]). The principles that underlie his explanation are akin to Hume's account of association. If objects are observed to have 'constantly presented themselves to the senses' in a particular order then they become associated so that it is 'the habit of the imagination' to pass from one to the other (40–1). Against this backcloth of imagined coherence anything that disrupts, or produces a 'gap', in the customary connections will produce initially 'surprise' and then 'wonder' at how the disruption occurred (40). Philosophy/science is the attempt to discover a 'connecting chain of intermediate events' such that the imagination can reassume its habits of association and in this way remove the wonder (42). As we noted above (p. 56) this language had been used by Kames (*HLT*: iv) and it was reproduced by Millar, who declared that 'in proportion as men are ignorant and destitute of civilization they are more liable to be impressed with admiration, wonder and surprise' (*HV*: IV, 320).

The history of astronomical systems is then outlined by Smith to illustrate this gap-filling, wonder-removing quality. The systems culminate in Newton's. Not unexpectedly Smith is fulsome. Newton's system not only excels all others in internal coherence but also its principles have a greater degree of firmness and solidity than any other (104–5 cf. *LRBL*: 146). As a consequence his system 'has advanced to the acquisition of the most universal empire that was ever established in philosophy' (104). Smith goes on to remark that so powerful is the system that he has been led to using language that speaks of the connecting principles as 'the real chains' which operate in Nature (105). This remark has led some commentators to regard Smith as a 'conventionalist' rather than a 'realist' in his understanding of science (see especially Lindgren (1969) and also Christie (1987), Reisman (1976: 45) and Raphael (1979: 89–90)). This is far-fetched. Smith had made it clear that his project in the essay is limited to a particular psychological perspective (cf. Campbell 1971: 35). He is concerned with how philosophical systems are 'fitted to soothe the imagination' and, quite explicitly, *not* concerned with their 'absurdity or probability, their agreement or inconsistency with truth or reality' (46). Sophisticated a thinker as Smith was it is a mistake to saddle him with the subtleties of twentieth-century philosophy. If nothing else, as a man of the Enlightenment he would (if it were possible) regard an 'anti-realist' view of science as undercutting the Baconian project.

C: Conjectural History

We noted above (Bi) that one of the striking facts about the Scots' social theory was its historical bent. Their history was of a distinctive kind. Dugald Stewart in his *Life of Smith* gave it the title 'theoretical or conjectural history' and the label has stuck.

i) Sources and Method

The 'experimental' subject-matter of Hume's science of man is 'human life'. This, he says, must be 'cautiously observed'. For the Scots there were three chief sources from which observations could be gleaned – the contemporary world of 'civilised' Scotland and Europe, the contemporary 'savage' world of the Americas, Asia and Polynesia and the world described by the ancient authors. Whereas for the first source personal experience could be a touchstone, for the other two the observations have to be indirect or secondary. Hence the need for the caution advised by Hume. This the Scots duly exercised. They were acutely aware of the pitfalls of indiscriminate use of evidence. This awareness is partly a fruit of a 'historiographical revolution' in early eighteenth-century Scotland[11] and partly a product of their social 'scientific' aspirations.

Of the Scots, Robertson is perhaps the most meticulous and self-conscious (cf. Black (1926: 118f.), Horn (1956)), although Gilbert Stuart extended his rivalry into this arena also. Robertson's sensitivity was established in his first major work, *The History of Scotland*. The contentiousness of this subject (cf. Kidd 1993) meant especial care had to be taken to vindicate his interpretation. In his Preface he itemised the scholarship that he had undertaken (*HSc*: 1–2). Similarly in his Preface to his *View of Progress*, he made a point of saying that he had carefully identified his sources and 'with a minute exactness' had cited his authorities (*VPE*: 307). One reason for this parade of scholarly virtue was that he was critical of those who were cavalier in this regard. Among those criticised was Voltaire. After having paid due to Voltaire's universal genius, Robertson confesses that he was unable to use his work precisely because of his failure to cite his sources (429).[12] Robertson had other targets. He also criticised contemporary chroniclers. He thought that 'little information' is to be obtained from them since they were 'ignorant of the true end and unacquainted with the proper objects of history' (312). He is more precise in the *History of Scotland*. There he declares that prior to the reign of Kenneth II Scottish history is a time of pure fable, which ought to be 'totally neglected or abandoned to the industry and credulity of antiquaries' (*HSc*: 4).

One mark of this credulity and ignorance was an indifference to anachronism. The role given to Legislators in these chronicles is a case in point. This role was the consequence of supposing the abilities of a later age to be present at an earlier date (see Stuart *Diss*: 226 quoted above p. 38). The sin of anachronism was more generally pervasive. For Kames, when studying 'original laws', 'nothing is more apt to lead into error' than 'prepossession derived from modern improvement'

(*HLT*: 91). Stuart similarly remarked that the conjugal ceremonies of the ancient Germans were 'suited exactly to the condition of a rude society' and 'must not be judged by the ideas of a refined age' (*VSE*: 17 cf. 50). In a striking phrase, Stuart elsewhere deemed anachronism 'to violate the laws of history' (though as befits his polemical temper he had Robertson, not chroniclers, in his sights at the time) (*PLS*: 211).

Anachronism is not the only mark of ignorance. These chroniclers were also indifferent to explanation (the 'proper object' of history). Instead they were propagandists. This same defect contaminated many of the ethnographical reports, the Scots' second source of observations. Robertson in his *History of America* commented upon the Spaniards, who, being the first Europeans in the Americas, had the opportunity of seeing the natives before the impact of European conquest and settlement. Alas they were mostly 'illiterate adventurers', ill-equipped for 'speculative inquiry'. The reports of later Spaniards were vitiated because, as participants in a long-running controversy, they either magnified the virtues or aggravated the defects of the natives. In each case the reports were unreliable (*HAm*: 812). Millar echoes these conclusions. The information about the 'rude parts of the world', he notes, stems from 'travellers whose character and situation in life neither set them above the suspicion of being easily deceived nor of endeavouring to misrepresent the fact which they have related' (*OR*: 180–1).

The judicious historian-cum-social theorist is not however at the mercy of propaganda, deception and misrepresentation. Scientific methodology is at hand to retrieve the situation. Two chief methods were employed. The first of these was implicit in the example of the die used by Hume in his *Essays* and Millar. The sheer recurrence of a particular finding has significance ('statistically' so, as we might say today). As Millar says:

> From the number, however, and the variety of those relations they acquire in many cases a degree of authority upon which we may depend with security and to which the narration of any single person how respectable soever can have no pretension. (*OR*: 181)

The second method is implicit in this statement and was openly mentioned by Hume when he remarked that the 'experiments' must be 'compared'.

The Scots were convinced practitioners of (what is now called) the 'comparative method' (cf. Stocking 1975: 73). Once again Millar's testimony can be given in evidence. When 'illiterate men, ignorant of the writings of each other' have described 'people in similar circumstances', so that 'the reader has the opportunity of comparing their several descriptions', then 'from their agreement or disagreement' he is able 'to ascertain the credit that is due to them' (*OR*: 181). For Robertson, it is through 'comparing detached facts' supplied by, among others, missionaries and 'vulgar travellers' that it is possible to discover 'what they wanted the sagacity to observe' (*HAm*: 812–13). To Kames, the best method (there is 'none more rational') of studying law is by a 'careful and judicious comparison of the laws of different countries' (*HLT*: xii) while Monboddo confessed that he had been at great pains to collect facts from travellers and 'to compare them with the facts related by ancient Authors' (*AM*: III, iii).

Monboddo's choice for comparison was widely shared. Robertson, in a discussion of the sources from which information about the 'ancient state of the barbarous nations' of Europe has to be derived, acknowledges that the historian has to rely not on the barbarians themselves but upon the descriptions provided by the Greek and Roman writers (*VPE*: 370). However he also observes that there is 'still one race of men nearly in the same political situation' as the barbarians, namely, the 'various tribes and nations of savages in North America' (371). He accordingly hypothesises that should there be similarity between the barbarous Europeans and Americans then 'it is stronger proof' that a 'just account' of the former has been given than 'the testimony even of Caesar or Tacitus' (371). After itemising five points of similarity Robertson concludes that, although not perfectly similar, the 'resemblance is greater perhaps than any that history affords an opportunity of observing' (372). While Dunbar comments unspecifically that the 'information of modern travellers' has been 'rendered credible by several passages of antiquity' (*EHM*: 21), Stuart makes specific use of the comparison between the Americans and the Germans throughout his *View of Society*. His principal source of information about the Americans was Lafitau. This is unsurprising since Lafitau took the comparison between the 'new' and the ancient world as the leitmotif for his entire study.[13]

A wider point lurks here. What this particular application of the comparative method contains is the idea of social change. Suppose you left your newly constructed town-house in Edinburgh's New Town and visited upper New York state, there you would encounter natives recognisably similar in their customs and way of living (in their 'manners') to those described by Tacitus. Suppose again you visited Weimar, there the Germans you would meet would be polite and civilised. Since Weimar is in the territory described by Tacitus it follows that the manners of the Germans have undergone a change. What this means for the relative importance of 'climate' or territory (Space) and history (Time) as explanations of diversity will be discussed in Chapter 4. What we must now discuss is how that change can be explained or what sort of history the Scottish social theorists wrote to achieve that explanation.

ii) The Scope of History

The titles of some of the key works of the Scottish Enlightenment are revealing. Kames' *Sketches on the History of Man* and Dunbar's *Essays on the History of Mankind* are unashamedly universal in their scope. Millar's *Origin of Ranks*, Ferguson's *History of Civil Society* and Monboddo's *Origin and Progress of Language*, though ostensibly particular in perspective are nonetheless unrestricted in historical sweep, and Stuart's *View of Society* and Robertson's *View of Progress* though confined (to a still broad) geographical area still survey it expansively, incorporating as we have just seen comparisons with the Amerindians. And in a similar fashion any reader of the *Wealth of Nations* quickly appreciates the breadth of Smith's ambition. Furthermore, even the seemingly more narrowly focused works, like Robertson's histories of Scotland, Charles V and America or Millar's *Historical View* and Hume's *History of England*, all include reflections or appendices and separate discussions of a wide-ranging character.

While there were of course local or parochial histories (cf. Allan 1993) the works written by the major theorists all exhibited this universality of scope. Indeed one of the chief factors that makes these theorists 'major' is precisely this ambition. What above all they sought to explain was the whys and wherefores of how the manners of the polite eighteenth century are distinct from those of the Iroquois or the Scythians or the Spartans. Since humans are social creatures then it means that the history of mankind is conterminous with the history of society. The universality of the former carries over into the latter. The Scots are putting forward a history of Society. As scientific social theorists they do not confine themselves to a detailed description of a particular society, say, the Huron or a Highland clan or the Etruscans. Rather they seek causes for the differences between these particular societies (what these 'causes' are will be the subject of Chapter 4) and in this quest Lafitau's account of the Iroquois and Tacitus' account of the Germans were both equally serviceable in tracing the steps of human history.

There is a further aspect. Given the universal scope of a history of mankind then particular histories can be drawn upon as the narrative requires. Should there be a gap in the story-line then it can be 'plugged' from a variety of sources. This was desirable since, as Smith openly prescribed, a narrative should not leave 'any chasm or gap' (*LRBL*: 100).[14] The Americans were especially important in this respect. Robertson states explicitly that they 'fill up a considerable chasm in the history of the progress of the human species' (*HAm*: 812). Kames similarly says 'we must endeavour to supply the broken links [in a 'historical chain']' by 'cautious conjectures' drawn from the 'collateral facts' supplied by 'poets and historians' (*HLT*: 25). In this passage Kames also supplies Stewart with his pretext for labelling this whole enterprise 'conjectural history' (see Civ below).

iii) The Shape of History

The history of mankind is a history of progress. History, the past, therefore has a definite contour or shape; there is, as Millar declares, 'a remarkable continuity in the several steps of his [man's] progression' (*OR*: 176). This is a progress from the rude to the cultivated (the sub-title of Dunbar's *Essays*) or from 'ignorance to knowledge and from rude to civilized manners' (Millar *OR*: 176). The general shape possessed by this progress is from simplicity to complexity or from uniformity to diversity or, again, as we will stress in Chapter 5, from the concrete to the abstract.

For Robertson this is a 'natural' progression (*HAm*: 812 cf. Stuart *PLS*: 11, Millar *OR*: 176 etc.). The 'model' for this progress was organic growth in general and the human life-process in particular. Hence, as we will explore at some length in Chapter 5, as the individual develops from childhood to adulthood so society develops from infancy to maturity. In both cases the development is 'natural' in the sense that it is predictable and normal. As you must walk before you can run so societies must, for example, develop private property before legal systems are necessary. (On this basis, anachronism is thinking you can run before you can walk.)

With this natural blue-print a particular social institution can be chronologically located. Also it makes possible reasonable conjecture as to the features of a particular society's institutions at the various stages of its development. This most reliably applies in the earliest ages where uniformity is greatest. Millar makes the point clearly. Echoing Hume's view of the relationship between variety and uniformity, he remarks that

> However such people [rude and barbarous] may happen to be distinguished by singular institutions and whimsical customs, they discover a wonderful uniformity in the general outline of their character and manners; an uniformity no less remarkable in different nations the most remote from each other. (*HV*: IV, 363)

Similarity of circumstances or conditions is a general cause that produces as an effect similarity of manners (cf. Robertson *HAm*: 806; Millar *HV*: I, 40). Hence the 'wonderful uniformity' of the manners of rude people is the product of similar circumstances. Stuart puts this 'principle' to polemical effect. He argues that feudal institutions were similar due to similar causal forces (the manners of the barbarians) and not because they were copied from one source to another (*PLS*: 3–4). Since, for reasons to be examined in Chapter 5, 'the attention of a rude people is confined to a few objects' (Millar *HV*: III, 3) then their manners are 'simple'. The various improvements of mankind serve to diversify their circumstances and, as a consequence, complicate their manners. Diversification and complication are thus marks of progress and are the correlative of knowledge and civilised manners, whereas uniformity and simplicity are the correlative of ignorance and rudeness. Robertson uses this 'principle' to argue that Indian society is 'highly civilized' (*India*: 1140). They are, for example, less superstitious than the Greeks and Romans (1152), exhibit 'extensive distinction of ranks' (1132) and, in the *Mahabarat*, have a composition that only a 'people of polished manners and delicate sentiments' could have produced (1142). (These institutions will be the focus of later chapters.)

iv) The Nature of History

So far conjectural history has been identified as universal in scope and progressive in shape. We now need to address the central question: what is the nature or defining characteristic of this history? There is a classic source for the answer in Dugald Stewart's *Life of Smith*. Since Stewart's characterisation has remained definitive we can use his account as our focus (and quote what he says at length).

We have already covered some of the points Stewart makes. It is, he declares, an 'interesting question' to discern by what 'gradual steps' the transition from the 'simple efforts of uncultivated nature' to a 'complicated' state has been made (in *EPS*: 292). He also remarks that little information can be gleaned, especially in the earliest ages, from 'the casual observations of travellers'. The consequence is that

In this want of direct evidence, we are under a necessity of supplying the place of fact by conjecture; and when we are unable to ascertain how men have actually conducted themselves upon particular occasions, of considering in what manner they are likely to have proceeded, from the principles of their nature, and the circumstances of their external situation. (293)

Conjecture thus rests on two pillars – the principles of human nature and external circumstances. Clearly Stewart does not believe that this licensed mere idle fancy. The 'principles' are fixed and constant (see subsection v below) and, given the uniformity of nature, the circumstances in a particular situation are inferable from what is known generally to be the case. Accordingly, he says that 'in examining the history of mankind' when 'we cannot trace the process by which an event *has been* produced, it is often of importance to be able to show how it *may have been* produced by natural causes' (293; Stewart's emphases).

The importance of this last phrase is worth underlining. To locate these causes, and as Kames said to 'join all in one regular chain' (*HLT*: 25), is to give an explanation. To seek them is to undertake a scientific enquiry; to refrain from such a search is to remain with the vulgar in a state of ignorance. This basic Humean contrast between science and ignorance, between the philosopher and the vulgar, or, again, between giving causes and invoking chance, is picked up by Stewart and placed in a significantly wider context. He says that the quest for natural causes gives a 'check ... to that indolent philosophy which refers to a miracle whatever appearances, both in the natural and moral worlds, it is unable to explain' (293).

This whole scientific approach to the history of mankind Stewart now says he will take the liberty of entitling

> *Theoretical* or *Conjectural History*; an expression which coincides pretty nearly in its meaning with that of *Natural History*, as employed by Mr Hume, and with what some French writers have called *Histoire Raisonnée*. (293)[15]

As examples of this approach Stewart cites Kames' *Historical Law Tracts*, the 'works of Mr Millar' and the pretext for this entire digression Smith's 'Dissertation' on the origin of language (294–5).

Had Stewart concluded his summatory characterisation at this point then this view of history would have been regarded as being, if not acceptable, at least intelligible. However, Stewart went further. He also stated that

> In most cases, it is of more importance to ascertain the progress that is most simple, than the progress that is most agreeable to fact; for paradoxical as the proposition may appear, it is certainly true, that the real progress is not always the most natural. It may have been determined by particular accidents, which are not likely again to occur, and which cannot be considered as forming any part of that general provision which nature has made for the improvement of the race. (296)

This further characterisation has been a butt of much criticism and has had the effect of denigrating the entire enterprise.[16] The crux of the matter for these critics is that history is precisely concerned with what actually happened and not with with some suppositious 'natural' progress. This view was established in the nineteenth century and still holds sway. But although there were contemporary critics of facile progressivism like Herder, this view is itself unhistorical.

The notion of history that Stewart is here summarising can be best understood not from present historicist sensibilities but as an expression of scientific social theory (or the Scottish aspiration thereto).[17] The contrast between 'real progress' and that which is 'most natural' and the contrast between the 'most simple' and the 'most agreeable to fact' is that between one roll and many rolls of a biased die. This is but another expression of the universalist scope of their history of mankind-in-society. Millar illustrates the point, 'it appeared unnecessary to give a separate detail of the laws of any one country or to take notice of any particular institutions further than they contribute to show the natural progress of human society' (*Observations concerning the Distinction of Ranks* [1771] i.e. 1st edition of *Origin of Ranks* p. xi). A particular society may as a matter of actual fact develop an agricultural economy before a pastoral one but from the perspective of the history of mankind the 'natural' order is the reverse of this, that is, most societies herd before they farm. On this basis Smith is able to argue simultaneously that the 'natural progress of opulence' is for the development of the countryside to precede that of towns but that the reverse occurred (to decisive effect as we shall see in Chapter 6) in the modern states of Europe (*WN*: 376–80).

One consequence of this is that chronology itself can in a particular instance be disregarded. Dunbar is here explicit. At the opening of his *Essays* he states that 'it is the order of improvement merely not the chronological order of the world that belongs to this enquiry' (*EHM*: 3). Somewhat similarly even the fastidious Robertson remarks that it is 'not necessary to observe the order of time with chronological accuracy, it is of more importance to keep in view their mutual connection and dependence' (*VPE*: 315). This 'view' is policed by the 'comparative method'. Robertson declares that by noting the 'general system' in Europe then Scotland's particular history will be clarified and, more pointedly, that 'where the bulk of historians have seen only the effects we may be able to discover the cause' (*HSc*: 25). Kames generalises this. He points out that through collecting and collating facts from different countries we can 'make a regular chain of causes and effects' so that we may then 'rationally conclude that the progress has been the same among all nations in the capital circumstances at least; for accident or the singular nature of a people or of a government will always produce some peculiarities' (*HLT*: 26).

The outcome is that the general structure and order of social development can be identified amidst the diversity of the reports. If the separateness or distinctiveness of the particular societies is emphasised then it means they are incomparable. And if the 'comparative method' is ruled out then it means each society must be studied discretely. But there is now no room for social science. There is an absence of constant conjunctions such that the institutions and behaviours of a multiplicity of societies can be explained as the effects of a few, simple, basic causes. (We will explore these questions more thoroughly in Chapter 4.)

As Stewart said the aim of the conjectural historians was to answer the question: how and in what way has the transition from rude to cultivated nations happened? Even though local histories might have pretensions,[18] the aim is not to give an account of the happenings in (say) Dumbarton from 1630 to 1660. To use Kames' terminology, such an account would be a mere 'geographical' compilation of facts. This history of Dumbarton may tweak antiquarian or purely parochial curiosity but it cannot in isolation be 'interesting' (always a benchmark of 'proper' history for the Scots). What is needed is the general context that a causal enquiry would provide. Not only is it important to know how Dumbarton at this time compares to Stirling (or Rennes or Naples) but also, bereft of some wider explanatory framework, what took place in Dumbarton during those years cannot be truly appreciated. Nor as a consequence, and as Kames also pointed out, can this localised list of facts be instructive. This is the key point. Conjectural history as a way of conducting social science was integral to the Baconian temper of the Scottish Enlightenment. Kames, for example, closes his Preface to the *Historical Law Tracts* by openly announcing that one of his motives has been to remedy the imperfection of England and Scotland still retaining different legal systems. And, as we will see in later chapters, these various histories while pointing up the superiority of the 'cultivated' over the 'rude' nevertheless contained criticisms of the former. These criticisms, and the policy prescriptions to meet them, were an indispensable ingredient of the historians' project and central to determining the scope, shape and nature of the history they wrote (cf. Redman 1993: 223).

v) The Assumptions of History

In order for conjectural history to 'work', one basic assumption has to be made. If human behaviour across space and time can be compared, if gaps can be plugged by conjecturing what may have happened, if it is feasible to write a history of mankind then there has to be a basic fixity or constancy in human nature. This constancy or uniformity of human nature is the governing assumption. This is scarcely radical and before the nineteenth century, before the so-called 'historicist revolution', would not have been considered contestable. It is not enough however just to point out its taken-for-granted status, more important is to establish how this assumption underpins the 'scientific' history written by the Scots.

The most celebrated exposition is given by Hume. Though Hume's remarks on the scope and function of history are scattered through his writings, we can focus on his account in the *First Enquiry*. It is there that he most unequivocally puts his case for the constancy and uniformity of human nature. Its precise location is in the chapter on 'Liberty and Necessity', and that is significant because it places the discussion within Hume's attempt to treat human nature scientifically, as susceptible to causal regularity or necessity.

Hume confidently asserts that 'it is universally acknowledged that there is a great uniformity among the actions of men, in all nations and ages, and that human nature remains still the same in its principles and operations' so that it now follows that

History informs us of nothing new or strange in this particular. Its chief use is only to discover the constant and universal principles of human nature by showing men in all varieties of circumstances and situations and furnishing us with materials from which we may form our observations and become acquainted with the regular springs of human action and behaviour. (*EHU*: 83)

Hume is quite explicit that these 'materials' provided by the historical record are 'collections of experiments' that enable the 'moral philosopher' to fix 'the principles of his science' just like 'the natural philosopher becomes acquainted with the nature of plants [etc.] . . . by the experiments which he forms concerning them' (84). And in his own *History of England* he did not forget to act like a 'philosopher' (cf. Stockton 1976: 297, Danford 1990: 88ff.). For example, he says that the crisis of the Scottish Reformation can, by 'whoever enlarges his view', be seen to mark 'the necessary progress of human affairs and the operation of those principles which are inherent in human nature' (*HE*: II, 336).

If we ask what these 'principles' are, they are the 'regular springs' of human behaviour. If we further ask what these 'springs' are, the general answer is the passions. In the *First Enquiry* Hume lists ambition, avarice, self-love, vanity, friendship, generosity and public spirit (83). These operate regardless of particular social context. If you want to know the Greeks and Romans then, he advises, study the French and the English (83). This independence of the principles of human nature from their particular social context (what I have elsewhere called a 'non-contextualist' theory (Berry 1982 cf. Berry 1986)) gives them authority. Hume supposes that a traveller's report which described a society of humans without avarice or ambition would be a falsehood, just as it would be if it reported the presence of centaurs and dragons (84).

Of course there are differences and variations but, as we said above, the comprehension of these is still founded on knowledge of constant uniformity. All human behaviour, even if it has a 'local' character, is explicable because it is governed by regular springs which have uniform effects. Thanks to Hume's non-contextualism, 'man' is a fit subject for a 'science' because his behaviour necessarily exhibits certain uniformities. Man is not some locally defined phenomenon that can only be understood parochially. It would be contrary to the first Newtonian rule of philosophising if these local phenomena could not be subsumed under and explained by a few simple causes but had, rather, to be accounted for in their own strictly non-comparable terms.

The scientific credentials which Hume bestows on his view give to it more than merely formal status.[19] That is to say, for Hume the constancy of human nature is not merely a necessary presupposition to make any historical knowledge possible (such as might be conceded by modern critics of conjectural history and its assumptions (cf. Walsh (1975), Pompa (1990)) it is also a normative or judgemental yardstick. That dimension was implicit in the authoritative dismissal of the traveller's report and we will meet further expressions, especially when we examine his view of religion in Chapter 7.

Though I have outlined Hume's argument at some length on this issue his stance was unexceptional. None of the social theorists of the Scottish Enlightenment doubted the constancy of human nature. And as with Hume this constancy was not merely formal but also judgemental. One such judgement is decisive in sustaining conjectural history. We have seen that conjectural history is both universal and progressive; it deals with the development (or improvement) of mankind. What enables this to be a developmental story is the assumption that human nature itself is progressive.

Hume himself does not explicitly include this principle in his extensive list of constant ingredients of human nature (see Berry 1982: 60–2) but many of his compatriots are less reticent. Hence Ferguson declares 'man is susceptible of improvement and has in himself a principle of progression' (*ECS*: 8 cf. *IMP*: 93, *PMPS*: I, 204, 249) and Millar proclaims that there is 'in man a disposition and capacity for improving his condition' (*OR*: 176). Smith for his part signals the presence of this trait in his oft-quoted comment that 'the natural effort of every individual to better his own condition' is 'a powerful principle' (*WN*: 540 cf. 674). This effort (or desire) 'comes with us from the womb and never leaves till we go into the grave' (341). Kames' writings are littered with references to human progressiveness (see e.g. *PMNR*: 97, 100; *HLT*: 64; *SHM*: I, 230) and it can be detected in many others (e.g. Stuart *Diss*: 217, Dunbar *EHM*: 16).

D: Conclusion

The Scottish social theorists had a 'mission to explain'. Humans are naturally social, and this sociality expresses itself institutionally. These are natural facts. They are just as much a part of experience as the spectrum created by passing light through a prism or apples falling to the ground. Though the latter two facts might be classified as 'physical' or 'natural' and the former as 'moral', they all cohabit the one experienced world. The natural aspect of that world has, since the Renaissance, been systematically investigated and causal explanations provided with great success. One mark of that success was that Nature could be made less recalcitrant. For example, knowledge of the properties of phosphate can be put to use to effect increased crop yields. The expectation throughout the Enlightenment was that a similar success, both theoretical and practical, beckoned for the moral aspect. It was in Scotland that the most systematic efforts were made to realise this expectation. This is a further testament to the significance of their contribution to the development of social theory. Due to the Scots' strong commitment to sociality, which we discussed in Chapter 2, they produced investigations that sought to explain human institutions causally. It is against this background that one of the great books in the entire history of social theory was written. That Smith was a key member of the Scottish Enlightenment is no coincidental fact and the full title of his book, *An Inquiry into the Nature and Causes of the Wealth of Nations*, succinctly captures how the Scots conceived of social theory. Two features of this conception stand out.

The first is that since to study society scientifically means tracing, in Kames' favourite though commonplace imagery, the chain of causes and effects, it builds into the study a temporal aspect: causes precede effects. Accordingly to understand (say) the emergence of liberty it is necessary to investigate what changes or events brought it about. This investigation is to be carried out by writing history. But this is history with a distinctive agenda.

The second feature underlies this distinctiveness. Sociality is true of all humans but it is evident to experience that its institutional expression is not uniform. Nevertheless by seeking a causal explanation for these expressions they can be revealed as non-random. Since the hallmark of successful natural science is the reduction of multiplicity to simplicity then the hallmark of successful social science is the reduction of the diversity of institutions to some intelligible pattern. What makes the history written by the Scots distinctive is that it is the search for this pattern. The key to it lies in the very universality of sociality, the source of which lies in human nature itself. Here is the second feature. The various properties and capacities of human nature provide the uniformity in terms of which the diversity can be rendered intelligible. How this was executed and what the pattern was that the 'history of Mankind' revealed is the subject of the next two chapters.

Notes

1. Cf. Dunbar *EHM*: 354–5 (discussed in Chapter 4). Wood interprets Kames' *Sketches* as collapsing Bacon's distinction (1989: 102). This was reflected institutionally: Marischal College, Aberdeen, established a professorship in natural and civil history in 1753 (Wood 1993: 92).
2. That this outlook was central is reflected in the presence of effectively this same proposition in Hobbes' *Leviathan* (1651) Ch. 5.
3. Hume received £1,400 for the last two volumes of his *History* (Mossner 1980: 315). Robertson got £4,000 for his *Charles V* (Graham 1901: 94). By comparison Smith as a professor earned £300 p.a. and a judge £700 p.a. (Ross 1995b: 81).
4. In his later *Elucidations* Kames repeats the clarion-call for law to be a 'rational science' though his emphasis is on reasoning from first principles – against reliance on authorities such as Stair – and not on causal/historical reasoning (*ELS*: Preface).
5. This phrase is Bolingbroke's (see *Letters on the Study and Use of History* [1735]: 18) but is in tune with a 'humanist tradition' from the Renaissance. Kames quotes Bolingbroke (though not that phrase) in the Preface to *HLT*. These sentiments were commonplace. For example, Blair 'The general idea of History is a record of truth for the instruction of mankind' (*LRB*: 482) or Hume 'The object of ... history is to instruct' (*E–ST*: 246) or Robertson 'History which ought to record truth and teach wisdom' (*HSc*: 3).
6. Cf. Bolingbroke, 'it is the business ... of others to separate the ore from the dross, to stamp it into coin, and to enrich and not encumber mankind. When there are none sufficient to this task, there may be antiquaries, and there may be journalists or annalists but there are no historians' (*Letters*: 37).
7. A simple introduction is Jenkins (1992). Useful short treatments include Rosenberg (1993), Robinson (1966) and Lenz (1966). All general books on Hume's philosophy discuss the topic, of these Livingston (1984), Passmore (1968) and Baier (1991) bring out the links with his social theory.
8. Cf. Newton: 'Nature is pleased with simplicity and affects not the pomp of superfluous

causes' so that the first rule of reasoning in natural philosophy is to admit only such causes as are 'true and sufficient to explain their [natural things] appearances' (*Method of Natural Philosophy* Rule I (1953: 3)). Hume's vocabulary frequently and indisputably echoes Newton. For example, he says of what he regards as his own key invention (the use of the association of ideas (*Abs*: 198)) that it is a 'kind of attraction' in the mental world with the same effects as in the natural world (*THN*: 12–13). Both Turnbull (*PMP*: 190) and Kames (*SHM*: I, 395) overtly associate Newton's account of attraction with mental attraction.

9. For the less than straightforward relationship between Hume and Newtonianism see Forbes (1975a) and for his relationship to Newton see, for example, Kemp Smith (1964), Noxon (1973), Capaldi (1975) and Wright (1983). Hume's own explicit opinion of Newton was that he was 'the greatest and rarest genius that ever arose for the ornament and instruction of the species' (*HE*: III, 780).

10. Cf. Kames, who likens the 'necessity' of the criminal on his way to the scaffold forseeing his execution to the expectation that a stone will drop to the ground when released (*PMNR*: 158). Hume, too, had used the example of an execution to make the same point (*EHU*: 90).

11. Cf. Kidd (1995: 146), who refers to the work of Thomas Innes (author of *A Critical History of the Ancient Inhabitants of the Northern part of Britain or Scotland'* [1729]). (Robertson cites Innes, *HSc*: 4.) Kidd also notes that in addition to this Catholic anti-Hanoverian enterprise there was a Protestant contribution and claims that Robertson's scepticism about the early Scottish past was inspired by his Leiden-educated teacher, Charles Mackie (153).

12. Hume apologised for not giving references in the first volume of his *History* (*Letts*: I, 284). He added these to later editions (*Letts*: I, 379). Cf. Wootton 1993: 283.

13. The title of his book makes this explicit, *Moeurs des sauvages ameriquains, comparées aux moeurs des premiers temps* (1724). The chapters of the large two-volume work go through the gamut of social institutions. In his Introduction Lafitau admits that the customs of the savages have helped him to understand the ancient authors' (I, 4) – though Robertson criticises him for his naivety (*HAm*: 806). Somewhat similarly the opening chapter of Charlevoix's *Journal historique* (1744) (the other major source of information about the Americans) discusses the much debated topic of their origin – a debate which necessarily entailed some comparison between selected European nations and American tribes. As a final illustration Colden's *History of the Five Indian Nations of Canada* (1750, 2nd edn) says that these Indians resemble nobody so much as the Spartans in their laws and customs (see Introduction).

14. Cf. Manuel (1959: 112): 'The eighteenth century was still unaccustomed to a segmented historical world with inevitable lacunae; it demanded a continuum ...' See text below for further discussion of the Enlightenment view of history.

15. Cf. Stewart: 'The application of this fundamental and leading idea [that the capacities of the human mind are the same in all ages and diversity is the result of different circumstances] to the natural or *theoretical history* of society in all its various aspects; – to the history of languages, of the arts, of the sciences, of laws, of government, of manners, and of religion, – is the peculiar glory of the latter half of the eighteenth century, and forms a characteristic feature of its philosophy, which even the imagination of Bacon was unable to foresee' (*Dissertation exhibiting the progress of Metaphysical, Ethical and Political Philosophy* in *Collected Works*: I, 70; Stewart's emphasis).

16. Cf., for example, Höpfl (1978), Collingwood (1961: 76–85) and Sampson (1956: 72, 74), who quotes that last extract from Stewart and calls it a 'damaging admission' and says that there is some justification for regarding the eighteenth century as 'fundamentally anti-historical'. A harbinger of this critique was Tytler, who in his *Life of Kames* remarked that 'the recording of authentic facts, the display of historical truth is much less an object with such writers than ingenious argument and plausible theory ... such

philosophers are bold enough to determine not only what men ought to be but to prove by a priori reasoning what in certain situations has been and in similar situations ever must be' (1807: I, 200n.).

17. Teggart had seen this when he described conjectural history as 'an attempt to lay the foundations of a strictly scientific approach to the study of man' (1925: 87). Bryson quoted this twice (1945: 92, 112).

18. For example, in his Preface to his continuation of Crawfurd's *The History of the Shire of Renfrew* (1782), William Semple says (in justification) that this is not a 'barren subject' because it can 'mark the progress of refinement from barbarous ages to the present enlightened period'. Rather more indicative of the book itself is that the first actual justification given is that the history paints the character of eminent persons.

19. Cf. Wertz (1975), who maintains (correctly) that the constancy of human nature is a 'methodological principle' and who criticises Black (1926) for not distinguishing between methodological and substantial uniformity and similarly Forbes (1975a: 119), who maintains (also correctly) that the universal principles are for Hume abstractions from concrete variety. Nevertheless, Hume did work with a normatively loaded and substantive view of human nature, see Berry (1982) for further discussion.

4

Social Diversity

A key finding of Chapter 3 was that human nature was, in Hume's words, 'constant and uniform in all its operations'. One facet of this uniformity is that human nature is progressive or developmental. Millar can, accordingly, write:

> There is, however, in man a disposition and capacity for improving his condition, by the exertion of which, he is carried on from one degree of advancement to another; and the similarity of his wants, as well as of the faculties by which those wants are supplied, has everywhere produced a remarkable uniformity in the several steps of his progression. (*OR*: 176)

However, just before this, Millar had commented upon the 'amazing diversity' of the laws and rules of conduct in different countries and at different times in the same country (175). And he swiftly proceeds to extend the diversity to encompass customs, taste, sentiments and the 'general system of behaviour' (176). The relationship between uniformity and diversity is the theme of this chapter; given that humans are the same across time and space then it is indeed prima facie 'amazing' that societies are so diverse.

At the very beginning of the opening chapter to the *Ranks*, Millar refers to 'the most wonderful variety' in the 'rank and condition of women' (183). We know from Chapter 3 that the 'wonderful' (or amazing) constituted a challenge – how is it to be *explained*, what *causes* are at work to account for it?[1] For Millar an investigation of these causes will be 'entertaining' for it excites 'our curiosity' that there are such different rules of conduct (175). Alongside this simple desire to explain, Millar is a fully signed-up Baconian, this causal investigation will also be useful; without the knowledge attained 'we cannot form a just notion of their [rules of conduct] utility' (*Ibid.*).

A: Relativism

In Chapter 2 we saw how much emphasis the Scots laid upon evidence. It was clear from the record, suitably sifted to weed out the prejudices of the recorders, that for every social institution from government to marriage to religion to ethical standards, reliable evidence could be found to indicate great differences in practice – whether it be, say, elected chiefs or polygamy or animism or probity. The acceptance of empiricism had one further consequence. The ubiquitous and powerful impact of the principle of habit (the process of socialisation) means that the inhabitants of a particular locale, exposed to a particular set of institutions, will grow up accepting those institutions as the way things naturally are. But the facts of diversity mean that what is naturally the done thing in, for example, the Congo (say female subservience) is very different from what is naturally the done thing in, say, the Ladrone Islands (The Marianas Islands), where females are dominant (see Millar OR: 193, 200 cf. Ferguson, who uses different examples to illustrate the same point, ECS: 115).

This would seem to suggest a form of cultural relativism, that is, the idea that each culture has its own specific standards that are not necessarily commensurate with the standards adopted by other cultures. However, Enlightenment thinkers were unwilling to follow that suggestion. It is true that there was some critical mileage to be got out of the variety of religious and sexual practices as a way of taunting traditional thinkers and casting doubt on the solidity of traditional institutions. Montesquieu's *Persian Letters* (1721) or Diderot's *Supplement to Bougainville's Voyage* (1773), for example, can be read in that light. But as Montesquieu himself put it in the Preface to *The Spirit of the Laws* (1748) 'amidst the infinite diversity of laws and mores [mankind] were not led by their fancies alone' (*SL*: xliii). Social institutions are not entirely the fruit of locally variable whim; there are universally applicable standards. No Enlightenment thinker (Scots included) would hesitate to label some practices 'superstitions' and convey by that anything other than hostility (see Chapter 7). Cultural relativists would (ideally) have no truck with this. In their eyes to call a practice a 'superstition' is to overlook the authenticity it enjoys in the experience of its practitioners. But to the Enlightenment that is tantamount to endorsing the darkness of ignorance not the light of science. In addition, and more pointedly, this relativism would render useless the very exercise of searching for the causes of diversity.

Because of the Scots' great stress on the process of socialisation the need to distance themselves from 'relativism' was important. We shall see in Chapter 7 how, for example, this informs their discussion of aesthetics, where the search for a standard of taste is central, but here we can usefully say something briefly about ethical standards. Robertson observes that 'in every stage of society, the faculties, the sentiments and desires of men are so accommodated to their own state that they become standards of excellence to themselves' (*HAm*: 811). This seems a clear illustration of a link between diversity, socialisation and relativism. Millar, somewhat similarly, writes 'individuals form their notions of propriety according to a general standard, and fashion their morals in conformity to the prevailing taste of the times' (*HV*: IV, 246/*HVL*: 386). Since Millar openly acknowledges his debt to Smith's *Moral Sentiments*, a closer look at (a portion) of Smith's discussion will help.

Since different societies, each with their own way of doing things, will generate their own internally valid norms then it would seem to preclude the possibility of any 'external' evaluative perspective. Smith, however, does not follow this line of argument. Indeed he devotes a whole Part of the *Moral Sentiments* to exactly this issue.[2] He admits that virtues differ between 'rude and barbarous nations' and 'civilized nations' (*TMS*: 204–5). In general, though, Smith believes that 'the sentiments of moral approbation and disapprobation are founded on the strongest and most vigorous passions of human nature; and though they may be somewhat warpt, cannot be entirely perverted' (200).

This statement is instructive for two reasons. First, it not only testifies again to the commitment to the uniformity of human nature but also lays the foundation of moral sentiments on this uniformity. This means that there is a uniform or universal structure to morality; ethical relativism is false. This conclusion could have been anticipated. For the Scots in general there is a moral order just as there is a natural order. These two 'orders' are in fact mutually supportive, each separately and both collectively bear witness to God's general superintendence of the cosmos (see Chapter 7). Second, *given* this universality, then particular practices may be judged 'warpt'; they are not all on a par each within their own internal standard, some deviate from an authoritative transcultural norm.

As an example Smith cites the practice (empirically well attested) of infanticide. He accounts for this by the fact that 'in the earliest period of society' infanticide was commonplace and the 'uniform continuance of the custom had hindered them [the practitioners] from perceiving its enormity' (210). Smith allows the practice to be 'more pardonable' in the rudest and lowest state of society than it was 'even among the polite and civilized Athenians', when it was inexcusable. Smith is adamant that just because something is commonly done does not mean it is condonable when the practice itself is 'unjust and unreasonable' (*Ibid.*). As we pointed out in Chapter 2, the Scots freely acknowledge that habits can be bad. Moreover, because of the strength of morality's foundations in human nature then these can only be divergent customs since 'no society could subsist for a moment' if this 'horrible practice' was an essential part of its way of living, or constituted the 'usual strain' of their 'conduct and behaviour' (211).

This rebuttal of relativism raises a couple of related issues. It is a matter of logic that diversity presupposes uniformity, that is, the ability to identify differences presupposes some basic common point of contact since without that commonality it is impossible to judge whether others do have beliefs or conceptual frameworks different from one's own (cf. Davidson 1984). This logical point aside, for the eighteenth-century Scots the crucial point is that their doctrine of human nature plays the role of providing this commonality. Yet, as Smith's account of infanticide reveals, this role is no mere formality; it carries a normative punch. That which is universal (in accord with human nature) carries, by virtue of that very trait, more moral weight than that which is 'merely' particular or local.

For the Enlightenment there is a practical dimension to this. Smith's argument serves not only to identify the 'warped' but also justifies straightening it. An arguable case in point is the literati's attitude to the Highlands. As we noted in Chapter 1 there were deliberate attempts, especially in the wake of the '45 to 'deal' with the Highlands. We quoted (p. 21) from the remit of The Board of Annexed Estates that (part of) its rationale was 'civilizing the Inhabitants'. And among explicit statements of the literati can be found Robert Wallace's remark that the present inhabitants of the Highlands were 'overwhelmed with ignorance and barbarity' and that they 'can only be civilized by being made industrious' (*Dissertation on the Numbers of Mankind*: 155, 157).[3] For the Scots this attitude was a relatively straightforward consequence of their rejection of relativism, on the one hand, and their Baconian outlook, on the other. Indeed, it illustrates neatly the link between their 'theory' and their 'practice'.[4]

B: Moral and Physical Causes

In a manner now familiar, Ferguson declares it necessary that we attend 'to the universal qualities of our nature before we regard its varieties'. And in that same passage he remarks, in language very similar to that Millar was to use, that it is indeed 'a task of great curiosity or signal utility' to account for this variety by 'principles either moral or physical' (*ECS*: 10). Ferguson is here alluding to a lively contemporary debate.

i) Explanation and Description

While Ferguson may here refer to 'principles' the standard terminology was physical and moral *causes*. We shall deal with each of those in turn (subsections ii and iii) before looking at accounts of their inter-relationship (subsection iv) but in this subsection I want underscore the significance of the reference to *causality*.

This we can do by returning to conjectural history. As we saw, on Dugald Stewart's reading, it was important to the conjectural historians to explain what happened by referring to natural causes. Explanations of that sort were important because they put a stop to an easy or indolent recourse to the miraculous. Miracles constitute (albeit as a special case – see Chapter 7) a 'one-off', or exceptional, case. One way of interpreting the central claim of relativism is that it denies that different cultural practices are just particular examples of some general condition – rather each practice is a one-off or sui generis. If that is the case then it follows that to explain a practice it is pointless to appeal to some external overarching or transcultural factors; the explanation must be sought internally within the practice.

The 'internal' and the 'external' here represent two very different philosophies. It will help us to understand the Scots if we briefly spell this out. Witchcraft is a convenient test-case. The argument pivots on the issue of causality. To an 'internalist' like Peter Winch (1958 cf. 1970) a Humean 'externalist' account of causality cannot explain the belief in witches. For Hume witchcraft was a superstition and its persecution an act of fanaticism (*HE*: II, 366; III, 416). Both superstition and fanaticism are for Hume the consequences of ignorance and the 'science of man' will account for them. An increase in knowledge will produce – as a causal regularity – a decrease in inhumanity (such as burning witches). Moreover, since this is a causal regularity then it holds good regardless of cultural differences; *whatever* the culture Hume claims that 'industry, knowledge and humanity' (*E–RA*: 271; see Chapter 6), *whenever* they occur, form an indissoluble chain. Winch, on the contrary, argues that in order to explain why a certain society acted in a certain way towards witches then such actions must be placed in the specific context of that society's way of life, its beliefs and so on. These beliefs do not, as Hume supposedly would have it,[5] cause some subsequent, separate, external behaviour (like billiard balls colliding) but are, rather, an inseparable, constitutive, internal element of the action (cf. MacIntyre 1967).

The intelligibility of Winch's own argument is not here at issue, the point of invoking his argument is (to repeat) to throw the Scots' own position into an enlightening relief. On the Winchian view the internal nature of beliefs makes them useless for any general social explanation; their explanatory power is confined to their own society. To the Scots this is tantamount to giving up on explanation altogether; all that it provides is what has been called 'thick description' (Geertz 1972). This is unacceptable in exactly the way that infanticide is unacceptable. The Greeks and savages had certain beliefs such that exposing infants was thought permissible. Not only do the Scots wish to condemn these beliefs as inhuman (as 'repugnant to the human heart', Ferguson *ECS*: 139, referring to the Chinese) they also wish to explain them. This explanation, like the condemnation, will be independent of the beliefs. Accordingly, Smith explains the practice of infanticide in savage society by referring to their 'extreme indigence' (*TMS*: 210). The implicit argument/explanation is that when resources are scarce, so that both child and parent cannot survive, then, in such circumstances, this will (causally) produce the effect of parental discretion as to whether or not to bring up the child. This is implicit because Smith assumes that these principles are self-evident. There is, however, an explicit clue that Smith is here operating 'scientifically' since he says that the presence of this discretion ought not to 'surprise' us because, given the circumstances, infanticide is not a source of 'wonder' (see Chapter 3). For the 'polite' Athenians, however, Smith's explanation, as we saw above, was the power of habit (Millar makes the same point in the same context, *OR*: 236). As noted in Chapter 3, this is one of the commonest explanatory principles put forward by the Scots. Why a particular set of habits is contracted is to be accounted for by some set of initial conditions. In the case of the Athenians, Smith's explanation is that they were themselves at one time savages, who acted then as those who are still savages now do. The crucial point is that the judgement and the explanatory principles – indigence and human nature – apply across cultures.

If, on Winchian grounds, such uniformly operating universal principles were precluded, then the diversity would remain 'amazing'. In Smith's terms we would remain, like the vulgar, in a pre-scientific state of 'wonder'. But this commitment to go beyond description (no matter how 'thick') and to find a causal explanation says nothing about what causes are applicable. Smith's own account draws on 'moral' causes; but that was not the only category, since recourse was also made to 'physical' causes.

ii) Physical Causes

Although Hume is very much *parti pris* he does provide clarity by giving definitions of both sets of causes. In his essay *Of National Characters* he defines physical causes as:

> Those qualities of the air and climate, which are supposed to work insensibly on the temper, by altering the tone of the body and giving a particular complexion,

which, though reflection and reason may sometimes overcome it, will yet prevail among the generality of mankind, and have an influence on their manners. (*E–NC*: 198)

We shall return to some phrases in that definition. Hume's aim in this essay is to argue *against* these physical causes as an explanation for differences in character. This supposes that there were advocates of such an explanation. Who does Hume have in mind?

This question does not have a straightforward answer. The most illustrious exponent of physical causes was Montesquieu in the *Spirit of the Laws*. That work, however, was published in 1748 and only a little before Hume's *National Characters* in that same year. Paul Chamley has argued that Hume's essay gives so a 'pointed reply' to Montesquieu's case that it must have been written intentionally as a rebuttal (1975: 286). Accordingly he conjectures how it may have been possible for Hume to have seen a copy of Montesquieu's manuscript. This remains circumstantial but Montesquieu was the not the sole advocate of physical causes. Hume could well have had in mind Abbé Dubos' *Réflexions critiques sur la poésie, peinture et la musique* (1719), to which he refers in other contemporary essays.[6] Indeed Hume's reference to 'air' in his definition is suggestive of Dubos, who had argued that air quality was the effect of 'emanations' from the soil (*Réflexions* [1755]: II, 230). Dubos, more generally, held that effects supposedly the product of moral causes were rather the result of physical causes (e.g. II, 140). This, as we shall see, is directly contrary to Hume.[7]

Hume's reference to 'climate' in his definition also calls for comment. The first preliminary point is definitional. In the eighteenth century, 'climate' does not have its present metereological denotation; instead, Dr Johnson, for example, in his *Dictionary*, defines it as: 'A space upon the surface of the earth, measured from the equator to the polar circles in each of which spaces the longest day is half-an-hour longer.' As we shall shortly see, climate was Montesquieu's chief physical cause. Although, according to his biographer, this position produced the greatest stir (Shackleton 1961: 302), climatic theories were far from new, particularly in Scotland. Thomas Blackwell in his *Enquiry into the Life and Writings of Homer* (1735) remarked that 'In the division commonly made of Climates, the Rough and Cold are observed to produce the strongest Bodies and most martial spirits; the hotter, lazy Bodies with cunning and obstinate Passions' (5–6). Blackwell cites as his chief authorities Galen and Hippocrates. Dedieu (1909: 206–11 cf. Fletcher 1980: 94) has demonstrated just how much Hippocrates was in vogue in the 1730s. His *Treatise on Air, Water and Situation* was translated into English and Thomas Simson (Professor of Medicine at St Andrews) investigated the effects of cold air on the human body. In addition, Dedieu argued that John Arbuthnot's *An Essay concerning the Effects of Air on Human Bodies* (1733) contains the germ of Montesquieu's theory, though as Glacken (1967: 563) points out, much of the climatic discussion in the book is a précis of Hippocrates.[8]

Clearly recourse to climate was no novelty and it was invoked to account for differences in a variety of contexts – from racial types (Buffon) to pronunciation

(Bullet) to artistic style (Dubos) – throughout the Enlightenment. Even if Montesquieu was not Hume's intentional target, he was for others. Given that Hume and Montesquieu stood in opposing camps on this issue (as openly acknowledged by Dunbar (*EHM*: 296)) a brief look at Montesquieu's argument will be helpful.

In Book 14 of the *Spirit of the Laws* Montesquieu maintains that in cold climates humans are more vigorous than they are in warmer zones. The explanation is that

> Cold air contracts the extremities of the body's surface fibers; this increases their spring and favors the return of blood from the extremities of the heart. It shortens these same fibers; therefore, it increases their strength in this way too. Hot air, by contrast, relaxes these extremities of the fibers and lengthens them; therefore, it decreases their strength and their spring. (*SL*: 231)

This is a direct physiological argument, which Montesquieu supports with evidence. He froze half a sheep's tongue and through a microscope compared the tissue in that state with the other half. He then declares that this experiment 'confirms' that in cold nations nerves are less exposed and 'therefore' sensations are less vivid (233). What follows from this is that 'In cold countries one will have little sensitivity to pleasures; one will have more of it in temperate countries; in hot countries, sensitivity will be extreme' (*Ibid.*). For Montesquieu this now explains a variety of diverse social practices. For example, with respect to their moral character, those in hot climates are timid like old men, while those in cold are courageous like the young (232). Climatic differences similarly explain the different reception afforded to the same opera in England and Italy or the fact that punishment has to be severe in cold climates because there the soul is less sensitive to pain ('A Muscovite has to be flayed alive before he feels anything' (233)).

Although Montesquieu's overall position is more complicated than this suggests,[9] it was this argument that was taken up by the Scots in the wake of Hume. To appreciate their position it is worth glossing Montesquieu's argument. We can label his argument from physical causes 'hard determinism'. This argument postulates a direct relationship between climate or air, as causes, and social institutions or national character and human behaviour, as effects. Just as the effect of freezing the sheep's tongue is to shrink its fibres so the effect of cold on a Muscovite is to make him insensitive and impervious to pain. There is no difference *in principle* between the two accounts. Diversity of institutions, such as differing punishment regimes, is thus explicable by an external physical cause; as Montesquieu says explicitly, 'as one distinguishes climates by degrees of latitude, one can also distinguish them by degrees of insensitivity' (232). Following Hume, the Scots, with one or two reservations, reject this argument.

Before we turn to Hume's own positive argument in support of moral causes, it is worth commenting on another physical principle. This principle is race. Though Hume's account is brief and stark there was a related debate, in which Kames is the chief Scottish participant, as to whether racial diversity means that there are distinct species of human being.

Hume devotes a Note to race (*E–NC*: 208n.). It is attached to his conclusion that national character is 'very promiscuous' in temperate climates so that generalisations are fallacious. Arguably the Note appears as a qualification (it was added in the 1753/4 edition of the *Essays*). Hume admits to the suspicion that Negroes are 'naturally inferior' to the whites since there 'scarcely ever' was a 'civilized nation' or 'eminent' individual of that complexion.[10] Nor can this difference be attributed to a lack of social development since 'the most rude and barbarous of the whites' (such as the ancient Germans and present Tartars) have 'something eminent about them'. Popkin points out that this seems to amount to moral causes only operating upon whites while some natural fact (what Hume refers to as an 'original distinction') precludes their operation upon Negroes (1977: 218). Popkin also traces the influence of this Note on later racist literature but Davis observes that Hume's reputation as an infidel meant that to defend the African was also to defend religion (1966: 458).

Davis draws attention to Beattie's role in this regard. As part of his general assault on Hume, Beattie fastened on to this Note. He accused Hume of merely asserting his position and pointed out that it was falsified by the examples of the ancient Mexicans and Peruvians (*Essay on ... Truth* (6th edn): 310–11). Indeed it would seem that despite his judgement that Beattie was 'a bigotted silly fellow' (*Letts*: II, 301), Hume on this point did pay heed (cf. Immerwahr 1992). In the last edition of the *Essays* (published posthumously in 1777) Hume amended the Note. He struck out 'never' and replaced with 'scarcely ever' (as quoted above) and, arguably side-stepping the Incas, he omitted all reference to non-whites other than Negroes (*E*: 629 [variants]).

One of the phrases that Hume omitted referred to there being four or five different species of man. This doctrine, known as polygenesis, was firmly upheld by Kames. As we shall see shortly, Kames was critical of Montesquieu's climatic theory, but in this context his chief target is Buffon's argument that climate could account for the vast differences in both the external appearance (stature as well as complexion) and temper of humans. Kames' alternative explanation is that 'it appears clear from the very frame of the human body that there must be different races of men fitted for different climates' (*SHM*: I, 40–1 cf. 13). This also entails the rejection of the 'diffusionist' hypothesis that humans peopled the globe from some single starting-point. Given that rejection then, for Kames, there must have been several 'different races or kinds of men' placed *ab origine* in their appropriate climate (I, 42). But this polygenetic conclusion ran into a serious snag; it is contrary to Scripture. Kames salvages his position by invoking the scattering of humans after the fall of the Tower of Babel; this, he believes, reconciles sacred and profane history (I, 44). Post-Babel mankind not only degenerated into savagery but also underwent 'considerable change of bodily constitution' (*Ibid*.). Yet when confronted with *terra australis incognita* it seems that even post-Babel diffusion is inadequate so that Kames has to admit after all that it was peopled by a separate 'local creation'. And once that has been allowed then the same explanation (once more *pace* Buffon) can be given for how

America was populated (II, 85),[11] this despite the fact that Robertson regards the migration from Siberia established beyond 'mere conjecture' by 'undoubted evidence' (*HAm*: 809).

Despite this argument for racial differences Kames does not use this as a physical cause to account for *social* differences. The reason why many (but significantly not *all*) Negroes have not developed is not due to their constitution but to circumstantial lack of opportunity to develop (*SHM*: I, 36). As we will see in subsection iv, this does allow climate a role as a 'circumstance' but, even so, the decisive explanation for social diversity is to be sought in moral causes.

iii) Moral Causes

Hume defines moral causes as

> All circumstances which are fitted to work on the mind as motives or reasons, and which render a peculiar set of manners habitual to us. (*E–NC*: 198)

We will also return to some phrases in this definition. As examples of what his definition includes, Hume supplies

> The nature of government, the revolutions of public affairs, the plenty or penury in which the people live, the situation of the nation with regard to its neighbours. (*Ibid.*)

Before he outlines his argument Hume announces that he is 'inclined to doubt altogether' that physical causes account for national characters and 'that men owe any thing of their temper or genius to air, food[12] or climate' (200).[13] Hume goes on in the body of the essay to give nine reasons to support his dismissal of the relevance of physical causation. A common argumentative strategy runs through this list of reasons. If climate and air are indeed causes of national character as an effect, then that can be disproved by citing cases where the requisite constant conjunction is absent. This can take two forms. Either the cause is the same but the effect is different or, conversely, the causes are different but the effect is the same. As instances of the former Hume supplies the case of England and Scotland (207) and of the latter the Chinese (204).

When we turn to the other Scots we find unproblematically in the cases of Kames and Millar an espousal of Hume's argument. Thus Millar writes that some philosophers have

> pretended that great heat, by relaxing the fibres, and by extending the surface of the skin, where the action of the nerves is chiefly performed, occasions great sensibility to all external impressions; which is accompanied with proportionable vivacity of ideas and feelings ... The inhabitants of a cold region are said, on the other hand, to acquire an opposite complexion. (*OR*: 179)

Although Montesquieu is not mentioned by name, the vocabulary makes it clear that he is the target. Kames is more explicit. After quoting Vitruvius at length, he openly identifies Montesquieu as the 'most formidable antagonist'. For Kames,

Montesquieu's argument is epitomised in his claim that in hot climates men are timid like old men, while in cold they are bold like the young (*SHM*: I, 33).

Kames has no doubt that Montesquieu's theory is wrong because although ingenious it is 'contradicted by stubborn facts' (I, 34). The 'contradiction' is made apparent by using these 'facts' in line with Hume's strategy. Hence, for example, Malays and Scandinavians are compared as being equally courageous while living in 'opposite climates' (*Ibid.*). Millar, too, adopts the same basic strategy, although all his examples are of climate as constant causes with opposite effects on character. Thus the 'mild' Chinese and 'rough' Japanese are contrasted while both are alleged to have the same climate and he repeats Hume's local example of the English and Scotch (*OR*: 180).

Ferguson is perhaps more equivocal. He appears to commit himself implicitly to a hard determinist position, like that found in Book 14 of *Spirit of the Laws*, when he comments 'The sun it seems which ripens the pine-apple and the tamerind, inspires a degree of mildness that can even assuage the rigours of despotical government' (*ECS*: 111). Nor is this an isolated comment (cf. *IMP*: 21, *ECS*: 112). Indeed this is one place where there is some passing reference to the fact of colonialism. Ferguson argues that 'The Hollander is laborious and industrious in Europe, he becomes languid and slothful in India' (*ECS*: 118). This is closer to Montesquieu, who had observed that 'the children of Europeans born in the Indies lose the courage of the European climate' (*SL*: 234), than it is to Hume, who had remarked that 'The Spanish, English, French and Dutch colonies are all distinguishable even between the tropics' (*E–NC*: 205).

Over against these sentiments Ferguson also declares that 'variations of temperament and character do not indeed correspond with the number of degrees that are measured from the equator to the pole' (*ECS*: 116). This, too, is not an isolated remark, for he goes on to say (in an extremely convoluted sentence) that the causal connection between the 'determining' nature of circumstances and a people's 'manner of life' is 'more familarly known' than the 'supposed physical source' of dispositions (118).

Ferguson's wording has echoes of Millar's reference to the relationship implied by physical causes as a 'secret influence'. Both Ferguson and Millar admit that the precise chain of causation whereby body and mind interact is unknown. Millar allows 'we are too little acquainted with the structure of the human body to discover how it is affected by such physical causes' (*OR*: 179) and in Ferguson's judgement 'we can never hope to explain the manner of those influences til we have understood the structure of those finer organs with which the operations of the soul are connected' (*ECS*: 118).[14] In this same vein James Dunbar refers to that 'mysterious influence' between mind and body (*EHM*: 319) and John Gregory to it being not understood (*CV*: 6). The medical dimension to this speculation is a likely background factor here (Gregory was a practising physician – recall the debate on the soul and place of instinct in animals and humans, Chapter 2 n. 4).

Cullen for example in his medical lectures (1770–1) declared that 'it is not less certain that the Conditions of the Mind do mutually affect the Body' than vice versa (quoted in Wright 1990: 251). Turnbull, in fact, much earlier, in his critique of Dubos had nonetheless admitted that simply because of our bodily constitution and the 'reciprocal Union and connection of our Mind and Body' then physical causes without doubt have an influence (*Painting*: 109).

Despite these concessions to uncertainty both Millar and Ferguson (even if to differing degrees) do regard moral causes as effectively explanatory. To see how we can return to Hume's two definitions. If we compare the definitions we can identify where the crucial difference lies. Physical causes work 'insensibly' on the 'temper' via the 'body'; moral causes work on the 'mind' as a 'motive' via making a set of manners 'habitual'. The same differential crux is identified in slightly different terminology by Robert Wallace. In his version physical causes 'depend utterly on the course of nature and are independent on mankind', while moral causes 'depend on the affections, passions and institutions of men' (*Dissertation*: 12).

Earlier we labelled Montesquieu's account as 'hard determinist'. This fits Hume's definition of physical causation as working insensibly on the body, with what Dunbar calls 'irresistible impulse on the fabric of our being' (*EHM*: 221). There is direct physiological 'natural' connection operating, as Wallace puts it, independently of mankind. Given that the aim of punishment is to inflict pain then it has to be of a high degree of intensity in Muscovy in order to fulfil that aim. It is not that the Muscovite is a masochist who likes extreme pain, since in that case it is not an independent but a dependent (on an individual's 'affections' or 'passions') relationship. Where Hume's argument decisively differs is in the explanation of why it is 'given' that punishment aims to inflict pain. Physical causes of themselves cannot explain a punishment regime, there needs to be some 'moral' intermediary such that effective punishment is required for social order.[15]

It is, however, important to note that Hume's support for moral causes is still deterministic. We can label his position 'soft' determinism. This is 'soft', as opposed to 'hard', because it operates not directly on the body, as a mere automatic reflex (such as the fibres on a sheep's tongue) but through the 'mind'. Yet this is still deterministic because the way the various circumstances that constitute moral causes operate is to establish a set of motives or reasons that 'render a peculiar set of manners habitual' or, as he puts it in the following paragraph, 'the manners of individuals are frequently *determined* by these [moral] causes' (*E–NC*: 198; my emphasis). The mode of determination Hume explains a little later. He declares that 'Whatever it be that forms the manners of one generation, the next must imbibe a deeper tincture of the same dye; men being more susceptible of all impressions during infancy, and retaining these impressions as long as they remain in the world' (203).

The argument here links up closely with the discussion of socialisation in Chapter 2. Habits and customs are so powerful in society precisely because they circumscribe the range of putatively 'free' actions. Of course any particular individual can in some aspect of their behaviour act idiosyncratically – a Muscovite can indeed be a masochist. But such behaviour is exceptional and is allowed for by Hume when he inserts the adverb 'frequently' before 'determined' in the quotation from *E–NC* p. 198 above. But precisely because there is such a phenomenon as 'national character' that case cannot be generalised; 'exceptions' must by definition be deviations from some norm. For most of the people for most of the time their 'reasons' for acting are a product of their pre-reflective childhood; they have always done it, it is second nature to them. Smith's explanation for infanticide is a case in point. According to Smith the polite Athenians exposed infants *because* (morally) this was their 'uninterrupted custom': even the great philosophers – Plato and Aristotle (who, we can gloss, in virtue of their strength of intellect, might be expected to be relatively immune to even soft determinism) – accepted it as normal (*TMS*: 210).

If there were not this ('soft') determinism at work then the attempt to *explain* diversity would collapse into some sort of descriptivism in the manner of Winch and Geertz. For Winch, no understanding of any particular society can be gained from subsuming it under some general framework such that it is a 'type' or 'instance' of some law-like regularity. Even the recurrence of certain combinations or presence of certain constant features cannot be comprehended by some universalist schema. Geertz allows that there may be universal existential problems but he is adamant that the solutions to them are culturally unique (1972: 363). The principles that underlie the arguments of both Hume and Montesquieu stand in opposition to this descriptivism. Where Hume and Montesquieu differ from each other is over the way 'circumstances' are supposed to determine 'character'.

It is important that this difference concerns the manner of the determination rather than different definitions of 'circumstance'. This importance is reflected in the fact that the Scottish advocates of moral causes did not altogether discount climate. One of Hume's examples of moral causation was 'the plenty or penury in which a people live'. A number of his compatriots explored what was involved in this case and this exploration revealed that physical and moral causes were not opposed in all respects.

iv) Progress and the two Causes

Millar, immediately after stating that the search for the causes of the 'amazing diversity' is 'useful as well as an entertaining', asserts that in that search 'we must undoubtedly resort, first of all, to the differences of situation'. These differences will, inter alia, include 'the fertility or barrenness of the soil' and 'the nature of its productions'. These are not physical causes as such because Millar believes that these differences suggest 'different views and motives of actions' so that the quality of the soil, for example, will affect the 'species of labour requisite for procuring subsistence' (*OR*: 175). Kames has a similar argument. He believes that climatic conditions affect the mode of subsistence. In cold climes, where the hardness of the ground makes cultivation of corn difficult, only hunting or herding are practised, while in the 'torrid zone' the inhabitants subsist only on vegetable food (*SHM*: I, 58). Kames also, seemingly independently, has climate play a significant role, as one of the two factors responsible for polygamy (see Chapter 5). Hume himself notes that 'the warmth of the weather in the torrid zone' is a 'probable cause' of the lack of industry of those who live there (*E–Com*: 267). Finally, Ferguson, for his part, thinks that the 'intermediate climates' are the most favourable to human nature. By this he means that 'the principal honours of the species' have always been attained 'within the temperate zone' (*ECS*: 108).

In each of these cases there is a shared subtext. Ferguson supplies a clue to its presence when he writes 'the torrid zone everywhere round the globe ... has furnished few materials for history' (110). The temperate zone is by contrast the scene of 'principal honours' because it is there that mankind has developed or progressed. For Kames climate has operated to preclude a development in the mode of subsistence. This idea that development can be measured in terms of modes of subsistence will the central subject of Chapter 5. The present agenda, however, is the connection between the idea of progress and social diversity. We have already outlined this in broad terms in Chapter 3, where, as we saw, it was one of the chief purposes of conjectural or natural history to place human social experience into a sequence. Millar provides an apt illustration of the point here at issue. He says of the 'natural history of legal establishments' that (inter alia) it provides 'evidence of the uniformity of those internal principles which are productive of such various and *apparently* inconsistent operations' (*HV*: IV, 285/*HVL*: 347; my emphasis).

In Chapter 3 we made use of Robertson's comparison of the *ancient* Germans with the *contemporary* Iroquois. Since contemporary Germans do not resemble the Iroquois then it demonstrates how diversity is temporal as well as geographic (as Millar recognised at the very beginning of his discussion (see p. 74)). This ability to accommodate change/progress is a further dimension of the relationship between moral and physical causes. Robertson's discussion of the Amerinds (of which much more in Chapter 5) illustrates this.

Much of what Robertson says echoes what has already been said. Climate operates with 'decisive influence upon [man's] condition and character' yet he has 'attained the greatest perfection ... in the temperate regions of the globe' (*HAm*: 850). There is indeed a 'law of climate' but when applied to human conduct it is open to 'many exceptions' (851). This openness supports the conclusion that 'moral and political causes ... affect the disposition and character of individuals, as well as nations, still more powerfully than the influence of climate' (*Ibid.*). More revealing, however, is Robertson's comment that the relative sway of moral and physical causes is itself an index of development; climate produces greater effects on 'rude nations' than in 'societies more improved' (850). 'Civilized men' are, through their 'ingenuity and inventions', able to 'supply the defects and guard against the inconveniences of any climate' (*Ibid.*). This last phrase underlines once more the greater explanatory power of moral causes. As they develop, humans are able increasingly to dominate Nature ('supply the defects') *because* they are not determined rigidly (or insensibly) by their environment. They have, rather, 'ingenuity', the capacity to use reason to 'invent' improvements. These are retained through habit and custom, and so improvement upon improvement – the process of 'civilisation' – becomes possible (if not certain). Montesquieu himself had made similar remarks (see *SL*: 310) but the Scot who devotes most attention to this question and indeed to the entire issue of the relationship between physical and moral causation is James Dunbar. Three of the thirteen essays that comprise his *Essays on the History of Mankind* deal with climate.

Dunbar rejects the argument that climate has a 'positive and direct influence' on the human mind (*EHM*: 239) but allows what he calls 'local circumstances', such as the division of a country by mountains or having an insular or continental situation, to have an impact. While these circumstances are 'physical' in nature yet they are 'often moral only in their operations' (296). For example, Britain's insular location meant at one time isolation from the rest of Europe and civilisation but this circumstance in the 'aera of navigation' was a source of wealth and power and, furthermore, it meant that Britain was able to avoid continental wars and consequent dissipation of wealth (281). The influence of the environment or climate (physical cause) on a society can change with the alteration in social conditions (moral cause). The change can be baleful (Britain's isolation from Roman civilisation) or beneficial (isolation from continental wars) depending on the particular instance. In short, Dunbar argues that 'the series of events, once begun, is governed more perhaps by moral than physical causes' (239).

In line with this argument, Dunbar, like Robertson, discerns a general pattern (cf. Spadafora 1990: 311). The impact of these local circumstances varies with 'the general state of human improvement' (297) so that they are of 'the least relative moment in the most flourishing stage of arts and sciences' (317). The explanation offered for this is the human capacity to control the environment so that (here openly employing Baconian language) the 'natural history of the terraqueous globe varies with the civil history of nations' (354–5). Soil and climate are susceptible of improvement and the extent of any improvement correlates 'in a high degree with the progress of civil arts' (360) (not that there are not some negative aspects also, such as the introduction of small-pox into rude nations by the cultivated (363 cf. 373)). By these means, Dunbar affirms, man becomes progressively 'in some degree the arbiter of his own happiness and perfection' (347).

Dunbar, in fact, stresses how, when compared to animals, man is 'more exempted from mechanical domination' (342). This is only relatively the case since the human external frame, like 'every system of matter', is subject to mechanical laws (322). Hence, because of the superior quality of its air people live longer in the Hague than they do in Amsterdam – this is a 'natural cause' that operates independently of the fact that both cities are within the same civil society (334–5). Yet that said, Dunbar still denies that 'national genius' can be calculated from bills of mortality (338). This indeed is the crux. It is the explanation of *social* diversity that is at issue. The Scots are seeking to explain the occurrence of differing social practices and institutions; these are '*moral* subjects' (that is, pertaining to *mores*, manners and customs) (cf. Hume *THN*: Preface) to which *moral* causes are appropriate.

C: Conclusion

It is scarcely a novel perception that the world contains a variety of social practices and institutions. And for all the Scots' self-conscious commitment to *evidence*, as the validation of that perception, they here follow one of the most venerable traditions in Western thought, stemming at least from the Platonic and Aristotelian critique of the Sophists. Without endowing that tradition with a false solidity, what endures is the conviction that these differences overlie some basic universality; indeed much of the purpose behind identifying universals emanates from the recognition of differences (cf. Berry 1986: Ch. 4).

While at this level of generality this is commonplace what differentiates the Enlightenment in general and the Scots in particular is a concern to place this diversity into some sort of order. Amazing as this diversity might well be, it will only remain so to the vulgar because the social theorist (what the Scots themselves would call the 'moral scientist') will dispel the amazement. This is a significant claim. For the Scots the social world is not a closed book but one that can be read. This reading can be more or less difficult but even the more recalcitrant texts – those that describe a form of society very different to one that is familiar – can, with proper application, be rendered intelligible.

As we saw in Chapter 3, the Scottish theorists aspire to achieve this intelligibility through the discovery of causes. While geographical location is undoubtedly a factor in why societies differ, that by itself could not constitute an adequate explanation. As we would expect, for the Scots, we have to turn to history to get the explanatory power needed. If geographical factors are the key species of physical cause then historical or temporal factors will consequently be the stuff of moral causation (cf. Stewart 1963: 10). The next chapter will discuss how this commitment to moral causes manifests itself in the proper subject-matter of history.

Notes

1. Cf. Bowles (1985), who picks up this reference to 'wonderful' and relates it to Smith's account in *Astronomy* – see Chapter 3 and text below.
2. Cf. Hume, who wrote 'A Dialogue' on the relationship between the variety of customs and moral standards. He concluded that 'different customs and situations vary not the original ideas of merit ... in any very essential point' (*EPM*: 341). In his correspondence he says of this discussion that his refutation of the sceptical position that there are no standards is sincere 'because [it is] drawn from the capital principles of my system' (*Letts*: I, 173).
3. Another 'local' example is the Irish. While the context is historical, Hume clearly commends, for example, James I's policy of 'civilizing' the Irish. In practice this meant reconciling them to 'laws and industry', thus making their subjection 'durable and useful to the crown of England', and to achieve that end it was necessary to 'abolish Irish customs which supplied the place of laws and which were calculated to keep that people for ever in a state of barbarism and disorder'. In particular, those customs which hindered 'the enjoyment of fixed property in land' (without which there is no incentive

'to enclose, to cultivate, to improve') were replaced (*HE*: III, 33, 34). I am grateful to Paul Smith for drawing this passage to my attention.

4. This position can be read as the expression of a 'bourgeois ideology' (see Chapter 8). We will see in later chapters that the Scots are not above criticising their own commercial society and while 'straightening the warped' might, in theory, ideologically fit the interests of a colonial power the Scots are forthright in their criticisms of European arrogance, see e.g. Robertson *India*: 1154; Dunbar *EHM*: 414; Millar *HV*: IV, 263–5.

5. Some interpretations of Hume (e.g. Farr (1978), Capaldi (1978)) in fact claim that he is a subscriber to an 'interpretativist' approach to social science requiring the use of subjective understanding (*verstehen*). Such interpretations stray too far to the 'other side' and fail to take sufficiently seriously the substantive, evaluative tenor of his thought.

6. Dubos' influence upon Hume, especially in aesthetics, is emphasised by Jones (1983).

7. Turnbull had in fact explicitly taken this line with Dubos in his *Treatise on Ancient Painting* (1740). According to Turnbull, Dubos (or rather the author of the *Réflexions*, who is never identified) has produced 'several very curious Observations to prove the power of physical Causes in producing Effects that may be properly called moral', these physical causes are listed as air, diet, climate, soil, bodily constitution (108). As a case in point Dubos claims that such causes must be evoked to explain the absence of English history painters, while Turnbull counters that it is the moral cause of the absence of fine arts in English liberal education that is decisive (109).

8. Arbuthnot was a Scotsman, who had a medical degree from St Andrews. In the *Essay* he does openly call Hippocrates 'this great man' (122). For doubts on Arbuthnot's influence on Montesquieu (when compared to Chardin and Dubos) see Gates (1967). It is clear though that the topic was well worn. For a survey of the tradition see Glacken (1967: Ch. 12).

9. For example climate is only cause among several in his summation of 'the general spirit' in *SL*: 19, 4. And outside *SL* in his *Essai sur les causes* he is clear that moral causes are more responsible for a nation's character and spirit than physical causes (1955: III, 421).

10. In an earlier essay Hume had noted that the Moroccan civil war between blacks and white occurred 'merely on account of their complexion'. His argument here was that when compared to controversies over articles of faith 'the difference of complexion is a sensible and real difference' (*E–PG*: 59).

11. Cf. Wokler for a discussion of Kames' relationship to Buffon. Wokler also claims that the theory of a separate creation of the American race forms 'Kames' principal contribution to eighteenth-century anthropological thought' (1988: 156). On polygenesis see Greene 1961: Ch. 8. Kames' account was explicitly challenged by James Adair, whose *History of the American Indians* (1775) strove to establish that the Amerinds descended from the Israelites. This he did in a comparative manner (see Chapter 3) endeavouring 'to prove' his case from the Amerinds' 'religious rites, civil and martial customs, their marriages, funeral ceremonies, manners, language, traditions and a variety of particulars' (15). Adair's *History* was cited by Stuart, which is unsurprising given Adair's view that the Amerind is 'governed by the plain and honest law of nature, their whole constitution breathes nothing but liberty' (407).

12. The incluson of 'food' probably alludes to William Temple's *Observations on the United Provinces of the Netherlands* (1673) in *Works* (1754) (though 'diet' was mentioned by Dubos, see n. 7 above). He refers to Temple explicitly later in this same essay in this context (212). Temple's views in this particular were also mentioned by Kames (*SHM*: I, 35, 197n.).

13. In a later essay Hume again affirms that *general* physical causes are irrelevant in determining whether or not the ancient world was more populous than the contemporary one, although he does concede that *particular* physical causes, such as disease,

had a part to play. Nevertheless it is moral causes to which he turns to answer the question (*E–PAN*: 378–9; Hume's emphases). Robert Wallace (Hume's target in this Essay) had argued similarly. He distinguished between 'constant' (for example, temperature of the air) and 'variable' (for example, famines) physical causes but thought moral causes decisive in explaining why the ancient world was more populous than the modern (*Dissertation*: 13).

14. Ferguson's wording is probably not coincidentally found in Hume's Essay, where he says even supposing there was a physical basis for love of drink in northern climes and love of women in the south yet 'we can only infer that the climate may affect the grosser and more bodily organs of our frame; not that it can work upon those finer organs on which the operations of the mind and understanding depend' (*E–NC*: 215).

15. This, of course, was Montesquieu's own position; physical causes did not determine laws but set conditions in terms of which 'good', i.e. effective laws should be framed. Hence he commends the legislators of China for making the laws and customs practical so that the enervating effects of their climate would be offset: 'The more the physical causes incline men to rest, the more the moral causes should divert them from it' (*SL*: 236).

5

Social History

We can best open this chapter by pulling together some earlier findings. From Chapter 3 we can pick up the idea of the human capacity to progress. Also from that chapter we can pick up the idea that 'scientific' history will deal causally with social institutions rather than with singular events like wars and conquests and, accordingly, that it deals with what is 'natural' rather than what is 'most agreeable to fact'. And from Chapter 4 we can pick up the idea that the most important source of social diversity is the various sets of moral causes and that these make their determining effect increasingly as mankind develops.

By and large this has been abstract and it is now time to look at the *content* of this development. The content of the history-of-mankind-in-society is principally a history of social institutions. To comprehend that history is, for the Scots, to remove 'wonder' by discovering connecting principles. A society's institutions, in other words, are not merely contingently connected either at any particular point in time (social statics) or between one period and the next (social dynamics) but reveal a necessary/natural pattern. It is this pattern that makes social history intelligible. As we will see, this intelligibility was achieved most characteristically by dividing the history of social institutions into four stages and, as we shall also see, the key social institution is property.

A: Locke, Empiricism and Primitive Psychology

Before we see how this was done we have to outline a crucial underpinning premise. Once again the way forward is to return initially to a point made earlier. We saw in Chapter 2 how much emphasis the Scots laid upon 'evidence'. Human sociality was an empirically established fact. This empiricism exploded all 'closet metaphysics' by relying upon what actually is the record of human experience. Humans 'experience' the world through the medium of their senses. This doctrine was put on the map, so to speak, by John Locke (see Chapter 1).

To Locke all our ideas come either from sensation or reflection, that is, either from 'sensible objects without' or from 'what we feel within ourselves from the inward workings of our own spirits' (*Essay*: Bk 1, Ch. 5 [1854: II, 3]). What is important for our current purposes is a feature of Locke's own way of arguing. In the context of language, he developed a genetic or historical argument. According to Locke, our words stem from common sensible ideas, and even words that refer to notions 'removed from sense' nevertheless 'have their rise from thence'. For example, the source of the word 'spirit' is 'breath' (*Ibid.*: II, 2).

Revealingly Locke refers frequently to the experience of children. Their first words – Locke mentions 'nurse' and 'mamma' – are, always particular, since their ideas are only particular (Bk 3, Ch. 3, Sect. 7 (II, 11)). Children's ideas as particulars are predominantly sense-derived; it is only later as they mature that they get ideas of reflection (2, 1, 8 (I, 210)). Observation of children, Locke believes, will show how the mind advances by degrees to exercise its faculties of enlarging, compounding and abstracting ideas (2, 1, 22 (I, 222)). While the ability to formulate general ideas 'puts a perfect distinction between man and brutes' (2, 11, 10 (I, 275)), it can, as with idiots and madmen, malfunction. This ability also, as with children, develops sequentially; reason is something attained. There is, however, another category of human. Like children and idiots, Locke says that 'savages and illiterate people' function without any capacity to refer to general maxims and universal principles (1, 2, 27 cf. 1, 2, 12 (I, 153 cf. 140)). This model of cognitive development will feature prominently in what is to come but the analogy between children and savages is where we begin.

At least since Thomas Peacock's sardonic crack[1] the Scots' predilection for using this analogy has been apparent. In itself it is of course not new, but it often underwrote a cyclicalism of birth–maturity–death–birth ... The Scots, however, stress the developmental aspect from infancy to maturity – though they are not averse on occasion to exploiting this imagery by talking also of decline (Ferguson is a notable case but he is not alone). For the present it is the analogy between the mental and emotional capacities of the child and those of the savage (that is, of one who lives in the infancy of society) that is centre stage.

The following passage from Robertson encapsulates what is at stake and it is, therefore, worth quoting at length:

> As the individual advances from the ignorance and imbecility of the infant state to vigour and maturity of understanding, something similar to this may be observed in the progress of the species. With respect to it, too, there is a period of infancy, during which several powers of the mind are not unfolded, and all are feeble and defective in their operation. In the early ages of society, while the condition of man is simple and rude, his reason is but little exercised, and his desires move within a very narrow sphere. Hence arise two remarkable characteristics of the human mind in this state. Its intellectual powers are extremely limited; its emotions and efforts are few and languid. Both these distinctions are conspicuous among the rudest and most unimproved of the American tribes ... (*HAm*: 819)

We can discern here the two ingredients necessary for conjectural or natural history, as identified by Stewart (see Chapter 3) – a view of human nature (as infant/savage) and a description of circumstances (unimproved America). What is now conjectured is that the 'first efforts of every people are naturally calculated to increase the means of subsistence' and (given what is known and what is conjecturable) these initial 'efforts' will take the form of 'catching and ensnaring wild animals or by gathering the spontaneous fruits of the earth' (Millar *OR*: 176). Savages are hunter-gatherers. This now establishes the first step in a four-fold progression.

B: Property and the Four-stages Theory

Before outlining these four steps, or stages, it is important to appreciate what the Scots are trying to do. In an oft-quoted passage Robertson declares:

> In every inquiry concerning the operations of men when united together in society, the first object of attention should be their mode of subsistence. Accordingly as that varies, their laws and policy must be different. (*HAm*: 823)

This is worth a closer look. Note, first, the focus of interest. Reinforcing the argument from Chapter 3, the enterprise is characterised as an 'inquiry' into social operations. Concerning this enquiry Robertson prescribes both a procedure and a purpose; examine the mode of subsistence first because it correlates positively with changes in 'laws and policy'. The latter are the social operations that are the object of the enquiry. Finally, Robertson's use of 'must' should not be overlooked if only because this passage has been the focus of an argument that the 'four-stages theory' is a proto-Marxian version of 'historical materialism'. I shall say something briefly about this argument later.

Though this passage from Robertson has figured prominently in that argument, this is because of its clarity not its novelty. He is here stating what he believes to be a well-established position. Certainly its sentiments were echoed throughout the Scottish Enlightenment. There is some uncertainty but it would appear that Adam Smith's formulation was crucial. Part of the uncertainty stems from the fact that his version of the enquiry (the four-stages theory) only appeared in print in 1776 in *The Wealth of Nations*. However, Smith had featured this doctrine in his Glasgow lectures and possibly before that in some public lectures in Edinburgh in 1750–1 (cf. Meek 1976: Ch. 4). Because we have records of Smith's Glasgow lectures, they are the source to which we can turn for an initial exposition.

In Smith's lectures of 1762/3 he unequivocally refers to 'four distinct states which mankind pass thro' – hunter, shepherd, agriculture and commerce (*LJ*: 14–16). In the 1766 version they are called hunting, pasturage, farming and commerce (459). It is of more than incidental significance that these professions of the four-stages doctrine occurred in lectures on *jurisprudence*. In both versions the context is the same, namely, the property rights of occupation. Similarly in, perhaps, the other most unequivocal expression, Millar's (unpublished) lectures on government, they are explicitly said to be 'stages in the acquisition of property'.[2] Smith's point, is the same as that implicit in Robertson (*HAm*: 823); regulations governing occupation vary according to the four states of society.[3]

Smith illustrates the difference between hunting and herding societies by their attitude to theft. In pastoral societies, as evidenced by the Tartars, theft is punished by immediate death but in hunter-gatherer societies, as evidenced by the Amerinds, theft is not much regarded for the simple reason that there is almost no property among them (*LJ*: 16). In agricultural societies while the severity of the punishment for theft will decline, more laws to regulate property are required since the ways in which 'property may be interrupted' (a phrase to which I shall return) are manifold. And commercial society, being the most improved of all, requires still more laws to prevent infringements of the right to property. (The recurrent references here to law and regulation will be taken up below.)

All these points were echoed elsewhere and by taking Smith's account as standard (even seminal as Duncan Forbes has called it (1954, 1982)), the pivotal role of property is clear. I will discuss how this role manifested itself in the Scots' discussions of ranks or subordination (section C), government and authority (section D) and manners, in particular the role of women in society (section E). However, before proceeding I want to explore the link between the discussion of property and the acceptance of the broadly Lockean version of the savage mentality.

The history of property as portrayed in the four stages rests on a particular model of 'natural' development. What develops are the human cognitive and emotional capacities. While that passage from p. 823 of the *History of America* is quoted many times, what is not quoted is the sequel. Robertson immediately continues:

> The institution suited to the ideas and exigences of tribes, which subsist chiefly by hunting or fishing, and which have as yet acquired but an imperfect conception of any species of property, will be much more simple than those which must take place when the earth is cultivated with regular industry, and a right of property, not only in its productions, but in the soil itself, is completely ascertained.

Not only does Robertson in this latter passage refer to 'ideas' [4] but he also links together the first 'mode of subsistence', hunting and fishing, with an 'imperfect conception of property', where one inferable criterion of imperfection is the absence of a 'right' to property. Millar makes a similar connection. He first states that the 'ideas and feeling' of savages 'in conformity to their situation must of course be narrow and constricted' (*OR*: 176) and then he outlines, though without here explicit enumeration, the four stages.

These initial ideas are 'narrow and constricted' because, as Millar says in a later work, in the mind of the 'poor savage' there are 'few traces of thought beyond what arise from the few objects which impress his external senses' (*HV*: IV, 206 cf. II, 354). To similar effect Robertson observes 'the first ideas of every human being must be such as he receives by the senses' and, he immediately continues, 'while in the savage state there seem to be hardly any ideas but what enter by this avenue' (*HAm*: 819). The savage indeed employs his reasoning powers 'merely on what is sensible' (820). Giving further testimony to the savage/child analogy Robertson openly compares these characteristics with the 'thoughtless levity of children' (819).

What bearing has this on property? The priority of the sensible to the thoughtfull means that initially property and possession are not distinguished and that their later separation marks the 'maturation' of cognitive abilities. In the *Lectures* Smith remarks that 'among savages property begins and ends with possession and they seem scarce to have any idea of anything as their own which is not about their own body' (*LJ*: 460 cf. 18). Kames says the same: 'independent of possession they [savages and barbarians] have no conception of property' (*ELS*: 228). Kames also explains why. The 'conception' of 'property without possession' is, he maintains, 'too abstract for a savage' and the reason for this, he further supposes, is that savages are 'involved in objects of sense' (*HLT*: 91).

A possession is something sensible – it is tangible or graspable. We can ask both 'why' and 'how' are objects possessed. Stuart provides a succinct answer to the first question when he declares that property's foundation lies in the use or pleasure accruing from objects to their possessor (*Diss*: 26). But as he makes clear later this is not the same as having a property-right because the 'abstract idea conveyed by that term and so little known in the beginning of society' had not yet 'gradually evolved' (115). All the Scots regard property as a relation between a person and object (cf. e.g. Hume *THN*: 310, 491, 522 etc.; Kames *HLT*: 88; *ELS*: 228) and it is because occupancy is the most immediate relationship between a person and a thing that Smith, following the precedent most recently of Hutcheson (*SIMP*: 155) but others in the Natural Law tradition behind him,[5] starts his discussion of property rights with that relationship. Ferguson usefully spells out the relevant point when he declares that 'occupancy is no more than ... possession ... [and] the effect of occupancy, therefore, ceases with the actual use, it does not amount to property' (*PMPS*: II, 204). The answer as to 'how' objects are possessed is, therefore, answered in the most general terms by what establishes occupancy.

We can shed more light on what is here at stake by illuminating the well-established distinction between natural and moral powers. Kames' use of this distinction can provide the promised enlightenment. Possessions as graspable objects are obtained through the exercise of natural powers. A beast caught in a trap or a fish by a hook, that is, through 'art and industry' (*HLT*: 90 cf. *SHM*: I, 65 where the reference is to 'labour or art'[6]) is, Kames believes, from the beginning considered to belong to the hunter or fisher. But should a trapped creature escape and be caught by another hunter, through his exercise of his natural powers, then this interruption in possession renders ownership problematic. The 'grossest savages', thanks to their inability to think abstractly, have no distinct conception of 'moral powers'; they are 'strangers' to the moral idea of property as something separate from physically or 'naturally' possessing it (*HLT*: 91).[7] We can detect here a distinctive extra dimension to the standard Natural Law version of this distinction. Pufendorf had argued that 'when a man takes inanimate objects or animals for his use he exercises only a purely natural faculty ... but this faculty takes on the nature of a real right at the moment when this moral effect [when it concerns other humans] is produced in the rest of mankind'.[8] What Kames (and the other Scots) have added is a cognitive developmental perspective, so that although Pufendorf allows for a 'history' of property he does not plot this history as a 'natural history of mankind'.

That savage hunter-gatherers are strangers to the idea of property is explicable by the fact that they live in a world of concrete immediacy, the 'here and now'.

Robertson produces an elaborate account of this world. Savages, because they prize things for present use or because they minister to present enjoyment, set no value on what is not immediately wanted; they act, as Kames puts it, 'by sense not by foresight' (*SHM*: I, 48). Similarly Robertson refers to 'their inconsiderate thought-lessness about futurity', which, for him, is the corollary of their limited understandings and inactive minds (*HAm*: 821). And again, Dunbar observes that man is 'at first possessed of few ideas and of still fewer desires. Absorbed in the present object of sense he seldom indulges any train of reflection on the past and cares not, by anxious anticipation, to antedate futurity' (*EHM*: 68 cf. 15, where he acknowledges Robertson's account). Following Locke's genetic argument, the confinement of savages to the world of immediate sensation means that they are unacquainted with all universal or abstract ideas. Both Robertson (*Ibid.*) and Kames (*SHM*: II, 377n.) note the absence of terms for time, space and substance from American languages (indeed following Locke's lead much of the speculation about cognitive development was conducted by means of an investigation of language, so what Smith, for example, says about the development of the idea of property is mirrored by his account of the development of parts of speech in his *Considerations* (see Chapter 2)). Robertson also draws attention to the Amerind's inability to count beyond three and he explains this inability by the fact that 'savage's have no property to estimate, no hoarded treasure to count, no variety of objects or multiplicity of ideas to enumerate' (*HAm*: 819). Their experience to which their ideas conform provides no opportunity for the exercise of such capacities.[9]

So much for the first stage. The Scots are not strong on explanation for the move from stage to stage. Millar only refers to 'experience' (*OR*: 176)[10] and Kames to 'necessities' (*HLT*: 100) of which hunger is the most important (*SHM*: I, 55). Smith, following a Natural Law commonplace, refers to population growth and consequent pressure on resources as the source of this necessity (*LJ*: 14–15). In line with the stadial hypothesis we know this will produce a herding 'economy' but, in line with the Lockean model of cognitive development, we can anticipate that the capacity for abstract thought will also gradually manifest itself. And a decisive manifestation of this is the emergence of a right of property distinct from physical possession.

The first extension beyond simple possession is alluded to by Smith in the context of Kames' problematic case of the escaped animal. Of such a case – which figures in Justinian's *The Institutes* (II–1–12) – Smith remarks that provided the original hunter still pursued his former catch (that is, in Kames' terminology continued to exert natural powers) with the probability of recapture it would be thought by others to be his. This 'thought' is for Smith the first step in extending the conception of property (*LJ*: 19). But it is not, he claims, until 'men come to think of taming these wild animals' that 'property would necessarily be extended a great deal further' (*LJ*: 20). Kames, too, sees the emergence of the second herding stage as the source of extension but Smith goes into more detail by following Roman Law (cf. Justinian: II–1–15) and distinguishing different steps. At first those animals that were tamed, such that they returned habitually to the proprietor, were deemed his property. A further extension occurred when some species (such as oxen) only existed in tamed form, so that they were regarded as the owner's not on the strength of their returning into his power but simply because they could be distinguished to be his. Smith does not explain how this would be realised. However, Stuart says that when animals are tamed and receive different marks then property is conceived distinct from possession (*Diss*: 27).

The presence of such 'marks' is suggestive of a capacity for symbolic representation – a capacity that would seemingly indicate the presence of some 'abstracting' cognitive capacity. But this itself is not yet full-blown. Kames and Sir John Dalrymple refer to 'symbolic possession' but argue that this was required precisely because transference of possession still needed some tangible token (cf. Hume, who refers to this as a 'superstitious practice' *THN*: 515). As an example, Dalrymple cites the account in the Old Testament whereby the land of Elemelech was granted to Boaz by the delivery of a shoe (*General History of Feudal Property in Great Britain* [1757]: 220) and Kames cites a case reported by Selden whereby a grant of land was sealed by laying a turf upon an altar (*HLT*: 108).

These two examples, by referring to land, bring us to the third stage. The third or agricultural age produces landed property. Kames refers (in the manner of Hume (*THN*: 310)) to the intimate mental connection between the ploughed field and the ploughman (*HLT*: 104). This, however, is a connection that manifests moral as well as natural power, because if I leave my land or house and I am dispossessed in my absence then an injustice is perceived. That is to say there is a clear right to property that survives any physical interruption; there is a clear distinction between property and possession. Smith's story is somewhat similar. However, he remarks that the cultivation of land would not have immediately produced private ownership (*LJ*: 20). Rather he believes there could have been communal ownership and a field only belonged to the cultivator so long as he occupied it (22). What is crucial for Smith is the development of cities. With a definite fixed abode then the contiguous land would be cultivated so that it came to appear easier to divide the land once and for all, rather than the chief magistrate dividing its product each year.[11] Millar's version of the story is essentially the same (*OR*: 252). Stuart, whom Millar acknowledges (251n.), makes great play of the presence among the Germans of a communal stage, and he openly criticises Kames and Dalrymple on this point (*Diss*: 29), but of greater interest is his invocation here of the cognitive aspect. He writes that a 'rude people' who were 'uninstructed in arts and not used to abstraction' would have difficulty apportioning property according to merit (33).

Unlike the earlier transitions, the emergence of a society based on commerce is not the product of external forces like the pressure of population on resources. Indeed exchange, as Smith makes clear, has always existed. Even in hunter societies (the first stage) there was some vestigial division of labour when an individual adept at making bows and arrows exchanged his product for the meat killed by those more skilled at using them to hunt (*WN*: 27). If, as Smith says, in a commercial society every man is a merchant (*WN*: 37) then it means in that stage every man lives by exchanging (see Chapter 6). In contrast to landed property therefore the characteristic of property in the fourth stage is mobility.

To Kames, property originally bestowed no power of alienation (*HLT*: 110); a fact that follows from it being originally conterminous with possession. Alienation presupposes a 'will' or 'intention'. This presupposition, as both Smith and Kames observe, has particular bearing on testamentary succession. Smith remarks that in 'the savage nations of Asia and America' such succession is unknown and the explanation for this is that 'piety to the dead' is 'too refined a doctrine for a barbarous people' (*LJ*: 65 cf. 462). Kames notes that inheritance by children was considered a 'sort of property' but that this 'right' existed independently of the will of the father (*HLT*: 110). Smith regards testamentary succession as a great extension of property (i.e. its conceptual separation from possession) since it implies a right of disposal on the part of one who being dead cannot properly be said to have a right (*LJ*: 466 cf. Kames *British Antiquities*: 128n.). To recognise the wishes of a dead man Smith regards as a 'considerable refinement in humanity' (467), or, as Dalrymple put it, such a recognition was 'no very natural conception' to a rude people (*Feudal Property*: 143).

What is distinctive about the fourth stage is that the alienation of property is unrestricted. The decisive extension is that land itself becomes alienable. That movable objects were alienable before immovable ones was a commonplace, and it is a special characteristic of the third agricultural stage that the extension is resisted through such practices as entails – an institution frequently attacked.[12] Kames declares that now in the age of commerce the power of alienation is 'universally held to be inherent in the property of land as well as movables' (*HLT*: 113) and Dalrymple makes clear that the source of this universality is the transactions between merchants (*Feudal Property*: 94, 114) and that a 'commercial disposition' had made it necessary to allow 'unbounded commerce in land' (159). Similarly for Millar it was 'the general advancement of arts' that rendered land an 'object of commerce' (*HV*: I, 308).

Somewhat later in the *Historical View*, Millar remarks of this process that it has occurred by means of 'the improvements of society ... enlarging the ideas of mankind with regard to property' (II, 191 cf. Stuart *Diss*: 119). Once again the underlying cognitive psychology helps us make sense of this remark. The idea of property, like all ideas, is originally concrete and, again like all ideas, it develops or becomes increasingly abstract. Kames states this clearly: 'in the progress of nations toward maturity of understanding, abstract ideas become familiar: property is abstracted from possession; and in our conceptions it is now firmly established that the want of possession deprives not a man of his property' (*ELS*: 229). This means that in the most mature (that is, commercial) society the idea of property is the most abstract. It is present in the form of credit notes and bills of exchange, for example, which rely on a series of beliefs. This reflects the general character of life in such societies, but since Chapter 6 is devoted to the Scots' treatment of commerce I shall postpone further discussion of this abstractness until that chapter. At the end of this chapter I shall return to the bearing of this Lockean-derived developmentalism on the proper interpretative status of the four stages. We now have to consider how these changes in property interact with changes in other institutions.

C: Ranks

We know that in the infancy of society there is no property distinct from possession and that possessions themselves are limited to what is occupable or graspable. In the *Wealth of Nations* (702) Smith states that in 'a nation of hunters' there is 'scarce any property' (in the *Lectures* he had supposed that property was 'at first' confined 'to what was about one's person, his cloaths and any instruments he might have occasion for' (*LJ*: 20)). He also characterised this period as experiencing both 'universal poverty' and 'universal equality' (712). These three facts of propertylessness, poverty and equality are interrelated – the absence of private property means no extensive exchange can take place and without that there can be no opulence; conversely the presence of private property enables inequality to be established.

While Smith says that in the first stage there was 'universal equality', in the same sentence he makes it clear that this did not exclude all grounds of subordination. He, in fact, identifies four 'causes', or 'circumstances', which 'naturally introduce subordination' (711/2 cf. *LJ*: 321). Of these four only two operate in the age of hunters. These two are types of personal quality or attribute. The first cause is superiority of either body or mind, the second is superiority of age. Smith proceeds effectively to discount bodily differences (even the weakest physically can still kill the strongest – as when Jael killed Sisera as he slept) while he regards mental differences as 'invisible' and thus disputable. This is what differentiates age as the second cause, since, according to Smith, it is a 'plain and palpable quality which admits of no dispute'. ('Palpability' is a quality which occurs more than once in this context and its presence can, perhaps, be connected with the prevalence of concrete over the abstract relationships in early ages.)

All the Scots argue that in the first age subordination was based on personal qualities. Millar states that in that 'rude period' of hunting and fishing (where there is no opportunity for acquiring considerable property) there are no distinctions except those which arise from 'personal qualities either of mind or body' (*OR*: 247 cf. 204). Robertson declares 'wherever the idea of property is not established' the only distinctions are those that arise from 'personal qualities' (*HAm*: 827/8). He mentions 'age' and 'courage' as examples of such qualities, while Kames refers to 'age' and 'experience' (*SHM*: I, 414), Hume to 'valour, force, integrity or prudence' (*E–OG*: 39) and Stuart to 'force of body and vigour of mind' (*VSE*: 37). Ferguson, for his part, believes that some 'mode of subordination' complies with 'an order established by nature' (*ECS*: 63) and, in the clearest expression of a stadial thesis in the *Essay*,[13] identifies as 'savages' those who hunt and fish and have no property and who experience only the subordination that 'follows from the differences of age, talents and dispositions' (84 cf. 7). Following

Montesquieu (cf. *SL*: 290–1), Ferguson distinguishes savages from 'barbarians' who do possess property and where the 'ground of a permanent and palpable subordination is laid' (98). The implication here that a distinction of ranks is prior to the establishment of property is emphasised by Stuart in his argument that the ancient Germans embodied public virtue (*Diss*: 130).

Smith's two remaining 'causes', however, establish a crucial link between property and subordination. The third is 'superiority of fortune', which is especially marked in the age of shepherds (*WN*: 712–13). His main example is the Tartar chief under whose rule occurs the greatest degree of subordination. This rests on the chief's possession of extensive herds with which he maintains a host of dependants. These retainers depend for their subsistence entirely upon the chief so that they 'must obey his orders in war and submit to his jurisdiction in peace'. As this implies, Smith here indicates that the creation of this subordination necessarily involves, also in this second stage, the emergence of government (see section D below).

Smith's fourth cause – superiority of birth – consolidates the third because it only has any social significance once inequality of fortune has been established (713). As a straightforward descriptive fact, Smith observes, all families are equally ancient and to regard birth as a cause of superiority can only mean being born into wealthy family. Given this it follows that this fourth cause is necessarily absent from the first age, where there is equality of fortune and that, once again, it is pastoral societies which embody this inequality to the greatest extent (714). Picking up the theme of the last section, it is worth observing that the possibility in the pastoral age of being the owner of property while not in possession of the object is an integral element in the development of the inequality that grows in that stage (cf. Horne 1990: 115). The limits to inequality in the first stage, being confined by physical capacity or natural power, are transcended when the size of the herd (the quantity of possession) is determinable by marks.

These third and fourth causes come together with considerable effect, a point made also by Ferguson when he comments that a chief enjoys a pre-eminence beyond that of the battlefield when 'the distinctions of fortune and those of birth are conjoined' (*ECS*: 100). In the discussion of ranks in the *Moral Sentiments* (see below) Smith remarks that the 'distinction of ranks' rests more securely on 'the plain and palpable difference of birth and fortune' than upon invisible factors like wisdom and virtue (*TMS*: 226). The Tartar chief thus 'on account of his great wealth, and of the great number of those who depend upon him for subsistence, and revered on account of the nobleness of his birth, and of the immemorial antiquity of his illustrious family has a natural authority over all the inferior shepherds and herdsmen of his horde or clan' (*WN*: 714).

We can exploit Smith's use of the term 'natural authority' (on which more below when it is considered in its own right) here to note that the effective basis of rule is not the 'brute' fact of material dependency but, rather, a set of beliefs about that rule. Hume had developed a version of this argument. It is a 'wonder' how easy it is for a few to rule over the many, especially since strength (of numbers) must always lie with the latter. All the governors (the few) can rely on is 'opinion' (*E–FPG*: 32). Hume then analyses 'opinion' distinguishing between 'opinion of interest', based on 'the sense of advantage reaped from government', and 'opinion of right', which is subdivided into 'right to power' and 'right to property' (33). He takes the latter of these two subdivisions to be well established, and his chief example of the former is attachment to 'ancient government' since 'antiquity always begets the opinion of right' (see p. 34 above).

If we return to Smith's account of pastoral societies we can see these Humean observations implicitly repeated. The social coherence of pastoral societies rests on custom. We saw in Chapter 2 how longevity of itself established in the minds of subjects a disposition to accept the status quo as legitimate. In this context Smith remarks that because there is no outlet for wealth in pastoral societies other than the maintenance of dependants (a situation that decisively changes in a commercial society) then it remains concentrated. The effect of this is a continuity in the pattern of relationships, and it is precisely such a continuity that permits the development of customary beliefs. It is, says Smith, a fact that 'men more easily submit to a family to whom they and their ancestors have always submitted' (713). Millar provides a particularly clear example of this chain of reasoning, 'thus the son, who inherits the state of his father, is enabled to maintain an equal rank … which is daily augmented by the power of habit and becomes more considerable as it passes from one generation to another' (*OR*: 250).

One question that remains unanswered is how did the Tartar chief come to be chief in the first place. Just as the account of the transition from stage to stage was relatively undertheorised – it is a matter of contingent fact – so this question is not considered at length. Three candidates can be identified. The first is implicit in the foregoing, namely, military prowess abetted by the principle of habit. Millar, following Hume (see *E–OG*), hypothesises that those adept at waging war will be conspicuous and that will be enhanced by others becoming 'accustomed to follow his banner' (*OR*: 247 cf. 254). For this to be effective presumes warfare to be endemic in the first stage but such a condition was widely accepted to be the case (e.g. see Hume *E–OG*: 40, Ferguson *ECS*: 101). With leadership thus already established when herding is introduced, the leader will claim ownership and thus underwrite further his power. The second candidate is 'industry'. Just as military ability in hunter societies produced chiefs so those who exhibit 'pre-eminence and superior abilities' in acquiring herds and flocks will become the richest and chiefs (Millar *OR*: 250). The final candidate is luck. Millar merely brackets this together with the second and provides no separate treatment. Ferguson is similarly unforthcoming; men 'arrive at unequal conditions by chance' and these 'conditions' are solidified before they realise 'subordination is a matter of choice' (*ECS*: 100 cf. 237).

The establishment of property in land, and thus the presence of the third stage, though it has a number of far-reaching consequences (such as the growth of cities and the emergence of a proper sentiment of patriotism (Kames *SHM*: I, 465)) does not produce any shift in the basis of subordination; it merely consolidates.

Just as the chief in pastoral times is the one with the largest herd (and thus most retainers) so the leader in agricultural societies is the one with the most land (and thus most retainers) (cf. Smith *WN*: 717). The same crucial relationship of dependency, and its root in customary obedience, applies in both ages. It is a further characteristic of a commercial society that this dependency is absent. Owing to the pervasiveness of exchange – including as we saw in land – then property is 'subjected to a constant rotation' and this 'prevents it from conferring upon the owner the habitual respect and consideration derived from a long continued intercourse between the poor and the rich' (Millar *HV*: IV, 131/*HVL*: 337).[14]

i) Social Psychology of Subordination

This plotting of the growth of dependency via its links with the control of livelihood has seemed to some to approximate or anticipate an 'economic' or 'materialist' theory of history.[15] If this is taken to mean that humans are motivated by economic self-interest then clearly the Scots do not have such a theory.[16] Their whole moral theory is against the primacy of self-interest (see Chapter 7) and their discussion of ranks is another clear case. In this discussion the Scots are again concerned to produce an account that is true to experience; they produce a social psychology of belief.

Smith provides the most worked-out account of these beliefs, although Hume had perhaps already sketched out the key principles (cf. *THN*: 365). A central element in human sociality is responsive interaction. (See Chapter 7 for the underpinning theory.) One manifestation of this is that, because people respond positively to our joy, we parade our riches but conceal our poverty (*TMS*: 50). It is in this 'regard to the sentiments of mankind' that Smith locates the incentive to 'pursue riches and avoid poverty' – in short, it is 'vanity' not 'ease' that motivates (*Ibid.*). The rich glory in their wealth because it 'naturally' draws upon them 'the attention of the world' (51). They are thus emulated and it is 'upon this disposition of mankind to go along with the passions of the rich and powerful' that the 'distinction of ranks and order of society' is founded (52 cf. Ferguson *ECS*: 237). Generally speaking, individuals do not 'go along' because of any 'private expectations of benefit' nor because of any 'regard to the utility of such submission' but rather because of their 'admiration for the advantages' of the superior's situation (*Ibid.*). As we will see in section D this same theory is used by Smith in his account of the effective basis of political obligation.

Millar refers to Smith's account and Lehmann speculates that the *Ranks* is likely to have been given its initial impetus by this chapter in the *Moral Sentiments* (1960: 167). Despite this reference Millar draws more obvious attention to the link between giving support and receiving maintenance and protection (*OR*: 250). In his later work Millar repeats the Smithian argument though, once again, after having acknowledged the reverence superiors receive, he remarks that the authority of the rich over the poor is 'doubtless chiefly supported by selfish considerations' (*HV*: IV, 289/*HVL*: 349)). In this same passage Millar hints at a criticism of this psychological acquiescence in rank distinctions when he comments that reverence and awe may reach such proportions that inferiors lose the 'exercise of their natural powers' and become 'sunk in abasement and stupidity'. Smith, too, is not averse to making critical judgements, but these can be best appreciated in the context of his remarks on the middling ranks.

ii) Middling Ranks

In that same chapter of the *Moral Sentiments* where he had outlined his theory of the origin of ranks, Smith comments upon the circumstances of a 'young noble-man'. He asks rhetorically, what makes this person 'worthy' of the superiority he possesses over his fellow citizens? To which he answers, it is not by exercising the virtues of knowledge, industry, patience or self-denial (53); rather, his highest exploit is 'to figure at a ball' and he 'shudders with horror' at the thought of having to exercise those virtues (55–6). The next chapter (one added to the sixth edition and one which some commentators have thought significant on that account (cf. Dickey (1986), Dwyer (1987)) opens by making explicit what this depiction implies: the disposition to admire the rich while necessary to establish and maintain the distinction of ranks is 'at the same time the great and most universal cause of the corruption of our moral sentiments' (61). We find a very similar argument in Ferguson. He observes that 'when mere riches or court-favour are supposed to constitute rank, the mind is misled from the consideration of qualities on which it ought to rely' (*ECS*: 238 cf. 250, 254). These desiderated 'qualities' are ability and merit (cf. 67).

This critique of aristocratic ethics (the 'young nobleman' and 'court-favour'), along with support for a meritocracy, appears to exemplify what is often termed a bourgeois ideology (see Chapter 8). Further apparently straightforward support for this interpretation comes from Smith's discussion of the middling ranks. In the next chapter we will examine directly his treatment of commercial virtues (and also his criticism of some aspects of the consequences of commercial practices) but this particular discussion is best considered here.

Since those born into the nobility scorn the virtues of industry it follows, for Smith, that in all governments the administration is executed by men who 'were educated in the middle and inferior ranks of life'. These are men who have had to make their way in the world 'by their own industry and abilities' (*TMS*: 56). Smith further endorses this meritocratic picture by remarking that in the 'middling and inferior stations of life' ability is generally rewarded with commensurate success – virtue and fortune 'happily in most cases' coincide (63). Their commitment to honesty and law-abidingness produces a circumstance where such virtues become the norm as they are adopted 'by far the greater part of mankind' (*Ibid.*). Though this is not here explicitly stated, the clear implication is that this happy situation obtains in a commercial society, and in the *Wealth of Nations* he says of post-Union Scotland that 'the middling and inferior ranks' have gained a 'compleat deliverance' from the previously oppressive power of the aristocracy (944).

It is worth noting that in all these references Smith includes the 'inferior' along with the 'middling'. A similar open endorsement of the middling ranks, though without this inclusion of the 'inferior', is made by Hume. In contrast to 'rude unpolished nations', by which he here means the third agricultural stage characterised by the rule of barons as 'petty tyrants', in commercial societies we find the 'middling rank of men who are the best and firmest basis of public liberty' (*E–RA*: 277). Another illustration of the same phenomenon is the twin absence among the Anglo-Saxons of 'true liberty' and a 'middle rank of men' (*HE*: I, 115, 116). Like Aristotle's account (cf. *Politics*: 1295b) of this stratum, they are neither too poor to submit themselves to abject dependence nor too rich to be able to tyrannise others – rather, they 'covet equal laws, which may secure their property' (*E–RA*: 278). This same 'classical' argument is propounded by Kames, to whom 'gentlemen of moderate fortune' (or 'of the middle rank') are the locus of 'the genuine spirit of liberty' since they abhor equally 'servility to superiors' and 'tyranny to inferiors' (*SHM*: II, 531). Dunbar is another who sees the 'middling ranks of life' not only possessing moral and intellectual endowments but also being less corrupt than the superior ranks (*EHM*: 436). In addition to these traditional commonplaces there is another well-established idiom with a somewhat different sociological message. Here the key is a notion of a 'middle power' that acts as a buffer between a monarch and the body of the people. In France this was associated with Montesquieu and the *thèse nobiliaire* (cf. Ford 1965) and, as this suggests, it was the aristocracy that was seen as playing this role. In British politics the landed gentry could occasionally be given this same role, and Hume, for example, sees the removal of this 'middle power' as infallibly producing a despotism (*E–PC*: 358).

The presence of these various idioms make it prudent not to erect too fixed an interpretation on references to the middling ranks.[17] Certainly to read them as the expression of bourgeois ideology is not a simple matter if only because that interpretation itself is far from simple. I will consider this interpretation, along with others, in Chapter 8.

D: Government and Authority

We have already indicated some of the issues to be discussed in this section. The first is the close link with the account of ranks and thence with property. There is an intimate connection between government and subordination because it is assumed to be part of the meaning of 'government' that it is a hierarchical relationship of ruler over ruled (cf. Millar *HV*: IV, 293/*HVL*: 350). The tie-in with property is of interest because it renews the Scots' encounter with Locke.

It was central to the strategy of Locke's normative theory (the extent of the 'true end' of civil government) that he trace government to its origin. As we saw in Chapter 2 an important thrust in the Scots' critique of Contractarian thought was to sever this link between origins and legitimacy. If government did not therefore originate in contract, where and how did it commence? The most general answer is supplied by Hume. On his account, as we noted in the last section, in the earliest societies 'long continuance' of the state of war at that time gave to the strongest and most prudent a leadership role (*E–OG*: 40). The people, being 'enured' to their submission, come to accept the leader's decisions as an arbiter during peace-time disputes. It is in this casual and imperfect way, as an unintended consequence, that government commences; it was not discovered by foresight as a remedy for inconveniences (39).

This same trajectory is traced by others. Both Kames and Ferguson illustrate this 'casual and imperfect' process by observing that government emerges gradually and is only restrained by rules after many 'errors in the capacities of magistrates and subjects' have been committed (Ferguson *ECS*: 63) or until the people have suffered under 'vicious government' (Kames *SHM*: I, 414). Millar follows Hume closely. The head of a rude society is at first the commander of forces who later turns his attention to settling internal disputes (*OR*: 254/5 cf. *HV*: I, 233/4). One important reason for this priority of external to internal affairs, which both Kames (*HLT*: 39, 306) and Ferguson (*ECS*: 100) also endorse, is that initially internal troubles were expected to be settled privately – the principle of revenge was accepted. The ceding of the right of revenge by the 'multitude' to the chief is remarked upon by Stuart (*VSE*: 37 cf. *Diss*: 90). It is also stressed by Robertson, who refers to it in several of his writings (see *HAm*: 828, *VSE*: 322, *HSc*: 97). Millar, too, joins in. He puts this process down to the 'progress of government' (*HV*: I, 192, 198) and in so doing reasserts the link with the distribution of property (I, 127).

This pattern is the same as traced by Locke in his formal account of the inconveniences of the state of nature. The natural right to execute the law of nature (the right to punish) is a major of 'inconvenience' because 'interested' humans are liable to punish beyond due proportion (see *Second Treatise*: §8). Lying behind this are disputes over property (both of the person and of goods) so that Locke is able to say that the end or purpose of government is the preservation of property (§§94, 95, 138). A striking illustration of the difference between Locke and the Scots is provided by how Smith (especially) explains the emergence of that same 'end'.

We recall from section C that social inequality emerges in the second stage and that this establishes dependency relationships. Smith now says that this also 'thereby introduces some degree of ... civil government' (*WN*: 715). This reference to 'civil' government not only underlines the traditional Lockean link but also, in so doing, takes for granted private/familial governance. Kames does acknowledge this point overtly, 'in the first state of men, viz, that of hunting and fishing, there obviously is no place for government, except that which is exercised by the heads of families over children and domesticks' (*HLT*: 56n.).

On Smith's account, the introduction of civil government is a self-interested move on the part of the rich. They require government to preserve 'that order of things which can alone secure them in the possession of their own advantages'. Those of inferior wealth go along with this because they depend on their superiors to give them protection. The consequence is that 'civil government so far as it is instituted for the security of property is in reality instituted for the defence of the rich against the poor, or of those who have some property against those who have none at all' (*WN*: 715). This same argument had been made in the *Lectures*, where property in the age of shepherds is said bluntly to make government 'absolutely necessary' and to be so because otherwise the poor would attack the rich (*LJ*: 208).

Three observations are worth making about this argument. First, it claims to be a descriptive account, to tell it as it 'really' is. The intention behind this claim is to discredit the cogency of a Lockean-type prescriptive account on the grounds that it is divorced from what 'actually happened' (cf. Hume *E–OC*: 487). Second, it establishes historically a strong connection between government and social inequality and attributes to the former a predominantly self-interested rationale rather than some (ideal) concern with the public good.[18] Finally, it establishes a benchmark. This is a description of how matters stand in the second, and effectively also in the third, stage. However, when these are set against the prevalent circumstances of the fourth stage – regular government and impartial administration of justice (see Chapter 6) – then a clear improvement can be discerned.

i) Obligation and Revolution

Locke's theory was centrally a theory of obligation. It provided criteria or principles to determine when rulers were entitled to obedience and, by the same token, when the citizens were entitled to disobey. As we would expect the Scots supply a naturalistic rather than an openly normative account of obligation. Smith neatly contrasts these accounts. The idea that 'kings are the servants of the people to be obeyed, resisted, deposed and punished as the public conveniency may require' is 'the doctrine of reason and philosophy' but, he adds, this normative Lockean position is 'not the doctrine of Nature'. Rather, it is natural to submit to kings for their own sake, 'to tremble and bow down before their exalted station' (*TMS*: 53). When resistance has occurred, in order to overcome this 'habitual state of deference', it must have been prompted by the 'bulk of the people' experiencing the highest degree of fear, hatred and resentment (*Ibid.*). But so deep-seated is this deference that it soon re-establishes itself (as English history demonstrates).

Elsewhere Smith generalises by identifying two principles of allegiance (*LJ*: 318). The first is the principle of authority. This is the natural disposition to respect an established authority in general. It applies to the respect given by the young to the old or by children to their parents or by subjects to their government. The second principle is utility or the general interest. Individuals support their magistrates beause they are the source of their security (and justice and peace (*LJ*: 402)). Because there is general benefit or public utility derived from this security then particular individuals are inclined to tolerate some loss of their own private utility. Yet because subjects are 'born and bred up under the authority of magistrates' then the power of custom means that their rule is accepted ('everything by custom appears to be right' (*LJ*: 322) cf. p. 35 above) and this stability conduces to security. It is seemingly on the strength of this inference that Smith is able to declare that 'the principle of authority is the foundation of that of utility' (*LJ*: 322).

This same terminology is employed by Millar. He reiterates Smith's general argument for authority and also lays appropriate emphasis on the force of habit ('the great controller and governor of our actions' (*HV*: IV, 291/*HVL*: 349)). He also regards government's 'general utility' as the chief principle that induces individuals 'to resign their own private interest, to subdue their opposite and jarring passions' (293/350). Millar also appears to give to utility a critical as well as supportive role. This can be seen in his treatment of Irish history. He first counsels against assuming approval from the mere quiescence. He couches this point in general terms, 'in every rude nation' those with authority are likely to indulge in 'arbitrary proceedings' with impunity (*HV*: IV, 56). Yet long custom cannot sanction measures incompatible with the 'great interests of society'. In the case of the Irish this means that they were justified in 'asserting their natural rights' against oppressive English rule (60).

This last phrase should be interpreted with some care.[19] The actual terminology should not be over-emphasised. In a very similar context Millar refers to subjects being justified in uniting 'in defence of their privileges' as well as in invoking their 'fundamental rights' (*HV*: IV, 261). More significant than terminology is that Millar is not here contradicting his critique of Contract theory and its individualistic assumptions. He is careful to point out that the issue of Anglo-Irish relations was not decided by 'abstract reasoning', it was, rather, another instance of the impact of general social progress. The English found that they could not withhold from Ireland that 'free spirit which the example of her constitution and the general advancement of commerce and manufactures contribute to inspire' (IV, 60). Indeed in the essay where he discusses authority and utility he remarks that there are natural rights antecedent to society which, though not lost, are modified by social life (such as the surrender of the right to revenge) (*HV*: IV, 294/*HVL*: 350/1).[20] This reads like Burke[21] but, as we have seen, Millar is clear (perhaps more so than others of his compatriots) that mere longevity or 'tradition' must still be assessed by the 'general interest'.

These theoretical concerns with the grounds of allegiance are never 'purely' theoretical, they have practical resonances. Perhaps the clearest case of this is the principle of the right to resist. This was well established in the jurisprudential/Natural Law tradition and, as we noted above, was central to Locke's *Second Treatise*.[22] The Scots were particularly sensitive to this issue. As we sketched in Chapter 1, they wished to establish their credentials as Britons, which meant in their eyes emphasising the legitimacy of the Hanoverian settlement and putting a great distance between themselves and the Jacobites. (We will discuss in Chapter 6 a significant aspect of this sensitivity in the debate over a Scottish militia.) Hume's early *Essays* exhibit this trait as he attempted, as Duncan Forbes has argued, 'to give the established regime, the Revolution Settlement, the Hanoverian succession the respectable intellectual foundation ... it had not got' (1975: 91 cf. 94). However, the resonance I wish to pick up illustratively is that generated by the American Revolution.

In their generality the Scottish literati were not favourably disposed to the American cause. Kames uses the conflict to continue the critique of Locke in as much as his view of 'no taxation without representation' had been used against the authority of the British government. To this view Kames replies that obligation (and hence the duty to pay tax) stems from protection (*SHM*: I, 492–3).[23] Ferguson was commissioned by the government to write a pamphlet in direct reply to Richard Price's *Observations on the Nature of Civil Liberty* and in 1778 was a member of a peace commission to Philadelphia (Fagg 1995: li–iv). Ferguson's *Remarks on a Pamphlet lately published by Dr. Price* (1776) fastened on to Price's Lockean notion of civil liberty (cf. Laboucheix 1970: 132, Thomas, 1977: 156). To Price, liberty originates with the people and consists of the power of a civil society to govern itself (*Observations* in *Political Writings* (1991): 22). In the American context this means that the British government are trying to rob them of that liberty – 'their natural and unalienable title' (21). According to Ferguson, this notion is inconsistent with the 'great end of civil government', namely, security (*Remarks*: 3). He then glosses 'security' to mean possession of rights while being restrained from invading the rights of others (5). Sher judges that this pamphlet is consistent with Ferguson's other writings and mentions this jurisprudential definition of rights as evidence (1985: 267). We shall see in Chapter 6 that Ferguson's view of 'rights' in the *Essay* and their relationship to liberty is less clear-cut than this gloss might suggest.

In the pamphlet Ferguson comments that despite all the talk of rights by the Americans the conflict is really about tax and property (*Remarks*: 28). A somewhat similar debunking of rhetoric is effected by Millar. He observes sardonically that it is a 'curious spectacle' to see those who speak so loudly about liberty and inalienable rights nonetheless making 'no scruple' of depriving a great proportion of their fellow creatures of 'almost every species of right' (*OR*: 321). On the subject of taxation Ferguson adopts a legalistic line – until there is a formal separation the Americans as members of the British Empire are obliged to contribute (*Remarks*: 31). The issue of representation is not vital since the key concern is who is elected not who can elect (13). Similar arguments were propounded by two Aberdonian professors/divines who both published sermons on the conflict. The text of Campbell's sermon was 'meddle not with them that are given to change'. He does not deny the possibility of lawful resistance but it can only ever be a necessary evil (*The Nature, Extent and Importance of the Duty of Allegiance* [1776]: 6, 13). While dismissing the terms 'natural' and 'inalienable' as nonsense (35), Campbell declares the rights of the people to be as real and valuable as those of the magistrate (15). Nonetheless the end of government is public utility (13). Campbell, like Ferguson, openly criticised Price's notion of liberty as self-government (25) and he was followed to similar effect by his fellow Aberdonian Alexander Gerard to whom this notion was tantamount to anarchy (*Liberty the Cloke of Maliciousness* [1778]: 8). Gerard, too, interprets the Americans as wanting immunity from any financial contribution to the upkeep of the Empire – a desire 'repugnant to the plainest principles of justice' (12). Nor is Gerard any more sympathetic to the American case over taxation since, he declares, taxes only encroach upon liberty if they are excessive or unequal not if they levied without consent (10).

Ferguson, Campbell and Gerard all not only affirm the rectitude of government policy they also eulogise the system and constitution. While not derogating the system, a view more critical of the policy was put forward by Dunbar. Without being an apologist for the Americans, Dunbar was, among the literati (as opposed to the evangelical wing of the Kirk (cf. Fagerstrom 1954)), one of the clearest opponents of the war.[24] For example, compared to the open assault on Price launched by Ferguson and the others, Dunbar notes that Price 'rightly' numbered colonial governments among those which deserve to be labelled tyrannical (*EHM*: 292).

Dunbar not only interpolates his view of the war in his book but he also wrote a pamphlet directly on the conflict.[25] The pamphlet is dedicated to Camden, who is also alluded to fulsomely in the book (*EHM*: 435), and who did regard taxation without representation as robbery (cf. Beloff 1960: 19–24). Dunbar openly criticised British high-handedness and miscalculation (292, 313) though he hoped some mutually acceptable reconciliation might still be possible (283). One theme in his argument is an adaptation of the popular familial metaphor to maintain that the relation between colonies and the 'ancient country' is 'rightly understood' that is, one of equality not that of mother to daughter (281). Britons and Americans share a common culture and both sides should compromise, true liberty lies midway between humble service and proud domination (*Oratio*: 20).

In the course of his argument Dunbar refers to Smith. Smith included a lengthy discussion of British colonial policy in the *Wealth of Nations*; indeed the one fault that Blair detected in that work was that the discussion of America made the book seem 'too much like a publication for the present moment' (*Corr*: 188). Smith speculates that if Britain gave up governance of the colonies and then entered into free trade with them, all would benefit, but he is well aware that 'interest' is less potent than pride and, even more significantly, that such a demission of power is 'always contrary to the private interest of the governing part [of a nation]' (*WN*: 616–17). Despite the extent of his discussion, Smith's treatment should be viewed in the light of his general economic argument rather than as a continuation of his historical account of government or of his account of the principles of obligation (cf. Skinner 1976).

E: Manners and Women

According to Kames, 'manners' signify a 'mode of behaviour' (*SHM*: I, 181). Because they depend on an 'endless variety of circumstances' they are 'too complex for law' yet it is upon them that 'chiefly depends the well-being of society' (*Loose Hints upon Education*: 21). Under this heading Kames included clothing, language and customs but he also wrote a separate Sketch on the subject of women. I want to follow his example and discuss this subject (and the related issues of marriage and family) under the heading of manners.

The most extensive account is provided by Millar, although an Edinburgh physician William Alexander wrote a large two-volume *History of Women*.[26] The first and longest of his chapters in the *Ranks* concerns the 'rank and condition of women in different ages'. As that title suggests, Millar is also the author who most explicitly treats this topic in line with the stadial thesis (Smith in the context of Domestic Law may well have done something not dissimilar – and be the inspiration for Millar – but we have an incomplete record[27]). In the rudest age of the hunters and fishers, with the absence of both leisure and property, there is nothing to 'interrupt the free intercourse of the sexes' (*OR*: 183). Sex took place for procreation and paid little regard to previous attachments. However, there was 'some sort of marriage' in as much as care for offspring became a joint task (184/5). Dunbar, who adopted a different (quasi Rousseauan) periodisation (see Chapter 2), thought this itself could not be taken for granted since the presence not only of paternal but also of maternal affection in the earliest ages may be doubted (*EHM*: 19). In Millar's version the attachments, through time, did solidify into marriage but he puts this down to expediency rather than the preference of a man for a particular woman. He infers from these circumstances that the 'manners' of the time 'must be extremely unfavourable to the rank and dignity of women' (*OR*: 192). Not being equipped physically for warfare, women have to perform 'all the inferior concerns of the household' and, since these are held in low esteem, so the 'women of a family are treated as the servants or slaves of the men' (*Ibid.*).

Robertson paints an identical picture of the Amerinds (Millar's sources range more widely). For Robertson the circumstance of women is one of 'mortifying inferiority'; the wife is 'no better than a beast of burthen destined to every office of labour and fatigue' so that her condition, and that of women generally, is 'humiliating and miserable' (*HAm*: 822). One mark of this humiliation was that women were bought and sold. Robertson cites Kames in support (*SHM*: I, 303f.) and Millar, too, had previously noted, that since women are little more slaves then 'it was natural' that they should be traded (*OR*: 195 cf. *HV*: I, 54). Hume had argued similarly (and luridly). In barbarous nations men exhibit their superiority by 'reducing their females to the most abject slavery; by confining them, by beating them, by selling them, by killing them' (*E–AS*: 133). Stuart is an exception to this consensus. He openly disputes Robertson, Kames and Millar by declaring that women were not in an abject state of servility before property (*VSE*: 11). He conjectures that in every period of society, not excluding that which precedes knowledge of 'extensive property', there is some tenderness and the male heart 'cannot be insensible to female attractions' (12).

Stuart also takes up what he believes to be a contrary position on the issue of polygamy. Kames had attributed polygamy to two sources – to savage manners and to voluptuousness in warm climates (*SHM*: I, 302). Regarding the former, polygamy is a corollary of women's low esteem and their availability for purchase. Stuart demurs. Polygamy, he declares, was unknown in an age of simple manners (*VSE*: 20). Kames' second cause had been propounded by Millar, who sees polygamy as properly belonging to voluptuous Eastern nations where the climate makes an easy life possible (and an opulent life feasible for a few) (*OR*: 225 cf. Ferguson *ECS*: 139, Hume *E–PD*: 183–4). Its practice in barbarian (European) nations was only introduced as a temporary expedient to replenish population (*OR*: 226n.), a view that was also shared by Dunbar (*EHM*: 50).

Millar and Stuart are here disputing the correct interpretation of Tacitus and Caesar. The former, especially, is Stuart's chief authority. This is not surprising given his basic project of tracing European institutions to the tribes of Germany. Stuart also draws on other sources, with the work of Lafitau and Charlevoix on the Amerinds (typically) prominent, and he cites all these to further his case for the higher status of women in early societies. As part of his evidence he notes their participation in public councils (*VSE*: 15). Millar accounts for this fact, which he explicitly regards as an exception to the general tenor of rude manners and is thus far from universal (*OR*: 199), by noting how before marriage was fully established mothers would have authority over children (*Ibid.*). (It is in this context that Millar cites the case of the Ladrone Islands – mentioned in Chapter 4 – where the wife is absolute mistress.) Female participation in public affairs is thus the offshoot of that authority (the likely source of the Amazon myth, he conjectures) (202). Ferguson drawing on the same sources remarks that women's familial role and matriarchal rule, is, rather, a mark of her subjection since it only shows that the warrior males cannot be bothered (*ECS*: 83). Dunbar explicitly acknowledges this argument and concedes some force to it but remarks nonetheless that this status is evidence of some improvement from an earlier state (*EHM*: 54).

For Millar, in spite of these matriarchal exceptions, the development of the pastoral stage produces, as an integral component of the 'very important alterations in the state and manners of the people' (*OR*: 203), a change in the treatment and status of women. Greater leisure, the emergence of property and the distinction of ranks interrupt the communication between the sexes (205 cf. *HV*: I, 120). Once again the effect of the third stage is to consolidate. Agriculture multiplies conveniences and also extends the causes of dissension and jealousy. A significant consequence of these developments is that the virtue of chastity comes to be recognised. Smith had remarked that where manners are rude and uncultivated there is no such thing as jealousy (*LJ*: 439) and for Millar in the first age the 'laws of chastity' are violated without any stain on a woman's character (*OR*: 187). But in these later stages, when 'love becomes a passion' rather than a 'sensual appetite', 'it is natural to think that those affections which are not dissipated by variety of enjoyment will be the purest and strongest' (204). Millar does not spell out the connection but Smith and Kames are more forthcoming. For Smith jealousy can only occur where there is 'that delicacy which attends the sentiments of love' (*LJ*: 439) and for Kames it is linked with the growth of esteem since a husband can only become jealous when 'by ripening sensibility' he feels 'pleasure in his wife's attachment to him' (*SHM*: I, 328). Kames is particularly fond of the organic imagery of 'ripening' and elsewhere he says to similar effect that 'law ripens gradually with the human faculties and by ripeness of discernment and delicacy of sentiment many duties formerly neglected are found to be binding in conscience' (*Principles of Equity*: I, 8 cf. *SHM*: II, 523; also Dunbar *EHM*: 24). In the light of the argument in section B it is possible to see implicit in this general change from 'sensual appetite' to 'love', or from 'rudeness' to 'delicacy', a further manifestation of the move from the prevalence of the immediately concrete to increasingly abstract and refined conceptions.

Despite such advances in esteem the relationships are not reciprocal. The 'double-standard' obtains: adultery is a worse crime in the wife than in the husband (Kames *SHM*: II, 283 cf. Beattie *Elements of Moral Science*: II, 136). Not only does the female naturally (which for both Kames and Beattie is an openly Providential arrangement) enjoy 'superior modesty' but she is liable to bring a 'spurious issue into the family' through 'betraying the husband to maintain and educate children who are not his own' (Kames *SHM*: II, 324). Smith refers to this latter argument (as does Millar (*OR*: 188)) but he regards the 'alienation' of preference rather than spuriousness as the crux (*LJ*: 438/9).

Smith does not deny the utility of the virtue of chastity in determining lawful succession and this is the focus of Hume's more formal account of the source of this virtue. The a priori argument that Hume explicitly puts forward is that men labour to maintain their children *because* they are persuaded that they are 'really their own'. In order to make that persuasion effective it is 'necessary' to give them 'some security in this particular' (*THN*: 571). In practice men 'naturally disapprove' of women's infidelity because they have an interest in their fidelity. This interest is itself most effectively furthered by restraining women through shame – through 'manners' not through a legal endorsement of a husband's right to rule (cf. Baier 1988: 774, 1989: 38 [28]). Women are led by education (it 'takes possession of the ductile minds of the fair sex') to adopt chastity as a virtue (572). For Hume, unlike for Kames (cf. *PMNR*: 145), chastity is thus an artificial not a natural virtue. Like the other artificial virtues, such as justice, it acts to restrain 'original inclinations' by means of rules or conventions. This restraint is in the 'interest of society'. However, while a woman benefits from having a husband to help her look after offspring, and men benefit from the greater (though not absolute) certainty that they are caring for their biological progeny, it is clear that this convention does not effect both sexes equally. Though it is, he declares, 'contrary to the interests of civil society' that men be completely free to indulge their 'appetites in venereal enjoyment' yet the obligation remains weaker in them than in women (cf. *EPM*: 207). This is Hume's version of the 'double-standard',[29] a state of affairs that is borne out 'by the practice and sentiments of all nations and ages' (*THN*: 573).

What Hume, of course, takes for granted under this universalism is that women are tempted strongly to infidelity (a particular instance, though heightened in the case of women, of the human tendency to prefer the immediate to the remote). Millar makes the same assumption when he observes, in passing, that rules of decency and decorum are 'peculiarly indispensable' to women, since of them 'for obvious reasons the greatest delicacy and propriety is required' (*OR*: 190 cf. Kames *SHM*: I, 289). Behind this lies a long tradition of male disparagement. Women are in Tertullian's infamous phrase 'the devil's gateway'. They are, at one and the same time, weak and therefore unable to resist their passions (and hence they are closer to animals/nature than are males) yet strong because they can seduce men away from stern duty (Eve persuaded Adam to eat the apple). The link between women and luxury was particularly strong as we shall see shortly (and as we shall consider more fully in Chapter 6).

Historically the laws of chastity reached their high point in the European Middle Ages (the third stage) when they were bound up with the notions of knightly gallantry, the code of chivalry and the convention of romantic love (Millar *OR*: 210–14 cf. Robertson *VPE*: 329). Women were effectively put on a pedestal and they learned, in return, to 'affect a delicacy and even a weakness' (Stuart *VSE*: 33). Yet with further developments (and the gradual shift to the fourth stage) women come, first, to be valued for their 'useful or agreeable talents' and wives come to enjoy the station of friend and companion rather than slave or idol (Millar *OR*: 219). Later, women come to be courted less for their practical skills than for their 'agreeable qualities' and as society becomes polished, they are led to 'distinguish themselves by polite accomplishments and to excite those peculiar sentiments and passions of which they are the natural objects' (224). Hume, too, remarks that in a refined age the sexes meet in an easy sociable manner (*E–RA*: 271); indeed, there can be no 'better school for manners than the company of virtuous women' (*E–AS*: 134). Elsewhere he goes further. He claims that women themselves have been able through 'insinuations' and 'charms' to break an original male tyranny based on bodily force and to share 'with the other sex in all the rights and privileges of society' (*EPM*: 191).

Though Hume's argument has a temporal aspect it is as part of a general history of civilisation and he does not provide a systematic account in the manner of the 'four stages' of this change (see also *E–PD*). While Millar in his account is in no doubt that the fourth stage sees a great improvement in the status of women he nonetheless expresses some traditional alarms (cf. Ignatieff: 1983). He notes how opulence and luxury produce 'licentious and dissolute manners' (*OR*: 225 cf. Beattie *Dissertations Moral, Critical and Literary*: 579). These tend to diminish the rank and dignity of women since the appropriate delicacy of sentiment is missing. In a perverse way the free intercourse of the first age is reprised, though now with deleterious consequences on good order. These consequences are expounded at great length by Kames, who draws on standard accounts of Roman decadence (*SHM*: I, 330). Millar, too, does not forbear from citing the satires of Horace and Juvenal and he believes that modern Europe (especially France and Italy) are exhibiting the same traits. Kames is typically forthright – states enriched by conquest and commerce decline into luxury and 'chastity becomes a mere name' (338). Even Hume observes that in polite ages libertine love is more frequent (*E–RA*: 272). That the age of commerce is at once an advance and yet one that has faults will be a major theme of the next chapter.

F: Conclusion

Social history as practised by the Scots is an account of the development of social institutions. Institutions are not fixed across time but by adopting development as their major organising principle the Scots are removing the 'wonder' that this variety inspires in the vulgar. The root of this development lies in human nature. The formal principle of progressiveness was given a definite shape in the specific guise of the natural history of human faculties – 'one of the most remarkable differences between man and other animals is that wonderful capacity for the improvement of his faculties with which he is endowed' (Millar OR: 218).

Following a broadly Lockean scheme, individuals and societies develop from a world of concrete immediacy to one of abstract relations. It is from that starting-point that the human concern with subsistence acquires its salience. This concern is, as Robertson said and as Millar similarly stated on several occasions, the first (that is, 'immediate') object of attention. This is not the same as being the 'sole object'. As development proceeds so the range and number of objects increases (without ever eradicating the 'first') to incorporate not only fine arts, science and philosophy but also an enhanced quality to daily life in the shape of humane relationships and a better standard of food, shelter and clothing.

Against this backcloth the 'four stages' acted as a heuristic. It was a tool to identify certain coherences in social institutions. As such it did not explain these institutions. Nowhere do the Scots say that the mode of subsistence *causes* the form that social insitutions take. Rather it was a device that highlighted the central role that property played since it was how property was organised that gave the coherence. Property played that role because its 'organisation' has to entail how ownership is identified and maintained and that in turn is inseparable from how law and power both formally (government) and informally (manners) function.

What the Scots have done here – and why many commentators have been impressed (see Chapter 8) – is not only to understand society as an interlocking whole but also to appreciate that change too occurs in an integrated manner. While they do, of course, have predecessors, such as Harrington, in seeing property as pivotal, it is in their conception of it as a social rather than a political institution that helps mark out the Scots as *social* theorists.

The distinctive character of their theory is also abetted by another aspect of their Lockeanism. It underwrites their 'determinism' and it does this in two ways. First, as Locke's famous image of the blank sheet suggests, the empiricist doctrine lent itself as a matter of course to deterministic imagery and language – we simply receive sensory input and since there are no innate ideas then we are each of us a product of our environment.[30] The general principle is enunciated by Millar when he remarks that 'the dispositions and behaviour of man are liable to be influenced by the circumstances in which he is placed, and by his peculiar education and habits of life is a proposition which few persons will be inclined to controvert' (HV: IV, 174/HVL: 383). The impact of 'education and habits', of the process of socialisation, was central to moral causation. These causes, we recall from Chapter 4, are 'all circumstances which are fitted to work on the mind as motives or reasons, and which render a peculiar set of manners habitual to us' (Hume E–NC: 198 cf. p. 82 above). This 'rendering' we called 'soft determinism'.

It was this 'determinism' the child/species analogy exploited and here is the second contribution of their Lockeanism. While there may be no innate *ideas* there were connatural 'principles' and 'powers' and these manifested themselves in a determinate or structured manner. Hence it is, to cite Millar, 'the similarity of his wants, as well as of the faculties by which those wants are supplied, has every where produced a remarkable uniformity in the several steps of his progression' (*OR*: 176). In 'the infancy of society', that is, at the time of the hunter-gatherers, humans '*must* have their attention directed to a small number of objects' (*Ibid.*; my emphasis) or, as Robertson puts it, the range of the savage's understanding '*must* of course be very confined' and employed 'merely on what is sensible' (*HAm*: 819; my emphasis). Yet when the 'seeds of improvement' are 'brought to maturity' then 'those wonderful powers and faculties' will 'have led to the noblest discoveries in art or science and to the most exalted refinement of taste and manners' (Millar *OR*: 198). (Recall also Kames' fondness for the idea of 'ripening'.)

It is this commitment to a determinate course of improvement that sustains the very idea of a 'natural history' or 'natural progress' from (in Millar's version) 'ignorance to knowledge and from rude to civilized manners' (*OR*: 176). The 'natural' here is that which is produced by natural causes, rather than that which is in any particular instance most agreeable to fact (cf. Dugald Stewart (*EPS*: 293-6) and Chapter 3). All institutions are susceptible to a natural history – religion, taste and science as Emerson pointed out (1984: 82). And to these three is, of course, to be added the subject-matter of the four stages – property, law, government, ranks and manners. Because the four-stages theory is a natural history there is no pretence that this progression must happen uniformly – as we saw in Chapter 4, climatic conditions have an impact and Smith notes how some North American nations cultivate the ground 'tho' they have no notion of keeping flocks' (*LJ*: 459). Neither is there a pretence that the stages are discrete modes of social organisation; Ferguson, for example, says explicitly that the savages of America mix hunting with 'some species of rude agriculture' (*ECS*: 82). Nor, again, is there a pretence that the progressiveness through the stages is irreversible; most obviously the city-states of Greece and the republic of Rome were 'civilised' but were succeeded by barbaric pastoral peoples.

This last point has particular bearing on commerce. Although Athens was a civilised commercial city and barter took place in the earliest ages, nonetheless commerce did constitute a separate stage. Why that should be so and what are its distinctive characteristics will be questions answered in Chapter 6.

Notes

1. '*Rev. Dr. Folliott*: Pray, Mr. MacQuedy, how is it that all gentlemen of your nation begin everything they write with the "infancy of society"' *Crotchet Castle*. This is quoted by Forbes (1954) and by Höpfl (1978).
2. Millar's list is 'Hunters and Fishers or mere Savages'; 'Shepherds'; 'Husbandmen'; and 'Commercial People'. Quoted in Meek (1976: 166). This quotation is from the

1787 version but it is repeated identically in the two other surviving versions (1789, 1790). All three are in Glasgow University Library.

3. As Stein (1988) has pointed out explicit reference to *four* stages is relatively rare and although he argues (405) that it was Kames who made the 'first unequivocal declaration' in *HLT* an explicit enunciation of four stages is only found in the much later *SHM*: (II, 92). One explanation for the frequent absence of an overtly four-fold depiction is that commerce is less obviously a primary mode, i.e. one can only exchange what has been previously caught, reared or grown (cf. Hont 1987: 254). See also Chapter 6.

4. Just before this passage Robertson had written, 'The ideas which seem to be natural to man in his savage state, as they result necessarily from his circumstances and condition in that period of his progress, affect the two capital relations in domestic life' (*HAm*: 823). Note that it is the 'ideas' that do the 'affecting'.

5. For the significance of *occupatio* in Grotius see Buckle (1991: 13–15). For a failure to appreciate this usage and thus misapprehend Smith's argument, see Werhane (1991: 69).

6. With the exception of Hutcheson (see *SIMP*: 150f.) and Ogilvie (see his *Essay on Property in Land*), who remain closer to a Lockean version of Natural Law theory, 'labour' is not endowed with any special weight in the Scots' theories and indeed explicitly criticised as too restrictive (see Hume *THN*: 505n.) and even Hutcheson is critical of the 'physical' origin of property (i.e. Locke's notion of 'mixing' (*Second Treatise*: §27)) (*PWD*: 170/*SIMP*: 152), while Ogilvie regards occupancy as constituting equally a valid title as labour (*Essay*: §§1, 7). Smith does in the context of restrictions on labour hold that everyman has property in his own labour (*WN*: 138)).

7. Smith's version rested the 'right' on the 'rational expectation' of the possessor/occupier that he would continue in possession, a sentiment with which the 'impartial spectator' (see Chapter 7) would concur (*LJ*: 17). Here Smith is explaining how possession can generate a sense of 'right'. But, as we have noted, this quite explicitly does not commit him to holding that originally this 'right' was thought separable from actual possession or that, at that time, there was juridical conception of a 'right'. This spectator theory resting on expectation was followed by Millar in his lectures.

8. *The Law of Nature and Nations*: III–5–3. The context is a critique of Hobbes' notion of 'natural right'.

9. One of Robertson's chief references here is LaCondamine (he who investigated the accuracy of Newton's predictions – see Chapter 1), who, in his report, on the South American Indians (1745) commented on the absence of abstract terms in their languages. LaCondamine was also cited on precisely this point by Condillac in his directly Lockean-inspired treatise on human knowledge (see *Essai sur l'origine des connaissances humaines* [1746] (1947) Pt. 2, Sect. 1, Ch. 10).

10. In his lectures Millar says there are two routes of improvement which correspond to man as carnivorous – hence herding, and as 'granivorous' – hence farming. However since the former is easier then mankind has 'generally arrived at the state of Shepherd before that of Agriculture'. Lectures 1789 (no. 4).

11. Arguably what makes this 'easier' is the association of an individual/family with a particular piece of contiguous land, given that contiguity is one of the natural principles of association (see Hume *THN*: 11).

12. See for example Smith (*LJ*: 467), Dalrymple (*Feudal Property*: 185f.) and Kames (*HLT*: 135ff., *ELS*: 334, *SHM*: II, 523–33). As befits a practising judge, Kames took more overtly practical steps on this issue – see, for example, his letter and submission to the Lord Chancellor reprinted in Lehmann (1971: 327–32). See further Lieberman (1989: 156–8), Horne (1990: 106–8).

13. In *IMP*: Introd. §9, Ferguson lists as 'the arts which men practise for subsistence' the standard first three stages and later in that same section refers to the progress of arts making commerce 'expedient or even necessary'. In the light of this discussion Chitnis

thus errs when he states that Ferguson did not accept the four-stages theory (1976: 102). Since *IMP* are Ferguson's Edinburgh lectures and since, too, the 'four-stages' theory was expounded by both Smith and Millar in their lectures, it does suggest that the theory was thought to possess some expository utility.

14. Cf. *OR*: 291, 'This fluctuation of property, so observable in all commercial countries, and which no prohibitions are capable of preventing, must necessarily weaken the authority of those who are placed in the higher ranks of life. Persons who have lately attained to riches, have no opportunity of establishing that train of dependence which is maintained by those who have remained for ages at the head of a great estate. The hereditary influence is thus, in a great measure, destroyed; and the consideration derived from wealth is often limited to what the possessor can acquire during his own life.'

15. The best-known exponent of this theory is Meek, who in 1954 published an essay entitled 'The Scottish contribution to Marxist sociology' (in that work he acknowledged Pascal's 1938 essay as 'pioneering'). Though Meek in subsequent writings did qualify his initial formulations, he nevertheless explicitly said, in a 1977 essay, about his earlier account that he didn't think he was 'all that wrong in describing this theoretical system [i.e. the four stages] as *a* if not *the* materialist conception of history' (1977: 19, quoting 1954: 90; emphases in the original). On Meek's presentation the 'essential idea' contained in the four-stages theory was that societies undergo development through successive stages which are based on different modes of subsistence and which were recognised to be 'if only vaguely in some sense determining elements in the total situation' (1976: 4 cf. Skinner 1965, 1967, 1975, but see next note).

16. Meek's views were criticised by Höpfl, who argued that the conjectural history written by the Scots gave no particular motive or interest automatic priority and Meek's interpretation that they thought that social change was explicable by 'economic' forces so that political and other ideational agencies were 'merely epiphenomenal was quite alien to the Scots' (1978: 33–5). Similarly Haakonssen explicitly denied that Smith's theory of motivation was materialistic and drew attention to the way Smith admitted non-economic factors, such as geography and religion as well as pure chance, into his account of social change (1981: 185). Skinner, seemingly influenced by Haakonssen, shifted the balance of his earlier argument to claim of Smith that he was neither a determinist nor a materialist (1982: 104). A thorough-going assault on the Scots' supposed materialism was launched by Roger Emerson, who argued that the Scots were committed to 'complex usually idealistic theories of social change' (1984: 82; see also Winch 1978, 1983). Salter (1992) argues *pace* Haakonssen that Smith is a materialist but not in the manner of Meek or Skinner. See Chapter 8 for a discussion of these various 'readings'.

17. Cf. Forbes (1975a: 176–7) for a discussion of Hume's various uses of the term as well as of its flexibility in contemporary usage. See also Giarrizzo (1962: Ch. 2), Miller (1980), Chisick (1989). More generally on eighteenth-century usage see Corfield (1987).

18. This argument seems to run counter to Hume's more formal account in the *Treatise*. In that work Hume had argued that government arose as a necessary means of constraining interested humans to adhere inflexibly to the rule of justice. The governors are those 'having no interest, or but a remote one, in any act of injustice'; they have rather an 'immediate interest in every execution of justice'. These governors are, accordingly, those who are 'satisfied with their present condition' (537). This *could* be read to mean that the Tartar chiefs as governors in the execution of 'justice' are in effect upholding their own material interests (as Smith implies). Or it *could* be read as a generalisation of the situation where a system of justice in the guise of the rule of law obtains, that is in an age of commerce, in which case the difference between himself and Smith is slight (see Chapter 6). In his late essay *Origin of Government* Hume says

that magistrates are 'often led astray by private passions', although he does think that ordinarily that they have a 'visible interest in the impartial administration of justice' (*E–OG*: 39).

19. Other references to 'natural rights' in Millar occur at *HV*: I, 375; III, 327. Haakonssen seizes upon this usage as constituting the main obstacle to the 'materialist' interpretation (1985: 65).

20. Cf. Ferguson 'the rights of men are modified by their condition' (*ECS*: 68) and Kames, who talks of the feudal system as a 'violent encroachment on the natural rights of man' and also declares that 'the right of the individual yields here [security of possession] to public utility, as every such right ought to do' (*ELS*: 334, 233).

21. Burke was a rector of Glasgow University when Millar was a professor. Millar indeed was charged with writing to Burke to encourage him to accept a second term – see Lehmann (1960: 399). Pocock judges Millar and Burke's views of British constitutional history to be 'not at bottom very far apart' (1985: 299). However, while, according to his son-in-law, Millar (in Burkean fashion) treated with contempt notions of 'metaphysical' rights – including the 'imprescriptible and indefeasible right in the people to conduct the affairs of government' – he was in favour of Parliamentary reform and a member of the Friends of the People (Craig 1990: cxiv–cxv). This critique contrasts with the views, from an earlier generation, of Turnbull to whom 'liberty' is imprescriptible, it is 'a right in the nature of things unalienable' (Commentary on Heineccius' *System of Universal Law*: I, 245).

22. Hutcheson given his closeness to Locke was a firm advocate of the right of resistance – Caroline Robbins calls it his most important political principle (1959: 188) and she has highlighted (1954) the prescience of his remark concerning 'when it is the colonies might become independent' (*System of Moral Philosophy* (1755): 308/*PWD*: 196). More generally, Natural Law theory played a role in underwriting a limited right of resistance in early eighteenth-century Britain – see Phillipson (1993).

23. As an aside in his *Gentleman Farmer* he remarked that though the present rebellion will soon be concluded, the era of the 'total separation' of the Americans 'cannot be at a great distance' (368).

24. Hume's observation in October 1775 that 'I am an American in my Principles' is perhaps best interpreted in the light of what else he says in that same sentence, namely, that is best to let the Americans govern – or misgovern – themselves (*Letts*: II, 303). Cf. Pocock (1985: 125–41) for a nuanced account of Hume's position.

25. *De Primordiis Civitatum oratio. In qua agitur de Bello Civili inter M. Britanniam et Colonias nunc flagranti* (1779). As its full title indicates, this pamphlet also contains a more general social philosophy, where a number of the themes common in the Scottish Enlightenment are to be found; e.g. earliest authority is in the hands of strong individuals (6), a critique of the social contract (13) and an acknowledgement of the power of custom (14). For an account of Dunbar's extra-literary opposition see Berry 1974b.

26. Alexander's book was deliberately written for 'the amusement and instruction of the Fair Sex' and is a compilation of what he calls 'anecdotes' that he has industriously pulled together. Lacking any sustaining theoretical organisation it is essentially a repository of received views, coupled with a fervent conviction that women's lot has been the effect of a faulty education. While some of his material inevitably echoes that of his compatriots, he pays no heed to their social theory and they none to him.

27. Rendall has pieced together what evidence there is of a stadial account in Smith (1987: 646–8).

28. Baier's nuanced account of Hume's view of women includes attributing to him 'radical feminist ideals' (1989: 45). See also her earlier essay (1979).

29. A good analysis of Hume's defence of the double-standard is given by Battersby (1981). She criticises Baier but is also critical of other treatments that regard Hume's sexism as a necessary implication of his philosophy (see Lacoste 1976: 425, who says she agrees

with Burns (1976) that the 'Humean female' is an expression of the 'male chauvinist position').

30. This premise did, of course, in the hands of Helvetius, and later in the work of Godwin and Owen, facilitate a strongly secular perfectibilism. But as we saw in Chapter 2 with their attention to the constraining power of habit and relative weakness of reason, the Scots (no more than Locke himself, who remained firmly wedded to a theological framework) did not follow that route. The occasional perfectibilist echo can be heard among the Scots e.g. Fordyce *Dialogues concerning Education* [1753] I, p. 151, Turnbull *Observations upon Liberal Education* p. 91 and Wallace *Prospects* p. 23.

6

Commercial Society

The fourth of the four stages is the Age of Commerce. Since the stages are progressive then this stage marks an advance. Its superiority is conveyed by its synonyms – it is 'civilised' or 'cultivated' or 'polished'. But we need also to recall some of the straws blowing in the wind of the earlier chapters. The Scots were not uncritical of this fourth stage, of their own society. While it is too strong to say that they were ambivalent, they nevertheless judge commercial society to be superior only 'on balance'; there is a downside. This chapter examines their overall assessment, both their positive and negative appraisals. This will prove to be a lengthy and involved task. An important reason for this is that on this issue the Scots appear more divided *and* that the divisions are not straightforward or clear-cut. The most appropriate image is that of points on a scale (differing shades of grey) rather than root and branch opposition (black or white). Even those, like Smith and Hume, who accentuate the positive do not eliminate the negative elements and conversely those, like Ferguson and Kames, who find much to debit do not withhold entries on the credit side of the ledger.

A: Prosperity

A student records Smith professing in his Glasgow lectures that 'opulence and freedom' were the 'two greatest blessings men can possess' (*LJ*: 185). This linkage is central to Smith's vindication of commercial society (cf. Berry 1989, 1992). I will discuss his view of 'freedom' in the next section; here I focus on 'opulence'.

i) The Division of Labour

For Smith one characteristic of a developed commercial society is the presence of a 'universal opulence which extends itself to the lowest ranks of the people' (*WN*: 22). A mark of this opulence is that these ranks are supplied 'abundantly' with what they have 'occasion for'. The source of this abundance is the division of labour. Smith conjectures that this practice is a consequence of a 'propensity' in human nature to 'truck, barter and exchange' (25). Since this is a 'propensity', an inclination or disposition, then this consequence (which results in 'so many advantages') is neither the fruit of deliberation nor an intended outcome. Furthermore, as a propensity it cannot be the prerogative of the fourth stage alone; the division of labour in a rudimentary form exists in the first stage. As we noted in Chapter 5 (p. 97), Smith cites the case of an individual skilled in bow-making who discovers that by exchanging his bows for the meat from deer slain by more adept hunters he can obtain more venison than from trying to kill his own beast (27). The reason why this is rudimentary is that the 'market' is limited. Why that in turn should be true of the earliest stages and untrue of the fourth stage hinges on the state of 'property and manners' and security generated by the rule of law (see section B below).

Smith illustrates how an extensive division of labour produces opulence with the famous example of a 'very trifling manufacture' – pin-making (14). Though, as he openly admits, this example has very often been used (it appears in the *Encyclopédie* in 1755), it was swiftly taken up by his compatriots.[1] Smith calculates that through the division of labour ten individuals could make 48,000 pins a day – equivalent to 4800 each – whereas if each performed all the tasks required 'not twenty each' would have been manufactured. He gives three reasons for this: increased dexterity that comes from reducing each individual's task to 'one simple operation'; time-saving that stems from not having to transfer from one task to the next and inventing better ways of executing the task prompted by the concentration on one task (17–20). We will return to these features – just as Smith does – when we consider (Cv) other less advantageous consequences of this specialisation.

A society where tasks like pin-making are minutely divided must necessarily be complex. (Recall here from Chapter 3 the shape assumed by the Scots' conjectural history; the progress from simple to complex.) The members of a commercial society are deeply interdependent. Smith illustrates this with the example of a coarse woollen coat. Even this humble product, he remarks, requires many contributing hands. After listing nine trades he firstly tacks on the phrase 'with many others' then goes on to note all those employed in transporting the materials, then those in manufacturing the transport, which is not to include those involved in making the tools used to make the coat (and so on), to the inevitable conclusion that 'many thousands' are implicated in this relatively simple garment (22–3). The fact of interdependence means that each individual 'stands at all times in need of the co-operation and assistance of great multitudes' (26). So extensive does this become that 'everyman thus lives by exchanging or becomes in some measure a merchant'. And when this has happened then this is 'properly a commercial society' (37). We will meet this 'proper' characterisation again.

ii) The Misery of Poverty

By being 'blessed' by opulence the members of a commercial society are able to enjoy a far better standard of living than those in earlier ages. In material terms their basic needs of food, shelter and raiment are better and more adequately met. For example, in passing, Smith notes how the Chinese regard the 'putrid and stinking' garbage discarded by European ships as wholesome food (90). Elsewhere he observes how the accommodation of a European peasant exceeds that of many an African king (24). But Smith is not alone. If we take up the third of those three basic needs, we can find Kames, a critic of many aspects of commerce, still commenting how, before the Europeans arrived, the Canadians were thinly clothed in a bitterly cold climate (*SHM*: I, 363).

However, more than basic material satisfactions are at stake. Where there is abundance then a greater range and 'quality' of goods are available. What earlier ages thought of as luxuries are now seen as necessities or 'but decent for a tradesman's wife' (Kames, *SHM*: I, 261 cf. Millar *HV*: IV, 205; Smith *WN*: 870). Similarly there has been a shift in the relative importance of occupations. Hunting and fishing, the most important activities in the first stage, have become by the fourth 'agreeable amusements' (Smith *WN*: 117). This enhanced 'quality of life' extends beyond 'goods' or things to relationships. In the Introduction to the *Wealth of Nations* Smith says that the inhabitants of 'savage nations of hunters and fishers' are 'miserably poor' so that, as a consequence, 'they are frequently reduced or, at least, think themselves reduced, to the necessity sometimes of directly destroying and sometimes abandoning their infants, their old people and those afflicted with lingering diseases, to perish with hunger or to be devoured by wild beasts' (*WN*: 10). This is a powerful and important argument. Contrary to Stoic 'frugality' or Christian asceticism, that is contrary to two deeply influential doctrines, Smith is firmly repudiating any notion that poverty is ennobling or redemptive. What Hobbes claimed for the 'natural condition of mankind' is, in fact, true of the savage, whose life tends to be nasty, brutish and short, and anything that improves upon that is unequivocally to the good. And since the abundance that commerce brings is precisely such an improvement then Smith's repudiation of the nobility of poverty is key factor in his vindication of commercial society.

This argument can be generalised. It is, for example, an element in the treatment of women that we discussed in Chapter 5. Their status improves along with 'the advance of opulence' (Millar *OR*: 203), though, as we also noted, there was some renewed cause for concern as commerce advanced (a 'concern' that is more generally symptomatic of the negative elements as we will see). As Millar spells out, what applies to women also applies to another vulnerable group – children. Like Smith, Millar noted the link between the 'misery' of the savage and the practice of abandoning children to 'perish by hunger or to be devoured by wild beasts' (230 cf. 236). It is very likely that Millar is following Smith's account in the *Moral Sentiments* where the 'extreme indigence' of the savage results in abandoning children 'to wild beasts' (*TMS*: 210 cf. *LJ*: 172) (see Chapter 4 p. 76). By contrast in 'those European nations which have made the greatest improvements in commerce and manufactures' children are subjected to the authority of their father only to the extent that 'seems necessary for their advantage' (Millar *OR*: 243).

B: Liberty, Justice and the Rule of Law

When Smith compared the European peasant's accommodation to that of the African king, he included in his description of the latter that he was the 'absolute master of the lives and liberties of ten thousand naked savages' (*WN*: 24). One of the major positive hallmarks of a commercial society is that not only are its members materially prosperous but they also enjoy a liberty denied to the subjects of that African monarch. There is a crucial if complex inter-relation between a commercial society and the operation of the rule of law, the primacy of 'strict' justice and liberty. Not unexpectedly there is a historical dimension to this linkage that several Scots either explore or accept.

i) The Emergence of Commerce

Though he acknowledges that he is following in Hume's footsteps, the most detailed account of the emergence of commerce is provided by Smith in Book III in the *Wealth of Nations*. In the second of the four stages the leaders are those with the greatest herds, and similarly in the third agricultural stage power lies with the landlords, or, as Smith calls them, the 'great proprietors'. These individuals use their surplus in the same way as a Tartar chief (cf. *WN*: 712) had done, namely, to maintain a multitude of retainers and dependants, and all they can offer in return for their keep is obedience (413).

> These proprietors necessarily became the judges in peace, and the leaders in war of all who dwelt upon their estates. They could maintain order and execute law within their respective desmesnes, because each of them could there turn the whole force of all the inhabitants against the injustice of any one. No other person had sufficient authority to do this. (415)

Since the king was only another proprietor, the administration of justice lay in the (local) hands of those with the means to execute it. At this point Smith observes that it is mistake to see the origin of these 'territorial jurisdictions' in feudal law (417). The source of this mistake, we can say, is faulty social science, a misunderstanding of social causation. The cause of feudal power lies not in the deliberative and purposive decrees of law but in 'the state of property and manners' (cf. Cropsey 1957: 63). The former are subordinate to the latter. This priority is not a singular event causing wonder and surprise (cf. p. 60 above) since it is duplicated in the histories of the French and English monarchies and is exemplified by the case 'not thirty years ago' of Mr Cameron of Lochiel 'a gentleman of Lochaber in Scotland' (416). It is therefore a regularity amenable to scientific explanation; as Smith says explicitly 'such effects must always flow from such causes' (*Ibid.*).

To explain the collapse of feudal power – both secular and ecclesiastical (803) – an appropriate social cause has to be found. Smith finds it in 'the silent and insensible operation of foreign commerce'. In a celebrated passage he outlines its effects:

> For a pair of diamond buckles perhaps, or for something as frivolous and useless, they [the great proprietors] exchanged the maintenance, or what is the same thing, the price of the maintenance of a thousand men for a year, and with it the whole weight and authority which it could give them. The buckles, however, were to be all their own and no other human creature was to have any share of them; whereas in the more antient method of expence they must have shared with at least a thousand people ... and thus for the gratification of the most childish, the meanest and the most sordid of all vanities, they gradually bartered their whole power and authority. (418–19)

As the 'effects' of a 'cause' there is an implicit 'regularity' here. Smith provides a counterfactual – no cause therefore no effects – when he observes that the sway of the Tartar chief stems from his using his surplus to maintain a thousand men *because* 'the rude state of his society does not afford him any manufactured produce, any trinkets and baubles of any kind for which he can exchange that part of his rude produce which is over and above his own consumption' (712). However, thanks to foreign commerce, the availability of these baubles (or 'domestic luxury' (*LJ*: 227 cf. 416, 420)) in the feudal era results ultimately in the members of a commercial society being free of the thrall of personal dependency:

> In the present state of Europe a man of ten thousand a year can spend his whole revenue, and he generally does so, without directly maintaining twenty people, or being able to command more than ten footmen not worth the commanding. Indirectly, perhaps, he maintains as great or even a greater number of people than he could have done by the antient method of expence ... He generally contributes, however, but a very small proportion to that of each, to very few perhaps a tenth, to many not a thousandth part of their whole annual mainten-ance. Though he contributes therefore to the maintenance of them all, they are all more or less independent of him, because generally they can all be maintained without him. (*WN*: 419–20)

Once the tenants had attained their independence then – and this is crucial – the proprietors 'were no longer capable of interrupting the regular execution of justice'. This process of social change, which Smith calls a 'revolution of the greatest importance to the publick happiness', is another example of 'unintended consequences'; it cannot be put down to any purposive individualistic explanation. Neither the proprietors nor the merchants had the 'least intention to serve the publick' and neither had 'knowledge or foresight of that great revolution' (422). The public happiness, the general good, was not brought about by deliberate human policy. This, for Smith, is a general truth about social life, and its signifi-cance will become apparent.

The essential ingredients of Smith's story were repeated elsewhere. For example, Hume in his essay 'Of the Refinement in the Arts' (1752) – one of those Smith would have had in mind as prefiguring his own account – depicts a 'rude unpolished' society divided between the 'proprietors of land' and their 'vassals or tenants'. The latter are 'necessarily dependent' on the former, who 'erect them-selves into petty tyrants'. This situation changes when the 'arts' are developed and where 'luxury nourishes commerce and industry', thus enabling the peasants to 'become rich and independent' (*E–RA*: 277 cf. *E–Mon*: 291). Hume is more specific in his *History*. It was in the reign of Henry VII when these events made a decisive impact. At that time the 'habits of luxury', which 'dissipated the immense fortunes of the ancient barons', developed and 'new methods of expense' were available that 'gave subsistence to mechanics and merchants who lived in an independent manner on the fruits of their own industry' (*HE*: II, 602 cf. III, 99). Hume explicitly refers to the 'manners of the age' as a 'general cause' of this change; a change that 'begat a new plan of liberty'. (The role of 'luxury' here, and in Smith, should be put on a back-burner since the whole issue will be re-heated later (see Ciii below)).

We can briefly note three other accounts. Millar closely follows both Hume and Smith. The progress in the 'arts' enabled more to live without 'the necessity of courting the favour of their superiors' so that they did not feel themselves 'greatly dependent upon them' (*HV*: III, 101/*HVL*: 375–6; cf. II, 81). This independence enabled them to 'indulge that love of liberty so congenial to the mind of man' (III, 102/376; cf. II, 434; IV, 168–9, *OR*: 299). Steuart sharply contrasts the 'necessary dependence of the lower classes' under feudal government with the 'modern liberty' of the same classes that derives from their 'independence' consequent upon the 'introduction of industry' (*PPE*: I, 208–9). This is an 'independence' from specific masters, not from the 'economic system', where, as we saw, 'interdependence' better describes the situation. Finally, Robertson draws attention to the formation of cities as the chief cause in bringing about the end of feudal 'oppression' (*VPE*: 318). (Smith's account appeared in a chapter entitled 'How the commerce of the Towns contributed to the Improvement of the Country.') By acquiring 'the right of community', these cities become 'so many little republics' which valued their liberty highly. This 'liberty' revived the 'spirit of industry' and 'wealth flowed' (319). This freedom and independence inspired others to attain it and the feudal superiors, with the expectation of the rewards they might reap, 'set their dependants at liberty' (320). The eventual outcome was the establishment of a 'more regular, equal and vigorous administration of justice' (321), or the rule of law.

ii) Markets and the Rule of Law

In Smith's account the feudal lords were judges as well as 'leaders in war'. The localised character of the power base meant there could be no consistency of decision between localities or any 'external' guarantee of consistency within a 'jurisdiction'. Lack of consistency meant lack of security (cf. *LRBL*: 170). As his reference to Cameron of Locheil suggests, Smith was well aware of this characteristic in his own country (cf. Hume *HE*: III, 182). One of the more important consequences of the failure of the '45 rebellion was the abolition of 'heritable jurisdictions' (see Chapter 1). These 'jurisdictions' had given to the clan chiefs the 'right' to exact taxes, hold courts and pass judgements (and raise troops). Stuart called them 'disgraceful' not only because they divorced offices of justice from talent and inclination but also because there was no 'uniformity' from the 'hand of the administrator' (*PLS*: 144). In short, there was 'the lack of any recognisable rule of law' (Kidd 1993: 155). The Highlands needed to be 'civilised' (see p. 76 above) and an important agent of civilisation was the introduction of commerce. What happens once commerce is introduced? The answer (to appropriate a phrase from Marx) is that it creates a world after its own image. Though 'fair', this image was not thought to be 'lovely' in all its aspects.

Commerce requires stability or consistency and security because it rests on a set of expectations and beliefs. Exchange presupposes specialisation. I will only specialise in making hats in the expectation that others are specialising in shoes, gloves, shirts and so on, so that when I take my hats to market I can, via the medium of money, exchange them for shoes and the rest. This means acting now in expectation of future return. Hume expresses this 'logic' when he writes:

> [The poorest artificer] expects that when he carries his goods to market and offers them at a reasonable price, he shall find purchasers and shall be able, by the money he acquires, to engage others to supply him with those commodities which are requisite for his subsistence. In proportion as men extend their dealings and render their intercourse with others more complicated, they always comprehend in their schemes of life a greater variety of voluntary actions which they expect, from the proper motives, to co-operate with their own. (*EHU*: 89)

What is required to underwrite this entire series is predictability or confidence (this passage from Hume comes from his chapter on 'Liberty and Necessity'). Where the actions of others are not predictable, then it is better (more rational) to be independent and self-sufficient and not rely on anyone – I make all my own clothes. But, of course, that option means forgoing the blessing of the opulence – poorer quality of clothing, even of hats, because I can no longer devote as much time to their manufacture – that comes from interdependence. That said, it is in the nature of expectations that they be dashed. The future is always uncertain. There are risks in specialising – my hats may not sell. This uncertainty at the centre of a system which seems to depend on predictability was thought by many to be its Achilles heel. As we will see later, many writers, drawing on classical precedent, thought a commercial society fundamentally unsound since it seemingly rests on nothing more substantial than a tissue of beliefs.

Expectation and belief are central. This is apparent in the credit system. We saw in Chapter 5 that property began as the concrete idea of possession and became increasingly abstract. Credit, a pivotal factor in commerce, is simultaneously, and for the same reason, abstract and belief-dependent. In commercial society money is, as Smith put it, 'the great wheel of circulation' (*WN*: 291). The substitution of paper for gold and silver increases the wealth of nations because it increases productivity and thus the number and quality of goods. Generically the paper constitutes a set of promissory notes (cf. *WN*: 292), which, contrary to any direct concrete 'experience', can be a substantial piece of property. Its substance obviously does not lie in the physical object and neither, like the shoe for Boaz (see p. 97 above), does it lie in the fact that it represents symbolically something tangible like land; rather it lies in the fact that *others believe* it to have value. It is evidence of that belief's substance that it supports action – possession of a promissory note can be used as surety to secure a loan.

This constitutes a contract. Smith argues that in the first periods of society, and even for some considerable time thereafter, contracts were not binding and the earliest forms required both parties to be present (*LJ*: 88, 91). The fragility of obligations among barbarous or uncivilised nations is also remarked upon by Kames (*HLT*: 66) and Dalrymple (*Feudal Property*: 106). Dalrymple also stresses that words were not then regarded as sufficient 'to dissolve the corporeal connection' between the proprietor and his property, so that instead elaborate ceremonies were needed to establish more concretely any transference (*Feudal Property*: 225 cf. Kames *HLT*: 107). However, when a 'very extensive degree of commerce' obtains then words expressed in writing are taken as sufficient indication of an intention to transfer (250). It is only in commercial society that contracts between strangers are central. Smith maintains that the obligatoriness of the contract arises 'entirely from the expectation and dependence which was excited in him to whom the contract was made' (*LJ*: 92). This now brings us back to stability.

What lies behind this obligation and what sustains the co-operativeness that these contracts embody is what Smith calls the 'regular administration of' (*WN*: 910), or Hume calls the 'inflexible principles of', justice (*THN*: 532). Hume and Smith on justice will concern us later, but we can here point out that a system of justice is an impersonal abstract order that operates through general rules and is the antithesis of the personal particular rule of the tribal chiefs or local landlords. At the heart of this system is the principle of the rule of law and, as Millar remarks, in 'opulent and polished nations' the 'impartial administration of justice is looked upon almost as a matter of course' (*HV*: I, 251). It is only through living under the rule of law that individuals will have 'confidence' in the 'faith of contracts' and 'payment of debts' (Smith, *WN*: 910). Only in 'commercial countries' is the 'authority of the law ... perfectly sufficient to protect the meanest man in the state' (Smith *TMS*: 223).

iii) Commerce and Constitutions

A 'properly' commercial society is one where every man is a merchant. For that society to function, the rule of law and the regular administration of justice are necessary. It is the job of government to do 'the necessary' and the execution of that task is the most important fact about it. This task, as we have just seen, is a reflex of a commercial, or 'civilised and thriving', society. The degree of civilisation now becomes the most informative criterion for distinguishing between types of government.

The force of this point is negative; it displaces from centre-stage talking about government in terms of constitutions. None of the Scots entirely jettison this talk and some continue to use this language more than others. But even those who still employ it, such as Ferguson, emphasise the 'sociological' element. This element had always been present – it was central to Aristotle's conception of oligarchy and democracy, for example. This also fits Montesquieu, though, given his great influence, it is his re-formulation of the standard language that established a powerful precedent for the Scots' own displacement.

The shift in emphasis that the Scots' approach represents can be succinctly grasped in Hume's comment that 'it may now be affirmed of civilized monarchies what was formally said in praise of republics alone, that they are a government of laws and men' (*E–CL*: 94 cf. *HE*: II, 15) (cf. Vlachos 1955: 169). By what criterion is that affirmation sustainable? Hume answers by declaring that in these monarchies 'property is there secure, industry encouraged, the arts flourish'. The monarch himself lives secure among his subjects (*E–CL*: 94), even though, as he admits in another essay, he 'alone is unrestrained in the exercise of his authority' (*E–AS*: 125). Yet because the regime here too is identified as a 'civilized monarchy' then all the other ministers or magistrates 'must submit to the general laws which govern the whole society'. The people depend on the sovereign alone for the security of their property, but since 'he is so far removed from them and is so much exempt from private jealousies' then 'this dependence is scarcely felt' (*Ibid.*). This entire line of argument is part of a polemic on Hume's part.[2] This is borne out by his next observation. Such a monarchy, he continues, is given 'in high political rant' the name 'tyranny' when, in fact, by its 'just and prudent administration' and provision of 'security to the people' it 'meets most of the ends of political society'.

Because the weight falls on the qualifier 'civilized' rather than the substantive 'monarchy', Hume can put forward two further arguments. First, he can accept as a historical argument that 'arts and sciences' can only be generated by free states or 'republics'. This argument relies on a series of causal connections: stability from a framework of law causes security, security is a causal precondition for the exercise of curiosity and that exercise is required if knowledge (whence arts and sciences) is to be obtained (*E–AS*: 118). But although republics are necessary at the beginning (they are the 'nursery' (119)), once the civilising process has begun it can be taken over and continued by monarchies (cf. Livingston 1990: 128–9). Second, a negative correlation between commerce, civilisation and the rule of law can be sustained. Absolute government, he claims, 'by its very nature' is 'hurtful to commerce' (*E–CL*: 92). This claim rests not on the threat of 'absolutism' to the security of property but, rather, on the social fact that commerce is not thought honourable in a society where 'birth, titles and place must be honoured above industry and riches' (93 cf. *E–AS*: 126). (The difference in 'virtues' here will be picked up later.) A consequence of this social disparagement of industry is that the 'poverty of the common people' is a 'natural if not infallible effect of absolute monarchy' (*E–Com*: 265).

The more typical argument was that liberty was precarious when it rested on what Steuart called 'the ambulatory will of any man or set of men', where the laws were liable to be changed 'through favour or prejudice to particular persons or particular classes' (*PPE*: I, 206). In contrast, where people are 'governed by general laws', which are 'established so as not to be changed but in regular and uniform way', there they are 'free' (*Ibid.*). Steuart also proceeds to make explicit what lurked in the principle if not in the language of Hume's argument.[3] To Steuart it is in line with his definition that a 'people may be found to enjoy freedom under the most despotic forms of government' (207). That is to say, Steuart distinguishes liberty under general laws (the rule of law) from liberty as a 'political right'. This distinction is the hallmark of 'modern liberty'.

iv) Modern Liberty

Since in a commercial society its members are not tied into relationships of dependence then they are, for example, able to change occupations as often as they please (Smith *WN*: 23). Smith labels as 'violent' the practice of forcing a son to follow his father's trade (80; he cites the 'police' of Indostan and ancient Egypt). He is explicit that it is the presence of a choice of occupation, along with the ablility to have one's children inherit and to dispose of one's property by testament, that makes individuals 'free in our present sense of the word Freedom' (and its absence is a principal attribute of 'villanage and slavery') (400).

What this modern liberty of choice taps are the deep wells of human motivation. Humans, declares Smith, have a natural desire to better their condition. For the 'greater part' this desire takes the concrete form of an 'augmentation of fortune' (341). In order to achieve this, individuals should enjoy the private liberty to decide for themselves how to deploy their resources (454). This is what Smith calls the 'obvious and simple system of natural liberty' where everyman is 'left perfectly free to pursue his own interest his own way' (687). From this perspective, sumptuary laws which aim to regulate consumption are the 'highest impertinence' and show up the presumptuousness of 'kings and ministers' as they attempt 'to watch over the economy of private people' (346 cf. 630).

According to Smith's system of natural liberty, government has only three tasks; protection from external foes; maintenance of public works, including importantly education (see Cv); and 'an exact administration of justice' (687). Provided individuals do not violate the laws of justice then they are to be left alone to pursue their own interests. On this understanding, which, as we have seen, is essentially shared by Hume and Steuart[4] and to which Millar also subscribes (cf. e.g. *HV*: IV, 109–11), modern liberty consists in living under equitable laws. Indeed, Hume, more than once, calls this 'true liberty' (*HE*: I, 115; I, 175, see above p. 104). What is important here is that this liberty is enjoyed by all. This inclusiveness demarcates it sharply from 'ancient liberty'. Ancient liberty was exclusive. It was enjoyed by those who had leisure and that was made possible, as Hume (*E–Com*: 257; *E–PAN*: 383) and Smith (*LJ*: 226) point out, by the presence of a class of slaves. The abolition of slavery was part of the civilising process brought on by the emergence of commerce. (Smith observes that slavery was economically unproductive (*WN*: 387, 684) – wealth was increased by diligent workers and diligence is enhanced by the 'liberal reward for labour' (99).)

This division between modern and ancient liberty is a significant faultline in the assessment of commercial society. While slavery was not advocated or condoned,[5] other Scots, notably Ferguson, wished to retain what they thought valuable in ancient political liberty and warned against the dangers in the Smithian/Humean line. We will explore these concerns in section C below, but there remains one final, closely related, theme to consider in this section.

v) Justice

We have already touched on justice in several places. This recurrence indicates its centrality. Further evidence of its key status is the basic fact that it was the subject of extensive analysis. Of these analyses Hume's in the *Treatise* is justly famous.[6]

The crux of Hume's argument is that justice is an artificial virtue. From Plato through to the great systems of Natural Law justice had been thought 'natural' – it was part of human nature to act justly. Hume, however, is careful to spell out what it is that he is affirming and what it is that he is here denying. In outline, his argument is that justice is a convention which arises 'necessarily' out of the concurrence of two facts: it is a uniform fact of human nature that humans have only a 'limited' or 'confin'd generosity' and that, in fact, 'external objects' are scarce relative to the desire for them (*THN*: 494–5). (These constitute what the twentieth-century political philosopher, John Rawls, in an explicit acknowledgement of Hume, calls the 'circumstances of justice'.) The constancy of this concurrence means that justice is necessary. Hume is emphatic: 'without justice society must immediately dissolve' (497 cf. *EPM*: 199). Although Smith has his differences with Hume, he is here equally uncompromising: 'justice is the main pillar that upholds the whole edifice. If it is removed, the great, the immense fabric of human society ... must in a moment crumble into atoms' (*TMS*: 86). Kames, too, is forthright: 'justice being essentially necessary to the maintenance of society' (*PMNR*: 65 cf. 42).

For Hume, justice upholds society by means of rules. Humans have agreed to restrain themselves. Justice is artificial because it is the product of this agreement. Hume gives a careful account of how these rules/agreements/conventions arise so that it does not fall foul of the criticisms he makes of Contract theory (see Chapter 2 p. 32).[7] Hume identifies three rules – stability of possession, its transfer by consent and promise-keeping (*THN*: 526). These are so necessary to society's cohesion that it is not, he says, 'improper to call them Laws of Nature', where 'nature' means what is 'common to' or 'inseparable from' any species (484). These rules have two important characteristics, and it is here where the more obvious link between Hume's analysis and our concern with commercial society is forged. These rules are both general and inflexible.

It is perhaps part of the meaning of 'rule' that it is 'general'. If everything was treated discretely, as a single event, then there could be no rule because no link could be forged between each unique case; it is merely 'one damn thing after another'. That, however, is impossible across the board. We can see here a clear connection between Hume's epistemology and his political and moral philosophy. The very coherence of the world (the cement of the universe – see p. 58 above) depended upon extending through habit the experience of one case to another. General rules are formed on the basis of expecting past occurrences to continue (*THN*: 362). They are indispensable; indeed Hume regards it as a truth about human nature that we 'are mightily addicted to general rules' (551).

In the case of justice these rules are artificial. Humans impose them upon themselves in order to establish order. These rules restrain them and are 'unchangeable by spite and favour, and by particular views of private or public interest' (532). This unchangeability, or inflexibility, is necessary so that there can be predictability and thence social coherence. When that is established, then individuals can act 'in expectation that others are to perform the like' (498). Such expectations, built up through 'repeated experience', are self-supporting because 'this experience assures us still more that the sense of interest has become common to all our fellows and gives us a *confidence* of the *future regularity* of their conduct. And 'tis only on the *expectation* of this, that our moderation and abstinence are founded' (490; my emphases).

These references to 'expectation' and 'confidence' reveal that it is a picture of commercial society that lies behind Hume's analysis. Justice has to be inflexible because the temptation to relax the rules is strong. He cites the case of a miser who justly receives a great fortune. He admits that a 'single act' of justice like this may 'in itself be prejudicial to society' (the money could have done more good elsewhere), but, nonetheless, the 'whole plan or scheme' is 'absolutely requisite' (497). If an exception is made in one case, if the rules are made flexible or made to forfeit their generality, then justice in the form of expectations that 'everyone will perform the like' will break down. And if that happens, then society, too, will collapse.

Although justice must on Hume's account be co-eval with society (it is present in the family (cf. *THN*: 493, *EPM*: 190)), the extent to which it sustains its generality and inflexibility improves. (Once again the move from the concrete to the abstract can be detected.) This dimension is a running theme in his *History* and is picked up by others. In Millar the institutional context is the focus. It is the 'advancement of commerce and civilization' that has tended to 'promote the virtue of strict justice'. This promotion was part and parcel of the cultivation of the science of law (*HV*: IV, 266/*HVL*: 340). The development of this 'science' is explicitly linked by Millar to the 'establishment of general rules of justice'. Echoing Hume's view of their addictiveness, Millar thinks the introduction of a general rule, and its extension by 'habit and analogy', originates in a 'propensity natural to all mankind'. Notwithstanding this foundation, it is the 'utility' of these rules that counts (IV, 278/344). This utility is two-fold. It enables every person to 'simplify his transactions' and it checks 'the partiality of judges' (*Ibid.*). (Hume had emphasised utility in the 'Second' Enquiry (*EPM*: 183, 188).) In broadly similar fashion, Robertson traces the development of the system of judicial procedure from its original dependence upon 'private persons', and thus 'capricious and unequal' character, to the establishment of a more 'regular course' (*VPE*: 321). Smith concludes the *Moral Sentiments* by contrasting the circumstances where the 'rudeness and barbarism of the people' make the system of justice irregular with those in 'more civilized nations', where the 'natural sentiments of justice' arrive at 'accuracy and precision' (*TMS*: 341).

While Smith's reference here to 'natural' sentiments distinguishes his account from Hume's, his emphasis on rules closely follows Hume. We have already seen that he shares Hume's view on the indispensability of justice and, in the same way that Hume had linked justice with restraint, Smith refers to justice as a negative virtue. Justice is negative because it requires forbearance, not hurting another. As a consequence Smith declares (importantly as we shall see) that 'we often fulfil all the rules of justice by sitting still and doing nothing' (82).

Smith likens these rules of justice to the rules of grammar since both possess the qualities of precision, accuracy and indispensability (175). This precision makes both grammar and justice amenable to instruction; in the same way that we can be taught how to conjugate verbs correctly so we 'may be taught to act justly'. Justice is now once again inclusively in the reach of all ('the coarse clay of the bulk of mankind') because:

> There is scarce any man ... who by discipline, education, and example, may not be so impressed with a regard to general rules, as to act upon almost every occasion with tolerable decency, and through the whole of his life to avoid any considerable degree of blame. (163)

The effect of this process of instruction or socialisation (see Chapter 2) is to establish certainty and predictability, for 'without this sacred regard to general rules there is no man whose conduct can be much depended upon'(*Ibid.*). Millar follows Smith closely. He, too, explicitly calls justice a negative virtue and remarks how its rules are capable of 'accuracy and precision' (*HV*: IV, 266–7/*HVL*: 340).

Smith objects to Hume's 'utilitarian' account of justice. For Smith, a concern for specific individuals rather than, as with Hume, a concern with a society's well-being is the effective source of justice. Smith does not deny utility a role, only that it is the 'first or principal source' (*TMS*: 188). On Smith's reading of human nature, humans 'delight' in seeing the unjust punished (89). This delight itself has its source in resentment at injustice (218 cf. Campbell 1971: 190ff.). This, too, is part of human nature; the sense of resentment 'seems to have been given us by nature for defence' since it 'prompts us to beat off mischief' or 'retaliate that which is already done' (79). In accord with Smith's moral theory (see Chapter 7 below), such actions would be approved of by the 'impartial spectator'.

The role given to resentment here was well established. Turnbull (*Discourse upon Moral and Civil Laws*: 293) gave voice to it early in the century and his pupil Reid followed suit (*AP*: 655). Less theoretical acceptance was given by Robertson. He gives a historical account of the development of justice from its source in the 'natural' desire to 'repel injuries and to revenge wrongs' (*VPE*: 321). On this account from being at first concerned (concretely) with wrongs done to individuals personally (or those to whom they are connected) this 'desire' develops over time, with the progress of civilisation, to express itself in regular (and abstract) procedure.

Other of Hume's contemporaries also criticised his account of the artificiality of justice. Kames denies that there is a distinction between gratitude to benefactors (which Hume regards as a natural virtue (see *E–OC*: 479)) and acting justly (*PMNR*: 40). For Kames, justice 'belongs to man as such' (48 cf. 54). He seemingly agrees with Hume that justice is the virtue that 'guards property and gives authority to covenants' (65) but believes that property and the obligation to keep our word are both natural principles (79). In Kames' eyes this is a consequence of natural sociability and in virtue of this he affirms, as we noted, along with Hume and Smith, that justice is necessary for the maintenance of society (65). Reid, for his part, also grants the utility and necessity of justice, and moreover allows that there is 'no animal affection in human nature that prompts us immediately to acts of justice as such' (*AP*: 652–3). Yet, notwithstanding these points, Reid regards it as a truth borne out by 'the sentiments of every honest man' that the 'turpitude in injustice' is perceived without any reference to utility (653). There is, he affirms, 'a natural judgment of conscience in man that injustice and treachery is base' (654). It is from the principle of conscience ('which nature has implanted in the human breast') that we derive the sentiment of justice (662). As we will see in Chapter 7, this final point also implicitly distinguishes Reid's account from Smith's.

C: Commerce, Virtue and Corruption

Not everything in the commercial garden is rosy. The pluses of the rule of law, of the opulence generated by the division of labour and of the benefits of credit can all be seen to have corresponding minuses. A common theme in this more critical assessment is that virtue is threatened. In this context 'virtue' refers to desirable character traits possessed by individuals (e.g. a 'brave man') and, in a reciprocal fashion, to the values upheld generally throughout society (e.g. patriotism). This theme owes much to the tradition of civic humanism (see Chapter 1).

i) Justice and Benevolence

Smith illustrates the indispensability of justice by the fact that it makes a society of merchants possible (*TMS*: 86). This example was chosen to identify quite deliberately a society where 'mutual love and affection' are absent. An important conclusion can be drawn from this, namely, 'beneficence is less essential to the existence of society than justice' (*Ibid.*). And since in commercial society 'everyman is a merchant' this further entails that a commercial society's coherence – its social bonds – do not depend on love and affection. You can coexist socially with those to whom you are emotionally indifferent.

This state of affairs is the reality of commercial life. The very complexity of commercial society means, on the one hand, that any individual needs the assistance of many others (the message of the coarse woollen coat), but, on the other, that only a few of these 'many' are personally known (*WN*: 26). In a commercial society we live predominantly among strangers (see Ignatieff 1984: 119). Relationships of mutual love and affection or friendship are correspondingly relatively scarce. Since the bulk of our dealings are impersonal then they must be conducted on the basis of adhering to the rules of justice. In a complex society a shopkeeper is unlikely to be also your friend; to you he provides something you want, to him you are a customer. This pattern of relationships lies behind Smith's famous passage:

> It is not from the benevolence of the butcher, the brewer or the baker that we expect our dinner, but from their regard to their own interest. We address ourselves not to their humanity but to their self-love and never talk to them of our own necessities but of their advantages. Nobody but a beggar chuses to depend chiefly upon the benevolence of his fellow-citizens. (*WN*: 26–7)

Nothing in this means that Smith is denying the virtuousness of benevolence. Indeed in the *Moral Sentiments* he is careful to say that a society of merchants would be 'less happy and agreeable' than one where beneficence was practised. Moreover, since just 'action' is 'inaction' (restraining from injury) then one who is 'merely' just is entitled to 'very little gratitude' and, possessing 'very little positive merit', will be treated without affection (*TMS*: 82).

That justice was distinct from other virtues such as benevolence was not Smith's argument alone. In fact the distinctiveness has a long pedigree and in the *Moral Sentiments* itself he refers (as the editors note) to Kames' *Principles of Morality and Natural Religion* for support for the view that we are under a stricter obligation to be just than we are to be generous (*TMS*: 8on.). Kames had said that 'benevolence and generosity are more beautiful and more attractive of love and esteem than justice' but that they are 'virtuous actions beyond what is strictly our duty', whereas 'performing our engagements' is our duty 'in the strictest sense' (*PMNR*: 41–2). Millar explicitly links up the distinctiveness of justice to its precision, its reducibility to accurate general rules, and contrasts it with the other virtues where their exercise depends so much on the particularities of circumstances that two cases are seldom sufficiently alike to establish 'room' for a general view (*HV*: IV, 266–8/*HVL*: 340–1 cf. IV, 283/346).

In spite of this distinction between justice and the other virtues, it is an important element in Smith's vindication of commerce that he does not regard them as inversely related. He argues that the concern 'not to hurt our neighbour' constitutes the character of the 'perfectly innocent and just man'. And such a character, he continues, can 'scarce ever fail to be accompanied with many other virtues, with great feeling for other people, with great humanity and great benevolence' (*TMS*: 218). Members of a commercial society can be both just and benevolent. These two virtues do, however, have a different focus. To see how, we can pick up the reference here to 'our neighbour'.

ii) Private Business and Public Action

Even if we admit that Smith was probably using the phrase 'our neighbour' as a synonym for 'our fellows', we can, with interpretative licence, take it to be symptomatic of the implicit emphasis on *private* life in his account. In fact, Millar, too, had used the same phrase in the same context and thus his version is open to the same interpretation (*HV*: IV, 267/*HVL*: 340). Justice is primary but negative; do nothing but abide by the rules. Any positive action – deeds of generosity or benevolence or mutual love – are reserved for 'our neighbours'. That is, they are reserved for those known personally to us. We exercise these positive virtues in a necessarily partial fashion; everybody cannot be our neighbour, everybody cannot be the proper recipient of our beneficence, everybody cannot be our friend. We treat 'everybody' impartially, we treat them in accordance with the rules of justice.

Alternatively put, justice is a matter of public interest, of *general* rules, while the other virtues are a matter of private concern, of *specific* deed. Understood in this way (and here is the justification for my interpretative licence) Smith's (and

Millar's and implicitly Hume's) account results in a re-scheduling of virtues. An 'active' life is founded on private relationships not on the public stage. Because commercial society has produced this outcome then it means that active public virtues – in particular a principled involvement with the public good – are not (now) to be expected. Those who valued that involvement with public issues (*rei publicae*) were imbued with 'republican', or civic, values. This is a powerful strain in Ferguson's *Essay*.

Ferguson does not deny the advantages and advances that a commercial society brings. He is, however, perturbed by some aspects of the accompanying rescheduling of the virtues. In particular, he is alarmed by the implicit devaluing of an active public life. What is at stake here can best be appreciated by returning to the issue of liberty. In his chapter on 'Civil Liberty', Ferguson seems to accept the link between liberty and the rule of law; 'where the citizen is supposed to have rights of property and station, and is protected in the exercise of them, he is said to be free; and the very restraints by which he is hindered from the commission of crimes are part of his liberty' (*ECS*: 156 cf. 161, *PMPS*: II, 459–61). Yet, even in this chapter, there are indications of disquiet. At the heart of Ferguson's misgivings is his antipathy to the passivity that he sees this 'modern' view of liberty engendering.

It is a basic ingredient in Ferguson's general philosophy that he holds that 'man is not made for repose' (*ECS*: 210 cf. 7, *PMPS*: II, 508). Man is naturally active. Ferguson believes that this activity should be exercised on the public stage (*ECS*: 214) and not confined to the 'improvement of fortune' (253) or 'separate pursuits of pleasure' (222). With this belief Ferguson is signalling his sympathy with the 'classical' position that 'politics' is what men do in contrast to 'economics' (the organisation and conduct of the household), which is the sphere of women, slaves and animals. In Aristotelian parlance – the ultimate source of this position – human nature is fulfilled in political action because man is by nature a creature of the polis (*Politics*: 1253a).

It is against this backdrop that Ferguson's misgivings are best understood. Despite the undoubted value of 'modern' liberty (thus clearly ruling out slavery (*ECS*: 161, *PMPS*: II, 472)), the values of 'ancient', or 'republican', liberty (cf. Goldsmith 1994) still have a place. It is the loss of these latter values in commercial society that Ferguson most fears. His concern is expressed at its sharpest when he sees dangers even within the key, modern principle – the rule of law. Liberty, he declares, is 'never in greater danger than it is when we measure national felicity ... by the mere tranquillity which may attend on equitable administration' (*ECS*: 270). The tranquillity, or passivity, is the problem. Individual citizens allow the 'administration' to get on with its public task of enforcing the general rules of justice while they get on with their own private business. And from their individual point of view, the less the administration interferes in the 'commercial and lucrative arts' the better. But the effect of this 'indifference' is to 'foster the vices' (256) with the consequence that a situation has been produced that is 'more akin to despotism than we are apt to imagine' (269).

By inculcating or permitting passivity, modern liberty fails to protect the true values of liberty. At *that* protection ancient liberty was much more effective. It is no accident that Ferguson wrote a multi-volume history of the Roman republic since early Rome was one of the standard models of a 'free' state. (Recall from Chapter 2 (p. 42) when discussing 'conflict', Rome's role as the model for how opposing forces maintained liberty.) Sparta, the other key model, is also invoked by Ferguson. He refers to it as a state whose 'sole object was virtue' (160) and where the 'preservation of civil liberty' was the 'disposition' in 'the hearts of its members' (158).[8] The source of ancient liberty's effectiveness was that it required active involvement by citizens in the running of the polis or republic, it required political participation (cf. *PMPS*: II, 509). Commercial society requires no such participation; there is a political deficit (cf. Medick & Batscha 1988: 79). All that it calls forth is 'merely' forbearing from injustice by abiding by the rules. But, once again, for Ferguson, this passivity is a danger. If the provision of security, which for moderns is the 'seeming perfection' of government, is all there is to politics then this can 'weaken the bands of society' (*ECS*: 191). Why? Because the citizen is not called upon 'to act for himself to maintain his rights' (223). Inactivity produces inadvertence. Through being too busy on private affairs the 'political spirit' is laid to rest, by chaining up the 'active virtues', commercial nations become 'unworthy of the freedom they possess' (221).[9]

In discussing this whole process, Ferguson uses the language of 'corruption'. He says, for example, that the rules of despotism (which, as we saw, he feared modern liberty approaches) are 'made for the government of corrupted men' (240). This is the authentic vocabulary of a 'classical republican'.[10] While this vocabulary with its stress on virtue can be contrasted with the typical jurisprudentialist talk of 'rights' (*virtus* not *ius* as Pocock put it (1983: 248)), language is elastic or fluid not rigid or solid. It is also possible to be bilingual. Ferguson's treatment of 'rights' is a seeming case in point.[11]

In apparently standard jurisprudentialist terms Ferguson refers, as we have already quoted, to 'rights of property' (156) and in his critique of Price (see Chapter 5 p. 108) he links security with the possession of rights, where these are understood negatively as restraining others from invading (cf. *IMP*: Pt. 5). We also noted that he refers to the 'right of the individual to act in his station for himself and the public'. This latter right he explicitly identifies as 'political freedom' (*ECS*: 167). It is this active, participatory right that is needed to keep a people free. Mere laws, mere forms of civil procedure will not do that job – 'the influence of laws where they have any real effect in the preservation of liberty is not any magic power descending from the shelves that are loaded with books but is in reality the influence of men resolved to be free' (263). Liberty is a 'right which every individual must be ready to vindicate for himself'; this vindication is a 'firm and resolute spirit' possessed by 'the liberal mind' (266). This means each citizen being 'willing to sustain in their own persons the burden of government and of national defence' and not leaving it to others (*Ibid.*). The reference here to 'defence' fuels Ferguson's support for citizen militias (see subsection vi below). More generally, it is against this backcloth that we can now make sense of Ferguson's reference to the 'rights of the mind' (167); these are (political) rights that only exist when exercised as the expression of a virtuous character.

We can clarify this entire line of argument by returning briefly to Smith. Though Smith's use of the image of the 'invisible hand' (see p. 45) in the *Wealth of Nations* is generally interpreted as part of an 'economic' argument against interference it also has a *political* meaning (it is after all political interference that is to be curtailed). For Smith the public good, since it is in a commercial society the product of individuals independently pursuing their own private interests, no longer requires distinctly *political* action. We noted above that the opulence generated by commerce makes for a better and happier society than in earlier times. Since this is an unintended consequence of commercial activity and the exercise of private (negative) liberty then it means Smith can· consistently attribute unprepossessing motivations to merchants (cf. *WN*: 267) while still seeing some more overtly political and supra-individualistic conception of the public good as superfluous. Ferguson's 'rights of the mind' can be seen to be out of place. This displacement has the far-reaching consequence of shifting not only the primacy of 'politics' over 'economics' (cf. Teichgraeber 1986: 10) but also the entire Aristotelian view of human nature that makes political activity its fulfilment (cf. Berry 1994: 166). In a different context Smith's comment on good citizenry in the *Moral Sentiments* carries a similar message. There, Smith says a good citizen should promote the welfare of his fellows as well as respecting and obeying the laws. He notes, however, that in 'peaceable and quiet times' these two principles coincide – 'support of the established government seems evidently the best expedient for maintaining the safe, respectable and happy situation of our fellow citizens' (*TMS*: 231). These requisite 'times' are, as a general rule, provided by a commercial society. To associate commerce with 'peace and quiet' is further evidence that a rescheduling of virtues has taken place and is, once again, a cause of alarm.

iii) Humanity and Courage

Like all other 'states of society' the age of commerce generates certain ways of acting, a distinctive set of manners. Indeed a distinct personality is fostered. Ferguson, in his pamphlet on the case for a militia (see subsection vi below), remarks that our ancestors 'were a people, in many respects, different from what we now are' (*Reflections previous to the Establishment of a Militia* [1756]: 5). This is no more than we would expect from the earlier discussion of the impact of socialisation. These two points are neatly juxtaposed in Millar. Directly echoing Smith's remark that every man is a sort of merchant, Millar declares that the 'mercantile spirit is not confined to tradesmen or merchants; from a similarity of situation it pervades in some degree all orders and ranks and by the influence of habit and example it is communicated, more or less, to every member of the community' (*HV*: IV, 247/*HVL*: 386). It is this diffusion that Ferguson fears. If the 'pretensions to equal justice and freedom should terminate in rendering every class equally servile and mercenary we make a nation of helots and have no free citizens' (*ECS*: 186).

What are the 'morals' fashioned by commerce? What are the 'commercial virtues'? Ferguson, in an aside, refers to 'punctuality and fair-dealing' as the 'system of manners' of merchants (189 cf. identically *IMP*: 39). Millar says that as social intercourse extends (as society gets more complex) it 'requires more and more a mutual trust and confidence, which cannot be maintained without the uniform profession and rigid practice of honesty and fair-dealing' (*HV*: IV, 237/*HVL*: 384). Once again a Smithian precedent is identifiable. In his lectures Smith observed that 'when the greater part of the people are merchants they always bring probity and punctuality into fashion' so that these are 'the principal virtues of a commercial nation' (*LJ*: 539). That these virtues are pre-eminent is a direct reflection of the abstract quality of commercial life and the need for predictability and certainty in future-oriented 'market' dealings. They can, therefore, be contrasted with the virtues or standards of earlier ages; for example, 'barbarians' have 'seldom any regard to their promises' (*HV*: IV, 239/*HVL*: 385). This contrast opens the way for a progressive history of 'civilisation'. (Recall from Chapter 5 the discussion of manners in the form of the changing status of women.)

Hume's essays of the 1750s can be instructively read from this perspective. The 'ages of refinement' are both the 'happiest and most virtuous' (*E–RA*: 269). Since Hume also says that these ages enjoy the 'arts of luxury' (*E–Com*: 256) then he is associating, not opposing, virtue and luxury. (The significance of this association will become apparent.) If individuals are now 'happier', in what does this happiness consist? Hume identifies three components – repose, pleasure and action (*E–RA*: 269–70). Of these the last is crucial. The first is merely derivative, only valued as a break from action. The second is integrally connected with action because 'being occupied' is itself enjoyable. But in contrast to the public or political gloss that Ferguson will put on 'activity', Hume observes that humans are roused to activity or industry by a 'desire of a more splendid way of life than what their ancestors enjoyed' (*E–Com*: 264).

This splendour manifests itself in refinement of behaviour and manners. Negatively it prevents 'habits of indolence' from establishing themselves. This is the same basic psychology that we covered in Chapter 5 where 'savages' were characterised by Robertson and Millar (among others) as languid and idle. However, in the present context, it is the positive manifestations that are important. The more refined a people become, the more they are able to cultivate the pleasures of the mind and body (*E–RA*: 271). Regarding the latter, they are, for example, able to enjoy the refinements of cooking and not indulge in gluttony like the Tartars who 'feast on dead horses' (272). Regarding the former, they are, of course, more knowledgeable as improvements abound in 'every art and science' and 'profound ignorance is totally banished' (271). In addition, there is an increase in sociability (including gallantry towards women). This sociability is a product of the increased density of population as they 'flock into cities'. For Hume there is more than a merely etymological link between city-dwelling, civility and civilisation. He sums up these improvements by stating that 'industry, knowledge and humanity are linked together by an indissoluble chain and are found ... to be peculiar to the more refined and, what are commonly denominated, the more luxurious ages' (271).

Hume's reference to 'humanity' carries a lot of freight. He, here, associates it with increased conversation and improvement in 'temper', or emotional dispositions. These are accompanied with a heightened sensitivity to the feelings of others (cf. Smith *TMS*: 207). By contrast barbarians are barbaric; they lack humanity – they are brutal, cruel and bloodthirsty. Smith notes how savages torture their victims and steel themselves not to express emotion when they are being tortured. Such hardiness diminishes their humanity (209). Their self-command when compared to that exercised by civilised peoples is more a matter of repression. Like a coiled spring that leaps unpredictably and uncontrollably once the tension is released, so the actions of savages when they lose their self-command are 'furious and violent', their recriminations 'always sanguinary and dreadful' (208). The humanity of a commercial people (along with their truthfulness and justice) is rewarded with the 'confidence, the esteem and love' of their fellows (166). And since Smith's moral theory hinges on responsiveness to others, then these three virtues will establish themselves and individuals will act accordingly. Since the 'good opinion' of others is always desired, then it will produce 'regular conduct' (63) or, in other words, the rule-governed, predictable behaviour necessary to the functioning of a commercial society.

Ferguson, too, remarks on the salience of humanity. He identifies it as the 'principal characteristic' of civilisation that the 'laws of war' have been 'softened' and that glory consists in protecting the vanquished not destroying them (*ECS*: 199–200). Nonetheless Ferguson fears that commercial states have a tendency to exhibit a 'contempt for glory' (258). Glory is essentially a military virtue – it is 'won' on the battlefield by exhibiting courage. Both Smith and Hume, however, throw doubt on the propriety of courage in the modern world; so, too, does Millar though he uses the term 'fortitude'.

Millar's doubts follow from his '(soft) determinism'; from his view that our dispositions are 'influenced' by our circumstances. Hence, fortitude or passive suffering (*HV*: IV, 177) is practised in the 'infancy of society' (181). Since it is 'the want of humanity' (178) that makes this practice effective, then it means, by contrast, that the 'lively sensibility and exquisite fellow-feeling which in opulent and polished nations take place among individuals are ... peculiarly unfavourable to fortitude' (185). This fellow-feeling is the product of the commercial 'mode of life', which comprises 'regular government', 'tranquillity', a 'secure and comfortable situation' and 'softness of manners' (185–6). In *these* social circumstances, fortitude is too random and individualistic. It is this element that Smith had picked up. The 'most heroic valour' can be used to equal effect to good or bad ends (*TMS*: 264). As such, it can be 'excessively dangerous' (241). Hume's remarks make this connection clear – 'it is indeed observable that among all uncultivated nations who have not as yet had full experience of the advantages attending beneficence, justice and the social virtues, courage is the predominant excellence' (*EPM*: 255). In his *History* he remarks, referring to sixteenth-century Scotland, that when 'arms' prevail over 'laws' then 'courage preferably to equity or justice was the virtue most valued and respected' (*HE*: II, 81 cf. I, 115 on the Anglo-Saxons). Courage is closely tied to the military virtues. If courage has only a limited role in a commercial society, then the martial virtues too would seem there to have only a limited relevance. This limitation was a source of worry. The anxiety was ultimately bound up with a complex of values that the issue of luxury evoked.

iv) The Luxury Debate

There was a far-reaching debate on the status of luxury in the eighteenth century (cf. Berry 1994: Ch. 6). The debate drew participants from across the whole world of letters and Scotland was not exempt. At stake was the character of 'modernity', and commerce and its consequences lay at its heart.

The traditional view, developed paradigmatically by Roman moralists and upheld by civic humanists among others, was that luxury was a corruption. On an individual level, men who live a life of luxury become effeminate. That is to say, they become 'soft', unable to endure hardship and act in a 'manly' fashion, where that means risking death and acting courageously. It is not mere coincidence that in both Greek and Latin the words for 'man' (*aner/andra* and *vir*) have the same root as those for 'courage' (*andreia* and *virtus*). To live luxuriously is to devote oneself to the pleasures of self-indulgence and greed. Such a life has social consequences. A society where luxury is established will devote itself to private ends since men will be unwilling to act (fight) for the public good. This society, it follows, will be militarily weak – a nation of cowards will easily succumb.

It was further assumed that pre-eminent among those who served their private interest were traders or merchants. Compared to a general or a statesman, that is, one who dedicated his life to the public good, a merchant lived a less fulfilling, less humanly worthwhile life. This disparagement, present in Aristotle for example, was sharpened once commerce began to spread. Moreover, commerce was suspect because of the uncertainty or risk that lies at its core – there is no guarantee that you will be able to sell your goods. And since the system rests on nothing more tangible than belief, opinion and expectation, then it seemed clearly too insubstantial to support a social order. These jeremiads were fuelled by the spectacular financial collapses of the late seventeenth and early eighteenth centuries (the Darien scheme, the South Sea Bubble). These worries were given a focus by the presence of a contrasting model in the person of the independent landowner or country gentleman. This individual enjoys stability and certainty. In sharp and deliberate contrast to the fluidity of a money economy, the giddy whirl of fashion and the evanescence of 'profit', the landowner with his commitment to a fixed 'place' is able to practise the virtues of loyalty, commitment and steadfastness. These are suitably 'masculine' traits[12] and they can be contrasted to the proverbial unreliability of women – not for nothing is it their 'prerogative to change their mind', truly '*la donna e mobile*'. Given its link with effeminacy, luxury now resurrects itself.

The only way a luxurious, soft nation could meet its military commitments or needs was by hiring others to play that role. To make that feasible, the nation had to have the wherewithal. Hence arose the important association between luxury, wealth (commerce) and mercenary armies. For civic humanists this was a negative association so that commerce, too, became tarred with the anti-luxury brush. This meant that to defend commerce required a deflection or subversion of the traditional case against luxury; hence the debate and its relevance.

One strategy was to exploit the connection between commerce and softness but to construe this positively.[13] Robertson neatly summarises what the positive case argued: 'commerce tends to wear off those prejudices which maintain distinction and animosity between nations. It softens and polishes the manners of men. It unites them by one of the strongest of all ties, the desire of supplying their mutual wants. It disposes them to peace ...' (*VPE*: 333). The growth of commerce – with its attendant 'civilising' traits of greater humanity and gentler, polished manners (cf. Hume *E–RA*: 271; Robertson *VPE*: 319; Stuart *PLS*: 57, 93; Millar *OR*: 176 etc.) – marked a move away from a hard 'Spartan' life, which for the traditionalists represented the virtuous life of frugality.

This 'move away' had begun in earnest in the seventeenth century. Several writers on trade, like Nicholas Barbon, began to 'de-moralise' luxury and argue that it was a useful because it promoted industry and the creation of wealth (cf. Berry 1994: Ch. 5). This strain of thought was given a fillip by Mandeville's deliberately provocative *The Fable of the Bees* (1721/1732), which, among other affronts to traditional or orthodox sensibilities, openly defended luxury. Many writers rose to the bait. Among these, and one of the most prominent as well as most astute, was Francis Hutcheson (see, for example, his *Observations on the Fable of the Bees* [1726]).

From the ground already covered the broad lines of the luxury debate and the stances of the various participants might seem to be predictable. However, as so often, matters are seldom as clear-cut as interpretative frameworks like to pretend. For example, Ferguson is indeed extremely chary of the commercial arts because they emphasise 'private advantage' and the individual becomes 'effeminate, mercenary and sensual' (*ECS*: 250), but his chapter on 'Luxury' was no blanket condemnation; he allowed that, as well as being censured, luxury has been praised as a means of adding 'national lustre and felicity' (244). What this chapter's balance-sheet approach reveals is an awareness on Ferguson's part that the meaning of 'luxury' has become too fluid. This same point had been made by Turnbull (*Principles of Moral Philosophy*: 341) and by Steuart, who attempted, as a consequence, to separate the moral from the 'political' sense of the term.[14]

One of the most telling Scottish contributions to the debate also starts from the term's 'uncertain signification'. That remark comes from the opening sentence of Hume's essay 'Of Refinement in the Arts' – an essay that on its first publication in 1752 was entitled 'Of Luxury'. In that essay, as well as its contemporary companion 'Of Commerce', Hume firmly rejects as misplaced much of the traditional 'moralised' disparagement of luxury. We have already hinted at the thrust of his argument by quoting his remark that ages of 'refinement', or luxury, are 'the most virtuous'.

Luxury, as an ally of commerce, when it is diffused among the population, diminishes the force and ambition of the sovereign (*E–Com*: 257). (Commerce, we recall, is antithetical to absolute government.) But this does not weaken the country. On the contrary, 'industry and arts and trade encrease the power of the sovereign' (260). Since a state's 'power' hinges on its military capacity, it means that Hume is contending that a commercial society is potent not impotent, is virile not emasculated. His contention has both a positive and a negative aspect. Negatively, he holds that the population of a non-trading society will be indolent and its soldiers will lack knowledge, skill and industry. These deficiencies make them fit for only sudden confrontations, regular attack or defence being beyond them (260). Positively, a civilised nation, precisely because it is industrious and knowledgeable, will be an effective military power. The root cause is that a nation's power increases in proportion as it increases labour employed 'beyond mere necessaries'. The effect of this cause is that the nation possesses a storehouse of labour (*E–RA*: 272; *E–Com*: 262). This store can be drawn on to meet military need. In a civilised nation an army is raised by imposing a tax, this reduces expenditure on unnecessary luxury goods thus releasing the manufacturers of such goods for military service (*E–Com*: 261).

There is a deeper dimension to Hume's analysis. This is revealed in his comment that the sort of society presupposed by the critics of luxury is contrary to the 'natural bent of the mind' (263). Hume's reference here is to Sparta – the paradigm of regime founded on hard, frugal virtues (for Hume on Sparta, see Berry 1994: 143–52). Spartan policy goes against the grain of human nature because its devotion to the 'public good' is too difficult to sustain (cf. Moore 1977: 820) given that humans are motivated by a 'spirit of avarice, industry, art and luxury' (*E–Com*: 263). To govern men along Spartan lines would require a 'miraculous transformation of mankind' (*E–RA*: 280). The government, however, is not in the business of miracles; it must deal with the world as it is and men as they are. Accordingly, the 'magistrate' can 'very often' only cure one vice by encouraging another, where the latter's effects are less damaging. It makes no sense to criticise the magistrate for not imposing, in line with 'classical' principles, some objective, rational doctrine of the 'good life'. Instead, the appropriate judgement is: does this policy promote the material well-being of those individuals subject to it? Understood in this way then luxury can be justly cultivated because it is superior to sloth. Moreover, by defending luxury in this way, Hume is still able to allow that luxury can be 'vicious' as well as innocent. Yet even then it might still be better to accept it than attempt vainly to eradicate it (279–80).

Other Scots were far less sanguine. Kames' writings, for example, are full of the traditional disparagement of luxury. He blames it for depopulation. In a direct manner it enervates the capacity in both sexes to procreate and, indirectly, it reduces then to slavery and destroys industry (*SHM*: I, 63–4). He follows the standard convention that Rome was corrupted by the import of 'Asiatic luxury' (I, 473) and laments that the 'epidemic distempers of luxury and selfishness are spreading wide in Britain' (I, 477). This implies a judgement of commerce. Kames allows that commerce is 'immediately' advantageous as it bestows wealth and power, but, echoing Ferguson, he fears the tranquillity engendered by 'strict and regular government' makes a 'warlike people effeminate and cowardly' (I, 459). Luxury is 'above all pernicious in a commercial state' (I, 373) as it eradicates both manhood (I, 487) and patriotism (I, 474).

In his Sketch on Patriotism Kames marries his traditionalist critique of luxury with his version of the 'four-stages' theory. In the 'original state of hunting and fishing' any notion of *patria* is absent, in the nomadic shepherd state there is an idea of common interest but not that of a *patria*, and it is only in the settled agricultural state that 'the sense of *patria* begins to unfold itself' (I, 465). When 'manufacture and commerce' begin to flourish, as in Tudor England, patriotism is still present (I, 468) but when 'power and riches become the sole object of pursuit' then, as happened in Rome and more recently with the Dutch, patriotism vanishes (I, 476). The only solution Kames sees is in 'pinching poverty', that is the introduction of sumptuary laws (I, 480). (Contrast this with Smith's view of sumptuary legislation – see above p. 129.)

Kames' unease about luxury and its diffusion into contemporary Scotland was widely shared. Journals carried laments about the 'luxury, effeminacy and debility' to which their country was prone.[15] Blair, as well as being an Edinburgh professor, was also an immensely popular preacher, and his sermons contain familiar reproaches against the 'evils' attending the 'habits of luxury'.[16] Other voices joining the anti-luxury chorus include Hutcheson (*Observations*: 81, *SIMP*: 321), Gregory (*CV*: xiii–xvii), Monboddo (*OPL*: V, 188, III, 453), Wallace (*Diss Numbers Mankind*: 13,19 et passim) and Blackwell (*Homer*: 63). In Stuart, in keeping with his general celebration of the liberty of the Germans 'in the woods', the growth of luxury is one ingredient in the emergence of cities, invidious distinctions and riches – a growth he describes in terms of the 'vices, venality and corruptions of mankind' (*Diss*: 36 cf. 95). Hence while luxury was, in the manner of Hume and Smith, a factor in the collapse of 'feudalism' for Stuart this same role was viewed as accelerating a corruption already set in (*VSE*: 2, 105; *PLS*: 119). Dunbar, more like Ferguson, opts for a balanced view. Luxury can be beneficial (as a motive for industry) or harmful (once obtained) (*EHM*: 368–9).

Millar is rather more intriguing. We have seen that he is a strong supporter of commerce as conducive to liberty, but, as we noted in Chapter 5, he was also worried about some of the effects of this 'liberty' upon women. In 'opulent and luxurious nations' the natural tendency of 'great luxury' is to 'diminish the rank and dignity of women' (*OR*: 225). Millar also voices disquiet about the competitiveness of commercial life, where the 'pursuit of riches becomes a scramble in which the hand of every man is against every other' (*HV*: IV, 249/*HVL*: 387). A further manifestation of Millar's awareness of a downside to commerce is his concern with the effects of the division of labour on the indivdual whose work is confined to extremely specialised or confined tasks. In this awareness he is not alone. It even seems he is here following no less an authority than Adam Smith himself.

v) 'Alienation' and the Division of Labour

The Scots' writings on the damaging consequences of the division of labour belong in two contexts – as a reason for government action/expense and as a further expression of the connection between commerce and the softening of manners. This duality has been insufficiently recognised. One explanation for this is that Smith, the dominant voice in this debate, in his argument within the first context, refers in passing to 'martial virtues' the seeming hinge of the second.

The fact that Smith's account of the advantages of the division of labour discussed in the opening chapters of the *Wealth of Nations* appears to sit oddly with the comments on its drawbacks that he makes in Book 5 has prompted much speculation.[17] Since some of the same phrases recur the difference in tenor between the two discussions is not plausibly attributed to inadvertence on Smith's part. Smith's strategy in Book 5 is to identify ailments and then recommend remedies. This discussion comes in Book 5 for the simple reason that the remedy recommended involves some government intervention and expense and *that* is the precise and explicit subject of that Part ('Of the Expence of publick Works and publick Insitutions') of that Book ('Of the Revenue of the Sovereign or Commonwealth').

Smith's diagnosis of the ailments focuses on the man 'whose whole life is spent in performing a few simple operations'. This individual, having 'no occasion to exert his understanding or to exercise his invention', loses the 'habit of exertion' to become

> as stupid and ignorant as it is possible for a human creature to become. The torpor of his mind renders him, not only incapable of relishing or bearing a part in any rational conversation, but of conceiving any generous, noble or tender sentiment, and consequently of forming any just judgment concerning many even of the ordinary duties of private life. (*WN*: 782)

Given the importance Smith attaches to 'private life', this is serious. Smith accentuates this account of the 'symptoms' by noting their pervasiveness and virulence. This individual's life is one of 'gross ignorance and stupidity' (788) that 'corrupts the courage of his mind' and renders him incapable of defending his country in war (782). In short his dexterity is bought at the cost of his 'intellectual, social and martial virtues' (*Ibid.*).

These individual ailments have social consequences. The mutilating deformation that accompanies the dulling of the intellect (788) and the atomised asocial life will reduce self-command, so that these individuals will be prey to 'enthusiasm' and 'superstition', which are a frequent source of 'the most dreadful disorders' (*Ibid.*). The enervation of martial virtue and instillation of cowardice ('a sort of mental mutilation, deformity and wretchedness' (787)) will clearly weaken the state's defensive abilities.[18] This grim picture has prompted commentators to see here a recognition by Smith of 'alienation' at the heart of the industrial process. This, however, is to read the past backwards in the light of Marx's celebrated discussion seventy years or so later.[19] However, if what Smith says is looked at in terms of his argument and not in terms of the very different metaphysics of a German philosopher then a clearer image can emerge.

What Smith says is that the above is the (sick) condition into which the 'labouring poor, that is, the great body of the people' necessarily fall 'unless government takes some pains to prevent it' (782). His basic remedy is education. The people of 'rank and fortune' have the leisure and inclination to fend for themselves but the 'common people' have neither of these (784). The 'publick', as a consequence, can (as in Scotland) establish a local school where children can be taught for a fee that 'even a common labourer may afford' (785). The public purse will pay the residue of the teacher's salary.[20] Smith's argument has a somewhat quixotic air; the (malign) unintended consequences of the specialisation of labour are to be offset intentionally by a specialised occupation.

But Smith's prescriptions go further. He also makes some recommendations as to what is to be taught. The essentials should be covered. This means the ability to 'read, write and account', plus, instead of the 'little smattering of Latin' they are sometimes taught, the 'elementary parts of geometry and mechanicks' (785). Smith thinks this sufficient for this 'rank of people'. There will be an incentive to acquire these basics. In order to set up trade or attain membership of a corporation then 'an examination or probation' in these essentials will first be made a requirement, it will be imposed by the 'publick' (786). In fact, Smith recommends a similar probation for those about to enter 'any liberal profession' or 'honourable office of trust or profit'. These individuals whom Smith explicitly identifies as members of the 'middling or more than middling rank and fortune' will receive instruction in 'science and philosophy'. Since science is the 'great antidote to the poison of enthusiasm and superstition' then these ranks will be relatively immune, and this will, Smith believes, forestall the contagion to the 'inferior ranks' (796).

Although Smith clearly sees education as functional both in its content and effects, it does not follow that his recommendations are straightforwardly an expression of social control (cf. Winch 1978: 120). Or, at least, he can be (sympathetically) read that way. He allows that geometry and mechanics learnt by the common people is a 'necessary introduction to the most sublime as well as most useful sciences' (786). And he writes (somewhat awkwardly) that 'though the state was to derive no advantage from the instruction of the inferior ranks of the people, it would still deserve its attention that they should not be altogether uninstructed' (788).

Education thus deals directly with the numbing of the intellectual virtues and indirectly with the weakening of the social virtues. What about the martial virtues? Here Smith's recommendations are not specific. What is apparent is that he does not see citizen militias as the obvious solution. The whole question of militias is the second context in which the deleterious consequences of the division of labour was discussed and will be dealt with in the next subsection.

Smith's general strategy of tying together these damaging consequences with the requirement that the government sponsor and subsidise education was taken up by others. Dunbar, after citing pin-making, virtually repeats Smith's phrase of the 'torpor of his mind' by referring to the 'torpor of intellect' suffered by the artisan. Dunbar further comments that this 'implies the absence or annihilation of every manly virtue'. But in that very same sentence he includes the qualifier 'if'. This annihilation will occur 'if the tendency of his occupation is not counteracted by some expedient of government' (*EHM*: 423–4). Millar, too, as so often, follows Smith's line. Workmen in the mechanical arts, confined to a 'single manual operation', are 'apt to acquire an habitual vacancy of thought' so that 'they become like machines'. And even in the intervals between work they draw little improvement from the company of companions similarly afflicted (*HV*: IV, 145–6/*HVL*: 380). Millar worries more openly than Smith that a gap will emerge in society between those with virtue and intelligence and those lacking them – a situation that might re-create the Europe of the Dark Ages, where ministers of religion were ever able to 'practise fraud and deception' (IV, 157).[21] However, Millar believes that 'it is plainly in the interests of the higher ranks to assist in cultivating the minds of the common people' and 'of the utmost consequence to the public' that the lower orders be 'conscientious in their domestic concerns, peaceable in their manners and adverse from riot and disorder' (IV, 158). The way to achieve this is by the 'public', as in Scotland, instituting 'schools and seminaries of education to communicate as far as possible to the most useful but humble class of citizens that knowledge which their way of life has in some degree prevented from acquiring' (IV, 160/382). Kames is another who uses the familiar language. Concentration 'on a single object' excludes 'thought and invention' so that the operator 'becomes dull and stupid' like 'a beast of burden' (he repeats the last phrase when characterising the harm of perpetual peace (*SHM*: I, 464)). But, unlike the others, this is not elaborated upon and no educational remedy is specified (I, 110–11).

vi) Militias and the Division of Labour

Although Adam Ferguson's comments on the division of labour in his *Essay* are standardly lumped in with Smith's, they are, I think, best viewed in the light of his more general disquiet about commercial society and the corruptions to which it is prone. Hence before some oft-quoted paragraphs on the effects of the mechanical arts, he has already indicated that the 'separation of arts and professions' applies to the 'higher departments of policy and war' (*ECS*: 181). When he comes to the 'inferior branches of manufacture' he observes that they 'prosper most where the mind is least consulted' and 'where the workshop may without any great effort of the imagination be considered as an engine, the parts of which are men' (182–3). (This was quoted by Marx in *Capital I*.) He goes on to remark – in the way Millar was later to do – that the 'master' of the workshop has more opportunity to take a wider view and cultivate an 'enlargement of thought' than the 'inferior workman' (183 cf. *PMPS*: I, 251).[22] Despite the concentration on these two paragraphs in commentary[23] it seems clear that *this* is not Ferguson's major preoccupation.

What really exercises Ferguson about the division of labour is that it compartmentalises society such that none of its various separated elements is 'animated with the spirit of society itself' (*ECS*: 218). He allows that the specialisation of the clothier and tanner gives us better clothes and shoes but – and this is the nub – to 'separate the arts which form the citizen and the statesman, the arts of policy and war, is an attempt to dismember the human character' (230). It is the 'political' rather than the 'working' class that concerns him (cf. Kettler 1977: 451).[24] This directly ties in with his support for the principles of 'ancient' liberty (a 'liberty' that always been the preserve of the landed, historically slave-owning, elite) and his desire to keep the active 'rights of the mind' alive. Commerce not only threatens to tie up the 'active virtues' but it also extends its specialisation into the very heart of the social spirit by making the art of war a technical profession. In a telling phrase he says this makes citizens and soldiers as distinguishable 'as women and men' (231).

The remedy is at hand within the resources of the tradition of ancient liberty, namely, the citizen militia. It is now not surprising to see that immediately after warning of the lack of social spirit (218) he quotes Pericles and immediately after that cites Rome. His multi-volume history of Rome can be read as one long recitation of this theme. For example, he exploits the set-piece of the war between Rome and Carthage to this end. Carthage was superior to Rome in commerce and every resource except 'that which is derived from national character and which is the consequence of public virtue'. The consequence was that the Carthaginians 'stifled the military character of their own citizens and had perpetual recourse to foreigners whom they trusted with their arms'. And, of course, in the ensuing struggle Rome, whose manners at that time were 'in perfect contrast', was victorious (*Rom*: I, 108–10).

The advantage of a citizen militia was that 'in the higher ranks' it kept together the 'talents for the council and the field', while at the same time it gave the 'body of the people' that 'zeal for their country, and that military character, which enable them to take a share in defending its rights' (*ECS*: 227 cf. 266). To rely on mercenaries is to play fast and loose with those rights; as commercial actors, mercenaries will fight where the pay is best, not where the cause is just. Similarly to rely on a professional 'standing' army will also threaten those rights, since this army can be used not only against an external foe but also against any perceived 'enemy within' (cf. 227).

Ferguson's concerns were not merely theoretical. He was one of the leaders of a campaign to establish a militia in Scotland (see Chapter 1) and, as we noted, wrote a pamphlet advocating its establishment.[25] Around this issue was formed the 'Poker Club', of which Ferguson was a member along with other literati, including Hume, Blair, Robertson, Dalrymple and Smith (see full list in Robertson 1985: 189–91), although the majority of members were nobles and gentlemen. It would appear that the Club had a 'social' as much as a 'political' character (Robertson,1985: 186 but cf. Sher 1989: 259n.).

Although Smith was a member of the Poker Club his views on the militia follow his positive rather than his negative assessment of the division of labour.[26] For Smith in 'modern armies', where artillery is a decisive factor (cf. Hume *HE*: I,

498), itself the product of technological advance, what matters is 'regularity, order and prompt obedience to command' (*WN*: 699).[27] Going by these criteria, a standing army is superior to a militia. As we saw (p. 142) this was also Hume's view.[28] And that a militia is not suited to a prolonged campaign was also the view of Millar (*HV*: IV, 195). For Smith in 'an opulent and civilized nation' a professional army is the means to preserve civilisation against invasion from a 'poor and barbarous nation'. Indeed Smith observed in his *Lectures* that had the few thousand 'naked unarmed Highlanders' in 1745 not been opposed by a standing army they would have seized the throne 'with little difficulty' (*LJ*: 540–1). But beyond this, Smith sees in its ability to enforce the laws of the sovereign throughout the 'provinces of empire' a way of bringing civilisation to barbarians (*WN*: 706). This has clear parallels with the emergence of the rule of law after the collapse of feudalism, as Millar pointed out (*OR*: 286).[29]

Smith, in fact, takes the argument into the camp of the 'militia-men'. Standing armies, he says, have been regarded by 'men of republican principles' as 'dangerous to liberty' (*WN*: 706). (Kames makes precisely that connection (*SHM*: II, 12, 37).) But, he goes on, they can 'in some cases be favourable to liberty'. These 'cases' include toleration of private activity even when that 'approaches to licentiousness' (707). This is admittedly qualified. It only applies in those circumstances where the chief officers in the army are drawn from the 'principal nobility and gentry', who have, in consequence, the 'greatest interest in the support of the civil authority' (706).

Yet what of the decline in martial virtue? As we saw in the last subsection, this was identified by Smith as a consequence of the division of labour. Smith regards the loss of this virtue or of the 'martial spirit' as a threat to a nation's security (787). The further message of the '45 was that the initial success of those naked Highlanders was because the 'unwarlike' inhabitants did not oppose them (*LJ*: 541). For these reasons the sickly condition of martial virtue (like the linked cases of intellectual and social virtue) deserves the 'serious attention of government' (*Ibid.*). If nothing else, the presence of a martial spirit would diminish the dangers to liberty ('whether real or imaginary') associated with a standing army and, at any rate, would require a less extensive (and thus less expensive) army.[30]

Quite what Smith does recommend the government to do is unclear (Donald Winch refers in this context to Smith's characteristic ambivalence (1978: 112)). He refers to the military exercises that the Greeks and Romans made the citizens perform (cf. Kames *SHM*: II, 20). But though he says these will decay with the progress of improvement 'unless government takes proper pains to support [them]' (786) he does *not* say (*pace* Robertson 1985: 216) that they should be made a compulsory part of public education (cf. Sher 1989: 285) – something Ferguson did seemingly advocate (see his unpublished *Essays* no. 15). What is certain is that Smith had earlier commented, referring explicitly to an 'industrious and wealthy nation', that to 'enforce the practice of military exercises' would require 'a very vigorous police' in the face of the 'interest, genius and inclinations of the people' (698). And in the later context he refers again to the 'continual and painful attention of government' that would be needed to maintain a militia (787). Millar puts the point succinctly when he notes that the difficulty of enforcing militias is 'sufficient evidence that they are adverse to the spirit of the times' (*HV*: IV, 189).³¹ (Even Ferguson in his pamphlet is conscious that 'to renew the habits of military men' would take time in an era of commercial manners (*Reflections*: 4).) *Perhaps* Smith puts his faith in indirect government measures. Government will 'support' the cultivation of the martial spirit by providing facilities and awarding 'prizes' for involvement (or making participation a condition of entry into the professions). A tincture of support for this speculation comes from the fact that it is immediately after the provision of such measures to combat the decline in intellectual/social virtues that Smith proceeds to discuss the practice of the Greeks and Romans.

vii) Public Credit

There is one final brushstroke to add to the chiaroscuro of commercial society. To the 'republicans' the sheer fickleness and illusory character of trade and exchange reached its acme in credit. The granting and foreclosing of credit was proof positive of the fragility of commercial society, of its flimsy foundations. It is some testament to the depth of the doubts raised by this issue that perhaps the two most prominent supporters of commerce – Hume and Smith – both express unease where public credit or debt is at stake.

For Hume public debt is a modern expedient. The ploy was to mortgage public revenues while trusting that posterity will pay off the debt. But, of course, the immediate 'posterity' will merely 'pass the buck' on to their successors and they to theirs, with the consequence that the expedient will lead to the accumulation of debt and eventual ruin (*E–PC*: 350 cf. Ferguson *ECS*: 234). In contrast to this 'ruinous' expenditure, ancient practice was to hoard treasure in peace-time in order to conquer or defend in time of war. This is Hume's opening point in his essay, and it shapes the ensuing argument. In particular it colours his declaration that 'either the nation must destroy public credit or public credit will destroy the nation' (360–1). National destruction follows from the abuses of mortgaging. These abuses 'almost infallibly' produce 'poverty, impotence and subjection to foreign powers' (351). The nation will become overburdened with taxes and eventually not enough will be raised to meet requirements. If the government is now confronted with an emergency then, acting like an absolute ruler (cf. *E–CL*: 96), it will seize the monies earmarked for interest repayment. Though it will swear to replace them, this abrogation of 'public faith' will bring the 'tottering fabric' to the ground. This scenario Hume calls 'the natural death of public credit' (*E–PC*: 363). But an even worse scenario is possible. This recourse to voluntary bankruptcy runs too much against the grain of 'popular government' (cf. *E–CL*: 96) with the result that no resources are left and the nation is easy meat for an external conqueror. This is the 'violent death of our public credit' (365). This conclusion brings his essay full circle since, as we noted, it opened by contrasting favourably the ancient practice of hoarding in order to be ready for war with the modern practice of borrowing.³²

For Hume commerce 'can never flourish but in a free government' (*E–CL*: 92) but, as we have now just seen, this combination of factors facilitates the contraction of public debt which eventually threatens the very survival of the state. This is a chain of events that produces an outcome scarcely envisaged by those who initiated the proceedings. Understood in this way, the operation of a system of public credit exemplifies the phenomenon of 'unintended consequences'.[33] It is this aspect of public credit in Smith's account that I want to highlight (see Chapter 2 p. 46).

Like Hume, Smith contrasts ancient and modern practice. In commercial nations the availability and attractive quality of luxury goods means that in peace funds are spent not hoarded. As a result, in time of war, in order to meet the extra costs there is a need to borrow revenue and contract debt (*WN*: 909). (Millar repeated the story (*HV*: III, 482).) But the operation of the 'moral cause' that produces this need also produces the means to meet it, that is, the presence of merchants and manufacturers with the wherewithal to lend (910 cf. Steuart *PPE*: I, 182). Given the regular administration of justice that commercial societies enjoy, then these merchants will have sufficient trust and confidence in the government to give credit. Since the government is in dire straits then the terms of the loan will be attractive (cf. *LJ*: 536). But since the government can now foresee a source of revenues it 'dispenses itself from the duty of saving' (*WN*: 911). A chain is set in motion which produces those 'enormous debts which at present oppress and will in the long run probably ruin all the great nations of Europe' (*Ibid.*). Smith proceeds at some length to itemise the various devices by which the debt is funded. Despite the ingenuity thereby shown, bankruptcy, when the revenues are insufficient to pay off the interest, let alone the capital, on past loans, is the ultimate consequence. This, Smith notes, is often 'disguised' by 'raising the denomination of the coin' (929). This only aggravates the situation and extends the 'calamity' to more innocent people. Smith thinks it 'vain to expect' the public debt ever to be paid back. At best it can be reduced by increasing public revenues (including tax from the colonies) and/or reducing public expenditure (933).

Smith's language is more temperate than Hume's (cf. Winch 1978: 135) and he is more inclined to regard indebtedness as a fact of commercial life, even if it is one that we would ideally be better off without. As we noted in Chapter 2, this entire episode illustrates how the unintended consequences of the emergence of commercial markets are not only beneficial in destroying feudal power and instigating the rule of law but also harmful in threatening via debt the ruin of the society that emerged in that manner.[34] There is no necessarily benign (Providential) outcome from human actions.

D: Conclusion

This has been a long and complex chapter. Both its length and complexity seem warranted in the light of the central place that the understanding of commercial society plays in the Scots' social theory. These adjectives also make a detailed summation impractical. Instead I wish here to make only two points of a general nature.

The first is that, despite their uncertainties, the Scots do think of commerce as creating or constituting a 'society', a distinctive interlocking set of institutions, behaviours and values. It is not that commerce itself is novel. Schooled in the classics as they all were, the Scots knew full well that there were antecedents in Athens or Phoenicia or Carthage. Yet they also knew that the 'modern' world was different. Here is where 'commerce' as a 'fourth stage' comes into play. It performs two roles.

Whereas in the past there was always a Sparta to counter Athens, or Rome to counter Carthage, in the contemporary world the stadial thesis firstly reveals there is no counter. All that there is are inferior 'savage' societies or unprepossessing 'empires' like the Chinese. Second, just as the other stages had their own institutional structure so too does a commercial society. It has its own mode of property and pattern of power relationships; it possesses a distinctive set of manners and upholds a particular code of moral conduct. Given that it is one of fundamental tenets of the Scots' social theory that humans are social and socialisation is a powerful force, then this configuration of institutions is bound to produce a distinctive *mentalité*. It is precisely because the Scots do see 'commerce' as capable of generating and sustaining a form of social life that their analysis is historically so important. This suggests a further observation. Commerce is not simply just another category. Its very centrality to the Scots' enquiry prompts the thought that the other, 'earlier', stages are understood in its light. It is because property, for example, is so important in commercial society that it is presumed to be similarly significant in the other stages.

Yet – and this is the second of my points – being able to develop a conception of commercial *society* does not mean that the actual conceptualisation is uniform and free from tensions. Indeed much of the content of this chapter should have conveyed that message. To repeat my opening imagery, we are looking at shifting points on a scale not polarities. Not only does this apply between different social theorists but also to any particular theorist himself. Hence, for instance, to identify Ferguson as a supporter of 'ancient' and Smith as a supporter of 'modern' liberty is I hope an illuminating way of coming to grips with aspects of their thought. But these are truly only 'aspects'. In no way does this identification make problematic the fact that Ferguson thought slavery morally wrong or that Smith genuinely thought cowardice unbecoming in a real man.

The Scots' theorising of commercial society was theorising about their own society, indeed about themselves. If there is any truth in Hegel's flight of fancy that the owl of Minerva (wisdom) only takes wing at dusk (after the event) then we should not perhaps expect them to come up with neat cut-and-dried answers. Nor, unless we are indeed Hegelians, should we pretend that our post-facto wisdom necessarily enables us to see clearly what was murky at the time. To produce an interpretation that resulted in sharp, clean lines with no blurred edges would be, despite itself, a distortion.

One point that has been clear is that the Scots' analysis of commercial society was no antiseptic value-free enquiry. In the next chapter we examine the various aspects of their analysis of values in their own right.

Notes

1. Cf. Dunbar *EHM*: 423, Ferguson *PMPS*: II, 424, Millar *HV*: IV,154/*HVL*: 381. Steuart also uses the example (*PPE*: I, 158) and though this predates *WN*, Smith had used the pin example in the 'Early Draft' of the early 1760s (in *LJ*: 564). The entry *Epingle* in the *Encyclopédie* was by Deleyre (see Lough 1971: 48).
2. This polemic is central to what Forbes' labels 'scientific whiggism'. This view questioned such 'holy cows of the Whigs' as the justification of the 1688 Revolution, the 'ancient constitution', the wickedness of Stuart kings and (pertinent here) the contrast between English 'liberty' and French 'slavery'. Forbes claims that the philosophical approach involved in 'scientific whiggism' gives 'Hume's thought its unity and continuity' (1975a: 139; cf. Forbes 1975b: 191, 1977: 41). Forbes (1954) had used the label with reference to Smith and Millar and in (1975b) applied it to Smith again.
3. Cf. Phillipson (1989: 59 cf. 50, 65), who argues that Hume regarded absolute, hereditary monarchs as the appropriate way to govern civilised polities. For an explicitly contrary view, see Stewart (1992: 171) and Wootton (1993: 296). Hume himself at one point thought a 'pure monarchy' (akin to the Chinese), which is distinct from an 'absolute' one, would be the 'best of all governments' (*E–AS*: 122n.).
4. Steuart's overall position is more complicated. The governing theme of his account is the supposition that at the head of government is a 'statesman' who will act so as to 'prevent the vicissitudes of manners and innovations, by their natural and immediate effects or consequences from hurting any interest within the commonwealth' (*PPE*: I, 12). See Skinner's (1966) editorial introduction for discussion.
5. Andrew Fletcher of Saltoun, whom we will meet again (n. 30 below), thought that estates should directly employ vagabonds who, if in surplus in one place, should be sold to another estate where there was shortage. Though he denies he is advocating slavery, he says that he is echoing the ancients where their slaves were better provided for than by current governments (*Second Discourse on the Affairs of Scotland [1698]* ed. Daiches (1979): 49–50). Fletcher has been thought a significant figure for the Scottish Enlightenment by Davie (1981) and Phillipson (1981). Hume is emphatic that those who live under arbitrary government are, because of the absence of slavery, still freer than those who lived in the 'most flourishing of ancient times'. Hume cannot forbear from adding (mischievously?) that the loss of slavery is regretted by 'zealous partisans of civil liberty' (*E–PAN*: 383).
6. As Whelan (1985: 5n.) notes, Hume's theory of justice is the only part of his political theory dealt with by 'philosophers' in their comprehensive treatments of his work. For more focused discussion see, in addition to Whelan, Harrison (1981) for a painstaking analytical examination, also Stewart (1963), Mackie (1980) and Miller (1981).
7. The conventions of justice are the effect of mutual agreement, which, when known to the participants, 'produce a suitable resolution and behaviour'. For example, 'two men who pull the oars of a boat do it by agreement or convention though they have never given promises to each other'. And it is through the operation of this same principle that 'gradually' and 'by slow progression' languages are formed and gold becomes the measure of exchange (*THN*: 490). Hume's account has been examined as an exercise in game-theory (e.g. Charron 1980).
8. Ferguson admits that Sparta cannot be re-created, and he is in that sense a more moderate devotee than Rousseau. He does, however, implicitly criticise Hume's treatment (see text below) and admitted in a letter his divergence on that issue (see *Correspondence*: I, 76). That Ferguson regarded Sparta as his 'ideal polity' is claimed by Jack (1989: 151).
9. When discussing the final events of the Roman republic, Ferguson remarks that Cato, Cicero, Brutus and others acted with a 'commendable zeal for liberty' to support their

fellow citizens when, in fact, they were unworthy of it (*Rom*: V, 71). More generally it is a recurrent theme in his *History* that with the relaxation of military and political virtues (which he closely associates – see further below) 'human nature fell into a retrograde motion' (V, 397).

10. Pocock called the *Essay* 'perhaps the most Machiavellian of the Scottish disquisitions on this theme [corruption]' (1975: 429). Cf. McDowell, 'Ferguson's undertanding of virtue was Machiavellian' (1983: 545), also Medick & Batscha (1988: 69).

11. Another striking example of bilingualism is Turnbull. In his Commentary to his translation of Heineccius' standard jurisprudential text (*System of Universal Law*) he sprinkles it with references to, and long quotations from, Harrington's *Oceana* (1656). Harrington was the major representative of seventeenth-century civic humanism (see Pocock's Introduction to his *Political Works* (1977)). Turnbull also upbraids Heineccius for making the common mistake of denigrating Machiavelli, when Machiavelli is for Turnbull an 'excellent politician' to whom Harrington has done justice by showing how he is 'friend of liberty' (*Commentary on Heineccius*: II, 124). On Turnbull in this context, see the passing comment by Miller (1995: 53).

12. This is not fanciful. Burke in his 'Speech on American Taxation' (1774) declaims '... the great and masculine virtues, constancy, gravity, magnanimity, fortitude, fidelity and firmness' (*Works* 1889: I, 427).

13. Hirschman (1977: 64) calls it the doctrine of 'the *doux* commerce' and sees Montesquieu as its most influential exponent (see *SL*: Bk 20, Chs. 1 and 2).

14. In *PPE* Bk I, Ch. 6 Steuart defines luxury 'in a political sense' where it is a 'principle which produces employment and gives bread to those who supply the demands of the rich' (I, 44n.). As such, he says, it produces 'good effects'. But in this same note he is at pains to dissociate this discussion from the 'doctrine of morals'. Much later in the book (Bk II, Ch. 20) he devotes a chapter to 'Luxury', where he supplies a list of stipulative definitions. He distinguishes luxury from sensuality and from excess. The point of his terminological manoeuvrings is that he is able to defend luxury (as above) without committing himself to upholding the desirability of either excess or sensuality; hence, 'luxury consists in providing the objects of sensuality so far as they are superfluous. Sensuality consists in the actual enjoyment of them and excess implies the abuse of enjoyment.' And by providing these 'objects' 'luxury' encourages 'emulation, industry and agriculture' (I, 266).

15. Cf. Dwyer and Murdoch (1983: 231). The quotation comes from the *Caledonian Mercury* (1764).

16. See his sermon 'On Luxury and Licentiousness' in *Sermons*: IV, 114. Blair's sermons were praised by the editor of the *Caledonian Mercury* (cf. Dwyer 1987: 15).

17. Cf. West (1975), Rosenberg (1965), Werhane (1991). For an antidote see Winch (1978).

18. Cf. *LJ*: 540, where he writes that 'another bad effect of commerce is that it sinks the courage of mankind and tends to extinguish martial spirit' (this 'effect' is caused by the division of labour). Hirschman (1977: 106) quotes this passage and announces that on its strength Smith is 'totally espousing the classical "republican view"'. This is to take the quotation out of context. Smith is here listing and not, as such, endorsing the 'inconveniences' of commerce as part of a general assessment of the 'influence of commerce on the manners of a people'. Others who detect civic humanism in Smith include (in a qualified way) Robertson (1983) and McNally (1988). Winch (1978), influenced by Pocock, casts much of his exposition in these terms, but his later essay (1983) makes clear the limits of this interpretation. A critique of the interpretation that focuses on Winch (1978) and which argues that Smith's 'liberal four-stage theory' sets him apart from the civic humanists (who, however, are thought to include Millar) is given by Harpham (1984). (Winch (1988) includes a reply which accuses Harpham of a 'blatant misreading' (88).) For a more extended discussion of these issues in Smith, see Berry (1994: Ch. 6).

19. Cf. West (1969,1975), Lamb (1973), Werhane (1991). Once again Winch (1978) is salutary.

20. Smith is against wholly public funding because it will encourage the teacher to 'neglect his business' (785); a maxim Smith extended to university education (760–1) comparing, implicitly, Scottish practice favourably with, explicitly, the Oxford system (see also *Corr*: 178).

21. Cf. Medick and Leppert-Fögen (1974: 31), although they support the presence of '*die Zweiklassentheorie*' with quotations from the *Letters of Sydney* (of which Millar's authorship is uncertain – see Haakonssen 1985: 42n.). This theory also in their view coexists with '*einer soziologische Dreiklassentheorie*' (i.e. based on rent, profit, wages as in Smith), which, to them, is further support for their interpretation of Millar as a theorist of the petty-bourgeoisie (34,47 et passim). See Chapter 8.

22. In some unpublished papers Ferguson uses Smithian language to make the same point – the master directs, while the artisan remains 'in some measure of torpor' (*Essays* in Edinburgh University Library (MS Dc1) no. 15). This essay has been published in Amoh (1989).

23. Cf. Brewer (1987, 1989), who sees Ferguson's civic humanism interfering with his sociology; Benton (1990), who reads Ferguson as a critic of 'enterprise culture'; McDowell (1983), who refers to Ferguson, foreshadowing Marx, sketching 'a vivid scene of class oppression' (543) or, like Tocqueville, seeing the 'potential hazards of the materialistic hedonism generated by the spirit of commerce' (537). Even Duncan Forbes (1967: 46) declares (originally in a radio broadcast) that in Ferguson can be discerned 'the first clear announcement of one of the most explosive themes in the history of modern thought; the idea of alienation'.

24. Cf. *ECS*: 260, 'we misapply our compassion in pitying the poor; it were much more justly applied to the rich who become the first victims of that wretched insignificance into which the members of every corrupted state … are in haste to plunge themselves'. In particular the rich cease to possess 'courage and elevation of mind' and in the 'absence of every manly occupation' they 'fly from every scene in which any efforts of vigour are required' (259–60).

25. In that pamphlet the link with the division of labour is also clear (*Reflections*: 12). Ferguson is also the author of another (anonymous) pamphlet *Sister Peg*, although this has been claimed for Hume (cf. Rayner 1982), but this seems unwarranted and is not proven.

26. Ferguson wrote to Smith after reading the *Wealth of Nations* and said that he supported him in much but opposed him over the militia (*Corr*: 193–4). The relationship between Smith and Ferguson on this issue is discussed by Sher (1989), who concludes they disagreed 'fundamentally' (208). See also Mizuta (1981).

27. Although true of modern armies, this general message applies in earlier times. Smith picks up the example of Rome and Carthage but focuses rather on the Second Punic War (Ferguson quoted above was referring to the First Punic War). The standing army of Hannibal and Hasdrubal was superior to the Roman militia, and the eventual success of the latter was due to its sheer permanence in the field so that it took on the character of a professional army (*WN*: 703). Ferguson judged this same development a sign of Roman corruption.

28. This is not to deny that Hume nonetheless had some sympathy with militias and some antipathy to standing armies, see Forbes 1975a: 212. Robertson also makes this point but he places too much emphasis on Hume's essay 'Idea of a Perfect Commonwealth' and strives too strenuously to locate Hume in a 'transformed' civic humanist tradition (1985: 70ff. cf. also 1983). That Hume should be disentangled from that tradition is an important theme in Stewart (1992).

29. Although on the Continent the use of mercenaries was associated with the rise of despotical government (Louis XIII and Philip II), in England this did not occur, despite

the pretensions of James I and Charles I. Millar's explanation for this difference is the role of the navy since, unlike a land army, it was less suited to act as a tool of the Court (*HV*: III, 119–20).

30. The attempt to marry the benefits of a standing army and a militia was the hinge of Kames' elaborate plan for a militia, to which end he devoted an entire Sketch (Bk II, Sk. 9). There would be periodic conscription so that everyone was bound to serve in the army. This would not only instil discipline (especially in persons of 'figure and fortune' since a military life is a cure for the diseases of vanity, profligacy and opulence) but also still allow manufacture to be kept up (Kames admits that it permits a country to be powerful). He refers to Fletcher of Saltoun's plan. Fletcher in typical 'republican' fashion praised militias as the 'true badges of liberty' and as a 'school of virtue' (*Discourse of Government with relation to Militias* (1698) in *Selected Writings* ed. Daiches: 19, 24).

31. Millar was more sanguine than even Smith at the prospect of the martial spirit declining as the arts progress. While he accepts the association between timidity and wealth (as manifest in the reluctance of the English to fight the Jacobites in the '45) he argues that there are limits to this, viz. a merchant would be valorous in defence of his property should any government aim at its destruction (*HV*: IV, 200).

32. This aspect of the argument is stressed by Hont (1993) in explicit contrast to Pocock's (1985: 132) interpretation where Hume is seen as condemning public credit as the agent of a commercial society's self-destruction. Pocock for his part was querying Forbes. Forbes (1975a: 174) had also stressed the foreign affairs aspect and used it to challenge the interpretation of Giarrizzo (1962) that this Essay signals Hume's increasing Toryism. Hont (346n.) thinks Forbes 'demolished' Giarrizzo's thesis.

33. Cf. Steuart, who, in a flight of fancy, depicted public credit as a 'most formidable monster striking terror into those who cherished it in its infancy' (*PPE*: I, 181).

34. Millar notes that the public debt could be a source of Crown patronage and dependency (cf. Pocock 1985: 132) but also thinks that this is counterbalanced by the independence that is spread by the extension of commerce (*HV*: IV, essay II ('Political consequences of the [1688] Revolution')).

7

Social Values

Whether applauding the rule of law or lamenting the dismemberment of human character, the Scots were not neutral about commercial society. And since that 'state of society' was deemed superior to earlier states then value-judgements may fairly be said to pervade the range of their social theory. This is only to be expected. The conviction that 'social science' should be 'value-free' is a twentieth-century preoccupation (even though Hume is often identified as a major source of that conviction[1]). In earlier centuries the notion of value-freedom would have seemed bizarre. For the Greeks their central concern was: 'how to live well'; for the Christians it was: 'know yourself as sinner and seek salvation in Christ' and for 'scientists' like Hobbes it was: 'heed the consequences of a failure to accept authority'. The Enlightenment marks no break in this. It was the leitmotif of Gladys Bryson's pioneering book that the Scots' social enquiry was a branch of moral philosophy. This chapter explores that motif. Taking the notion of 'social values' as an umbrella-concept, we can, under its shade, link together three areas of concern – morals, religion and taste.

A: Moral Theory

i) Context

Leaving aside the specific treatments of Hume and Reid's epistemology and of Smith's economics, the Scots' moral theory is perhaps the most studied aspect of their thought. In keeping with my agenda I shall be selective. This selectiveness can be justified crudely by a page count. Millar's remarks in moral theory are few and undeveloped. Ferguson in his *Essay* only devotes one perfunctory chapter to it, and even in his other works any moral theory is basically a digest of the views of others. Robertson, Stuart and Dunbar are essentially silent on this question. Of the remainder Smith and Hume, followed by Kames, have most to say and it is on their theorising that this section will concentrate. However, Francis Hutcheson, who has made only an intermittent appearance in the earlier chapters, will here receive a more sustained, if still brief, exposition. The touchstone throughout will be the relationship between the moral and social theory.

The key question for the Scots is: how do I know what is the morally right thing to do? The emphasis here is on *know*. The Scots are empiricists, and just as it is necessary to consult experience, the evidence, in order to know about society so experience is the baseline when moral issues are at stake. It follows that any account of morality that discounts experience is to be rejected. The alternative to empiricism was rationalism, here meaning the view that reason was the proper source and instrument of moral knowledge such that, for example, it could discern moral properties or relations in the same way that it discerns geometric relations. All the Scots dismiss rationalism thus understood.

This was a live issue since there were rationalists to be confuted. Hume in particular confronts them head on, as does Smith in his survey of systems of moral philosophy. They are both unequivocal; for Hume ' 'tis impossible that the distinction between moral good and evil can be made by reason' (*THN*: 462) and for Smith 'it is altogether absurd and unintelligible to suppose that the first perceptions of right and wrong can be derived from reason' (*TMS*: 320). Their forthrightness is echoed by Kames (*PMNR*: 100), even though, as we shall see, he is in turn critical of the alternatives put forward by both Hume and Smith.

The rationalists and empiricists agreed on one point, however. For both, morality and theology are distinguishable, even if connected. As Balguy, a typical rationalist, put it, 'the Divine will itself is certainly subject to the original Law or Rule of Action' so that the obligation to 'act conformably to Reason' is superior to acting in conformity with God's will (*The Foundation of Moral Goodness* [1728] in *SB*: II, 76). The Scots agreed with the implication of this. They, too, deny that some reference to God's will as manifest in Scripture is sufficient to determine moral duties. This is not to deny God a role, as we will see in the next section, but it does signal a significant break from Calvinist scripturalism (cf. Emerson 1989: 79). This break was evident to their orthodox compatriots who criticised them for assimilating morality to social politeness rather than Divine law.[2]

While the Scots' empiricism can thus distance them from rationalism as well as from any monopoly of virtue claimed by Christianity (since many societies function with recognisably moral norms without benefit of the Word), it itself provided no clear-cut moral theory. Indeed so open was it that much of the actual argument was 'in house', so to speak: what did the evidence of human moral experience actually establish? This question was not merely 'live', it was lively. This added vitality stemmed from the powerful provocation of two thinkers in particular – Hobbes and Mandeville. These two set the agenda in as much as it is responses to their reading of the 'evidence' that best characterises the Scots' position.

For Hobbes *the* fact about human nature was its egocentricity. Moved by their passions, humans called 'good' what they desired and 'evil' what they hated. But what *I* call good can be what *you* call evil (see *Leviathan*: Ch. 6). Moreover, in the 'state of nature' I have a 'natural right' to what *I* judge I need to preserve myself (which can consistently include a right to your possessions and even your life) (*Lev*: Ch. 14). The consequence Hobbes draws from this is the necessity of an authorised sovereign to establish with appropriate sanctions unequivocal definitions of good and evil (*Lev*: Chs. 16, 17). Contemporaries and successors read this to mean that morality meant no more than forced compliance to a sovereign's edict. Many critics took the rationalist road (e.g. Samuel Clarke) but another route was travelled by Anthony Ashley Cooper, 3rd Earl of Shaftesbury. Shaftesbury thought Hobbes' philosophy, like much 'modern' speculation, rested on a faulty reading of human nature. Humans were not irreducibly self-centred; they also possessed what he called a 'natural moral sense' (*Characteristics*: I, 262). Here Shaftesbury introduced the terminology that the Scots would adopt.

The Scots openly acknowledge their debt to Shaftesbury, but this is mediated by the impact of Mandeville. Like Hobbes but even more openly provocative, Mandeville declared that 'Moral Virtues are the Political Offspring which Flattery begot upon Pride' (*The Fable of the Bees*: I, 51). Mandeville was thought by his contemporaries to be claiming that all upholders of virtue (all right-thinking individuals, in other words) were hypocrites. Certainly he continually pointed out the difference between what humans actually *do* (they *enjoy* the comforts of life) and what they *say* (often in Stoic language) is truly pleasurable (I, 166). Shaftesbury was a frequent target for such jibes. But what was so potentially damaging was Mandeville's claim that Shaftesbury's theory is untrue because it is 'inconsistent with our daily Experience' (I, 324).

Pre-eminent among the defenders of Shaftesbury against Mandeville was Francis Hutcheson (see especially his *Observations on the Fable of the Bees* [1726]). While there is more to Hutcheson than a negative reaction to Mandeville, this context is, nonetheless, central to his own positive moral theory, and that theory is, in its turn, central to all the Scots. This does not mean they agree with him but their own thoughts are shaped by the ways in which they disagree.

ii) Hutcheson and Moral Sense

In the very first sentence of his *An Inquiry concerning Moral Good and Evil* (1725) Hutcheson defines 'moral goodness' as 'our idea of some quality apprehended in actions which procures approbation and love toward the actor, from those who receive no advantage by the action' (*PWD*: 67). In contrast to Hobbes and Mandeville, Hutcheson firmly separates morality from 'advantage' or self-interest.[3] He then proceeds to state that his intention is to seek to discover the 'general foundation there is in Nature' for moral goodness (and moral evil) (*Ibid.*).

He finds this foundation in the moral sense possessed by all humans. This sense he defines as, 'a determination of our minds to receive amiable or disagreeable ideas of actions, when they occur to our observation antecedent to any opinions of advantage or loss to redound to our selves from them' (75). To say this is a 'determination' is to indicate that it is involuntary (it 'occurs to us independent on our will' (71cf. *Essay on Passions* [1728]: 4)). One of his examples neatly captures what is at stake. He supposes we benefit equally from two men; the first does so 'from delight in our happiness', the second from 'views of self-interest or by constraint'. Although the benefit is the same, Hutcheson declares that we have 'quite different sentiments of them' (*PWD*: 71). That 'difference' is perceived by the moral sense.[4]

Hutcheson believes that this account is not only true to the facts of human experience ('human nature as it is' *PWD*: 129) but also shows up the inadequacies of both the rationalist and egoistic accounts of morality. Against the rationalists he firmly accepts Locke's rejection of innate ideas (*PWD*: 75) and regards reason's operation as 'too slow, too full of doubt and hesitation' to direct our actions (109).

That 'direction' is given by the moral sense and it operates prior 'or previous to reason' (*SB*: I, 116). The argument here is the same as that used by Kames and others to maintain that sociality is instinctive not rational. Hutcheson himself links together benevolence, kindness and 'sociability (see *On Human Nature* tr. p. 137 cf. Turnbull *Discourse upon Moral and Civil Laws*: 275; Turnbull called Hutcheson an 'admirable moralist' (312)). Moreover, he frequently links the moral sense to instinct (see e.g. *SB*: I, 87, 94, 116; *Passions*: 24, *SIMP*: 16 etc.). By contrast he regards reason's role as instrumental; it finds the 'proper means' of promoting public and private good (*SB*: I, 116 cf. 122; *PWD*: 135).

But Hutcheson's chief target are the egoistic systems. The whole thrust of his argument is that the principle of self-interest is insufficient to explain the reality of morality. Of course, he does not deny that humans are motivated by self-love. Indeed it is this notion that obstructs universal benevolence (*SB*: I, 97), and it is, more generally, mistaken self-love that is the source of the corruption of manners (I, 143) and vice (*PWD*: 84). (Hutcheson thinks that 'malicious, disinterested hatred' is something that 'human nature seems scarce capable of' (*Ibid.* cf. *Passions*: 108).) Yet this is grist to his mill. Self-love can only be understood as 'obstructing' or 'interfering' with something already supposed, namely, moral conduct (*SB*: I, 97). Time and again he insists on the facts of benevolence; the desire for the public good, the exercise of generosity and other virtues is inexplicable on the assumption that humans are solely motivated by a sense of their own advantage. And if nobody ever did 'love the publick or study the good of others' then 'we could form no idea' of such conduct (I, 133–4). It is consistent with this categorical separation of benevolence from self-interest to hold that acting benevolently is, in fact, in our own interest (cf. Campbell 1982: 169). Hence the passage quoted above (p. 41) where Hutcheson claims that in intending the good of others we 'undesignedly promote our own greatest private Good' (*PWD*: 75 cf. *Illustrations upon the Moral Sense* [1728]: 300).

This affirmation of the reality of moral judgements and behaviour is accepted by all of Hutcheson's Scottish successors. Where they differ, as we shall see, is over the need to invoke a distinct moral sense to justify that reality. Before turning to his successors the use made of 'human nature' in his own account is worth underlining. The moral sense as an attribute of human nature can only do the work required of it by accepting that human nature itself is constant and uniform. It is in virtue of this uniformity that we can show concern for those in distant countries and ages (when it is again plain that we can have no 'interest' in the proceedings). This means that while diversity of moral opinion might well tell against any theory of innate ideas (*SB*: I, 120), it is mute when it comes to the moral sense. Hutcheson's account of infanticide (compare Smith above p. 76) is that it is either a sudden passion that overwhelms benevolence or if it is commonly done then it is done 'under some appearance of benevolence' (I, 121).[5] In either case Hutcheson believes the reality of benevolence is not compromised and the demonstrable fact that infanticide did not result in the destruction of Sparta or Athens means that 'natural affection' was still present (I, 122). Hutcheson also uses this argument to show that the moral sense operates prior to all instruction (*PWD*: 99) but here Hume and Smith withdraw their support.

iii) Hume, Sympathy and Justice

Despite their disagreements, Hume's moral theory occupies the 'space' opened up by Hutcheson. He firmly rejects rationalism and sees the egocentrism of Mandeville as inadequate. However, Mandeville is not the *bête noire* for Hume that he was for Hutcheson.[6] He is explicitly identified, along with Hutcheson, as a pioneer in the 'science of man' (*THN*: xxi). The chief interest of Hume's moral theory for our purposes is how it supports his account of justice. And since this was the topic where Smith most clearly departs from Hume then it is here, too, where his moral theory diverges.

Hume's argument that morality is 'more properly felt than judg'd of' (*THN*: 470) stems definitionally from his basic axioms. Given that all perceptions are either impressions or ideas, then if moral perceptions are not ideas (the province of reason) they must be a feature of sentiment. He then claims that 'every man's experience must convince us' that the impression arising from virtue is 'agreeable' or pleasurable while that from vice is 'uneasy' or painful (*Ibid*. cf. 439, 276). While the agreeable impression that 'arises from' virtue is a given of human nature (an ultimate fact in the science of man that cannot be explained (cf. xxii)) there is nothing similarly given about what gives rise to virtue. Simply to state that all virtues originate in 'nature' is too imprecise (474). More than that it is actually false if 'natural' is taken to mean the operations of physiological/physical causes (like temperature on a sheep's tongue). Crucially for Hume, much of human life is necessarily governed not by knee-jerk reactions but by conventions, rules or artifices, and these are inventions or learned responses (484, 489). The most important of these conventions is justice. For Hume, justice is an artificial virtue (471).

Since without justice society would dissolve (see above p. 130), then the importance of this virtue can hardly be underestimated. Justice (we recall from Chapter 5) arises necessarily from the fact that humans possess only a 'confin'd generosity' and that they are confronted with scarce resources. Hume is here openly accepting that universal benevolence, which was for Hutcheson the summit of moral goodness (cf. *PWD*: 88–9, 100), is contrary to these facts. Yet Hume does *not* accept Hobbes' argument that humans are *only* self-interested, and in many passages he stresses human sociality and its importance (cf. e.g. *THN*: 352, 363, 421, 424). The support for this is 'common experience' since if that is consulted, then the finding is that 'kind affections' outweigh the selfish (487). Such kind affections as meekness, beneficence, charity, generosity, clemency and the like are both *natural* and social virtues (578 cf. *EPM*: 214, *E–OC*: 479). The undeniable evidence of their existence means that Hume is forthright in dismissing the Hobbesian/Mandevillean view that *all* moral distinctions are the product of the 'artifice of politicians' (*EPM*: 214, cf. *THN*: 500, 578). Yet all this granted, these social virtues cannot sustain society. For that task, justice and other artifices are needed. Justice is thus useful, but Hume has to explain why it is also 'virtuous'

and that explanation is needed because, as he admits, it was established out of
self-interest (*THN*: 499).

The closeness of social relationships, characteristic of the early stages of social
development, made it possible to identify directly with others. The consequence
of this proximity was that I could see that my restraint (my observation of the
rules of justice) was reciprocated to all our benefit. This circumstance 'pleases'
and we thus label ('denominate' is Hume's favourite term) this restraint/justice
virtuous. But once society has become more complex, this direct identification
with others is lost. It follows from this that (say) the burglary of a stranger's house
is of no material interest. Nevertheless the facts are that this burglary still displeases
and we still therefore say it is an injustice. But as matters now stand it is hard to
see why. Displeasure is a feeling, but that stranger as a stranger is someone to whom
I am indifferent. There has to be a means whereby the stranger's fate engages my
sentiments. Hume supplies that 'means' through the principle of 'sympathy'.

Hume first introduces 'sympathy' in Book II of the *Treatise*, where it has a
precise, 'technical' meaning (cf. Mercer 1972: 44). Sympathy is the process whereby
an 'idea' is converted into an 'impression' (the difference between these being one
of degree not kind (*THN*: 2)). It is, as Hume affirms, 'an object of the plainest
experience' that the 'idea' in our minds of another's passions is 'converted into
the very impressions' that those passions represent (319). We now feel as they do.
In line with this, the idea we form of the stranger's 'unease' at being burgled is
by sympathy converted into our 'partaking' of that unease. And since 'every thing
which gives uneasiness in human actions upon the general survey is call'd Vice'
then we label the burglary an injustice (499). Correspondingly all actions which
uphold the rules of justice give satisfaction and are labelled virtuous.

Sympathy takes us 'out of ourselves' so that the pleasure or uneasiness of others
is also felt (579). In this way sympathy '*produces* our sentiment of morals' in all
the artificial virtues (577; my emphasis). It is not itself a moral principle. We do
not therefore, unlike Hutcheson, require a direct moral sense to identify the virtue
of justice. For sympathy to achieve this considerable feat it also means that it has
to be a 'very powerful principle of human nature' (618, 577). As a principle of
human nature we know that it will be constant and uniform in operation. This is
why we are justified (as 'in any other matter of fact' (319)) in causally inferring
from the observation of another's behaviour that they are experiencing certain
passions (the burgled stranger's anger and grief, for example).[7]

The very technicality of Hume's account rendered it vulnerable. Kames, for
example, in direct rebuttal, thinks sympathy alone too weak a principle 'to control
our irregular appetites and passions' (*PMNR*: 39–40 cf. *SB*: II, 308[8]). A 'more
solid foundation' is needed. This Kames finds in the moral sense. In Kames'
version, this sense is the means by which 'we perceive some actions as being fit,
right and meet to be done and others as being unfit, unmeet and wrong' (40/II,
308). Kames also finds fault with Hutcheson because he reduces all morality to
benevolence (44, 147) and is thus unable to explain why we *have to* be just (41/II,
309).[9] As we noted in Chapter 6 (p. 130), Kames, like Hume, thinks justice

indispensable but unlike Hume he believes a sense of justice 'belongs to man as such' (46/II, 311). This, for Kames, is openly part of a Providential scheme. The very indispensability of justice, when coupled with the facts that humans possess social (see Chapter 2) and hoarding appetites (67/II, 320), means that it is part and parcel of the overall Design.

While Hume rejected this Kamesian gloss, he did in his later discussions of justice drop the references to sympathy. There is no need, he now remarks, for 'abstruse' systems, it is sufficient to accept as a fact the presence in human nature of 'humanity or fellow-feeling' so that no one is indifferent to the happiness or misery of others (*EPM*: 219–20n.). This later vocabulary was commonplace. Ferguson, for example, in the one chapter in the *Essay* ('Of Moral Sentiment') explicitly devoted to 'moral questions', sees in the 'amicable disposition' the foundation of our moral nature as our 'sense of a right' is extended by a 'movement of humanity' to our fellow creatures (*ECS*: 35, 37). In the later systematic *Principles* he states that 'humanity' is the name given to a 'principle of sympathy and indiscriminate concern in the condition of a fellow creature' (*PMPS*: I, 125). Virtually Millar's only reference to moral issues in his published work is his remark that it is 'feelings of humanity' that dispose mankind to abstain from injustice (*HV*: IV, 236/*HVL*: 384).[10] The probable explanation of this similarity is a common root in Cicero and natural jurisprudence (cf. Haakonssen 1990: 314). As Reid made clear in his jurisprudence lectures, that part of practical ethics which concerned the duties that men owe to each other 'as social creatures' falls under the 'general heads of Justice and Humanity' (*Practical Ethics*: 112–13).

While there was a relatively self-contained debate stimulated by Hutcheson's moral epistemology, it was never divorced from wider questions. The relationship between the nature of morality and the nature of society was always close and intimate. Hume on justice exemplifies this, as does Ferguson's linkage between amicability and humanity, but nowhere is this more evident than in Smith.

iv) Smith, Sympathy and the Impartial Spectator

Smith's key principle of sympathy is closer to the later than the earlier Hume since when he first refers to it he stipulates its meaning as 'our fellow-feeling with any passion whatever' (*TMS*: 10). This divergence from the early Hume not unexpectedly follows his disagreement over justice. As we saw in Chapter 6 (p. 132), Smith traces justice to the (approved) natural sentiment of resentment at the injustice suffered by individuals. He does not therefore require Hume's convoluted recourse to sympathy to account for the virtue attached to the artifice of justice.

In outline Smith's argument is as follows.[11] Through our imagination we are able to conceive what we would feel if we were in the situation of another. In this way we can bring 'home to ourselves', though in a necessarily weaker form, the other's sensations (9). It is how *we* would feel that is crucial. Smith stresses that the sympathy comes from our view of the other's situation not from their actual passions (12). He dramatically underlines this by declaring that it is possible to sympathise with the dead! Unlike Hutcheson, to whom sympathy was a 'sort of contagion or infection' (*SIMP*: 14), and also unlike Hume, to whom, too, sympathy was contagious (*E–NC*: 204), Smith's sympathy was not a form of empathy (cf. Campbell 1971: 95). (In this Smith was followed by Beattie (*Elements of Moral Science*: I, 173).)

For Smith it is a fact that 'nothing pleases more than to observe in other men a fellow-feeling with all the emotions of our own breast' (*TMS*: 12). This pleasure, he notes, cannot be explained by those who would derive all our sentiments from self-love. This is all the more significant since it is this fellow-feeling that is the root of moral judgement. If we, as spectators, replicate through sympathy the passions emoted by others in their situation then we approve (16). To give one of Smith's own examples: if I see a grief-stricken stranger and am informed that he has just learnt of his father's death then I, via sympathy, approve of his grief. What makes this possible is that I have learnt from experience that such misfortune excites such sorrow (18). The experience can only come from 'common life', from the fact that humans are social creatures. This sociality is decisive.

Smith illustrates this by likening society to a mirror (110 cf. Hume *THN*: 365). In a passage with strong echoes of Rousseau's *Second Discourse (of Inequality)* he remarks

> Were it possible that a human creature could grow up to manhood in some solitary place, without any communication with his own species, he could no more think of his own character, of the propriety or demerit of his own sentiment and conduct, of the beauty and deformity of his own mind, than of the beauty or deformity of his own face. All these objects which he cannot easily see, which naturally he does not look at, and with regard to which he is provided with no mirror which can present them to his view. Bring him into society and he is immediately provided with the mirror which he wanted before ... and all his own passions will immediately become the causes of new passions. He will observe that mankind approve of some of them and are disgusted by others. He will be elevated in the one case, and cast down in the other; his desires and aversions, his joys and sorrows, will now often become the causes of new desires and new aversions, new joys and new sorrows: they will now, therefore, interest him deeply, and often call upon his most attentive consideration. (110–11)

It is this responsiveness to others – pleasure in their approval, pain in their disapproval – that Smith used to explain why the rich parade their wealth while the poor hide their poverty. The rich value their possessions more for the esteem they bring than any utility (51). And not only, as we saw in Chapter 5 (p. 102), was this disposition to 'go along with the passions of the rich and powerful' the foundation for rank distinctions (52) but the desire to attain that enviable state was the incentive to better our condition (50 cf. 183). By closely linking morality with sociality and socialisation, Smith's theory was at odds with that offered by both Hutcheson and Kames. This divergence was even more marked, as we shall see, when Smith comes to discuss conscience. But we need, first, to explain more precisely how Smith's own theory is supposed to work.

It is a given fact of human nature that a spectator's sympathetic emotions are less intense than those of the party observed (the actor). It is equally a fact that the actor wishes the spectator's sympathy. In response to these facts the actor, in order to induce 'harmony and concord' between his emotions and those of the spectator, 'lowers his passion to that pitch in which the spectators are capable of going along with him' (22). This has direct bearing on Smith's analysis of commercial society. As we saw in Chapter 6 the very complexity of that society meant that the bulk of inter-personal dealings were with strangers. It was also the defining feature of that society that there everyone was a merchant with the result that concord rested on justice rather than benevolence. Smith's account of sympathy serves to explain how this is achieved.

In an argument reminiscent of Hume, he supposes that in earlier simpler ages, where dealings with family and friends dominate, plenty of sympathy will be forthcoming. Given this, then less effort is needed to 'tone down' the emotions. Strangers, however, are less obliging (23) and much greater effort is required. This effort serves to strengthen character and enables the actor to attain to a greater degree than is possible in more intimate times the virtue of self-command (146). This individual is (in general terms) able to act 'according to the dictates of prudence, justice and proper beneficence' (241). Not only is adherence to the 'sacred rules of justice' – the foundation of a commercial society – made possible but the distinctively commercial virtues of 'industry and frugality' (242) flourish.

The habitual effect of living among strangers is that individuals identify themselves (almost) with the 'impartial spectator' (147). The 'impartial spectator' is another vital brick in the wall. The emphasis upon morality as learnt seems to entail a conflation of social conformity and ethical standards. We met this concern in Chapter 4 (p. 75). Smith, however, denies that his account of morality precludes criticism. We covered his argument against cultural and ethical relativism in the earlier chapter, here we need to focus on intra-social assessment.

Another of the facts that Smith attributes to human nature is that humans wish 'not only to be loved but to be lovely ... not only praise but praiseworthiness' (113–14). One consequence of this is that we are pleased with having acted in a praiseworthy manner even if nobody praises us. We do not, therefore, rely on actual praise or blame but seek to act in such a way that an 'impartial spectator' would approve of our conduct (116). This spectator is an internalised standard of rectitude – he is 'the man within the breast, the great judge and arbiter' (130) whose jurisdiction covers the desire for praiseworthiness and blameworthiness (131). It is 'only by consulting this judge' that we can ever get a proper evaluative distance on our actions (134). Every man, he says later, is able to form gradually from his own 'observations upon the character and conduct of both himself and other people' an idea of 'exact propriety and perfection' (247). In other words, we are all able, though to varying degrees, to establish an ideal or benchmark. By implicit extension this benchmark, in principle, enables us to obtain a distance on social practices. Individuals and institutions can be judged as, for example, too heavily swayed by praise and insufficiently attentive to the praiseworthiness of their endeavours. Hence the criticism of the court of Louis XIV for making that monarch's mediocre talents and virtues estimable and conversely for causing 'knowledge, industry, valour and beneficence' to lose respect (54).

This same scope for criticism can be applied closer to home. Not only can contemporary politicians be found wanting but we can also detect here the grounds of Smith's concern for the 'virtues' of pin-makers. We noted in Chapter 6 (p. 144) that those whose lives were spent performing a 'few simple operations' were rendered incapable of 'any just judgment' about even the duties of their 'private life' (WN: 782). The 'morality' into which they are socialised is defective; the 'mirror' in which they see themselves reflects back to them to their 'mutilated' condition. The all-enveloping nature of their shared work experience means a lack of distance and the weakening of the impartial spectator's jurisdiction. Their self-command is attenuated and they are prey to enthusiasm and superstition (788).[12] Such at any rate is the probable course of events unless 'the public' takes remedial steps. Here we can see Smith's social and moral theory meshing to support his policy prescriptions.

v) Conscience

As an 'inhabitant of the breast' the impartial spectator is explicitly identified by Smith with the principle of conscience (TMS: 130, 137).[13] For Smith the authority possessed by conscience is the effect of 'habit and experience' (135). The fact that it is habitual, so that 'we are scarce sensible' that we do appeal to it, means that it is a learnt resource. (Although, as we have just seen, that does not mean that it is a mere reflex of prevalent social norms (cf. Raphael 1975: 90, Hope 1989: 105).[14]) This sharply distinguishes his account from Hutcheson and Kames.

Whereas Smith had linked morality with learnt behaviour Hutcheson had stressed that the very universality of the moral sense meant that it was 'antecedent to all instruction' (PWD: 99). This difference is symptomatic of Smith's wider divergence. He openly assessed Hutcheson in his review of moral theories or systems. In this review Hutcheson is identified as the advocate of the view that there is a 'peculiar' sentiment or 'particular power of perception' – the moral sense – that is the foundation of approbation (TMS: 321). Smith makes three criticisms. Hutcheson can neither explain why we approve of both tenderness and daring, though the sentiments in these two cases are different, nor why it is that this supposed universal sense has been so little noticed that it has no name in any language (324–6). Third, it is superfluous. There is no need to invoke a special sense since – and this is as we have seen the nub of Smith's own account – the agreement of sentiments between spectators and actors is sufficient to produce the judgement of approval.

Kames, for his part, openly criticises Smith's theory. He fastens on to the role given to imagination. He doubts that it will 'raise' the passion of the spectator (PMNR: 110). He alleges only a few will be able to make moral judgements because only a few will have sufficiently developed their imaginative capacities so as to be able to sympathise. Like Hutcheson, Kames invokes the counter-example of children. Children lack imagination (he claims) yet still have sympathy. The force of the example is that it 'shows clearly that sympathy must proceed from some natural principle inherent in all human beings' (111 cf. 47/*SB*: II, 312). As with his assessment of Hume, Kames believes that Smith's reliance on sympathy fails to give morality a sufficiently solid foundation (112).

For Kames himself this foundation lies in our moral sense. This sense is not a principle of action (here he departs from Hutcheson) but a regulator of action (53/II, 313). This 'regulation' can improve, just like other 'powers and faculties' (97). Polished nations are more 'refined' than savages, they are less selfish and more sociable. This is of a piece with Kames' Lockean psychology that we recorded in Chapter 5 (and which we will meet again in the next section). Savages have a moral sense, but it is relatively defective since they are governed by 'their appetites and passions more than by general principles' and have not acquired a 'facility in forming complex ideas and abstract propositions' (94–5).

Kames associates the moral sense-as-regulator with the operation of conscience (43/II, 310 cf. *SHM*: II, 269). In language that has echoes of Smith it is the voice of God within us. But whereas for Smith conscience is the forum of the internalised impartial spectator, for Kames 'it arises from a direct perception' (43/II, 310). In similar fashion, for Reid, conscience (or moral faculty) by which we perceive merit in honesty is not 'the effect of education or acquired habits' (*AP*: 662 cf. Beattie *Elements*: II, 57). In Reid, as in Kames though even more so, the proper comprehension of morality is inseparable from a just acknowledgement of the place of man in God's creation.

B: Religion

In at least all Christian cultures the link between religion and morals is close without being precise. One of the hallmarks of the Enlightenment was to challenge the link itself. The Scottish Enlightenment was not exempt, even though, with the exception of Hume, it was not as openly confrontational as in France. In part this quieter, more eirenic, stance can be put down to the close institutional links between the Kirk and many members of the literati (see Chapter 1 (Biv)). Nevertheless, as is apparent from the internal opposition to the Moderates (the 'enlightened party'), they were still judged to be dangerously heterodox.

Their moral theorising was one element of this alleged heterodoxy since the various arguments that located the basis of moral judgement in a moral sense or sentiment supposed that morality could have a footing independent of revealed Truth. Hutcheson was accused by the presbytery of Glasgow with heresy – for contravening the Westminister Confession [15] – and had to be acquitted publicly. Hutcheson, of course, was no atheist. It was a fundamental and constitutive part of his philosophy that his naturalism (that humans possess naturally a moral sense) supposed a Divine schema; humans would, he believed, through use of their natural faculties come necessarily to the 'knowledge and love of the Deity' (*Illustrations on the Moral Sense*: 328 cf. *SIMP*: 75).

While making all due allowances for nuance, this is the standard view across the Enlightenment. Ferguson is typical when he argues that the foundation of the difference between right and wrong does not rest directly or immediately on Divine will because it pleased God that the first intimations of His will should be declared 'by means of the order established in His works' (*PMPS*: I, 166–7). While Christian revelation in this way loses much of its prerogative, there remains a justified conviction that the universe is so orderly, so evidently 'designed', that it must be the product of an informing, superintending Intelligence. This meant that, unlike the nineteenth-century confrontations between 'science' and 'religion', in the Enlightenment increases in scientific knowledge and understanding were thought to demonstrate the perfection of the Design ever more clearly and conclusively. Good scientists were true believers, as Newton demonstrated beyond any shadow of doubt (cf. Gregory *CV*: 248). Denials of Design were very few and far between. Of these 'few' the most subversive of all is Hume. I shall touch on this subversion (see subsection iv below) but in keeping with the focus of this study, my chief concern is with the Scots' understanding of religion as a social institution.

i) The Natural History of Religion

Hume published a lengthy essay with that title in 1757. Since Dugald Stewart had used the term 'natural history' as a synonym for 'conjectural history' and had cited Hume as an exponent (see Chapter 3) then we can reasonably expect this essay to exhibit the characteristic traits of that genre. This is borne out by Hume's explicit aim in the essay; it is, he says, an enquiry into the origin of religion in human nature.

While 'in all places and in all ages' the belief in an 'invisible intelligent power' has been 'very generally diffused' it has not been so universal that there are no exceptions (*NHR*: 31). Moreover, where such a belief is found it is rarely the same across the places and ages. This lack of both universality and convergence prompts Hume's first conclusion. Religion, unlike 'self-love, affection between the sexes' and the like, is not the product of an 'original instinct or primary impression of nature'. It follows from this that 'the first religious principles must be secondary' (*Ibid.*). Kames, whose own natural history is a useful foil to Hume's, disagrees. On Kames' reading of the evidence, the belief that there exist beings 'powerful above the human race' is universal (*SHM*: II, 377 cf. Ferguson *IMP*: 120, Gregory *CV*: 243). He allows that there are travellers' tales to the contrary but, unlike Hume, who accepts them, he discounts them. Kames' reasoning is that these travellers are illiterate (see above p. 62) and that the savages lack the linguistic resources to refer to these (abstract) beings (see above p. 96).

Granted that the belief is indeed universal, Kames proceeds to look for its cause. The very universality and primacy of the belief means that it cannot be put down to 'chance' (II, 378) and Ferguson agrees that it cannot be attributed to 'peculiar circumstances' (*IMP*: 120). This is exactly Hume's position also: to explain the variety of religious beliefs and practices is to identify causes and distinguish them from chance (*NHR*: 54 cf. *E–RA*: 111, see above p. 56). Kames dismisses fear as the cause because it is insufficient and he dismisses reasoning from cause to effect because that is beyond the (un)developed capacities of savages. He concludes that the only explanation for this universal belief in a deity is that 'the image of the Deity must be stamped upon the mind of every human being' (*SHM*: II, 383). Ferguson is much less definite. The universality may be the 'result of human nature' but it may also be the 'suggestion of circumstances that occur in every place and age' (*IMP*: 120). But for Kames (and for Gregory (*CV*: 241)), in a directly analogous fashion to the moral sense, there is in humans an 'internal sense, which may be termed the sense of Deity' (*SHM*: II, 383).[16]

Because Hume thinks the source of religious belief is secondary, he must reject this argument. He agrees with Kames' rejection of this belief as the product of reflection, it is beyond the 'narrow conception' of savages (*NHR*: 42 cf. 39, 40). Instead its origin lies in the passions or 'ordinary affections of human life'. The 'first obscure traces of divinity' emerge from the hopes and, most especially, from the fears of 'barbarians'(39). Whereas Kames' dismissal of the universality of fear rests on its association with intermittent localised events like eclipses and earthquakes (*SHM*: II, 380), Hume is able to assert universality by fastening on to the quotidian fears and anxieties inseparable from human life. Though they differ, Kames and Hume do agree in tracing religion back to human nature. Both the 'difference' and the 'agreement' are significant. Whereas Kames' source implicates Divinity, so that a semblance of orthodoxy can be retained, Hume's source looks human-all-too-human. Yet, since human nature is constant and uniform then this not only provides the 'ingredients' for a 'scientific' causal account but also forms the premise from which a natural history can be written.

While not identical, Hume and Kames tell a basically similar story. Lockean psychology provides the common developmental framework. Religious belief moves from the particular and concrete to the general and abstract. Hence it is no surprise to find Kames referring to the sense of Deity 'ripening' (*SHM*: II, 404 cf. *PMNR*: 340). Hume for his part refers to the 'natural progress of thought' as the 'mind rises gradually from inferior to superior; by abstracting from what is imperfect it forms an idea of perfection' (*NHR*: 34 cf. Robertson *HAm*: 840). This shared framework produces the agreed position that 'polytheism was and *necessarily must have been* the first and most ancient religion of mankind' (*NHR*: 33, my emphasis; cf. Kames *SHM*: II, 390). This position was widely adopted. It can be found, for example, in Smith (*EPS*: 49), Stuart (*VSE*: 6) and Ferguson (*PMPS*: I, 168).

Hume and Kames divide the development of religious belief into stages. Kames identifies six. After polytheism is a stage – like that of the Greeks – where there is a mix of gods, some superior others inferior, and that is followed by the same mix but now the gods are conceived as invisible powers. The fourth stage is a belief in one supreme benevolent deity with several inferior ones; the fifth stage differs by having only one inferior. Finally 'through a long maze of errors men arrive at true religion, acknowledging but one Being supreme in power, intelligence and benevolence' (*SHM*: II, 404). In Hume, polytheism gives way to theism though he makes a point of noting that a relapse is possible; indeed there is a 'natural tendency' to rise from idolatry and then sink back into it (*NHR*: 62). Hume concludes that the presence of a purpose or design being evident, we are 'naturally if not necessarily' led to conceive of a single undivided intelligence as the author of this design (96). This Deistic view is the one, that is most widely shared in the Enlightenment, the Scots included. Hume however does not join in this consensus. Even in the *Natural History* he remarks that religious principles are just as likely to be as absurd as sublime, so that in his final paragraph he declares that religion is a 'riddle, enigma, an inexplicable mystery' (98).

ii) Ignorance and Belief

Hume defines polytheism as the 'primitive religion of uninstructed mankind' (37). That savages are ignorant is a point made again and again by Hume (cf. e.g. 35, 43, 44; *E–PG*: 61; *E–RA*: 274; EHU: 119). It is because they are ignorant of the connexions between causes and effects (cf. Kames *SHM*: II, 389) that they call upon the immediate action of gods to explain phenomena (especially those that frighten them). This ignorance is attributable to their circumstances. Primitive man is a necessitous creature, pressed by 'numerous wants and passions' (*NHR*: 35). These pressing needs mean a lack of leisure, and that shortcoming means no time to acquire instruction. 'Free' time is required to enable humans to begin the process of tracing causal links (cf. Smith *EPS*: 50). This now fits religious speculation into the broader schema of the development of civilisation. As humans become civilised so 'science and literature' as the 'natural fruit of leisure, tranquillity and affluence' have grown (Millar *HV*: III, 144/*HVL*: 375; *OR*: 176).

By sitting the history of religious belief alongside the history of civilisation it, too, can be plotted on the Lockean graph. But the relationship between these histories and the graph should not be misunderstood. More particularly we should not be tempted to attribute to the Scots a historicist perspective, as some commentators perhaps imply.[17] From that perspective, human nature itself would undergo a change – it is different in different times (and places). It would follow that the differences between a polytheist and a believer in Kames' true religion are more profound than any difference in external circumstances like lack of leisure. There is a close connection between this historicist argument and the cultural relativism discussed in Chapter 4 and the Scots' rejection of the latter is thus pertinent here also.

This last point is worth pursuing because the chase will lead us to a significant argument about the 'vulgar'. Hume explicitly identifies as the 'chief character' that distinguishes a 'civilized age from times of barbarity and ignorance' the former's humanity (*E–RA*: 274). This humanity is the product of the softening of their 'tempers' and is indissolubly linked with knowledge and industry (271 cf. p. 138 above). These are 'sociological' differences and relate only to the 'tempers' and, as Hume had made clear in the *Treatise*, differences in the 'tempers and complexions' of men are 'very inconsiderable' (*THN*: 281). Perhaps the clearest expression of the non-historicist cast of the Scots' thought is their attitude towards the 'vulgar'.

The vulgar and the ignorant are one and the same (Hume *E–AS*: 111). Hence, for Hume, the polytheist is not only uninstructed but 'vulgar' (*NHR*: 51 cf. 60, 63). The vulgar are those who go by first appearances and are to be contrasted with the 'wise' or 'philosophers' (*EHU*: 86, *THN*: 150). Kames in the Preface to the *Law Tracts* says the vulgar, unlike 'readers of solid judgment', relish a history of 'singular events', of wars, conquests and the like (*HLT*: iv). The crucial point is that the vulgar are not some historically removed group; they are also with us here and now. Kames is explicit. Immediately after having pronounced in good Lockean language that property without possession is too abstract a conception for a savage (see p. 95 above), he remarks, 'to this day the vulgar can form no distinct conception of property' (*HLT*: 91). There has been no change in human nature. The vulgar of today are akin to the savage in the past in that both are relatively uninstructed. On this basis Hume's remark that the 'vulgar *in nations which have embraced the doctrine of theism* still build it upon irrational and superstitious principles' (*NHR*: 57; my emphasis) makes perfect sense.[18] As he says appositely elsewhere, the 'propensity of mankind toward the marvellous', though it may 'receive a check from sense and learning can never be thoroughly extirpated from human nature' (*EHU*: 119). What makes this so apposite is that the context is a discussion of miracles. Before turning to a brief examination of that question superstition, the inseparable bedfellow of ignorance, needs an airing.

iii) Superstition and Priestcraft

For all their differences, the Scots' affiliation to the Enlightenment family is nowhere clearer than in their denunciation of superstition. Voltaire's battle-cry '*écrasez l'infâme*' is echoed, if rather more *sotto voce*. For Hume the true sources of superstition are 'weakness, fear, melancholy together with ignorance' (*E–SE*: 74). And although he labels superstition (along with enthusiasm) as a corruption of 'true religion', he yet remarks that it is 'a considerable ingredient in almost all religions' (75). This means that despite a prevalence of superstition in early ages it is never completely eradicated. He notes – from the evidence of both history and 'daily experience' – that men who are 'endowed with the strongest capacity for business and affairs' have yet lived 'lives crouched under the slavery to the grossest superstition' (*E–Sui*: 578). Kames makes explicit, and here reinforces the argument made earlier (in Bii), that while in 'an age of superstition' men of the 'greatest judgment are infected' in an 'enlightened age, superstition is confined among the vulgar' (*SHM*: II, 417). This is further grist to the Enlightenment mill. There is no opposition between true religion and science; the opposition is rather between superstition and science. Robertson is thus able to declare that true religion 'is the offspring of reason, cherished by science and attains to its highest perfecton in an age of light and improvement' (*India*: 1147).

For Hume superstition is a 'pestilent distemper' and 'false opinion', for which the remedy is 'true philosophy' (*E–Sui*: 579 cf. *E–SE*: 75, *THN*: 271, *EHU*: 12, 16 etc.). True philosophy is provided by the science of man. The philosopher or moral scientist is able to penetrate beneath the 'pretexts and appearances' that deceive the vulgar and uncover 'the uniform and constant principles of human nature' (*EHU*: 85). This is central to Hume's anti-relativism. There is no room for the 'descriptivist' claim (see Chapter 4) that distinct cultures have their own internally authentic and valid 'forms of life'. The Koran is 'a wild and absurd performance' that bestows praise on inhumanity, cruelty, bigotry and more; it is, in short, 'utterly incompatible with a civilized society' (*E–ST*: 229).[19] Moreover, as we have just seen, for Hume most religions contain large doses of superstition – the beliefs of weak and uninstructed minds. Here Hume follows a long tradition which had recently come into prominence in the writings of Toland, Trenchard and other advocates of 'rational religion'.[20]

Hume is not alone here in making this contrast between philosophy and ignorance/superstition. It is, for example, strongly echoed by Smith. His most unequivocal statement occurs in Book 5 of *Wealth of Nations* where he refers to 'science' as the 'great antidote to enthusiasm and superstition' (*WN*: 796).[21] This is stated in the context of his account of the relationship between the State and the religious beliefs and practices of its citizens. As a probationary requirement before entry into a liberal profession Smith advocates the State making 'almost universal among all people of middling or more than middling rank' the 'study of science and philosophy'. This study will render these ranks immune to superstitious poison and given that immunity the inferior ranks will be unlikely to catch the infection. (*Ibid.*).

Smith has a second antidote. The State can allow 'publick diversions', such as drama, poetry, music, dancing and the like. The effect of these will be to lift 'melancholy and gloomy humour'. This lifting of the spirits will dissipate the superstition, enthusiasm and fanaticism that melancholy nurtures. Smith links this melancholy with austere sects whose zealotry tends to make their 'morals' frequently 'disagreeably rigorous and unsocial' (796). The link between 'public spectacles' and support for the social affections had been made also by Kames. He believes these spectacles and amusements by being available to all ranks help counteract the divisiveness of the 'separation of men into different classes by birth, office or occupation' (*EC*: II, 443).

Smith, too, links these melancholic potentially disruptive 'enthusiastic' sects with the division of labour. This link is implicit in his account of the State's role as a provider of remedies to the ailments of extensive division of labour (see above p. 145). Smith paints another of his narrative pictures. He depicts a 'man of low condition' who when he comes into a 'great city' is 'sunk in obscurity and darkness'. We can exploit Smith's use of ocular language to gloss this to mean that he lacks the mirror of society and, in its absence, he is apt to 'abandon himself to every sort of low profligacy and vice' (*WN*: 795). The only place he can gain attention is by joining a small religious sect. Here he finds his mirror. But while his conduct becomes 'remarkably regular and orderly', the very austerity of these sects, as we have seen, makes them a breeding ground of fanaticism.

Smith's general concerns here appear to be motivated by historical sensibilities. European history (not least that of Scotland) bears eloquent testimony to the havoc wrought by religious conflict. A multitude of sects seems the best state of affairs. Their troublesome zeal is only serious when they are few in number, while the very fact of multiplicity might indeed induce 'that pure and rational religion, free from every mixture of absurdity, imposture or fanaticism' (793). Where there is an established religion then to prevent clerics from conspiring against the sovereign's authority it is necessary, for the sake of 'publick tranquillity', that the State should exercise a 'considerable degree' of influence over the 'greater part of the teachers of religion' (797). This 'influence' will be indirect (the hinge appears to be career structure); it will not directly concern the actual 'articles of faith' (798). The dangers of not exercising influence are borne out by the record of the Church of Rome (cf. 802). So it is that in his long discussion of Church–State relations most attention is paid to Catholicism. Not only is this historically justified but it also enables the strongest associations between superstition and priestcraft[22] to be made.

It is in this spirit that we find Robertson in his *History of Scotland* commenting that 'popery is a species of false religion, remarkable for the strong possession it takes of the heart ... and arrived at last to a degree of perfection which no former system of superstition had ever attained' (*HSc*: 93).[23] Similarly forthright or dogmatic (we might well say), is Millar, who proclaims that 'the Roman Catholic religion may be regarded as a deep-laid system of superstition, which took a firmer hold of the human mind than any other that has appeared in the world' (*HV*: III, 134/*HVL*: 341 cf. I, 149). Kames curtly dismisses the Athanasian creed as a 'heap of unintelligible jargon' (*SHM*: II, 432). And Smith himself was equally uncompromising – the Church of Rome was the 'most formidable combination' against 'the liberty, reason and happiness of mankind' (*WN*: 802–3). This antipathy to reason was the corollary of its support for 'the grossest delusions of superstition' (803). It took the improvements of 'arts, manufacture and commerce' (not the 'feeble efforts of human reason') to undermine this power (*Ibid.* cf. Millar *HV*: III, 144/*HVL*: 375; II, 474). That is, the same forces that broke the power of the feudal lords also destroyed the clergy, who were of course great landowners in their own right. Kames in a similar fashion sees religious toleration as the product of commerce rather than reason (*SHM*: II, 514n.).

What Catholicism exhibits is the more general self-serving connection between the priesthood and the maintenance of superstition. There is a positive correlation: the greater the superstition then the greater also the authority wielded by priests (cf. Hume *E–SE*: 75, *NHR*: 75). Since in 'ages of credulity and ignorance the ministers of religion are the objects of superstition and veneration', then the priesthood wants to keep things that way (Robertson *VPE*: 327). Accordingly they inculcate doctrines that 'contribute most effectually to their own aggrandizement', which is to say they 'promote and regulate' the superstitions on which their authority rests (Millar *HV*: I, 136/*HVL*: 372). Kames, immediately after his disparagement of the Athanasian creed, remarks that the creed 'seems purposely calculated' to require the 'slavish submission to the tyrannical authority of a proud and arrogant priest' (*SHM*: II, 432). Hume takes a similar view of priestly intent.

Speaking more generally than either Kames or Millar (whose context is still Catholicism), he comments that priests instead of correcting the 'depraved ideas of mankind' have 'often been ready to foster and encourage them' (*HNR*: 95).[24]

iv) Miracles, Providence and Design

'Miracles' were a delicate subject. On the one hand, belief in them is a mark of an ignorant and superstitious mind. As Dugald Stewart said, it was an 'indolent philosophy' that referred to miracles whenever it was stuck for an explanation (*Life of Smith* in *EPS*: 293 cf. p. 66 above). It is the mark of science conversely that it uncovers causal connections. As we have already observed, the fact that Nature could be shown by science to be systematic underwrote the Design Argument. Ferguson expresses the common view that 'it is proofs of design from which we infer the existence of God' (*ECS*: 6). This was easily coupled with the idea of benign superintending Providence. The geometric properties of honeycombs were for Reid the work of the 'great Geometrician' who designed the bee rather than the bee itself (*AP*: 546–7; Ferguson, too, cites the bee to the same point *ECS*: 182; it had in fact been the subject of a paper by Maclaurin, as Reid acknowledges). And Kames' writings abound with references to 'final causes'. On the other hand, over against these professions of faith based on the designed regularity of the universe with seemingly no place for miracles was, for Christians, the fact that belief in the miracles associated with Christ was apparently mandatory. One way round this was to distinguish between general and particular Providence or Revelation. God revealed Himself generally in the beauty and systematic quality of His Creation but revealed Himself particularly in Christ as the redeemer of mankind.

While there was an internal debate over the relative weight to be attached to the general vis-à-vis the particular,[25] Hume, by sceptically taking issue with the argument from miracles, put himself on the 'outside'. This confirmed his status but, as with other 'religious' questions, his contribution was part of a long-running debate (cf. Wootton 1993). For our limited purposes Hume's essay on 'Miracles' (included in the *First Enquiry*) is of importance for the connections it reveals to his related views of human nature and history.

A wise man, he says, proportions his belief to the evidence (*EHU*: 110). In line with the argument from the biased die (*E–RA*: 112) the findings of a 'greater number of experiments' constitute a probability. A particular instance of this general proposition is the weight to be attached to testimony: what are the grounds for believing the reports of eye-witnesses? By applying this to the case of miracles Hume is switching the focus away from whether they can ever occur to whether it is ever rational (or 'wise') to believe they have occurred. We recall that Hume had confidently dismissed a traveller's tale if it reported discovering a human society where ambition was absent among its people (*EHU*: 84 cf. above p. 69). This dismissal was on a par with that adopted to tales of dragons and centaurs. Exactly the same principles can be applied to miracles. Experience, and experience alone, gives authority to human testimony, just as it does to the law of nature (127). Since miracles are, by Hume's definition, violations of the laws of nature (114) then their occurrence cannot be established by human testimony (116, 127). Hume proposes a test: if the falsehood of the testimony would be more miraculous than the event related then, and only then, is the testimony credible (116). The consequence is that the Christian religion cannot be believed by 'any reasonable person' without a miracle; faith 'subverts all the principles of his understanding' and constitutes, in effect, a 'continued miracle in his own person' (131).[26]

Not surprisingly, Hume's essay provoked the orthodox. However, the only member of the literati to take direct explicit issue was George Campbell, Principal of Marischal College, Aberdeen. (Of course the paucity of this response would only confirm to the more traditional and evangelical that the Kirk's leaders had 'sold out' to the new-fangled rational religion.) Campbell published a *Dissertation on Miracles* (1762) in direct rebuttal. Campbell fastened on to the issue of testimony, which he thought in line 'with the common sense of mankind' sufficient to establish the evidential support for miracles (*Dissertation*: 288 cf. 14).[27]Hume thought sufficiently well overall of Campbell's arguments to defend himself in a letter to Hugh Blair (*Letts*: 348–51).

If Hume's critique of the case for a particular Providence was contrary to orthodox sensibilities, his critique of the entire argument from Design or general Providence would be even more startling. Hume was so well aware of this that he arranged for his *Dialogues on Natural Religion* to be published only after his death. So incendiary was this work that Smith declined that responsibility (see *Corr*: 211).[28] Of all Hume's writings the *Dialogues* is the most deliberately artful, and its stylistic features, almost as much as its argument, have stimulated extensive discussion. Perhaps his key observation is that we cannot know whether this supposedly designed machine (the universe) is perfect; it may rather (for all we know) be 'very faulty and imperfect', being the product of an infant or inferior or superannuated deity (*DNR*: 142). We cannot know how good the design is because we don't know what a badly designed universe would be like. This is the only universe we've got, it is unique; to invoke design is thus to beg the question (152).[29]

C: Taste

Criticism was one of the subjects identified by Hume, in the Preface to the *Treatise*, that the 'science of man' would put on a new footing (*THN*: xx cf. *EHU*: 90). To establish the principles of criticism, or the standard of taste, was one of the most widely debated topics in the Enlightenment. Many of the leading writers – including Montesquieu, Voltaire and Kant – entered the lists. The Scots too were conspicuous competitors. Hume wrote one of the most celebrated essays and Kames one of the most influential books but others joined in.

The ubiquity of this discussion can be put down to the 'public world' of debate in the eighteenth century, but the explanation for the debate's existence in the first place lies in the importance attached to maintaining 'standards'. Just as superstition cannot be allowed to represent an authentically valid 'form of life' so the ignorant and vulgar could not be allowed authority to determine aesthetic appreciation. The idea that 'art' was not a free-for-all was a long-established critical position stretching from Aristotle, through various Romans to the spokesmen of seventeenth-century classicism such as Boileau (author of *L'Art poétique* (1674)). And yet despite the equally long-standing recognition that artistic judgements varied (*de gustibus non disputandum est*), it took the typical Enlightenment mix of Lockean epistemology and sensitivity to the diversity of social experience to produce the context for 'taste'.

The aim of (neo)-classicism had been to make aesthetics an exact science. Its central assumption was that beauty was objective – it existed independently of the observer. There were, accordingly, precise rules which laid down the criteria of what was beautiful. But Lockeanism led in aesthetics towards subjectivism. Beauty was now held to be an experience – it was 'something' felt by the observer – and not an inherent quality of the object being observed. The logical outcome of this empiricism was that just as every person is unique (has different non-reproducible experiences) so every person will have a different idea of what is beautiful. Voltaire, for example, in his entry under *Beau* in his *Philosophical Dictionary* [1764] (1971) tr. p. 63) remarked:

> Ask a toad what beauty is, absolute beauty, the *to kalon*. He will answer that it is his female, with two large round eyes sticking out of her little head, a large and flat snout, a yellow belly, a brown back. Question a Negro from Guinea: for him beauty is a black oily skin, sunken eyes, a flat nose.

Though Voltaire seems to conclude by having a philosopher (a purveyor of grandiloquent nonsense) announce that beauty is relative that is not Voltaire's own considered view. For example, in his later entry under *Goût* (in *Oeuvres Complètes* (1877) vol. XIX p. 270) he distinguishes between sensual taste (about which there truly can be no dispute) and intellectual taste (which involves discernment and is capable of instruction and correction).

i) The Standard of Taste

Voltaire's distinction between sensual and intellectual taste reappears in various guises throughout the Enlightenment discussions. Hume's essay on 'Taste' pivots on the relationship between what he calls 'understanding' and 'sentiment'; he states that his aim is 'to mingle' the 'light' of the former with the 'feelings' of the latter (*E–ST*: 234; Blair repeated this almost verbatim *LRB*: 20). Hume (226), Kames (*EC*: II, 434) and Gerard (*Essay on Taste* 3rd edn: 199) each open their discussions by acknowledging the variety of taste and then quickly proceed to state that the blanket acceptance of this variety is unnatural. It flies in the face of the fact that 'it is natural for us to seek a Standard of Taste; a rule by which the various sentiments of men may be reconciled' (Hume *E–ST*: 229). This is 'natural' because it is universal to criticise according to standards (Kames *EC*: II, 437–8 cf. Horn 1965, who calls this 'anthropological criticism'). Hume is explicit that the 'general principles of taste are uniform in human nature' (*E–ST*: 243). The locus of the standard of taste is thus in human nature (Gerard *Essay*: 220; Blair *LRB*: 19; Gregory *CV*: 207; Beattie *Dissertations Moral, Critical and Literary*: 191 etc.).

Having laid down a solid foundation, construction can commence. The distinction between intellect and sentiment, or in Gerard's version 'discernment' and 'sensation' (*Essay*: 214), is a crucial building block. The facts of experience mean that a sentiment is self-referential – that coffee tastes sweet to me but bitter to you. Just as – following Locke – sweetness or bitterness are not features of the coffee but our sensations then so too with beauty and works of art (Hume *E–ST*: 230, Hutcheson *PWD*: 14).[30] Yet, thanks to the nature of human nature that is not all there is to say. Gerard puts the key point neatly when he argues that men 'who are *affected* differently may notwithstanding *judge* alike' (*Essay*: 219; Gerard's emphases). Judgement is a question of intellect or discernment. Here, unlike sentiment, there is reference beyond personal experience to 'real matters of fact' (Hume *E–ST*: 230).

Where are the relevant 'facts' to be found? The short answer is: in the possession – open to public scrutiny (cf. Jones 1976: 57) – of critical acumen. Hume outlines five characteristics of that acumen (largely similar lists are provided by Kames *EC*: II, 447–8; Beattie *Dissertations*: 166; Gregory *CV*: 132, 206). These five are (in Hume's own summary) 'strong sense, united to delicate sentiment, improved by practice, perfected by comparison and cleared of all prejudice' (241). He now claims when individuals (critics) who possess these characteristics concur in their judgements then that concurrence 'is the standard of taste and beauty' (241). For example, to equate Ogilby and Milton would be equivalent to claiming a mole-hill was as a high as a mountain and only 'pretended critics' (or 'cavillers' (Beattie *Elements*: I, 192)) would make such a claim (they would as a result be ignored) (*E–ST*: 231).[31] Not unexpectedly Blair (*LRB*: 21) closely follows Hume, and the crucial role of critics or judges is similarly upheld by Kames (*EC*: II, 227) and Gerard (*Essay*: 227).

Painting with a broad brush in bold strokes we can produce the following picture. Unlike the objectivism of classicism, where the beautiful was such because it truthfully obeyed the rules of harmony, proportion, regularity, and unlike the subjectivism of Romanticism, where the beautiful was the authentic expression of the artist's own vision, for the Enlightenment the beautiful was what the critics agreed upon. There seems to be a vicious circularity about the Enlightenment position: good art is defined by good critics and a good critic is one who defines good art (cf. Kivy 1976: 143). But this agreement between critics was not thought to be arbitrary. Such virtue as there is in the Enlightenment case lies in the conviction/argument that human nature, because of its very constancy and uniformity, is itself not arbitrary in its operations. The critics themselves only agree because the *principles* of taste are indeed, as Hume said, 'uniform in human nature'. The 'laws of criticism' are 'discovered' (*E–ST*: 231) and the 'general rules of art' are 'founded' on the experience of the 'common sentiments of human nature' (232). By using this 'experience' in this way good art may be said to pass the test of time; 'simplicity and true taste sooner or later gain the ascendant and prove their rectitude by their permanency' (Beattie *Dissertations*: 192 cf. *Elements*: I, 192). If Homer and Virgil are still admired, it shows that their quality is rooted in the 'genuine taste of human nature' and not in some temporary fashion (Blair *LRB*: 23 cf. Hume *E–ST*: 233).

ii) Critics and Authority

Abetted by the key role played by human nature, taste and morals were closely linked. Hutcheson again is a powerful influence (cf. Kivy 1976). Gerard, for example, opens his prize-winning *Essay on Taste* (1759 1st edn),[32] with a lengthy footnote discussion of Hutcheson and he is explicitly followed by Beattie (*Dissertations*: 172). Just as moral judgement condemns what deviates from a common standard in human nature so too, on the same principle, does aesthetic judgement (the standard of taste) (Kames *EC*: II, 443–4). This similarity enables the cultivation of taste to give 'new force to the sentiments of the moral faculty' (Gerard *Essay* 1st edn: 206 cf. 201, Beattie *Dissertations*: 189). For Turnbull, since all truths are 'strictly' bound together then all the arts have the same rule or standard and 'good taste' in 'Nature, Conduct and Art' must be the same (*A Treatise on Ancient Painting*: 143 cf. xxiii).

Taste was a 'civilising' agent (cf. Flynn 1980: 7). Kames remarked that to cultivate a taste in fine arts cannot fail to 'embellish ... manners and to sweeten society' (*EC*: II, 448n.). This tuned into the whole literature on civility and politeness that Shaftesbury had promoted (cf. Klein 1994), which not only via the work of Hutcheson but also as mediated by the *Spectator* and other periodicals had spread into Scottish society (see Chapter 1). This close link between the ideal of politeness and moral theory gives a crucial clue to the selection of 'good critics'. The moral sense is dull in savages (Gerard *Essay* 1st edn: 206; Kames *EC*: II, 445; Blair *LRB*: 21). We do not therefore appeal to their barbarous practices to ascertain the 'rules of morality'. These rules must be obtained from 'men in their more perfect state' (Kames *EC*: II, 445). The same holds true for aesthetics. According to Blair, taste has 'no materials on which to operate' in 'rude and uncivilized nations'; reference should thus be had to the 'sentiments of mankind in polished and flourishing nations' (*LRB*: 21).

This has two dimensions. First, it is the standards expressed in such nations that count. But second, within these nations not all judgements are to be heeded. Since these are truly two dimensions then we can expect the similarity between the savage and the vulgar, which we met in the last section, to reappear. We are not disappointed. Gerard explicitly makes that connection: as the savage is distinct from the civilised so the 'vulgar in every nation are distinguished by the same circumstance fom the polite' (*Essay* 1st. Ed 200).

Taste is subject to education and has therefore a cognitive component, what Hume refers to as 'understanding'. Today this same conception is conveyed in the notion of connoisseurship (which etymologically signals the key point). The vulgar and ignorant are thus by definition not qualified to be critics. Hume, immediately after summarising the five characteristics, says that only some will (as 'a matter of fact') possess them; indeed the 'generality of men' will be deficient (*E–ST* 241). Gerard puts this deficiency down to lack of opportunity (*Essay* 1st edn: 208) and Campbell to 'total want of education' (*Philosophy of Rhetoric*: 11). Kames is more sociologically exact and candid. We should not, he asserts, heed everyone's opinion equally; in fact the 'greater part of mankind' should be excluded, that is all those 'who depend for food on bodily labour'. These individuals are devoid of taste, so far as judgement 'in the fine arts is concerned' (*EC*: II, 446). Only those who have the leisure to study these arts will possess the requisite knowledge; something the 'rude and untaught vulgar' in the same nation lack (Blair *LRB*: 12). Gregory similarly moves from observing that by taste is meant the 'improved use of the powers of imagination' to concluding that 'the servile condition of the bulk of mankind ... deprives them of the means of improving the powers either of imagination or reason' (except where their own particular employment is concerned) (*CV*: 132–3).[33] This reinforces the earlier argument that the crucial variable is sociological. It is presence (or not) of leisure and education that is decisive and not any historicist argument that the savage is in some sense a different human being in virtue of living in a different 'culture' from that of a civilised society.

There seems a clear-cut connection here between the critic's role in maintaining standards and the social status of the educational elite. The ideological veil of the Enlightenment is seemingly rendered transparent. This has been duly pointed out by commentators (e.g. Pittock 1973; Barrell 1986; Copley 1987). Yet so transparent is this that nothing surprising is revealed. The Scots would no more think of allowing the aesthetic opinions of the vulgar to count than they would think of giving them the vote (cf. Kames *SHM*: II, 55). The same reasoning applies in each case. To regard the exclusion of the vulgar from the domain of taste as an insightful revelation of the Scots' shaky democratic credentials only stems from having myopic vision in the first place.

iii) Manners and Literature

This assimilation of the vulgar to the savage should produce a devaluation of their 'artistic' attempts. We, of an 'enlightened' and civilised perspective, do not turn to them for moral guidance (savages, after all, practise human sacrifice (Kames *EC*: II, 445)), nor given their superstitions do we look to them for insight into true religion and so we may comfortably judge that they lack 'delicacy of taste'. True though this is, matters are a little more complicated. Homeric verse, for example, is of undeniably high 'quality'. This fact differentiates aesthetic merit from moral and religious judgement. The idea that certain early pristine artistic expressions were of special worth has been called 'primitivism'. A number of the Scots, thanks largely to the status of and role played by 'Ossian', were key advocates of this idea (cf. Whitney 1924, Pearce 1945, Foerster 1950). Several strands are intertwined here but we only need to unravel one or two. Our guiding thread is the link with manners.

The most important early work is Thomas Blackwell's *An Enquiry into the Life and Times of Homer* (1735). In an attempt to account for the character of Homer's work, Blackwell (Principal of Marischal College) searches for formative principles: what it is that makes us what we are. He concludes that the most important 'principle', or force, is manners, which comprise 'the constitution (civil and religious)', 'the ordinary way of living' and the 'prevalent humours and professions in vogue' (*Enquiry*: 12). The guiding assumption is that 'every kind of writing, but especially the Poetick depends upon the Manners of the Age' (68–9). And since (following received wisdom) the 'best Poets copy from Nature' (69) then we can in a mutually reinforcing way infer the manners from the poems and the poems from the manners. In short, epic poetry can only be written in epic times. Comparative studies, Blackwell believes, will confirm this; the oracles and myths of Orpheus are, for example, akin to the verses of Homer and Hesiod (72).

Blackwell had, as it turned out, laid down the principles to authenticate Ossian, the supposed Scottish bard. In 1760 James Macpherson (a former student of Blackwell's) published *Fragments of Ancient Poetry collected in the Highlands of Scotland*. These fragments he claimed to have translated from the Gaelic and to have been the tales of a bard named Ossian.[34] Blackwell's principles were applied by Ossian's champions, notably Hugh Blair. To Blair, since 'poetical products' are characteristic of an 'age', rather than a country, then the 'fit' between Ossian's descriptions and other epics is not coincidental. Following Blackwell's 'comparative method', the resemblance between Homer and Ossian authenticates the latter. Further proof of this authenticity is the absence of general terms and the lack of religious ideas (*A Critical Dissertation on the Poems of Ossian* [1763] 1819: 76, 78). A similar comparative exercise is undertaken by William Duff in his *Essay on Original Genius* (1767). Both Homer and Ossian, he argues, display 'original genius in poetry'[35] since they both were writing in the least cultivated ages (261).

In this last point we can see a connection with the wider aspects of the Scots' social theory. On to Blackwell can be grafted the principles of 'conjectural history'. Blair is, therefore, also able to claim that such poetry is the product of the first of the 'four great stages' (*Diss on Ossian*: 73). In the 'Early Draft' of the *Wealth of Nations* Smith, too, makes this link, though by way of contrasting Homeric society as more advanced (*LJ*: 573). For Kames, part of the grounds for believing Ossian to be authentic is that every scene 'relates to hunting, to fighting or to love, the sole occupations of men in the original state of society' (*SHM*: I, 244). While Kames leaves the reader in no doubt as to Ossian's credentials, Millar does not enter into the debate over authenticity, but since he cites the poems as evidence (though of the second pastoral stage e.g. *OR*: 206) the presumption has to be that he, too, accepts their validity.[36]

Not all the Scots 'bought' Macpherson's story that he simply collated and translated. Some like Dunbar were non-committal (*EHM*: 198–9), others were unpersuaded. Hume dismissed it as a 'tiresome and insipid performance'. Indeed if had been seen in 'its real form', namely, the 'work of a contemporary, an obscure Highlander' nobody would have paid it any attention. (This is not included in *E*: see *Essays* in *Works* eds. Green & Grose: IV, 415). This dismissal was, however, accompanied by close rebuttal that included a refutation of Blair's case for authenticity, and it was in deference to his friendship with Blair that Hume did not publish this essay (Mossner 1980: 420).

To Dunbar, the connection between manners and language is 'obvious' (*EHM*: 115) and one significant aspect of the Ossian debate was the attention paid to language. As Dunbar implies, this itself was part and parcel of the more general discussion of the place of language in the history of mankind (see pp. 26 above). Blair, as part of the comparative approach, refers to similarity of imagery and metaphor (*Diss on Ossian*: 133). According to Duff, in uncultivated times poetry is at its most vigorous because of its novelty and the attendant feelings of wonder (*Original Genius*: 286, 265). This produces the spontaneous expression of 'vivid ideas in bold and glowing metaphors; in sublime animated and picturesque description' (267). The dominance of metaphor in early speech was explained by claiming that early speech was passionate and/or poverty-stricken (cf. Berry 1973). The dual explanation is put forward by Blair (*Diss on Ossian*: 58–9) and Ferguson. To Ferguson, man is 'a poet by nature' since the savage 'clothes every conception in image and metaphor' and this because of the 'scantiness of proper expressions' (*ECS*: 172). Exponents of the 'passionate' origin include Blackwell (*Enquiry*: 37), Duff (*Original Genius*: 267), Beattie (*Elements*: II, 483) and Dugald Stewart (in *Collected Works*: IV, 50) while upholders of the 'poverty' source include Monboddo (*OPL*: III, 40), Reid (*IP*: 493) and Dunbar (*EHM*: 111). From either starting-point the progress of the human mind/civilisation could be traced in the evolution of linguistic expression. Language moves from obscurity to perspicuity (Dunbar *EHM*: 129); figurativeness, which is suitable for poetry and oratory, gives way to the precision more suitable for philosophy and understanding (Stewart *Collected Works*: IV, 50; Blair *LRB*: 79; Campbell *Rhetoric*: Bk 3 Ch. 1).[37]

D: Conclusion

Although this chapter has looked at the more self-evidently evaluative topics of the right, the good and the beautiful, it has aimed to do so with an eye on the overall social theory. The best use of this conclusion is, therefore, to characterise in sweeping fashion the ways in which these links between the specific and the general are forged.

The Scots are moralists. Questions of judgement and value are not confined to just one room, they inhabit the entire building. This is only to be expected from a group of thinkers who, as social theorists, take the 'social' seriously. Human experience is experience of social life. Since the Scots uniformly accept an experiential starting-point, then a proper account of moral experience must be consonant with the facts. A genuine and disinterested concern for the well-being of others was just as much a fact as the fact that humans have always been found in 'troops and companies'. Nor were these two facts discrete. On the contrary, the sociable and the societal were, effectively, one and the same. This is straightforwardly evident in the value attached to friendship or the benevolence extended to the less fortunate. It is also discoverable in the various ways that the socially indispensable requirement to be 'just' is judged valuable. This meshing of the moral and the social means that what holds good in explaining the latter applies equally to the former.

The diversity of social experience and thence the diversity of moral beliefs, is explicable by reference to the uniformity and universality of human nature. In their infancy societies are rude; life is hard and there is no room for sentiment (as we might say). This savagery could express itself in infanticide or cannibalism. It can also express itself in worshipping suitably fiercesome gods who demand sacrifices or self-mutilation (cf. Dunbar *EHM*: 389, Kames *SHM*: II, 437). What is especially notable about the Scots' writing on religion is that so much of it can be described without undue distortion as more sociology of religion than theology. Without in any way compromising the validity of their theistic and Christian belief, the Scots treat religion in the same way that they treated other social institutions such as property or government. In every case the institution is plotted on to a temporal grid and then is 'read across' to discern the ways in which the different institutions cohere.

We can see again here how the Scots' social theory generated a conception of society as a set of interlocked institutions and behaviours. A society of hunter-gatherers will, thus, have little in the way of personal possessions, nothing to speak of in the form of governmental machinery, few status distinctions (except the inferiority of women) and will live in a world populated with a multiplicity of gods, whose actions make their feelings plain. These savages would also respond to these events in a speech abounding in vivid and animated images. They would likely bedaub themselves and represent their gods in idols (Kames *SHM*: II, 453). They would have standards – only the best-wrought statues are fitting as idols. In this way even these savages show that aesthetic considerations are a truly universal aspect of human nature. Of course what they do is crude and, by definition, lacking in refined taste, but refinement comes with cultivation. And cultivation whether moral, religious or aesthetic, comes along with the success of mankind in triumphing over the dictatorship of needs. Cultivation in its metaphorical sense is linked to its more literal meaning. As humans win the time to contemplate, so they leave the kingdom of necessity and enter the realm of freedom. Life in a free and civilised society is a better life than all that has gone before. The enlightened social theorist is not only justified in making that judgement, it is inescapable; it is human nature.

Notes

1. The source (often called 'Hume's Law') is a passage where he remarks that it 'seems altogether inconceivable' that 'ought' can be deduced from 'is' when they are 'entirely different' (*THN*: 469). This passage has produced an enormous quantity of literature – though a good deal of it has only passing reference to Hume. Chappell (ed.) (1966) contains a sample of the debate and most books on Hume's moral thought devote attention to it, e.g. Harrison (1976), Mackie (1980), Flew (1986).

2. Referring to Hutcheson among others, Elizabeth Mure recalled that, about 1730, there was a change such that ministers 'taught that whoever would please God must resemble

Him in goodness and benevolence, and those that had it not must affect it by politeness and good manners' (quoted in Hont & Ignatieff. (eds) 1983: 103).

3. The opening sentence of Smith's *Moral Sentiments* makes the same point, 'How selfish soever man may be supposed, there are evidently some principles in his nature which interest him in the fortune of others, and render their happiness necessary to him, though he derive nothing from it except the pleasure of seeing it' (*TMS*: 9).

4. For a thorough analysis of Hutcheson's complicated account of perception, see Norton 1982: 78–86. The proper characterisation of Hutcheson's theory has been the subject of debate. Norton (1982: Ch. 2) argues that Hutcheson is a moral realist, i.e. the moral sense apprehends an independently existing feature of the world (virtue is real) and not a subjectivist. As exponents of a subjectivist interpretation Norton identifies Kemp Smith (1964), Raphael (1947), Frankena (1955) and Jensen (1972). A later subjectivist account is given by Mackie (1980) and Norton's interpretation is explicitly criticised by Winkler (1985) – to which Norton has rejoined (1985). That Hutcheson is a realist is also upheld by Haakonssen (1990), though his approach differs from Norton's. According to Campbell, Hutcheson wants a *via media* between 'naive realism' and non-cognitivism (1982: 171 cf. Blackstone 1965: 67–9) and, to MacIntyre, Hutcheson attempts to unite two incompatibles – the particularity of sense-certainty with the universality of general moral truths (1988: 277). That Hutcheson wants to avoid purely subjectivist accounts is claimed by Buckle (1991: 207) and Stewart (1992: 90). On contextual grounds the 'realist' case seems the stronger.

5. Hutcheson allows for the propriety of the 'utilitarian' argument that if putting the aged to death really does tend to the public good then it is justifiable (*PWD*: 97). Cf. Mackie 1980: 30. Hutcheson is the originator of the utilitarian formula: 'that action is best which procures the greatest happiness for the greatest numbers' (*PWD*: 90). He does, however, deny that humans are motivated by some 'abstract conception of all mankind' for the happiness of 'any one particular person is an ultimate end', we 'do not serve the individual only from love of the species' *SB*: I, 406–7. Turnbull, too, makes this point (*Discourse*: 254).

6. Hutcheson criticised Hume, and in a well-known reply Hume considered himself as an 'anatomist' rather than a 'painter', that is, concerned with the 'most secret springs and principles' rather than the 'grace and beauty of its actions' (*Letts*: I, 32–3). This distinction is made also in the final paragraph of the *Treatise* (*THN*: 621). On Hutcheson and Hume, see Moore (1994), who emphasises (polemically) their divergence.

7. Though Hume allows that sympathy is responsible for the uniformity in the 'humours and turn of thinking of those of the same nation' (316) and this resemblance is more significant in forming national character than 'soil and climate (317 cf. *E–NC*) it is not restricted since the principles of the science of man apply universally; it is a matter of degrees of facility not possibility.

8. My citations from *PMNR* are from the third amended edition; the extracts in *SB* are from the second. Since the text is generally the same, I also give the location of the corresponding passage in *SB* as the marginally more accessible work.

9. That Kames in this way separated benevolence from justice is implicitly acknowledged by Smith, who calls Kames 'an author of very great and original genius' (*TMS*: 80).

10. In his Glasgow lectures Millar, as part of his duties, covered Ethics and its relation to Jurisprudence – see 'Notes on Lectures on *Institutes of Justinian according to Heineccius*' (1789) in Glasgow University Library (MS Gen 812). The influence of Smith is apparent.

11. For discussions of Smith's theory, see especially Campbell (1971), also MacFie (1967), Hope (1989), Phillipson (1983b) and several essays by Raphael (e.g. 1975, 1979).

12. Cf. Smith's remarks on the difficulties of keeping one's judgement untainted when a nation is 'distracted by faction', so that the non-partisan is held in 'contempt and derision, frequently in detestation, by the furious zealots of both parties'. 'Faction' and

'fanaticism' have always been the greatest 'corrupters of moral sentiments' (*TMS*: 155-6). As we will note later, Smith associates superstition and enthusiasm with religious sects and religious controversies with factions and fanaticism (*WN*: 793-4).

13. Raphael judges Smith's extension of the idea of the impartial spectator to an agent's own actions to be 'original' (1975: 87). He later adds that Smith's account can certainly stand comparison with the best-known modern psychological explanation of conscience, Freud's account of the super-ego (97).

14. Smith himself was alive to this objection, which may have been put to him after the publication of *TMS* by Gilbert Elliot. In his reply to Elliot (whose letter has not survived) Smith comments of an addition made to the Second Edition that it is intended to show that 'real magnanimity and conscious virtue can support itself under the disapprobation of all mankind' (*Corr*: 49 cf. *TMS*: 111).

15. The charges were that he taught that the promotion of the happiness of others was the standard of moral goodness and that knowledge of good and evil was available without prior knowledge of God. Cf. Scott 1966: 84. The Westminster Confession (1647) proclaimed basic Calvinist theology such as predestination and salvation by grace. It was ratified in Edinburgh in 1690 as official doctrine and university professors had to subscribe to its tenets (a provision only repealed for non-Divinity professors in 1853).

16. This was in fact an orthodox Calvinist position – see *Institutes*: Bk 1, Ch. 3, Sect. 3.

17. For example Pocock (referring to the 'four stages') judged it as an 'important stage in the historicisation of human personality' (1985: 116 cf. 1983) but the Lockean model pertains to human nature which is constant and uniform and the 'principle of improvement' that the Scots see in human nature is itself a non-historical principle.

18. Just before that statement Hume had observed, 'Even at this day, and in Europe, ask any of the vulgar, why he believes in an omnipotent creator of the world; he will never mention the beauty of final causes of which he is wholly ignorant.' Why is he ignorant? Because 'an invisible spiritual intelligence is an object too refined for vulgar apprehension, men naturally affix to some sensible representation' (*NHR*: 55, 54).

19. Cf. Dunbar, who, while decrying the Koran (along with the 'Vedam [and] the Shaster') for affording striking examples of 'credulity and fanaticism', says they may, from another point of view, be regarded as 'monuments of human sagacity'. Dunbar even goes so far as to claim that 'even superstition on some occasions has proved a guardian of public manners and an auxiliary to legislative power' (*EHM*: 372, 271).

20. Trenchard wrote *The Natural History of Superstition* (1709); the title and contents of which suggest to Manuel that Hume 'probably perused' it (1959: 72). Toland planned a commentary on Plutarch's essay *On Superstition*, which he regarded as an 'admirable treatise' (cf. Redwood 1976: 142). Hume would have known Plutarch's work, and he himself cites Cicero on the superstitious man (*E-Sui*: 579 citing *On Divination*: 2. 72).

21. Cf. *EPS*: 114, (Physics) 'as ignorance begot superstition, science gave birth to the first theism that arose among those nations who were not enlightened by divine Revelation'.

22. Cf. Goldie (1993) for a discussion of the origin of the term 'priestcraft' and its development in the context of Whig anticlericalism (Toland and Tindal were participants).

23. Robertson similarly berates canon law for 'establishing the dominion of popes' and being 'one of the most formidable engines ever formed against the happiness of civil society' (*VPE*: 327).

24. Cf. Tindal, '[most of mankind] are alike bound in all places to pin their faith on their priests and believe in men who have an interest to deceive them' (*Christianity as Old as Creation* (1730) excerpted in Waring 1967: 153).

25. For example, Ebenezer Erskine, who led a 'secession' prompted by the increasing intellectualism of the Kirk's leaders, spoke in a sermon in 1736 of 'a natural kind of religion' being preached in which 'the supernatural mysteries of the Gospel' are 'generally exploded as unfashionable among many of our young ministers' (quoted in Henderson 1920: 215).

26. In a typical ploy Hume has subverted the so-called (rational) 'external evidences' of Christianity and thrown the onus on to the (inner feeling of faith) 'internal evidences', which enthusiastic 'High-Flyers' and seceders like Erskine emphasised. But it is, of course, the vulgar who are prey to enthusiasm and whose views are not to be taken seriously by 'any reasonable person'.

27. Campbell judged Hume's conclusion (*EHU*: 131, quoted above) unintelligible, a 'strange assemblage of words' (*Dissertation*: 285). It is likely that Campbell was influenced by Duncan (a professor at Marischal), who had spelt out carefully the basis of historical knowledge and its relationship to testimony and its evaluation (*The Elements of Logick* [1748]: Bk 4, Ch. 3). For the link between Campbell and 'Common Sense' philosophy, see Voges 1986: 148.

28. Smith, however, was the subject of much adverse comment when after Hume's death he described him as 'approaching as nearly to the idea of a perfectly wise and virtuous man as perhaps the nature of human frailty will permit' (*Corr*: 221). Smith's own beliefs are enigmatic. His most recent biographer can only bring himself to observe that 'there is no great evidence that Smith put stock in an after-life' (Ross 1995a: 401).

29. That Hume accepts design is argued by Livingston (1984: 172). Gaskin thinks 'attenuated deism' ('a dim possibility that some non-providential God exists') with very little bearing on any 'real religion' is the most that Hume can subscribe to (1993: 322). For Flew, Hume is an 'aggressive agnostic' (1986: 61) while Mossner, in his *Life*, thinks Hume sincere in his sceptical unbelief (1980: 598 cf. Mossner 1977).

30. Not surprisingly in view of his general rejection of the Lockean 'way of ideas' Reid contests this in his own essay on 'Taste' (*IP*: 490 cf. 499).

31. Hume's second example, Bunyan and Addison, is less fortunate. Hume's point regarding the first case is effectively made by us today asking 'Ogilby who?' but we are supposed to think that Addison is a good author and Bunyan not; if anything, it is the latter who has lasted better. Longevity, as we will see, is a mark of value.

32. The prize (a gold medal) was offered by 'The Edinburgh Society for the encouragement of arts, sciences, manufactures and agriculture' (i.e. 'The Select') and awarded to Gerard in 1756. For discussion of the *Essay*, see e.g. Grene (1943), MacKenzie (1949).

33. Gregory, though, warns against criticism falling into the hands of 'men possessed of mere learning and abstract philosophy [who] condescend to bestow their attention on works of taste and imagination' (212). His chief target here are those (the neo-classicists) who 'dream of applying always the square and compass to such thin and delicate feelings as those of the imagination' (209). Cf. Beattie, who accuses the French critics of condemning without further enquiry 'what is contrary to established rule' with the consequence that, to them, only French authors 'write in taste' (*Dissertations*: 183).

34. For a brief summary, see Colgan, who states that the whole episode 'must be regarded as the most successful forgery in literary history' (1987: 346). For a fuller discussion and appreciation of the wider context, see MacQueen 1982: Ch. 4. Nonetheless at the time 'Ossian' had enormous impact, especially in Germany.

35. 'Genius' was a much debated issue. Aside from Duff, Gerard wrote an important *Essay on Genius* (1774). Gerard linked genius with 'imagination', with the capacity to 'invent' through 'assembling ideas' (27).

36. Macpherson himself developed a stadial theory of society. Society was based, first, on consanguinity and family then, second, when property is established, on mutual defence and, third, on subservience to laws and government. He places Ossian at the transition from the first to the second stage but, makes great play of the inadequacy of records (see *Dissertation* prefaced to *Temora* (1763)).

37. It is against this more general concern with language that the lengthy discussions of rhetoric by Smith, Blair, Campbell and others are to be placed. See Howell (1971) for a full discussion.

8

Reading the Scottish Enlightenment

Texts, we have been told, are inherently 'open', they defy 'closure'. Certainly interpretations of texts, thinkers, intellectual movements and the like are multivarious and change over time, and the Scottish Enlightenment is thus not remarkable in having produced a variety of readings. This concluding chapter – rather like the first – is an overview; it sketches the outlines of some of this variety. I make no claims to be comprehensive, but the readings can, for purely expository reasons, be divided into the explanatory and the significatory. The former is subdivided into the ideological, the cultural and the intellectual; the latter into the sociological and the liberal. These divisions and subdivisions are rough and ready, as we will see there is much blurring at the edges. My classificatory schema like the grid of a map is there as reference point to help the traveller. To continue the cartographic metaphor, the schema is a projection which can never be free of distortion as it attempts to represent the global reality on a flat surface.

A: Explanatory

i) Ideological

'Ideology' is a term that means different things to different people. The meaning I choose to use is the following: an argument is ideological when it presents as an impartial statement (of the truth) what in fact is the expression of a partial interest. Thus understood, an ideology is the object of criticism, where the strategy of the critic is to demystify or unmask or reveal the partiality 'behind' the impartial surface. Though Marx's views on ideology are not uniform, this critical perspective conforms to his basic usage. What underlies it is his materialist conception of history. The partial interest is a class interest, and that is formed around the ownership of the dominant forces of production. This owning class has a material interest in maintaining the status quo, and its ideology functions to legitimate this state of affairs by claiming that it is for the common (impartial) good.

When applied to the bourgeoisie, this claim expresses itself in two ways. First, it opposes the (feudal) landed aristocracy. The interest of these barons lay in keeping social mobility to a minimum in order to retain their own favoured position as the uppermost rung in a stable hierarchy. Examples of this putative aristocratic interest would include primogeniture, entails and sumptuary laws. These would be justified with reference to such ideas as the 'great chain of being' (where hierarchy is a necessary feature of the created order) and *noblesse oblige* (that social rank has duties as well as privileges) which function to legitimate these practices as 'natural'. But these practices are contrary to the bourgeois interest and its theorists would unmask them, and their justifications, as (if they had the word) 'ideological'. However, the second expression of bourgeois ideology is an opposition to the claims for economic or political power by the poor (the 'working class'). The interest of the bourgeoisie thus lies in investing private property with exclusionary rights and supports such practices as enclosures and clearances. These would be justified with reference to such ideas as equality of opportunity with all careers open to the talents or the necessity of incentives and actual inequality to encourage industry so that everybody enjoys a higher standard of living.

For Marx himself the first expression predominates in the transition from feudalism to capitalism, when the bourgeoisie is rising, while the second takes over once capitalism is established, when the bourgeoisie has gained its ascendancy (about 1830, see the Preface to *Capital* (1967: I, 15)). His view of Smith supports this. Referring to Smith's distinction between productive and unproductive labour, Marx argues that Smith used 'the language of the still revolutionary bourgeoisie which has not yet subjected to itself the whole of society, the state etc.' (*Theories of Surplus Value* (*Works* 1989: 31, 197)). Smith represents a bourgeoisie 'still struggling with the relics of feudal society' (*Poverty of Philosophy* [n.d.: 105]). Smith might be thought to be a special case, but he is (for Marxists) only the most articulate representative not a unique genius. Accordingly this view of the Enlightenment as the intellectual counterpart to the rising bourgeoisie can be applied generally.[1] There have, however, been a number of accounts that apply a Marx-derived framework to the Scots.

For Hiroshi Mizuta the function of Enlightenment ideas was 'to legitimise bourgeois civilization at an early stage of its growth' (1976: 1459). This function differed in its execution in different countries, each 'reflecting the specific way of the capitalist development within each national economy' (*Ibid.*). To Mizuta, in Scotland this produced (principally in the work of Smith) a union of moral philosophy and political economy that justified the activities of 'embryonic industrialists' (1975: 115) and its characteristic 'historical consciousness' was 'a product of the fast development of the Scottish society from tribal to capitalist stage' (1976: 1461). This latter point is often made. It is invoked by Giarrizzo in his interpretation of Hume (1962: 55) and both Pascal and Meek in their ascription of a materialist theory of history to the Scots (see Chapter 5) refer to it. Pascal notes that Smith and Millar, being based in Glasgow, had 'before their eyes the effects of rapid economic development' (1938: 169). Meek argues that it was the rapidity of the economic advance that facilitated the observable contrast between areas of differential economic development, a contrast that lay at the root of the Scottish Historical School (1954: 98). A similar relationship between 'ideas' and economic environment (material base) is inherent in Hobsbawm's comment that the 'rapidity and the dramatic character of this transformation is *reflected* in Scottish theory' (1980: 5; my emphasis).

In the process of ideological demystification the social role and status of the Scots themselves is not incidental. They were members of the educated elite and in 'material' terms this meant they inhabited a 'middle-class milieu' (Meek 1954: 99 cf. Pascal 1938: 169). Their 'class origins' are analysed more precisely – at least with respect to Smith and Millar- by Hans Medick.[2] He sees Smith's work as legitimising the striving after riches and luxury, although he stresses that for Smith the resultant socio-economic inequality is not an end in itself but, in keeping with Smith's 'enlightened humanism', was part of a progressive refinement of social needs and increase in human happiness (1973: 222 cf. 224, 227). Thus understood, the doctrine of 'natural liberty' functions as a harmonious overcoming of social conflict, and this viewpoint, according to Medick, makes Smith an ideologist of the petty-bourgeoisie (288-9 cf. 1988: 85). Millar is similarly located. His petty-bourgeois foundation is revealed in his assumption that idleness (and hence the need for incentives) is an anthropological constant (1974: 35 cf. 47). As with Smith, so too with Millar there is an implicit universalisation of this assumption in the form of a harmonious 'class-less' society of independent individuals (39).

While sharing the same analytical thrust, the ideological interpretation is not homogeneous. Hence, in contrast to Medick, Lawrence sees the philosophy of improvement as an ideological campaign destined to legitimate (and thus further) the interests of the landed class (1979: 21). The literati were patronised by the improving gentry (22) and in Smith there is an 'implicit defence of landed paternalism against mercantile interest' (32). Somewhat similarly McNally sees Smith's model as that of the agrarian capitalist (1988: 233) while Giarrizzo locates a 'nostalgia' in Hume for the period before the interests of the agricultural and mercantile classes diverged (1962: 47). Whether this heterogeneity undermines this entire line of interpretation is debatable, but it is not a minor matter if there is no agreement as to which class interest it is that the Scots are supposed to be furthering.

Those who read the Scots as ideologists do acknowledge their criticisms of commercial society. The acknowledgement is, however, grudging in as much as the criticisms are judged to be vitiated by their class position. Hence, Medick thinks Smith's criticisms could only go so far before he fell back into an apologetic for the middling-ranks and small-landed proprietors (1973: 288). For McNally, despite Smith providing no apology for industrial capitalism, his critique was 'seriously compromised' by his acceptance of the 'necessity of the basic social relations of capitalism'. His educational remedy to combat the ill-effects of these relations is accordingly judged to be 'little more than an attempt to resist the symptoms of capitalist development' (1988: 264-5). More generally, Pascal regards the Scots' 'most serious weakness' to be 'their ignoring of the dialectics of social progress'; an ignorance stemming from their 'middle-class' position (1938: 179).

Another facet of the Scots' situation – their relationship to England – has also been the focus of an ideological reading. As we shall shortly see, this relationship is the crux of the 'cultural' reading and thus represents a blurring of the edges. Lawrence in developing his argument for the alliance between the literati and the improving gentry interprets the latter as sanctioning the former as 'articulators of a specific *Scottish* cultural identity' (1979: 22; author's emphasis). This comes out most starkly in the treatment of the Highlands. The Highlanders were typified as savages and in need of 'civilisation'. This need is met by 'improvement' (23,31).

An extreme variant of this view is put forward by J. D. Young. According to Young, in the eighteenth century Scotland became an 'English cultural colony' with an 'economy peripheral to the core of English capitalism' (1979: 11). The intellectuals of the Enlightenment surrendered to this culture and their view of the Highlands demonstrates this (16). They exaggerated the barbarity of the Highlanders 'in order to rationalise their support for the cultural genocide they were engaging in' (26).[3] A more nuanced account is given by Keith Burgess. He emphasises the Scots' desire not to appear provincial even while their actual status was that of a dependent client of the English (1980: 125). The intelligentsia 'consciously or not' became 'legitimating agents ... for the hegemony enjoyed by the dominant English interests' (128). Once again the treatment of the Highlands is supporting evidence. Among other expressions of this dominance noted by Burgess is the development of a legal system 'attuned to the needs of a developing capitalist economy' and he cites both Smith[4] and Ferguson[5] in evidence (113 cf. 110, 126). And, among these needs, Burgess includes 'social control' (110, 120).[6]

The strength of the ideological reading is that it does offer a coherent interpretative package. Opposition to entails is a characteristic of the Scots' social theory and it is indisputable that they did think of themselves as more civilised than and superior to other less developed societies. Moreover, the actual remit of the Board of Annexed Estates did include 'civilising' the Highlands (see Chapter 1) and both the 'philosophy' and the composition of that Board can be reasonably be linked to the 'Enlightenment'. All that said, the weaknesses of the reading are formidable. The most basic is that the presence of these practices and ideas does not itself demonstrate that they are 'ideological' and that they have been *explained* by invoking class-analysis. To identify the idea of 'civilisation', for example, as an 'effect' depends on having already identified a prior cause. However, that prior identification is itself the product of the theoretical assumption that ideas 'reflect' more basic material circumstances. One consequence of the reading is that it is difficult to account for the presence of debate *within* the ideology. Ex hypothesi Smith and Kames share the same material circumstances, yet while the former does indeed oppose sumptuary laws (see *WN*: 346) – as the reading 'predicts' – the latter proposes them (*SHM*: I, 486). Of course there is considerable scope for sophisticated readings beyond a crude reductionism, but the greater the sophistication the more the explanation comes to resemble the increasingly complex cycles and epicycles of pre-Copernican astronomy. And, as with Copernicus, there comes a point when the very complexity generated by the sophistication produces the thought that perhaps the initial premise is mistaken. The other two explanatory readings to different degrees fit this pattern.

ii) Cultural

The common focus in these interpretations is on the Scottishness of the Scottish Enlightenment. This shared perspective divides into two basic camps: those who emphasise the Union with England as a decisive formative force and those who emphasise the continuity between the seventeenth and eighteenth centuries.

Hugh Trevor-Roper is a leading member of the former persuasion. In two articles (1967,1977) he set out his stall with a stark simplicity. For him the the nub of the 'Scottish Enlightenment' is the historical analysis of human progress. This constitutes 'the most authentically Scottish of all intellectual achievements' (1977: 374). To explain that achievement the focus has to be on the 'peculiar character of Scottish society' (375). For Trevor-Roper Scottish society was perceived, by its articulate members, to be backward so that the Union was an 'economic necessity' (376). The Union brought about a 'social revolution' (383). There developed a new elite centred on the law, the Church and the universities who – unlike the previous century – were involved in the official institutional life of the country (378). Aware of the barbarousness of their own country, this group sought to enquire how they might 'catch up'. They enquired, in other words, if there were 'rules of progress' (386). And, according to Trevor-Roper, it is out of this enquiry that political economy and sociological history were developed (1967: 1658).

Trevor-Roper thus shares with the 'ideologists' the emphasis on the Scots' theory being a reflex of socio-economic circumstances. The difference lies in the explanatory model. For the former theorists, this reflex has the form it does *because* 'ideas' are the bearers of class interests, while Trevor-Roper (we can impute – but cf. 1958) would baulk at the dogmatic simplification that this underlying historical scheme supposes and at the arrogance of thinking Marx was a pioneer in the 'economic interpretation' of history.

The general impact of Trevor-Roper's reading can be discerned in Horne's comment that 'the Scottish Enlightenment was dominated by the attempt to understand and promote the progress of society, specifically the economic growth and the cultural changes that had to occur for economic and moral improvement to take place ... [and] was prompted by the backward state of Scottish economic development' (1990: 73). Horne himself cites here the work of Nicholas Phillipson, and it is his work that has provided the fullest and most nuanced account of the links between the Scottish Enlightenment and the effects of the Union.

In a series of articles (especially 1973a, 1973b, 1976, 1978, 1981, 1983a) he has a charted a moving course, which nonetheless takes its bearings from 1707. The Union was traumatic. Scotland was bereft of a Parliament and the economically parlous condition of the country kept all but the very wealthiest from following the Parliament to London. The aristocratic elite that remained needed to establish a new identity for itself. This was initially fashioned from the numerous clubs and associations that sprang up. In addition to fostering a morality of politeness (see Chapter 1) they served the para-Parliamentary function of giving this elite an activist role that befitted their status as leaders of the community. This activism took the initial form of the campaign for agricultural improvement but soon widened its horizons into a general programme for economic and commercial advance. This elite thus attained its new civic identity as modernisers, which was in sharp contrast to the frugal austerity that the anti-Unionist Fletcher had offered.

On Phillipson's reading, the mid-century saw a great transformation. Scotland was now prospering and this new-found prosperity enabled a new generation of the elite to afford a metropolitan life. This became a new identity crisis (Phillipson draws on Erikson's psychology (1973a: 127n.; 1973b: 411n.)[7]). The new elite still wanted to see themselves (and be seen) as leaders yet also wanted not to tie themselves so closely to a life in Scotland. This crisis was resolved by joining and fastening on to the intellectual clubs that had existed off and on alongside the 'improving' clubs from the 1720s onwards. The dominant philosophy in these intellectual clubs was that of Hume and Smith, and what this philosophy taught was determinism. It taught that men were shaped by the economic and social circumstances in which they found themselves. This teaching harmonised with the continuing importance attached to manners and social intercourse but also, and crucially for Phillipson, it meant that improvement was not necessarily the product of deliberate intention. In this way Phillipson sees Smith's doctrine of the 'invisible hand' (first appearing in 1759 in the *Moral Sentiments*) fitting the needs of this elite.

Phillipson identifies a third phase, which takes the story from 1780. The landed elite, through its increased metropolitanism, has become less significant and leadership has passed to the distinctively Scottish professions. For these lawyers, ministers and professors an activist language of virtue was more appropriate to their role as leaders than the passive determinism of Hume and Smith. In this way Phillipson interprets the growth and popularity of the anti-Humean Common Sense School led by Reid, popularised by Beattie and culminating in Dugald Stewart.

Hence, while not interpreting the Scottish Enlightenment in materialist, class terms, Phillipson (in these essays) focuses on the elite and identifies its problems in terms of its response to circumstances. The social theory is at the service of resolving elite crises of identity. The resolution is achieved by means of a 'new understanding of civic virtue' and, also, by the development (the Scottish Enlightenment's unique contribution) of the '"sociological" understanding of the Science of Man' (1981: 22).[8] Phillipson's reference to 'virtue' here indicates another blurred edge. His 'cultural' interpretation links with the 'intellectual' reading that focuses on the Scottish Enlightenment as the transformation of the civic humanist tradition. However, the salience assumed by 1707 means that his account, like Trevor-Roper's, has drawn the fire of those who emphasise cultural continuity.

This latter camp disputes the crucial status given to the Union. Neither was Scotland as economically backward as Trevor-Roper claims nor was the Union as traumatic as Phillipson maintains. On the contrary the Enlightenment was penetrated and permeated by the Scots' own native intellectual tradition. R. H. Campbell argues that the seemingly quintessential Enlightenment focus on improvement was in fact established in the seventeenth century (1982: 23).[9] This same point is made by Chitnis in explicit confutation of Phillipson (1987: 79). Chitnis' article, which follows up his earlier books (1976, 1986), emphasises the general institutional roots of the Enlightenment. For him since the law, church and universities each have a long history, then the Enlightenment itself is not a rupture; the Union was only a catalyst (1976: 4, 249). In support of this reading of the Union Chitnis cites G. E. Davie. Davie, for his part, developed a view of the Enlightenment that saw it as a 'crisis of national existence' in that the 'threat or reality of assimilation to England brought home to the Scots the value of their native inheritance of institutions' (1967: 25). Seen in this light, the Enlightenment was a complex response to Fletcher's nationalism (1981: 22).[10]

Chitnis also detects intellectual as well as institutional roots and continuities. He especially emphasises the religious/theological context, arguing that this 'paved the way', given that the theology encouraged social action (1976: 252, 254). However, the most commonly cited case for intellectual continuity is the legal theorising of Lord Stair. He enjoys a prominent place in Meikle's pamphlet, and MacCormick, for example, thinks he prefigured the four-stages theory (1982: 160).[11] That these citations are more than dues-paying scholarship but, rather, polemical engagements is illustrated by Gordon Donaldson. Donaldson uses Stair's work to claim uncompromisingly that too many of those 'who babble about "The Enlightenment"', and thus imply that before 1707 was an uncultured backwater, have not bothered to investigate the seventeenth century (1981: 144–5). Stair was not alone and the intellectual scientific roots of the Enlightenment have been traced by Roger Emerson to the work of Sibbald (1988b).

Emerson's work represents another blurring of the edges and I will examine his reading in the next section. Another work at the blurred edge is Allan (1993). To him the Enlightenment was 'generated and sustained to a large extent' from the 'resources provided by Scotland's peculiar social and intellectual heritage' (235 cf. 128). The Enlightenment's intensified interest in manners and property relations 'built solidly' on the earlier Scottish political tradition (166). For Allan there was indeed a 'substantial degree of obvious continuity' because the purpose in writing history remained edificatory, the moral education of social leaders (169 cf. 65). On Allan's reading, therefore, the Enlightenment was founded on 'the assertion of the immense social utility of learning' (232). And this was put into effect by the scholars themselves, pronouncing that they were the 'moral and social leaders of their community' (191 cf. 207).

This final point demonstrates how Allan's and Phillipson's cultural readings simultaneously converge and diverge.[12] It also neatly illustrates what is at stake in the cultural reading. This interpretation is contextual. Its guiding assumption is that the Enlightenment is explained by its setting. Quite how that is supposed to work as an *explanation* is rarely spelt out. Frequently it seems to rely on the truism that social theory cannot occur in a vacuum. The dispute within this reading, as a consequence of its contextualism, is largely a historical matter over such issues as the depth of the economic depression in the 1690s or the extent to which the landed elite's influence continued after the Union. Beyond these debates it is easy to reject the extreme viewpoints – of course the Union made a difference and of course institutions and values persisted. In the last analysis it comes down to judgement. While it is always wise not to take all protestations at face value, that the Scots did think of themselves as distinctive in their 'enlightenment' is (in my judgement) a significant pointer to their divergence from their forbears.

iii) Intellectual

The focus here is on ideas, on intellectual rather than cultural or socio-economic history. These readings concentrate on the proposition that the Enlightenment in general is an intellectual movement and argue – more or less self-consciously – that an intellectual movement is only properly understood in intellectual terms and cannot (and should not) be reduced to some extra-intellectual context.

The most self-conscious of such readings is provided by J. G. A. Pocock. He has a distinctive approach to the study of (political) thought. He emphasises the role of 'a language' or 'languages'. These structure thought but do so in a fluid manner; discourse is 'polyvalent' (1985: 9 cf. 1987 and also his earlier formulations 1962, 1973). Pocock has explored just such a language at great length in his book *The Machiavellian Moment* (1975) and he has, in later essays, continued his story into eighteenth-century Scotland (see especially 1982). The story he tells is the story of civic humanism from Aristotle onwards. The guiding thread in the narrative is the practice of citizenship and the need to possess a properly virtuous character in order to engage in that practice. The threats to this are labelled corruptions and in the eighteenth century these centred on credit and stock jobbing. The Scots are now read as participants in this discourse. As we noted, Phillipson is indebted to this reading and much has now been written along these lines.[13] Pocock as part of his methodological self-consciousness takes explicit issue with Marxist readings because of their historical inaccuracy. The defenders of commerce were the Whig oligarchs (the aristocratic interest) not the rising bourgeoisie. Pocock also distances himself from the other major intellectual reading. This interpretation sees the Scottish Enlightenment in the light of jurisprudential theorising.

The most important author here is Duncan Forbes. His pivot is Hume. While his interpretation of Hume by no means 'de-contextualises' him, since it is the leitmotif of the interpretation that Hume was seeking to give the new Hanoverian regime a 'proper intellectual foundation' (1975a: x cf. 1977), his thrust is that the framework of his thought is a modernisation of the Natural Law theory (1982: 191). Forbes has ventured out beyond Hume (his original foray was an essay on Smith and Millar (1954)). As well as work on Smith (1975b) and Ferguson (1966, 1967), he has generalised his argument to claim that the Natural Law theory of Grotius and Pufendorf was the 'matrix of the Scottish Enlightenment' (1979: 97). This brand of Natural Law was not conducted on a deductive a priori basis but was one that started from the 'basic fact of human nature in society' (1982: 189). Understood from this perspective, the Scots' thought is to be interpreted as a 'more intensive and sophisticated continuation' of this jurisprudence along the 'same empirical and social, even social-evolutionary axis of advance' (1982: 201).

Another writer who treats the Natural Law backcloth in serious depth is Knud Haakonssen (cf. also Hont 1987). He states openly that Millar, for example, is in 'the jurisprudential tradition' (1985: 60). However, he is also (later) concerned to query the use of the definite article here (1990: 85) and has sought to distinguish Hume and Smith on the one hand from the bulk of their contemporaries. This distinction he believes is a 'basic feature of the *moral* thought of the Scottish Enlightenment' (1990: 62; my emphasis). More generally Haakonssen has tried to bridge the apparent gap between the civic humanist and jurisprudentialist accounts. In a clear expression of the intellectual approach he declares that through a 'delineation of basic connections at the level of pure theory' (1988: 98) he can discern how the moral and the juridical meet. The meeting-place (arrived at from an interpretation of Cumberland and Hutcheson) is a neo-Ciceronianism. Haakonssen supposes that this provides a common ground for, on the one hand, the civic concern with the proper discharge of life's duties and, on the other, the juridical concern with the proper constitution of the offices to be discharged (1988: 110).

Two other readings are worthy of a mention in their own right. Over a number of essays Roger Emerson has criticised interpretations of the Scottish Enlightenment for failing to give sufficient salience to the place of 'science' (cf. Wood 1989). For him, the 'Enlightenment' is properly understood as the search for, discovery and application of 'rationally-grounded natural knowledge to improve the human condition in this world' (1988a: 338). While Emerson has done important work on cultural history (especially on the universities – see Chapter 1) he can be placed in the intellectual camp. His general perspective can be gleaned from his remark that the conjectural historians were 'rooted in aesthetic, scholarly, literary and philosophical contexts which were often very old' (1985: 82). He stresses that natural philosophy shaped moral philosophy by making it more empirical and thus opening the way to history and, beyond that, to social theory (1988a: 356 cf. 1990: 34–5). While firmly underlining the links with similar movements in continental Europe, he uses this interpretation to hold to a version of the 'continuity' argument (he has influenced Allan, for example). Hence (he claims) 'Scottish enlightened thought during the eighteenth century never lost sight of its natural philosophical roots' (1986: 285). These 'roots' he further maintains, and this is another distinctive feature of his reading, lie in the work and attitudes of late seventeenth-century *virtuosi*. The endeavours of men like Sibbald and Pitcairne 'shaped the intellectual life of the Scots until at least the 1720s' (1988a: 356 cf. 1986: 288); indeed the Enlightenment (and not only in Scotland) 'clearly emerged from the world of the *virtuosi*' (1995: 19).

The second noteworthy reading is Alasdair MacIntyre's. The Scots, for MacIntyre, are a case in point of a more general argument. MacIntyre argues that thinking about justice and rationality is inextricably bound up with traditions of thinking about those issues. These traditions are always culturally specific in their expression. One such expression is the seventeenth-century Scottish synthesis between Calvinism and Aristotelianism (1988: 9–10). MacIntyre recounts the fate of this synthesis in the Enlightenment. As he tells it, in eighteenth-century Scottish thought this distinctively Scottish tradition was continued (and here he is seemingly in debt to Davie (cf. 240)) as a 'third way' between Fletcher and subversive Anglicizers, like Hume (258). The key role in this continuity was played by the professor of moral philosophy whose task it was to elaborate the principles that underlay the distinctively Scottish practices in law, education and theology (*Ibid.* cf. 239). The key player of that role was Hutcheson but in the Enlightenment itself there was divergence between Hume and Smith on the one hand and Reid and Dugald Stewart on the other. The former retained Hutcheson's moral epistemology but rejected his view of morality, the latter conversely took up his moral and theological position but rejected his epistemology (280).

On the intellectual reading the identity of the 'Scottish Enlightenment' is to be found in texts, and these embody thought. The primary focus is thus on understanding that thought. While Pocock and Forbes, say, might disagree on what constitutes the best understanding, they share a commitment to reaching that understanding through an investigation of the issues or topics with which the 'thought' is engaged. The thought is explained when it is in that way made intelligible. As was the case with the cultural reading, which intellectual context (or contexts) supplies the best explanation is in the end a matter of judgement. From the perspective of this reading, the cultural or socio-economic setting is not irrelevant but its textual focus provides a narrower treatment than is given in the other readings. This can be both a strength and a weakness. The strong point is that due weight is paid to the fact that members of the Enlightenment were involved in *argument*. Whether there is or ever was a social contract did involve interpreting and evaluating what Locke or Pufendorf had to say. The weak spot is that the argument can easily be assumed to inhabit some unreal rarified realm that talks only to itself. Hume may have argued with Locke but what was at stake was the basis of post-Revolutionary political stability.

Of course these readings of the Scottish Enlightenment need not be mutually exclusive – I have admitted as such with my allowance that the edges are blurred. This book has developed its own reading and in the terms of my own classification it belongs, because of its emphasis on the Scots' writings, most obviously in the intellectual camp. But the militaristic imagery of a 'camp' should not be taken to mean that I have taken up some oppositional posture to the other readings. It is rather a matter of 'horses for courses' and, as I said in my Preface, I'm not running in the same race as Chitnis or, for that matter, in the same as, say, Phillipson or Burgess.

B: Significatory

Interest in the Scottish Enlightenment is not confined to explaining its origins or delineating its basic ideas. Much as some scholars would disdain it, the work of the Scots has been of interest because of what it signifies.[14] That is to say, what is significant about the Scots is how they contributed to subsequent developments. Two particular contributions stand out. The Scots have been seen to play an important role in the emergence of sociology and in the formulation of a strand of liberalism.

i) Sociology

The neologism 'sociology' was coined by Auguste Comte in the nineteenth century, and that fact alone has coloured the history of the subject. That this colouring has had the effect of covering up other lineages is pithily conveyed in Donald MacRae's remark that 'Comte named the discipline but distorted its growth' (1969: 25). In that same article MacRae declares that Ferguson was 'the first sociologist' (*Ibid.*). A pupil of MacRae's, Alan Swingewood, wrote a thesis on the Scottish Enlightenment and the rise of sociology, the main lines of which he summarised in an article. In that article Swingewood is explicitly concerned with what is 'sociologically significant' in the Scots' analyses. By 'significant' he means not the accuracy of their discussions but the extent to which they anticipate later concerns (1970: 169). This understanding of significance echoes that of Louis Schneider, who, in a lengthy introduction to a series of extracts from the Scots, claims that what is of interest is to draw from their work 'sociological analyses, conceptions and descriptions that are of on-going significance in the work that sociologists do' (1967: xv). One example of this is how their thinking contains 'anticipations' of structural-functional analysis (xlvii). For his part Swingewood claims that the Scots developed a 'radically secular and remarkably scientific interpretation of the social world' that was concerned with issues of social class and power, conflict and 'the social and human implications of the division of labour' (1970: 165).

Swingewood and MacRae are aware that other earlier writers have seen a similar significance in the work of the Scots (Schneider closely follows Bryson's view of them as moral philosophers and like her excludes Millar from his survey). Comte himself in his *Positive Calendar* in the eleventh month (Descartes) had a week with Hume at its head and days allotted to Robertson and Smith, with Ferguson as a 'reserve' for Condorcet (1966: 270). W. C. Lehmann wrote a book in 1930 on Ferguson and the beginning of modern sociology where he interprets Ferguson as the most typical representative of the Scots' development of sociology and a naturalistic method (1930: 233). Lehmann pays particular attention to Ferguson's appreciation of the role of conflict (98–106) and he cites the earlier verdict of Ludwig Gumplowicz that this appreciation entitles Ferguson to be labelled one of the fathers of sociology. Lehmann was also one of the first to draw attention to Millar as a sociologist. Before his 1960 edition of the *Ranks* he wrote an article on Millar as a 'historical sociologist' where his 'most highly developed contribution' was judged to be his theory of the dominance of 'techno-economic factors' (1952: 41). Once again Lehmann acknowledges a significant predecessor in Werner Sombart, who regarded the *Ranks* as an 'astonishing book' for its formulation of 'a techno-economic social theory' (cf. Forbes 1954: 664n. Pascal 1938).

Ferguson and the Scots are now commonly seen as significant players in sociology's history. Bottomore can write that 'claims that Adam Ferguson is the real father of sociology are now so numerous that ... they have become monotonous' (1978: 27). And Evans-Pritchard in his history of anthropology devotes a chapter each to Kames, Ferguson and Millar and judges the *Ranks* 'nearer to a modern sociological treatise than any other eighteenth century book' (1981: 33). Yet, for all this, the Scots' sociological significance has been queried. Fletcher in his mammoth account of the 'makings of sociology' relegates the Scots to an appendix on the grounds that they produced no systematic conceptual schema of sociological analysis or theory (1972: 646). And even Swingewood in his own history of sociology thinks the 'real history of sociology begins with the work of Saint Simon and Comte' (1984: 28). Away from such grand sweeps, the Scots' significance is found to lie in more particular facets. Ferguson and conflict we have already mentioned and Burrow thinks their conjectural history was an 'anticipation' of the comparative method as understood in the nineteenth century (1970: 11). Strasser explicitly sees their sociological significance in their attempt to overcome the antagonism between the State and the individual (1976: 45) and Hamowy regards their 'single most significant sociological contribution' to be the notion of 'spontaneously generated social orders' (1987: 3).

Perhaps the most frequently cited aspect of their thought is their awareness of 'alienation'. Marx has been crucial here. Given that, in almost alchemical fashion, anything Marx refers to has 'significance' bestowed upon it then his citation of Ferguson on the effects of the division of labour in *Capital* (see Chapter 6) has brought this aspect to wide attention. (Similarly the work of Pascal and Meek discussed above was inspired by seeing in the Scots a prefigurement of the materialist theory of history – see also Skinner (1965, 1975, 1982).) On a wider front, Brewer treats Ferguson's account of 'alienation' (and other topics) as caught between the moralism of civic humanism and a sociological treatment of 'social structure' (1987: 24 cf. 1986, 1989). While Strasser, using Habermasian terminology, links Ferguson with Marx in having a 'social emancipatory interest' and dissociates him from Comte's 'social technological interest' (1976: 9).

All these accounts think the Scots significant because they contributed to the formulation of sociological thinking. Since sociology itself is a comparatively recent academic discipline then it has seemed to some important to establish its credentials. One way of doing that is to find its roots in older (respectable) thinking. This approach culminated perhaps in Alvin Gouldner (1967) writing a whole book on Plato as the first sociologist. The Scots feature instrumentally in this credential-hunting enterprise, but in their case there is perhaps more. Whereas Plato was obviously a ready-made star, some of whose lustre might be thought to rub off if he could be associated with sociology, the same cannot be said of Ferguson or Millar. In their case they have largely been discovered in the course of excavating sociology's foundations. Sociology cannot, however, claim sole credit. There is another avenue down which the Scots' significance has been seen to travel.

ii) Liberalism

Schneider in the Preface to his collection of the Scots' sociological writings acknowledges the direction of Friedrich Hayek, and in the Introduction he declares at one point that Hayek has 'without any doubt been directly influenced' by the Scots (1967: xlvi). This view has Hayek's own endorsement. Other commentators have picked up this endorsement and thought it a significant factor in his thought (for example, Gray 1984, Kukathas 1989). Whether Hayek's reading of the Scots is correct (his interpretation is criticised by Winch (1988)) or whether he can adequately assimilate them along with other components in his overall theory (that he cannot is the thrust of Kukathas' argument) are not here strictly relevant. Rather what is at stake is that Hayek was a leading and very influential representative of a particular strand in liberal thought.

I say a 'particular strand' because liberalism is a fabric woven from many threads. Hayek's thread is what is sometimes referred to as 'classical liberalism' and in that line Smith stands tall as its greatest figure. So tall does Smith stand that he has cast a long shadow. One consequence of this is that while Smith features in histories of liberalism it is rarely mentioned that he is a member of the Scottish Enlightenment. In a related fashion while it is true that Smith's significance is inseparably associated with free-market economics, that association has resulted in a particular reading of his overall thought. Historical re-assessments of his work (see especially the work of Donald Winch (1978, 1983, 1988) and also Teichgraeber (1986)) have sought to cast doubt on any simple view of Smith as 'alive and well in Chicago'. Just as there is more to Smith's liberalism than a defence of 'natural liberty' so there is more to the social theory of the Scottish Enlightenment than Smith; it does not all fall under his shade. Hayek was well aware of these points and because of that, as well as because of his influence and importance, the Scottish Enlightenment in general is held to be significant for 'liberal' thinking.[15]

Hayek distinguished two streams or traditions of liberal thought – one based on continental rationalism (but including Bentham) and one based on British empiricism (but including Tocqueville). He thought the former aberrant, the latter correct. Among those on the right course, pride of place goes to the Scots, not only Smith but also Hume, Millar and Ferguson. It is their work on the growth of civilisation that is 'still the indispensable foundation of the argument for liberty' (1972: 57). For Hayek, Smith was never completely the apostle of laissez-faire (a 'rationalist' idea), rather, like Hume,[16] his argument was about the proper functions and limits of the state (60 cf. 1978: 134, 1982: I, 4).

What Hayek kept on returning to was the Scots' anti-rationalism (or anti-constructivism). In illustrating their argument he almost invariably quoted Ferguson's remark that 'nations stumble upon establishments which are indeed the result of human action, but not of any human design' (*ECS*: 122). (He even wrote a whole essay with that quotation as its title (1967: 96–105).) On one such occasion he glossed the quotation as providing 'the best definition of the task of all social theory' (1978: 264). This gloss explains how Schneider could acknowledge Hayek's contribution in directing him toward the Scots. Similarly Hamowy openly acknowledges Hayek's impact in identifying the Scots' sociological significance as lying in the notion of 'spontaneous order' (see above).

The significance of the Scots in Hayekian liberalism is that of establishing a pedigree. In his lights they embody the true understanding of liberalism against a faulty view. The latter, by virtue of its rationalist commitment to problem solving, is kindred to his great enemy, namely, social collectivism in all its forms from Soviet planning to the so-called 'welfare liberalism' of 'social justice'. What he detects in the Scots is a sensitivity to institutional continuity and complexity. They are the founders of 'true' liberal theory because they make no false assumptions about a natural harmony of interests; rather, they recognise diversity and realise that the only way to accommodate that in a free society is through just conduct between individuals supported by the general rule of law (cf. 1978: 135; 1982: II, 162).

As with their 'sociology' their claim for significance in liberalism is contingent upon some subsequent condition. Hence, as Hayek's star waxed in the 1970s with the emergence of the New Right, so the Scots took on a significance not previously assigned. Given that this is a contingent relationship then it is not improbable (indeed it is likely) that with the eclipse of the New Right so the Scots' perceived significance in this area may subside.

This book is no bulwark against subsidence. I have, however, attempted to tell a reasonably straight story, the gist of which will remain useful independently of the whims of retrospectively imputed significance.

Notes

1. Goldman, for example, identifies a 'basic structure' that all the 'fundamental categories' of Enlightenment thought possess. This structure is analogous to that of a market economy, which 'constitutes in its turn the social basis of the evolving bourgeoisie' (1973: 20). As a consequence there is within the structure a 'fundamental contradiction' between its adoption of the principles of private property and those of equality (36). Although pitched in these general terms, Goldman in fact focuses on the French Enlightenment. An even more sweeping account is given by Adorno and Horkheimer. For them, the 'Enlightenment' was a general orientation to the natural world, namely, 'what men want to learn from nature is how to use it in order wholly to dominate it and other men' (1973: 4). It lacks a properly critical attitude because it accepts what is directly given to experience – it worships 'facts' and numbers (26–7). Another influential general account of bourgeois ideology is given by C. B. Macpherson. He developed the notion of 'possessive individualism' (1962), which assumes that the individual is 'the absolute proprietor of his own capacities' (1973: 199). Bourgeois ideologists make this assumption, which they derive from their own environment, and postulate it as a characteristic of human nature as such. It thus legitimates the right of unlimited appropriation as an incentive to increase wealth, which a 'new enterprising class' saw in prospect for itself (1973: 19). Macpherson (1978) makes a passing reference to Smith and Hume (for a critique see Miller (1980)).
2. In his (shared) introduction to his translation of Ferguson's *Essay*, Medick pays less overt heed to class analysis. His basic frame of reference is the same, namely, that early social science emerges in the transition from feudalism to capitalism (1988: 8) but he stresses Ferguson's 'civic humanist' perspective (see below). He views that perspective as backward-looking (90) and quotes Marx's verdict that it is an 'antique standpoint' (88).
3. Cf. Hobsbawm, who refers to the 'destruction' and 'abolition' of the traditional peasant economy (1980: 18–19). He also refers to the Scottish reformers' militant hostility to the human and moral values of clan society (7).
4. Regarding Smith's separation of law from morality, Burgess comments (citing Stein

(1970) citing *TMS*) that this 'awareness of the competitive character of the law fitted well with the outlook of an increasingly commercial age' (110).

5. He quotes *ECS*: 155–6 and comments thereon that Ferguson's conception of law was 'well-suited to the requirements of a relatively backward society committted to capitalist development' (126).

6. Cf. Copley, who interprets Hume's *Essays* as revealing a 'partisan discussion of the nature and place in society of the bourgeois political culture' in which the 'passions' are 'manipulated as a mechanism of social control' (1987: 182, 190). A different model of social control that owes its debt to Foucault has been applied by T. A. Markus, in the context of an architectural programme designed to exhibit order and reason and to suppress manifestations of unreason (1982: 105–6 cf. Markus 1988).

7. Cf. the rather different psychological model invoked by Daiches. Referring to lawyers – but generally applicable to his interpretation that focuses on the 'cultural consequences of the Union' – he says that to be successful they had to develop 'cultural schizophrenia' (1964: 66).

8. Cf. Sher, who has a similar elitist focus. He defines the Scottish Enlightenment as 'the culture of the literati of eighteenth century Scotland', that is, the values and outlook of 'middle and upper-middle professional men' (1985: 8, 11).

9. In support of pre-Union roots Campbell quotes approvingly a lecture by Meikle (1947), which Phillipson, for his part, judges to have perpetrated the myth that sundry seventeenth-century authors were ancestors of the Enlightenment (1973b: 431n.). Cf. Chitnis (1987: 79), who also gives a positive assessment of Meikle's argument.

10. As we noted the response to Fletcher was also picked up by Phillipson (1987) but Chitnis, for all his acknowledgement of Davie, holds that it is a distortion to give Fletcher such a prominent role (1987: 88 cf. Withrington 1987: 14).

11. But cf. Burgess, who in his 'ideological' reading makes a point of observing that Stair's moralistic conception of property and contract 'steadily succumbed during the eighteenth century to the forces of secularism unleashed in a developing capitalist society' (1980: 110).

12. Allan's work can be juxtaposed to Kidd's (1993), which is also concerned with the Enlightenment's view of its past. Whereas Allan points up the continuity, Kidd focuses on the post-Union transformation of the Scottish Whig tradition, which recognised the benefits of its integration with its more civilised neighbour (7,181). See also Kidd (1996).

13. Among the most notable contributions, particularly because they also engage with Pocock, aside from Phillipson (see in addition to the earlier articles his studies of Smith (1983b) and Hume (1979, 1989)), are Winch (1978, 1983) and Robertson (1982, 1983, 1985).

14. Cf. Q. Skinner's (1969) assault on the ahistorical character of such enterprises. Skinner's work, which has developed, has prompted a large literature that is conveniently contained in Tully (1988). For a relevant application by Skinner of his approach, see his review of Meek's *Social Science and the Ignoble Savage* in *Times Literary Supplement* 13 February 1976.

15. The only attempt, independent of either Hayek or of the standard Smithian story, that seeks to link the Scots with liberalism generally (as opposed more narrowly to J. S. Mill – for which see Cumming (1969)) is the work of John Hall. Hall emphasises Smith and Hume's rejection of civic virtue and their endorsement of the link between commerce and liberty and sees them as contributing to liberalism as an ideology at the heart of which is a sense of 'openness, contingency and choice' (1986: 181, cf. Ch. 2 passim. See also Hall (1986) where he regards 'the brilliant thinkers of the Scottish Enlightenment' as an influence on his own work (3)).

16. Hayek depicts Hume as giving us 'probably the only comprehensive statement of the legal and political philosophy which later became known as liberalism' (1966: 340).

Bibliography

Primary: Scottish

Alexander, W. *The History of Women from the Earliest Antiquity to the Present Time*, 3rd edn, 2 vols., London, 1782.

Arbuthnot, J. *An Essay concerning the Effects of Air on Human Bodies*, London, 1733.

Beattie, J. *Dissertations Moral, Critical and Literary* (1783), Hildesheim: Olms reprint, 1975.
  Elements of Moral Science (1790–3), 2 vols., Hildesheim: Olms reprint, 1975.
  Essay on the Nature and Immutability of Truth (revised edn 1776), Hildesheim: Olms reprint, 1975.
  Scotticisms arranged in Alphabetical Order, designed to correct Improprieties of Speech and Writing, Edinburgh, 1787.

Blackwell, T. *An Enquiry into the Life and Writings of Homer* (1735), Menston: Scolar Press reprint, 1972.

Blair, H. *A Critical Dissertation on the Poems of Ossian* (1763), appended to *Poems of Ossian*, ed. A. Stewart, Edinburgh, 1819.
  Lectures on Rhetoric and Belles Lettres (1783), in one volume, London, 1838.
  Sermons, 5 vols., London, 1777–1801.

Campbell, G. *Dissertation on Miracles*, Edinburgh, 1762.
  Philosophy of Rhetoric, 2 vols., Edinburgh, 1776.
  The Nature, Extent and Importance of the Duty of Allegiance, Aberdeen, 1776.

Carlyle, A. *The Autobiography of Dr. Alexander Carlyle of Inveresk 1722–1805*, ed. J. Burton, Edinburgh: Foulis, 1910.

Craig, J. *Account of the Life and Writings of John Millar* (1806), prefixed to Millar's *Origin of Ranks*, Bristol: Thoemmes Press Reprint, 1990.

Dalrymple, J. *Essay toward a General History of Feudal Property in Great Britain*, London, 1757.

Duff, W. *Essay on Original Genius*, London, 1767.

Dunbar, J. *De Primordiis Civitatum oratio. In qua agitur de Bello Civili inter M. Britanniam et Colonias nunc flagranti*, London, 1779.
  Essays on the History of Mankind in Rude and Cultivated Ages (1781), 2nd edn, Bristol: Thoemmes Press reprint, 1995.

Duncan, W. *The Elements of Logick*, London, 1748.

Ferguson, A. *Correspondence*, 2 vols., ed. V. Merolle, London: William Pickering, 1995.
  An Essay on the History of Civil Society (1767), ed. D. Forbes, Edinburgh: Edinburgh University Press, 1966.
  The History of the Progress and Termination of the Roman Republic (1783), new edition, 5 vols., Edinburgh, 1813.
  Institutes of Moral Philosophy (1769), 3rd edn, London, 1785.
  Principles of Moral and Political Science (1792), 2 vols. repr. New York: AMS Press, 1973.
  Reflections previous to the Establishment of a Militia, London, 1756.
  Remarks on a Pamphlet lately published by Dr Price, London, 1776.

Fletcher, A. *Selected Writings*, ed. D. Daiches, Edinburgh: Scottish Academic Press, 1979.

Fordyce, D. *Dialogues concerning Education*, 2 vols., Belfast, 1753.

Gerard, A. *Essay on Genius*, London, 1774.

Essay on Taste (1759), 1st edn, Menston: Scolar Press reprint, 1971.

Essay on Taste, 3rd edn, Edinburgh, 1780.

Liberty the Cloke of Maliciousness both in the American Rebellion and the Manners of the Times, Aberdeen, 1778.

Gregory, J. *A Comparative View of the State and Faculties of Man with those of the Animal World* (1765), in *Works*, vol. 2, Edinburgh, 1788.

Hume, D. *An Abstract of a Treatise of Human Nature* (1740), ed. C. Hendel, Indianapolis: Bobbs Merrill, 1955.

Dialogues concerning Natural Religion (1779), in *Hume on Religion*, ed. R. Wollheim, London: Fontana books, 1963.

Essays: Moral, Political and Literary (1779), ed. E. Miller, Indianapolis: Liberty Press, 1987.

Enquiries concerning Human Understanding and concerning the Principles of Morals (1777), eds. L. Selby-Bigge & P. Nidditch, Oxford: Clarendon Press, 1975.

The History of England (1786), 3 vols. London: Routledge, 1894.

The Letters of David Hume, ed. J. Greig, 2 vols., Oxford: Clarendon Press, 1932.

The Natural History of Religion (1757), in *Hume on Religion* ed. R. Wollheim, London: Fontana books, 1963.

A Treatise of Human Nature (1739/40), ed. L. Selby-Bigge, Oxford: Clarendon Press, 1888.

Philosophical Works, eds. T. Green & T. Grose, London: Longmans, 1889.

Hutcheson, F. *An Essay on the Nature and conduct of the Passions and Affections, with Illustrations on the Moral Sense* (1728), Menston: Scolar Press reprint, 1972.

An Inquiry in to the Original of our Ideas of Beauty and Virtue (1725), Hildesheim: Olms reprint, 1971.

Observations on the Fable of the Bees (1726), Bristol: Thoemmes Press reprint, 1989.

On Human Nature (1730), tr. inaugural lecture *De naturali hominum socialitate*, ed. T. Mautner, Cambridge: Cambridge University Press, 1993.

Philosophical Writings, ed. R. Downie, London: Everyman Library, 1994.

A Short Introduction to Moral Philosophy (1747), Hildesheim: Olms reprint, 1969.

System of Moral Philosophy (1755), 2vols., Hildesheim: Olms reprint, 1990.

Innes, T. *A Critical History of the Ancient Inhabitants of the Northern part of Britain or Scotland* (1729), Edinburgh: W. Paterson, 1879.

Kames, Lord *The Elements of Criticism* (1762), 9th edn, 2 vols., Edinburgh, 1817.

Elucidations respecting the Common and Statute Law of Scotland, Edinburgh, 1778.

Essays on the Principles of Morality and Natural Religion (1751), 3rd edn (corrected and improved), 1779.

Essays upon several subjects concerning British Antiquities, Edinburgh, 1747.

The Gentleman Farmer: Being an attempt to improve Agriculture by subjecting it to the Test of Rational Principles, Edinburgh, 1776.

Historical Law Tracts (1758), 3rd edn, Edinburgh, 1776.

Loose Hints upon Education, Edinburgh, 1781.

Principles of Equity (1760), 3rd edn, 2 vols., Edinburgh, 1778.

Sketches of the History of Man (1774), 3rd edn, 2 vols., Dublin, 1779.

Macpherson, J. *Fragments of Ancient Poetry collected in the Highlands of Scotland* (1760), 2nd edn, reprinted in *The Poems of Ossian*, ed. F. Stafford, Edinburgh: Edinburgh University Press, 1996.

A Dissertation in *The Poems of Ossian*, ed. F. Stafford, Edinburgh: Edinburgh University Press, 1996.

Millar, J. *An Historical View of the English Government* (1803), 4 vols., London, 1812.

Observations concerning the Distinction of Ranks in Society, London, 1771.

The Origin of the Distinction of Ranks (1779), 3rd edn, repr. in *John Millar of Glasgow*, W. Lehmann, Cambridge: Cambridge University Press, 1960.

Monboddo, Lord *Of the Origin and Progress of Language*, 6 vols., London, 1773–92.

Antient Metaphysics, 6 vols., London, 1779–99.

Ogilvie, W. *Essay on the Right of Property in Land*, London, 1781.

Pennant, T. *A Tour in Scotland*, 3rd edn, Warrington, 1774.

Ramsay, J. (of Ochtertyre) *Scotland and Scotsmen in the Eighteenth Century*, 2 vols., ed. A. Allardyce, Edinburgh, 1888.

Reid, T. *Essays on the Active Powers of the Human Mind* (1788), in *Works*, ed. W. Hamilton, in one volume, Edinburgh, 1846.

Essays on the Intellectual Powers of Man (1785), in *Works*, ed. W. Hamilton, in one volume, Edinburgh, 1846.

Practical Ethics, ed. K. Haakonssen, Princeton: Princeton University Press, 1990.

Robertson, W *An Historical Disquisition concerning Ancient India* (1791), in *Works*, ed. D. Stewart, in one volume, Edinburgh, 1840.

The History of America (1777), in *Works*, ed. D. Stewart, in one volume, Edinburgh, 1840.

The History of Scotland (1759), in *Works*, ed. D. Stewart, in one volume, Edinburgh, 1840.

A View of the Progress of Society in Europe (1769), in *Works*, ed. D. Stewart, in one volume, Edinburgh, 1840.

Semple, W. Preface to *The History of the Shire of Renfrew* by G. Crawfurd, Paisley, 1782.

Smith, A. *Correspondence of Adam Smith*, eds. E. Mossner and I. Ross, Indianapolis: Liberty Press, 1987.

Essays on Philosophical Subjects (1795), ed. W. Wightman, Indianapolis: Liberty Press, 1982.

Lectures on Rhetoric and Belles Lettres, ed. J. Bryce, Indianapolis: Liberty Press, 1985.

Lectures on Jurisprudence, eds. R. Meek, D. Raphael and P. Stein, Indianapolis: Liberty Press, 1982.

The Theory of Moral Sentiments (1759, 1st edn), eds. A. Macfie and D. Raphael, Indianapolis: Liberty Press, 1982.

An Inquiry into the Nature and Causes of the Wealth of Nations (1776), ed. R. Campbell and A. Skinner, Indianapolis: Liberty Press, 1981.

Somerville, T. *My Own Life and Times 1741–1814*, Edinburgh, 1861.

Stair, Lord *The Institutes of the Laws of Scotland* (1693), 2nd edn, ed. D. Walker, Glasgow & Edinburgh: The University Presses, 1981.

Steuart, J. *An Inquiry into the Principles of Political Oeconomy* (1767), 2 vols., ed. A. Skinner, Chicago: University of Chicago Press, 1966.

Stewart, D. *Collected Works*, 10 vols., ed. W. Hamilton, Edinburgh, 1854.

Stuart, G. *Historical Dissertation concerning the Antiquity of the English Constitution* Edinburgh, 1768.

Observations concerning the Public Law and the Constitutional History of Scotland, Edinburgh, 1779.

A View of Society in Europe in its Progress from Rudeness to Refinement (1792), 2nd edn, Bristol: Thoemmes Reprint, 1995.

Turnbull, G. *A Discourse upon Nature and Origine of Moral and Civil Laws*, London, 1740.

Heineccius' Methodological System of Universal Law (editor), 2 vols., London, 1740.

Observations upon Liberal Education, London, 1742.

The Principles of Moral Philosophy, 2vols., London, 1740.

A Treatise on Ancient Painting, London, 1740.

Tytler, A. *Life of Henry Home of Kames*, 2 vols., Edinburgh, 1807.

Wallace, R. *Dissertation on the Numbers of Mankind in Antient and Modern Times*, Edinburgh, 1753.

Various Prospects of Mankind, Nature and Providence, London, 1761.

Primary: Non-Scottish

Adair, J. *History of the American Indians* (1775), New York: Argonaut Press, 1966.

Aristotle *The Politics*, tr. E. Barker, Oxford: Clarendon Press, 1946.

Bacon, F. *Physical and Metaphysical Works*, ed. J. Devey, London: Bohn Library, 1853.

Balguy, J. *The Foundation of Moral Goodness*, in ed. L. Selby-Bigge *The British Moralists*, Indianapolis: Bobbs Merrill, 1964.

Bayle, P. *Historical and Critical Dictionary* (1697), tr. R. Popkin, Indianapolis: Bobbs Merrill, 1965.

Beccaria, C. *On Crimes and Punishments* (1764), tr. H. Paolucci, Indianapolis: Bobbs Merrill, 1963.

Boileau, N. *L'Art poétique* (1674), ed. R. D. Hermies, Paris: Larousse, 1949.

Bolingbroke, Lord *Letters on the Use and Study of History* (1735), London, 1870.

Buffon, Comte de *Natural History: General and Particular* (1749–89), 20 vols., tr. W. Smellie, London, 1812.

Burke, E. *Works*, 6 vols., London: Bohn Library, 1889.

Calvin, J. *Institutes of the Christian Religion*, 2 vols., tr. H. Betteridge, London: J. Clarke, 1953.

Charlevoix, P. *Journal of a voyage to North America* (1744), 2 vols., tr. London, 1761.

Colden, C. *A History of the Five Indian Nations of Canada*, 2nd edn, London, 1750.

Comte, A. *Catéchisme positiviste*, ed. P. Arnaud, Paris: Garnier-Flammarion, 1966.

Condillac, E. *Oeuvres* 3vols., ed. G. LeRoy, Paris: Presses Universitaire de France, 1947–51.

Condorcet, N. *Sketch for a Historical View of the Progress of the Human Mind* (1795), tr. J. Barraclough, London: Library of Ideas, 1955.

D'Alembert, J. *Preliminary Discourse to the Encyclopedia* (1751), tr. R. Schwab, Indianapolis: Bobbs Merrill, 1963.

Diderot, D. *Political Writings*, ed. R. Wokler & J. H. Mason, Cambridge: Cambridge University Press, 1992.

Dubos, J-B *Réflexions critiques sur la poésie, la peinture et la musique* (1719), 2 vols., Paris, 1760.

Grotius, H. *On the Law of War and Peace* (1625), tr. F. Kelsey, Oxford: Classics of International Law, 1925.

Harrington, J. *Political Works*, ed. J. Pocock, Cambridge: Cambridge University Press, 1977.

Helvetius, C. *A Treatise on Man* (1773) tr. W. Hooper, London, 1810.

Hobbes, T. *Leviathan* (1651), ed. R. Tuck, Cambridge: Cambridge University Press, 1991.

Johnson, S. *Dictionary of the English Language*, 10th edn, London, 1792.

Justinian *The Institutes*, tr. J. Moyle, 5th edn, Oxford: Clarendon Press, 1913.

Kant, I. *Kant on History*, ed. L. Beck, Indianapolis: Bobbs Merrill, 1963.
    The Philosophy of Kant, ed. C. Friedrich, New York: Modern Library, 1949.

Lafitau, P. *Moeurs des savages ameriquains, comparées aux moeurs des premiers temps*, 2 vols.,
    Paris, 1724.

La Mettrie, J. *Man a Machine* (1748), ed. G. Bussey, LaSalle, Ill.: Open Court, 1912.

Locke, J. *Philosophical Writings*, 2vols., London: Bohn Library, 1854.
    Two Treatises of Government (1689), ed. P. Laslett, New York: Mentor Library, 1963.
    Some Thoughts concerning Education (1693), Menston: Scolar Press reprint, 1970.

Machiavelli, N. *The Prince* (1513), tr. R. Price, Cambridge: Cambridge University Press,
    1988.

Mandeville, B. *The Fable of the Bees* (1732), 2 vols., ed. F. Kaye, Indianapolis: Liberty
    Press, 1988.

Marx, K. *Capital* (1857 vol. 1), tr. S. Moore & S. Aveling, New York: International Pub-
    lishers, 1967.
    Poverty of Philosophy (1847), London: M. Lawrence, n.d.
    Theories of Surplus Value, London: Lawrence & Wishart, 1989.

Montesquieu, C. *The Spirit of the Laws* (1748), tr. A. Cohler et al., Cambridge; Cambridge
    University Press, 1989.
    Oeuvres complètes, Paris: Nagel, 1955.

Newton, I. *Newton's Philosophy of Nature: Selections from his Writings*, ed. H. Thayer, New
    York: Hafner, 1953.

Price, R. *Political Writings*, ed. D. Thomas, Cambridge: Cambridge University Press, 1991.

Priestley, J. *Writings on Philosophy, Science and Politics*, ed. J. Passmore, New York: Collier
    Books, 1965.

Pufendorf, S. *On the Law of Nature and Nations* (1672), tr. C. & W. Oldfather, Oxford:
    Classics of International Law, 1934.

Rousseau, J-J. *The Social Contract and the Discourses*, tr. G. Cole. London: Everyman
    Library, 1968.

Sallust *The Conspiracy of Catiline*, tr. S. Handford, Harmondsworth: Penguin Books, 1963.

Shaftesbury, 3rd Earl of *Characteristics of Men, Manners, Opinions, Times etc.* (1711), ed.
    J. Robertson, London: Grant Richards, 1900.

Temple, W. *Works*, 4 vols., Edinburgh, 1754.

Voltaire, A. *Philosophical Dictionary* (1764), ed. & tr. H. Bestermann, Harmondsworth:
    Penguin Books, 1971.
    Oeuvres complètes Paris: Garnier, 1877.

Secondary Sources

Aarsleff, H. (1974) 'The Tradition of Condillac', in D. Hymes (ed.), *Studies in the History
    of Linguistics*, Bloomington: Indiana University Press, pp. 93–156.

Adorno, T. & Horkheimer, M. (1973) *The Dialectic of the Enlightenment*, tr. J. Cumming,
    London: Allen Lane.

Aldridge, A. (1975) *Voltaire and the Century of Light*, Princeton: Princeton University Press.

Alexander, H. (ed.) (1956) *The Leibniz–Clarke Correspondence*, Manchester: Manchester
    University Press.

Allan, D. (1993) *Virtue, Learning and the Scottish Enlightenment*, Edinburgh: Edinburgh University Press.

Amoh, Y. (1989) 'Ferguson's "Of the separation of departments, professions and tasks resulting from the progress of arts in society"', *Eighteenth Century Scotland*, 3.

Ashcraft, R. (1968) 'Locke's state of nature: historical fact or moral fiction?', *American Political Science Review*, 62, 898–915.

(1987) *Locke's Two Treatises of Government*, London: Unwin Hyman.

Baier, A. (1979) 'Good men's women: Hume on chastity and trust', *Hume Studies*, 5, 1–19.

(1988) 'Hume's account of social artifice', *Ethics*, 98, 757–78.

(1989) 'Hume on a woman's complexion' in P. Jones (ed.), *The Science of Man in the Scottish Enlightenment*, pp. 33–53.

(1991) *A Progress of Sentiments: Reflections on Hume's Treatise*, Cambridge, Mass.: Harvard University Press.

Baker, K. (1975) *Condorcet: From Natural Philosophy to Social Mathematics*, Chicago: University of Chicago Press.

Barfoot, M. (1990) 'Hume and the culture of science in the early eighteenth century' in M. A. Stewart (ed.), *Studies in the Philosophy of the Scottish Enlightenment*, pp. 151–90.

Barraclough, G. (1962) 'Universal history' in H. Finberg (ed.), *Approaches to History*, London: Routledge, pp. 83–109.

Barrell, J. (1986) *The Political Theory of Painting from Reynolds to Hazlitt*, New Haven: Yale University Press.

Basker, J. (1991) 'Scotticisms and the problem of cultural identity in eighteenth century Britain', *Eighteenth Century Life*, 15, 81–95.

Battersby, C. (1981) 'An enquiry concerning the Humean woman', *Philosophy*, 56, 303–12.

Beloff, M. (ed.) (1960 2nd edn) *The Debate on the American Revolution 1761–83*, London: A. & C. Black.

Benton, T. (1990) 'Adam Ferguson and the enterprise culture' in P. Hulme & L. Jordanova (eds.), *The Enlightenment and its Shadows*, London: Routledge, pp. 63–120.

Berry C. J. (1973) 'Approaches to the origin of metaphor in the eighteenth century', *Neuphilologische Mitteilungen*, 74, 690–713.

(1974a) 'Adam Smith's "considerations" on language', *Journal of the History of Ideas*, 35, 130–38.

(1974b) 'James Dunbar and the American War of Independence', *Aberdeen University Review*, 45, 255–66.

(1982) *Hume, Hegel and Human Nature*, The Hague: M. Nijhoff.

(1986) *Human Nature*, London: Macmillan.

(1987) 'James Dunbar and the Enlightenment debate on language' in J. Carter & J. Pittock (eds.), *Aberdeen and the Enlightenment* pp. 241–50.

(1989) 'Adam Smith: commerce, liberty and modernity' in P. Gilmour (ed.), *Philosophers of the Enlightenment*, Edinburgh: Edinburgh University Press, pp. 113–32.

(1992) 'Adam Smith and the virtues of commerce' in J. Chapman & W. Galston (eds.), *Virtue* New York: New York University Press, pp. 69–88.

(1994) *The Idea of Luxury: A Conceptual and Historical Investigation*, Cambridge: Cambridge University Press.

Black, J. B. (1926) *The Art of History*, London: Methuen.

Blackstone, W. (1965) *Francis Hutcheson and Contemporary Ethical Theory*, Athens, Ga.: University of Georgia Press.

Bottomore, T. & Nisbet, R. (1978) *A History of Sociological Analysis*, London: Heinemann.

Bowles, P. (1985) 'The origin of property and the development of Scottish historical science', *Journal of the History of Ideas*, 46, 197–209.

Brewer, J. D. (1986) 'Adam Ferguson and the theme of exploitation', *British Journal of Sociology*, 37, 461–78.

(1987) 'The Scottish Enlightenment' in A. Reeve (ed.), *Modern Theories of Exploitation*, London: Sage, pp. 6–29.

(1989) 'Conjectural history, sociology and social change in eighteenth century Scotland: Adam Ferguson and the division of labour' in D. McCrone et al. (eds.), *The Making of Scotland*, Edinburgh: Edinburgh University Press, pp. 13–30.

Brown, S. (ed.) (1979) *Philosophers of the Enlightenment*, Brighton: Harvester Press.

Brown, V. (1994) *Adam Smith's Discourse: Canonicity, Commerce and Conscience*, London: Routledge.

Brownsey, P. (1978) 'Hume and the social contract', *Philosophical Quarterly*, 28, 132–48.

Brumfitt, J. (1958) *Voltaire – Historian*, Oxford: Oxford University Press.

(1972) *The French Enlightenment*, London: Macmillan.

Bryson, G. (1945) *Man and Society: the Scottish Inquiry of the Eighteenth Century*, Princeton: Princeton University Press.

Buckle, S. & Castiglione, D. (1991) 'Hume's critique of Contract Theory', *History of Political Thought*, 12, 457– 80.

Buckle, S. (1991) *Natural Law and the Theory of Property: Grotius to Hume*, Oxford: Clarendon Press.

Burgess, K. (1980) 'Scotland and the first British Empire, 1707–1770s: the confirmation of client status' in J. Dickson (ed.), *Scottish Capitalism: Class, State and Nation from before the Union to the present*, London: L. Wishart, pp. 89–135.

Burns, S. (1976) 'The Humean female', *Dialogue*, 15, 415–24.

Burrow, J. (1970) *Evolution and Society: A Study in Victorian Social Theory*, Cambridge: Cambridge University Press.

Cairns, J. (1995) 'Famous as a school for law, as Edinburgh ... for medicine: legal education in Glasgow 1761–1801' in A. Hook & R. Sher (eds.), *The Glasgow Enlightenment*, pp. 133–59.

Cameron, J. (1967) 'Church of Scotland in the Age of Reason', *Studies in Voltaire*, 58, 1939–52.

(1982) 'Theological controversy: a factor in the origins of the Scottish Enlightenment' in R. Campbell & A. Skinner (eds.), *Origins and Nature of the Scottish Enlightenment* pp. 116–30.

Camic, C. (1983) *Experience and Enlightenment: Socialization for Cultural Change in Eighteenth Century Scotland*, Edinburgh: Edinburgh University Press.

Campbell, R. (1982) 'The Enlightenment and the economy' in R. Campbell & A. Skinner (eds.), *Origins and Nature of the Scottish Enlightenment*, pp. 8–25.

Campbell, R. & Skinner, A. (eds.) (1982) *Origins and Nature of the Scottish Enlightenment*, Edinburgh: John Donald.

(1985) *Adam Smith*, London: Croom Helm.

Campbell, T. (1971) *Adam Smith's Science of Morals*, London: G. Allen & Unwin.

(1982) 'Francis Hutcheson: "Father" of the Scottish Enlightenment' in R. Campbell & A. Skinner (eds.), *Origins and Nature of the Scottish Enlightenment*, pp. 167–85.

Cant, R. (1982) 'Origins of the Enlightenment in Scotland: the universities' in R. Campbell & A. Skinner (eds.), *Origins and Nature of the Scottish Enlightenment*, pp. 42–64.

Capaldi, N. (1975) *David Hume the Newtonian Philosopher*, Boston: Twayne.

(1978) 'Hume as a social scientist', *Review of Metaphysics*, 38, 99–123.

Capaldi, N. & Livingston, D. (eds.) (1990) *Liberty in Hume's 'History of England'*, Dordrecht: Kluwer Academic.

Carter, J. & Pittock, J. (eds.) (1987) *Aberdeen and the Enlightenment*, Aberdeen: Aberdeen University Press.

Cassirer, E. (1955) *The Philosophy of the Enlightenment*, tr. F. Koelln & J. Pettegrove, Boston: Beacon Press.

Chamley, P. (1975) 'The conflict between Montesquieu and Hume' in A. Skinner & T. Wilson (eds.), *Essays on Adam Smith*, pp. 274–305.

Chappell, V. (ed.) (1966) *Hume*, London: Macmillan.

Charron, W. (1980) 'Convention, games of strategy and Hume's philosophy of law and government', *American Philosophical Quarterly*, 17, 327–34.

Chisick, H. (1989) 'David Hume and the common people' in P. Jones (ed.), *The Science of Man in the Scottish Enlightenment*, pp. 5–32.

Chitnis, A. (1976) *The Scottish Enlightenment: A Social History*, London: Croom Helm.

(1986) *The Scottish Enlightenment and Early Victorian English Society*, London: Croom Helm.

(1987) 'The eighteenth century Scottish intellectual inquiry: context and continuities versus civic virtue' in J. Carter & J. Pittock (eds.), *Aberdeen and the Enlightenment*, pp. 77–92.

Christie, J. (1987) 'The culture of science in eighteenth century Scotland' in A. Hook (ed.), *The History of Scottish Literature*, Aberdeen: Aberdeen University Press, vol. 2, pp. 291–305.

Clark, I. (1970) 'From protest to reaction: the moderate regime in the Church of Scotland 1752–1805' in N. Phillipson & R. Mitchison (eds.), *Scotland in the Age of Improvement*, pp. 200–24.

Clive, J. & Bailyn, B. (1954) 'England's cultural provinces: Scotland and America', *William and Mary Quarterly*, 11, 200–13.

Cloyd, E. (1972) *James Burnett: Lord Monboddo*, Oxford: Clarendon Press.

Colgan, M. (1987) 'Ossian: success or failure for the Scottish Enlightenment', in J. Carter & J. Pittock (eds.), *Aberdeen and the Enlightenment*, pp. 344–9.

Colley, L. (1992) *Britons: Forging the Nation 1707–1837*, London: Pimlico Books.

Collingwood, R. (1961) *The Idea of History* (1946), Oxford: Clarendon Press.

Copley, S. (1987) 'Polite culture in commercial society' in A. Benjamin et al. (eds.), *The Figural and the Literal*, Manchester: Manchester University Press, pp. 176–201.

Corfield, P. (1987) 'Class by name and number in eighteenth century Britain', *History*, 72, 38–61.

Cranston, M. (1991) *The Noble Savage: J-J Rousseau 1754–62*, Harmondsworth: Penguin Books.

Crocker, L. (1963) *Nature and Culture: Ethical Thought in the French Enlightenment*, Baltimore: Johns Hopkins University Press.

Cropsey, J. (1957) *Polity and Economy: An Interpretation of Adam Smith*, The Hague: M. Nijhoff.

Cumming, R. (1969) *Human Nature and History: A Study of the Development of Liberal Political Thought*, Chicago: University of Chicago Press.

Daiches, D. (1964) *The Paradox of Scottish Culture – The Eighteenth Century Experience*, London: Oxford University Press.

Danford, J. (1990) *David Hume and the Problem of Reason*, New Haven: Yale University Press.

Darnton, R. (1971) 'In search of the Enlightenment', *Journal of Modern History*, 43, 113–32.

Davidson, D. (1984) 'On the very idea of a Conceptual Scheme' in his *Inquiries into Truth and Interpretation*, Oxford: Clarendon Press, pp. 183–98.

Davie, G. (1967) 'Hume, Reid and the passion for ideas' in D. Young (ed.), *Edinburgh in the Age of Reason*, Edinburgh: Edinburgh University Press, pp. 23–39.

(1981) *The Scottish Enlightenment*, London: Historical Association, pamphlet no. 99.

Davis, D. (1966) *The Problem of Slavery in Western Culture*, Ithaca: Cornell University Press.

Dedieu, J. (1909) *Montesquieu et la tradition politique anglaise*, Paris: Lecoffre.

Devine, T. (1985) 'The Union of 1707 and Scottish development', *Scottish Economic and Social History*, 5, 23–40.

Dickey, L. (1986) 'Historicizing the "Adam Smith Problem"', *Journal of Modern History*, 58, 579–609.

Dickinson, H. (1977) *Liberty and Property: Political Ideology in Eighteenth Century Britain*, London: Weidenfeld & Nicolson.

Dilthey, W. (1927) *Das Achtzehnte Jahrhundert und die Geschichtliche Welt* in his *Gesammelte Schriften*, Stuttgart: Teubner, vol. 3, pp. 209–68.

Donaldson, G. (1981) 'Stair's Scotland: the intellectual inheritance', *Juridical Review*, 26, 128–45.

Donovan, A (1982) 'William Cullen and the research tradition of eighteenth century Scottish chemistry' in R. Campbell & A. Skinner (eds.), *Origins and Nature of the Scottish Enlightenment*, pp. 98–114.

Durie, A. (1979) *The Scottish Linen Industry in the Eighteenth Century*, Edinburgh: John Donald.

Dwyer, J. (1987) *Virtuous Discourse: Sensibility and Community in Late Eighteenth Century Scotland*, Edinburgh: John Donald.

Dwyer, J. & Murdoch, A. (1983) 'Paradigms and politics: manners, morals and the rise of Henry Dundas, 1770–1784' in J. Dwyer, R. Mason & A. Murdoch (eds.), *New Perspectives on the Politics*, Edinburgh: John Donald, pp. 210–48.

Emerson, R. (1973) 'The social composition of Enlightened Scotland: the Select Society of Edinburgh 1754–64', *Studies in Voltaire*, 114, 291–329.

(1984) 'Conjectural history and the Scottish philosophers', *Historical Papers of the Canadian Historical Association*, 63–90.

(1986) 'Natural philosophy and the problem of the Scottish Enlightenment', *Studies in Voltaire*, 242, 243–88.

(1988a) 'Science and the origins and concerns of the Scottish Enlightenment', *History of Science*, 26, 333–66.

(1988b) 'Sir Robert Sibbald, The Royal Society of Scotland and the origins of the Scottish Enlightenment', *Annals of Science*, 45, 41–72.

(1988c) 'Lord Bute and the Scottish universities, 1760–92' in K. Schweizer (ed.), *Lord Bute: Essays in Re-interpretation*, Leicester: Leicester University Press, pp. 147–79.

(1989) 'The religious, the secular and the worldly: Scotland 1680–1800' in J. Crimmins (ed.), *Religion, Secularization and Political Thought*, London: Routledge, pp. 68–89.

(1990) 'Science and moral philosophy in the Scottish Enlightenment' in M. Stewart (ed.), *Studies in the Philosophy of the Scottish Enlightenment*, pp. 11–36.

(1992) *Professors, Patronage and Politics: The Aberdeen Universities in the Eighteenth Century*, Aberdeen: Aberdeen University Press.

(1993) 'Medical men, politicians and the medical schools at Glasgow and Edinburgh, 1685–1803' in R. Passmore (ed.), *William Cullen and the Medical World of the Eighteenth Century*, Edinburgh: Edinburgh University Press, pp. 186–215.

(1995) 'Did the Scottish Enlightenment emerge in an English cultural province?', *Lumen*, 15, 1–22.

Evans-Pritchard, E. (1981) *A History of Anthropological Thought*, London: Faber & Faber.

Fagerstrom, D. (1954) 'Scottish opinion and the American Revolution', *William and Mary Quarterly*, 11, 252–75.

Fagg, J. (1995) 'Biographical introduction' in V. Merolle (ed.), Ferguson's *Correspondence*, pp. xix–cxvii.

Farr, J. (1978) 'Hume, Hermeneutics and history: a "sympathetic" account', *History and Theory*, 17, 285–320.

Fletcher, F. (1980) *Montesquieu and English Politics 1750–1800* (1939), Philadelphia: Porcupine Press.

Fletcher, R. (1972) *The Making of Sociology: vol. 1*, London: Nelson.

Flew, A. (1986) *David Hume: Philosopher of Moral Science*, Oxford: Blackwell.

Flynn, J. (1980) 'Scottish aesthetics and the search for a standard of taste', *Dalhousie Review*, 60, 5–19.

Foerster, D. (1950) 'Scottish primitivism and the historical approach', *Philological Quarterly*, 29, 307–23.

Forbes, D. (1954) 'Scientific Whiggism: Adam Smith and John Millar', *Cambridge Journal*, 7, 643–70.

(1967) 'Adam Ferguson and the idea of Community' in D. Young (ed.), *Edinburgh in the Age of Reason*, Edinburgh: Edinburgh University Press, pp. 40–47.

(1975a) *Hume's Philosophical Politics*, Cambridge: Cambridge University Press.

(1975b) 'Sceptical Whiggism, commerce and liberty' in A. Skinner & T. Wilson (eds.), *Essays on Adam Smith*, pp. 179–201.

(1977) 'Hume's science of politics' in G. Morice (ed.), *David Hume: Bicentenary Papers*, Edinburgh: Edinburgh University Press, pp. 39–50.

(1979) 'Hume and the Scottish Enlightenment' in S. Brown (ed.), *Philosophers of the Enlightenment*, pp. 94–109.

(1982) 'Natural Law and the Scottish Enlightenment' in R. Campbell & A. Skinner (eds.), *Origins and Nature of the Scottish Enlightenment*, pp. 186–204.

Ford, F. (1965) *Robe and Sword: The Regrouping of the French Aristocracy after Louis XIV*, New York: Harper.

(1968) 'The Enlightenment: towards a useful definition' in R. Brissenden (ed.), *Studies in the Eighteenth Century*, Canberra: Australian National University Press, pp. 17–29.

Frankel, C. (1948) *The Faith of Reason*, New York: Octagon Books.

Frankena, W. (1955) 'Hutcheson's moral sense theory', *Journal of the History of Ideas*, 16, 356–75.

Gaskin, J. (1993) 'Hume on religion' in D. Norton (ed.), *Cambridge Companion to Hume*, pp. 313–44.

Gates, W. (1967) 'The spread of Ibn Khaldun's ideas on climate', *Journal of the History of Ideas*, 28, 415–22.

Gauthier, D. (1979) 'David Hume: Contractarian', *Philosophical Review*, 88, 3–38.

Gay, P. (1967) *The Enlightenment: The Rise of Modern Paganism*, London: Weidenfeld & Nicolson.

(1970) *The Enlightenment: The Science of Freedom*, London: Weidenfeld & Nicolson.

Geertz, C. (1972) *The Interpretation of Cultures*, New York: Basic Books.

Giarrizzo, G. (1962) *David Hume: Politico e Storico*, Turin: Einaudi.

Gierke, O. (1934) *Natural Law and the Theory of Society*, 2 vols, tr. E. Barker, Cambridge: Cambridge University Press.

Glacken, C. (1967) *Traces on the Rhodian Shore: Nature and Culture in Western Thought*, Berkeley: University of California Press.

Goldie, M. (1993) 'Priestcraft and the birth of Whiggism' in N. Phillipson & Q. Skinner (eds.), *Political Discourse in Early Modern Britain*, pp. 209–31.

Goldmann, L. (1973) *The Philosophy of the Enlightenment: The Christian Burgess and the Enlightenment*, tr. H. Maus, London: Routledge & Kegan Paul.

Goldsmith, M. (1994) 'Liberty, virtue and the rule of law, 1689–1770' in D. Wootton (ed.), *Republicanism, Liberty and Commercial Society 1649–1776*, pp. 197–232.

Gouldner, A. (1967) *Enter Plato*, London: Routledge & Kegan Paul.

Graham, H. (1901) *Scottish Men of Letters in the Eighteenth Century*, London: A. & C. Black.

Grave, S. (1960) *Scottish Philosophy of Common Sense*, Oxford: Clarendon Press.

Gray, J. (1984) *Hayek on Liberty*, Oxford: Blackwell.

Greene, J. (1961) *The Death of Adam: Evolution and its Impact on Western Thought*, New York: Mentor Books.

Grene, M. (1943) 'Gerard's "Essay on Taste"', *Modern Philology*, 41 , 45–58.

Gusdorf, G. (1971) *Les Principes de la pensée au siècle des lumières*, Paris: Payot.

Guthrie, D. (1950) 'William Cullen and his times' in A. Kent (ed.), *An Eighteenth Century Lectureship in Chemistry*, Glasgow: Jackson pp. 49–65.

Haakonssen, K. (1981) *The Science of a Legislator*, Cambridge: Cambridge University Press.

(1985) 'John Millar and the science of a legislator', *The Juridical Review*, 30, 41–68.

(1988) 'Moral philosophy and natural law: from the Cambridge Platonists to the Scottish Enlightenment', *Political Science*, 40, 97–110.

(1990) 'Natural law and moral realism: the Scottish synthesis' in M. A. Stewart (ed.), *Studies in the Philosophy of the Scottish Enlightenment*, pp. 61–85.

Hall, A. R. (1970) *From Galileo to Newton 1630–1720*, London: Fontana Books.

Hall, J. A. (1986) *Powers and Liberties: The Causes and Consequences of the Rise of the West*, Harmondsworth: Penguin Books.

(1988) *Liberalism: Politics, Ideology and the Market*, London: Paladin Books.

Hamilton, H. (1963) *An Economic History of Scotland in the Eighteenth Century*, Oxford: Clarendon Press.

Hamowy, R. (1987) *The Scottish Enlightenment and the Theory of Spontaneous Order*, Carbondale: Southern Illinois University Press.

Hankins, T. (1985) *Science and the Enlightenment*, Cambridge: Cambridge University Press.

Harpham, E. (1984) 'Liberalism, civic humanism and the case of Adam Smith', *American Political Science Review*, 78, 764–74.

Harrison, J. (1976) *Hume's Moral Epistemology*, Oxford: Clarendon Press.

(1981) *Hume's Theory of Justice*, Oxford: Clarendon Press.

Hastings, H. (1936) *Man and Beast in French Thought in the Eighteenth Century*, Baltimore: Johns Hopkins University Press.

Hayek, F. (1966) 'The legal and political philosophy of David Hume' in V. Chappell (ed.), *Hume*, pp. 335–60.

(1967) *Studies in Philosophy, Politics and Economics*, London: Routledge & Kegan Paul.

(1972) *The Constitution of Liberty* (1960), Chicago: Gateway.

(1978) *New Studies in Philosophy, Politics, Economics and the History of Ideas*, London: Routledge & Kegan Paul.

(1982) *Law, Legislation and Liberty* (3 vols. in 1), London: Routledge & Kegan Paul.

Henderson, H. (1920) *Religion in Scotland*, Paisley: A. Gardner.

Hirschman, A. (1977) *The Passions and the Interests: Political Arguments for Capitalism before its Triumph*, Princeton: Princeton University Press.

Hobsbawm, E. (1980) 'Scottish Reformers of the eighteenth century and capitalist agriculture' in his *Peasants in History*, Calcutta: Oxford University Press, pp. 3–29.

Hont, I. (1987) 'The language of sociability and commerce: S. Pufendorf and the theoretical foundations of the "four stages" theory' in A. Pagden (ed.), *The Languages of Political Theory in Early Modern Europe*, pp. 253–76.

(1993) 'The rhapsody of public debt: Hume and voluntary state bankruptcy' in N. Phillipson & Q. Skinner (eds.), *Political Discourse in Early Modern Britain*, pp. 321–48.

Hont, I. & Ignatieff, M. (eds.) (1983) *Wealth and Virtue: The Shaping of Political Economy in the Scottish Enlightenment*, Cambridge: Cambridge University Press.

Hook, A. & Sher, R. (eds.) (1995) *The Glasgow Enlightenment*, East Linton: Tuckwell Press.

Hope, V. (1989) *Virtue by Consensus*, Oxford: Clarendon Press.

Höpfl, H. (1978) 'From savage to Scotsman: conjectural history in the Scottish Enlightenment', *Journal of British Studies*, 7, 20–40.

Horn, A. (1965) 'Kames and the anthropological approach to criticism', *Philological Quarterly*, 44, 211–33.

Horn, D. (1956) 'Robertson as historian', *University of Edinburgh Journal*, 18, 155–68.

Horne, T. (1990) *Property Rights and Society: Political Argument in Britain 1605–1834*, Chapel Hill: University of North Carolina Press.

Howell, W. (1971) *Eighteenth Century British Logic and Rhetoric*, Princeton: Princeton University Press.

Hunter, M. (1992) 'Aikenhead the atheist: the context and consequences of Articulate Irreligion in the late seventeenth century' in M. Hunter & D. Wootton (eds.), *Atheism from the Reformation to the Enlightenment*, Oxford: Clarendon Press, pp. 221–54.

Ignatieff, M. (1983) 'John Millar and individualism' in I. Hont & M. Ignatieff (eds.), *Wealth and Virtue*, pp. 317–43.

(1984) *The Needs of Strangers*, London: Chatto & Windus.

Immerwahr, J. (1992) 'Hume's revised racism', *Journal of the History of Ideas*, 53, 481–86.

Jack, M. (1989) *Corruption and Progress: The Eighteenth Century Debate*, New York: AMS Press.

Jenkins, J. (1992) *Understanding Hume*, Edinburgh: Edinburgh University Press.

Jensen, H. (1972) *Motivation and Moral Sense in Francis Hutcheson's Moral Theory*, The Hague: M. Nijhoff.

Jones, P. (1976) 'Hume's aesthetics re-assessed', *Philosophical Quarterly*, 26, 48–62.

(1983) *Hume's Sentiments*, Edinburgh: Edinburgh University Press.

Jones, P. (ed.) (1988) *Philosophy and Science in the Scottish Enlightenment*, Edinburgh: John Donald.

(ed.) (1989) *The Science of Man in the Scottish Enlightenment*, Edinburgh: Edinburgh University Press.

Kemp Smith, N. (1964) *The Philosophy of David Hume* (1941), London: Macmillan.

Keohane, N. (1980) *Philosophy and the State in France*, Princeton: Princeton University Press.

Kenyon, J. (1977) *Revolution Principles: The Politics of Party 1689–1720*, Cambridge: Cambridge University Press.

Kettler, D. (1965) *Social and Political Thought of Adam Ferguson*, Columbus: Ohio State University Press.

(1977) 'History and theory in Ferguson's *Essay on the History of Civil Society*: a reconsideration', *Political Theory*, 5, 437–60.

Kidd, C. (1993) *Subverting Scotland's Past: Scottish Whig Historians and the creation of an Anglo-British Identity 1689–c1800*, Cambridge: Cambridge University Press.

(1995) 'Antiquarianism, religion and the Scottish Enlightenment', *The Innes Review*, 46, 139–54.

(1996) 'North Britishness and the nature of eighteenth century British patriotisms', *The Historical Journal*, 39, 361–82.

Kivy, P. (1976) *The Seventh Sense: A Study of Francis Hutcheson's Aesthetics*, New York: Burt Franklin.

Klein, L. (1994) *Shaftesbury and the Culture of Politeness*, Cambridge: Cambridge University Press.

Knight, I. (1968) *The Geometric Spirit: The Abbé de Condillac and the French Enlightenment*, New Haven: Yale University Press.

Knight, W. (1900) *Lord Monboddo and some of his Contemporaries*, London: John Murray.

Kukathas, C. (1989) *Hayek and Modern Liberalism*, Oxford: Clarendon Press.

Labouchiex, H. (1970) *Richard Price: théoricien de la révolution américaine*, Paris: Didier.

Labrousse, E. (1983) *Bayle*, tr. D. Potts, Oxford: Oxford University Press.

Lacoste, L. (1976) 'The consistency of Hume's position concerning women', *Dialogue*, 15, 425–40.

Lamb, R. (1973) 'Adam Smith's concept of alienation', *Oxford Economic Papers*, 25, 275–85.

Land, S. (1977) 'Adam Smith's "considerations concerning the first formation of languages"', *Journal of the History of Ideas*, 38, 677–90.

Landsman, N. (1991) 'Presbyterians and provincial society: the Evangelical Enlightenment in the west of Scotland, 1740–55, *Eighteenth Century Life*, 15, 194–209.

Lawrence, C. (1979) 'The nervous system and society in the Scottish Enlightenment' in B. Barnes & S. Shapin (eds.), *Natural Order*, London: Sage, pp. 19–40.

Lehmann, W. (1930) *Adam Ferguson and the Beginnings of Modern Sociology*, New York: Columbia University Press.

(1952) 'John Millar – historical sociologist', *British Journal of Sociology*, 2, 30–46.

(1960) *John Millar of Glasgow*, Cambridge: Cambridge University Press.

(1971) *Henry Home, Lord Kames and the Scottish Enlightenment*, The Hague: M. Nifhoff.

Lenman, B. (1981) *Integration, Enlightenment and Industrialization: Scotland 1746–1832*, London: E. Arnold.

Leith, J. (1971) 'Peter Gay's Enlightenment', *Eighteenth Century Studies*, 5, 157–71.

Lenz, J. (1966) 'Hume's defense of causal inference' in V. Chappell (ed.), *Hume*, pp. 169–86.

Lessnoff, M. (1986) *Social Contract*, London: Macmillan.

Lieberman, D. (1989) *The Province of Legislation Determined: Legal Theory in Eighteenth Century Britain*, Cambridge: Cambridge University Press.

Lindgren, J. (1969) 'Adam Smith's theory of inquiry', *Journal of Political Economy*, 77, 897–915.

Livingston, D. (1984) *Hume's Philosophy of Common Life*, Chicago: University of Chicago Press.

(1990) 'Hume's historical conception of liberty' in N. Capaldi & D. Livingston (eds.), *Liberty in Hume's 'History of England'*, pp. 105–53.

Longuet-Higgins, C. (1992) '"The History of Astronomy": a twentieth century view' in P. Jones & A. Skinner (eds.), *Adam Smith Reviewed*, Edinburgh: Edinburgh University Press, pp. 79–92.

Lough, J. (1971) *The Encyclopédie*, London: Longman.

MacCormick. N. (1982) 'Law and Enlightenment' in R. Campbell & A. Skinner (eds.), *Origin and Nature of the Scottish Enlightenment*, pp. 150–66.

McDowall. G. (1983) 'Commerce, virtue and politics: Adam Ferguson's Constitutionalism', *Review of Politics*, 45, 536–52.

McElroy, D. (1969) *Scotland's Age of Improvement*, Pullman: Washington State University Press.

MacFie, A. (1967) *The Individual in Society: Papers on Adam Smith*, London: G. Allen & Unwin.

(1971) 'The invisible hand of Jupiter', *Journal of the History of Ideas*, 32, 595–99.

MacIntytre, A. (1967) 'A mistake about Causality in Social Science' in P. Laslett & G. Runciman (eds.), *Politics, Philosophy and Society (II)*, Oxford: Blackwell, pp. 48–70.

(1985) *After Virtue*, 2nd edn, London: Duckworth.

(1988) *Whose Justice? Which Rationality?*, London: Duckworth.

Mackenzie, G. (1949) *Critical Responsiveness: A Study of the Psychological Current in later Eighteenth Century Criticism*, University of California Publications, no. 20.

Mackie , J. (1980) *Hume's Moral Theory*, London: Routledge & Kegan Paul.

McManners, J. (1985) *Death and the Enlightenment*, Oxford: Oxford University Press.

McNally, D. (1988) *Political Economy and the Rise of Capitalism*, Berkeley: University of California Press.

Macpherson, C. (1962) *The Political Theory of Possessive Individualism*, Oxford: Clarendon Press.

(1973) *Democratic Theory: Essays in Retrieval*, Oxford: Clarendon Press.

(1978) 'The economic penetration of political theory', *Journal of the History of Ideas*, 39, 101–10.

MacQueen, J. (1982) *The Enlightenment and Scottish Literature: Progress and Poetry*, Edinburgh: Scottish Academic Press.

MacRae, D. (1969) 'Adam Ferguson' in T. Raison (ed.), *Founding Fathers of Sociology*, Harmondsworth: Penguin Books, pp. 17–26.

Malson, L. (1972) *Wolf Children*, tr. E. Fawcett, London: New Left Books.

Manuel, F. (1959) *The Eighteenth Century confronts the Gods*, Cambridge, Mass.: Harvard University Press.

(1962) *Prophets of Paris*, Cambridge, Mass.: Harvard University Press.

Markus, T. (1982) 'Buildings for the sad, the bad and the mad in urban Scotland 1780–1830' in T. Markus (ed.), *Order in Space: Architectural Form and its Context in the Scottish Enlightenment*, Edinburgh: Mainstream, pp. 25–114.

(1988) 'Buildings and the orderings of minds and bodies' in P. Jones (ed.), *Philosophy and Science in the Scottish Enlightenment*, pp. 169–224.

Mason, S. (1975) *Montesquieu's Idea of Justice*, The Hague: M. Nijhoff.

Mathew, T. (1966) 'Origins and occupations of Glasgow students 1740–1839', *Past and Present*, 33, 74–94.

Medick, H. (1973) *Naturzustand und Naturgeschichte der bürgerlichen Gesellschaft*, Göttingen: Vandenhoeck & Ruprecht.

Medick, H. & Leppert- Fögen, A. (1974) 'Frühe Sozialwissenschaft als Ideologie des kleinens Bürgertums: J. Millar of Glasgow' in H. Wehler (ed.), *Sozialgeschichte Heute*, Göttingen: Vandenhoeck & Ruprecht, pp. 22–48.

Medick, H. & Batscha, Z. (1988) *Einleitung: A. Ferguson Versuch über die Geschichte der bürgerlichen Gesellschaft*, Frankfurt-am-Main: Suhrkamp.

Meek, R. (1954) 'The Scottish contribution to Marxist sociology' in J. Saville (ed.), *Democracy and the Labour Movement*, London: Lawrence & Wishart, pp. 84–102.

(1976) *Social Science and the Ignoble Savage*, Cambridge: Cambridge University Press.

(1977) 'Smith, Turgot and the "four stages" theory' in his *Smith, Marx and After*, London: Chapman & Hall, pp. 18–32.

Meikle, H. (1947) 'Some aspects of later seventeenth century Scotland', David Murray Lecture, Glasgow: Jackson.

Mercer, P. (1972) *Sympathy and Ethics*, Oxford: Clarendon Press.

Miller, D. (1980) 'Hume and possessive individualism', *History of Political Thought*, 1, 261–78.

(1981) *Philosophy and Ideology in Hume's Political Thought*, Oxford: Clarendon Press.

Miller, T. (1995) 'Francis Hutcheson and the civic humanist tradition' in A. Hook & R. Sher (eds.), *The Glasgow Enlightenment*, pp. 40–55.

Mitchison, R. (1962) *Agricultural Sir John: The life of Sir John Sinclair of Ulbster 1754–1835*, London: G. Bles.

Mizuta, H. (1975) 'Moral philosophy and civil society' in A. Skinner & T. Wilson (eds.), *Essays on Adam Smith*, pp. 114–31.

(1976) 'Toward a definition of the Scottish Enlightenment', *Studies in Voltaire*, 154, 1459–64.

(1981) 'Two Adams in the Scottish Enlightenment: Adam Smith and Adam Ferguson on progress', *Studies in Voltaire*, 191, 812–19.

Moore, J. (1977) 'Hume's political science and the classical republican tradition', *Canadian Journal of Political Science*, 10, 809–39.

(1994) 'Hume and Hutcheson' in M. Stewart &. J. Wright (eds.), *Hume and Hume's Connexions*, Edinburgh: Edinburgh University Press, pp. 23–57.

Moore, J. & Silverthorne, M. (1983) 'Gershom Carmichael and the natural jurisprudence tradition in eighteenth century Scotland' in I. Hont & M. Ignatieff (eds.), *Wealth and Virtue*, pp. 73–87.

(1984) 'Natural sociability and natural rights in the moral philosophy of Gershom Carmichael' in V. Hope (ed.), *Philosophers of the Scottish Enlightenment*, Edinburgh: Edinburgh University Press, pp. 1–12.

Morrice, G. (ed.) (1977) *David Hume: Bi-centenary Papers*, Edinburgh: Edinburgh University Press.

Mossner, E. (1977) 'Hume and the legacy of the *Dialogues*' in G. Morrice (ed.), *David Hume: Bi-centenary Papers*, pp. 1–22.

(1980) *Life of David Hume*, 2nd edn, Oxford: Clarendon Press.

Müller, M. (1875) *Lectures on the Science of Language*, 8th edn, 2 vols., London: Longmans Green.

Murdoch, A. (1980) *The People Above: Politics and Administration in mid-eighteenth Scotland*, Edinburgh: John Donald.

Murdoch, A. & Sher, R. (1989) 'Literary and Learned Culture' in T. Devine & R. Mitchison (eds.), *People and Society in Scotland*, vol. 1, Edinburgh: John Donald, pp. 127–42.

Norton, D. (1982) *David Hume: Common Sense Moralist, Sceptical Metaphysician*, Princeton: Princeton University Press.

(1985) 'Hutcheson's moral realism', *Journal of the History of Philosophy*, 23, 397–418.

(ed.) (1993) *Cambridge Companion to Hume*, Cambridge: Cambridge University Press.

Noxon, J. (1973) *Hume's Philosophical Development*, Oxford: Clarendon Press.

Oz-Salzburger, F. (1995) *Translating the Enlightenment: Scottish Civil Discourse in Eighteenth Century Germany*, Oxford: Clarendon Press.

Pagden, A. (ed.) (1987) *Languages of Political Theory in Early Modern Europe*, Cambridge: Cambridge University Press.

Pascal, R. (1938) 'Property and society: the Scottish historical school of the eighteenth century', *Modern Quarterly*, 1, 167–79.

Passmore, J. (1968) *Hume's Intentions*, revised edn, London: Duckworth.

(1970) *The Perfectibility of Man*, London: Duckworth.

(1971) 'The malleability of man in eighteenth century thought' in E. Wassermann (ed.), *Aspects of the Eighteenth Century*, Baltimore: Johns Hopkins University Press, pp. 21–46.

Payne, H. (1976) *The Philosophes and the People*, New Haven: Yale University Press.

Pearce, R. (1945) 'The eighteenth century Scottish Primitivists: some reconsiderations', *Journal of English Literary History*, 12, 203–20.

Phillipson, N. (1973a) 'Culture and society in the eighteenth century province: the case of Edinburgh and the Scottish Enlightenment' in L. Stone (ed.), *The University in Society*, vol. 1, Princeton: Princeton University Press, pp. 407–48.

(1973b) 'Towards a definition of the Scottish Enlightenment' in P. Fritz & D. Williams (eds.), *City and Society*, Toronto: Hakkert, pp. 125–47.

(1976) 'Lawyers, landowners and the civic leadership of post-Union Scotland', *Juridical Review*, 21, 97–120.

(1978) 'James Beattie and the defence of common sense' in B. Fabian (ed.), *Festschrift für Rainer Gruenter*, Heidelberg: C. Winter, pp. 145–54.

(1979) Hume as moralist: a social historian's perspective' in S. Brown (ed.), *The Philosophers of the Enlightenment*, pp. 140–61.

(1981) 'The Scottish Enlightenment', in *The Enlightenment in National Context*, R. Porter & M. Teich (eds.), Cambridge: Cambridge University Press, pp. 19–40.

(1983a) 'The pursuit of virtue in Scottish university education', in N. Phillipson (ed.), *Universities, Society and the Future*, Edinburgh: Edinburgh University Press, pp. 87–109.

(1983b) 'Adam Smith as Civic Moralist' in I. Hont & M. Ignatieff (eds.), *Wealth and Virtue*, pp. 179–202.

(1987) 'Politics, politeness and the anglicisation of early eighteenth century Scottish culture' in R. Mason (ed.), *Scotland and England 1286–1815*, Edinburgh: John Donald, pp. 226–46.

(1989) *Hume*, London: Weidenfeld & Nicolson.

(1993) 'Propriety, property and prudence; David Hume and the defence of the Revolution' in *Political Discourse in early modern Britain*, N. Phillipson & Q. Skinner (eds.), pp. 302–20.

Phillipson, N. & Mitchison, R. (eds) (1970) *Scotland in the Age of Improvement*, Edinburgh: Edinburgh University Press.

Phillipson, N. & Skinner, Q. (eds) (1993) *Political Discourse in Early Modern Britain*, Cambridge: Cambridge University Press.

Pittock, J. (1973) *The Ascendancy of Taste*, London: Routledge & Kegan Paul.

Pocock, J. (1962) 'The History of Political Thought: A methodological enquiry' in P. Laslett & G. Runciman (eds.), *Philosophy, Politics and Society* (2nd series), Oxford: Blackwell, pp. 183–202.

(1973) 'Languages and their implications' in his *Politics, Language and Time*, New York: Atheneum, pp. 3–41.

(1975) *The Machiavellian Moment*, Princeton: Princeton University Press.

(1983) 'Cambridge paradigms and Scottish philosophers' in I. Hont & M. Ignatieff (eds.), *Wealth and Virtue*, pp. 235–52.

(1985) *Virtue, Commerce and History*, Cambridge: Cambridge University Press.

(1987) 'The concept of a language and its *métier d'historien*' in A. Pagden (ed.), *The Languages of Political Theory in Early Modern Europe*, pp. 19–38.

Pompa, L. (1990) *Human Nature and Historical Knowledge: Hume, Hegel and Vico*, Cambridge: Cambridge University Press.

Popkin, R. (1977) 'Hume's racism', *Philosophical Forum*, 9, 211–26.

Porter, R. & Teich, M. (eds.) (1981) *The Enlightenment in National Context*, Cambridge: Cambridge University Press.

Rae, J. (1965) *Life of Adam Smith* (1895), J. Viner (ed.), New York: Kelley Reprints.

Raphael, D. (1947) *The Moral Sense*, London: Oxford University Press.

(1975) 'The impartial spectator' in A. Skinner & T. Wilson (eds.), *Essays on Adam Smith*, pp. 83–99.

(1979) 'Adam Smith: philosophy, science and social science' in S. Brown (ed.), *Philosophers of the Enlightenment*, pp. 77–93.

(1985) *Adam Smith*, Oxford: Oxford University Press.

Rayner, D. (1982) *Sister Peg: A Pamphlet hitherto unknown by David Hume*, Cambridge: Cambridge University Press.

Redman, D. (1993) 'Adam Smith and Isaac Newton', *Scottish Journal of Political Economy*, 40, 210–30.

Redwood, J. (1976) *Reason, Ridicule and Religion: The Age of Enlightenment in England 1660–1750*, London: Thames & Hudson.

Reisman, D. (1976) *Adam Smith's Sociological Economics*, London: Croom Helm.

Rendall, J. (1978) *The Origins of the Scottish Enlightenment 1707–1776*, London, Macmillan.

(1987) 'Virtue and commerce: women in the making of Adam Smith's political economy' in E. Kennedy & S. Mendus (eds.), *Women in Western Political Philosophy*, Brighton: Wheatsheaf, pp. 44–77.

Robbins, C. (1954) 'When it is that colonies may turn independent', *William and Mary Quarterly*, 11, 214–51.

(1959) *The Eighteenth Century Commonwealthman*, Cambridge, Mass: Harvard University Press.

Robertson, J. (1982) 'The Scottish Enlightenment at the limits of the civic tradition' in I. Hont & M. Ignatieff (eds.), *Wealth and Virtue*, pp. 137–78.

(1983) 'Scottish political economy beyond the civic tradition: government and economic development in the *Wealth of Nations*', *History of Political Thought*, 4, 451–82.

(1985) *The Scottish Enlightenment and the Militia Issue*, Edinburgh: John Donald.

Robinson, J. (1966) 'Hume's two definitions of cause' in V. Chappell (ed.), *Hume*, pp. 129–47.

Rosenberg, A. (1993) 'Hume and the philosophy of science' in D. Norton (ed.), *Cambridge companion to Hume*, pp. 64–89.

Rosenberg, N. (1965) 'Adam Smith on the division of labour: two views or one?', *Economica*, 32, 127–49.

Ross, I. (1972) *Lord Kames and the Scotland of his Day*, Oxford: Clarendon Press.

(1995a) *The Life of Adam Smith*, Oxford: Clarendon Press.

(1995b) 'Adam Smith's "Happiest" years as a Glasgow professor', in A. Hook & R. Sher (eds.), *The Glasgow Enlightenment*, pp. 73–94.

Salter, J. (1992) 'Adam Smith on feudalism, commerce and slavery', *History of Political Thought*, 13, 219–41.

Sampson, R. (1956) *Progress in the Age of Reason*, London: Heinemann.

Schneider, L. (1967) *Introduction to the Scottish Moralists on Human Nature and Society*, Chicago: University of Chicago Press.

Scott, W. (1966) *Francis Hutcheson: His Life, Teaching and Position in the History of Philosophy* (1900), New York: Kelley Economic Reprints.

Selby-Bigge, L. (ed.) (1964) *British Moralists* (1897), 2 vols. in one, Indianapolis: Bobbs-Merrill.

Shackleton, R. (1961) *Montesquieu: A Critical Biography*, Oxford: Clarendon Press.

Shaw, J. (1983) *The Management of Scottish Society 1707–64*, Edinburgh: John Donald.

Shepherd, C. (1982) 'Newtonianism in Scottish universities in the seventeenth century' in R. Campbell & A. Skinner (eds.), *The Origins and Nature of the Scottish Enlightenment*, pp. 65–85.

Sher, R. (1985) *Church and University in the Scottish Enlightenment*, Edinburgh: Edinburgh University Press.

(1989) 'Adam Ferguson, Adam Smith and the problem of national defense', *Journal of Modern History*, 61, 240–68.

(1994) 'From troglodytes to Americans: Montesquieu and the Scottish Enlightenment on liberty, virtue, and commerce' in D. Wootton (ed.), *Republicanism, Liberty, and Commercial Society 1649–1776*, Stanford: Stanford University Press, pp. 368–402.

Shklar, J. (1987) *Montesquieu*, Oxford: Oxford University Press.

Simpson, J. (1970) 'Who steered the gravy train, 1707–66' in N. Phillipson & R. Mitchison (eds.), *Scotland in the Age of Improvement*, pp. 47–72.

Skinner, A. (1965) 'Economics and history – the Scottish Enlightenment', *Scottish Journal of Political Economy*, 12, 1–22.

(1967) 'Natural history in the age of Adam Smith', *Political Studies*, 14, 32–48.

(1974a) *Adam Smith and the Role of the State*, Glasgow: University of Glasgow Press.

(1974b) 'Adam Smith, science and the role of imagination' in W. Todd (ed.), *Hume and the Enlightenment*, Edinburgh: Edinburgh University Press, pp. 164–78.

(1975) 'Adam Smith: an economic interpretation of history' in A. Skinner & T. Wilson (eds.), *Essays on Adam Smith*, pp. 154–78.

(1976) 'Adam Smith and the American economic community', *Journal of the History of Ideas*, 37, 59–78.

(1982) 'A Scottish contribution to Marxist sociology?' in I. Bradley & M. Howard (eds.) *Classical and Marxian Political Economy*, London: Macmillan, pp. 79–114.

Skinner, A. & Wilson, T. (eds.) (1975) *Essays on Adam Smith*, Oxford: Clarendon Press.

Skinner, Q. (1969) 'Meaning and understanding in the history of ideas', *History and Theory*, 9, 3–53.

Spadafora, D. (1990) *The Idea of Progress in Eighteenth Century Britain*, New Haven: Yale University Press.

Smout, T. (1969) *A History of the Scottish People 1560–1830*, London: Collins.

Stein, P. (1970) 'Law and society in eighteenth century Scottish thought' in N. Phillipson & R. Mitchison (eds.), *Scotland in the Age of Improvement*, pp. 148–68.

(1988) 'The four stages theory of the development of societies' in his *The Character and Influence of the Roman Civil Law*, London: The Hambledon Press, pp. 395–409.

Stewart, J, (1963) *The Moral and Political Philosophy of David Hume*, New York: Columbia University Press.

(1992) *Opinion and Reform in Hume's Political Philosophy*, Princeton: Princeton University Press.

Stewart, M. (ed.) (1990) *Studies in the Philosophy of the Scottish Enlightenment*, Oxford: Clarendon Press.

Stocking, G. (1975) 'Scotland as the model of mankind: Lord Kames' philosophical view of civilization' in T. Thoresen (ed.), *Toward a Science of Man*, The Hague: Mouton, pp. 65–89.

Stockton, C. (1976) 'Economics and the mechanism of historical progress in Hume's *History*', in D. Livingston & J. King (eds.), *Hume: A re-evaluation*, New York: Fordham University Press, pp. 296–320.

Strasser, H. (1976) *The Normative Structure of Sociology*, London: Routledge & Kegan Paul.

Stromberg, R. (1951) 'History in the eighteenth century', *Journal of the History of Ideas*, 12, 295–304.

Struthers, G. (1848) *History of the Rise, Progress and Principles of the Relief Church*, Edinburgh: Fullarton.

Swingewood, A. (1970) 'Origins of sociology: the case of the Scottish Enlightenment', *British Journal of Sociology*, 21, 164–80.

(1984) *A Short History of Sociological Thought*, London: Macmillan.

Teggart, F. (1925) *Theory of History*, New Haven: Yale University Press.

Teichgraeber, R. (1986) *'Free Trade' and Moral Philosophy*, Durham, NC: Duke University Press.

Thomas, D. (1977) *The Honest Mind: The Thought and Work of Richard Price* Oxford: Clarendon Press.

Thompson, M. (1976) 'The reception of Locke's *Two Treatises of Government* 1690–1705', *Political Studies*, 19, 184–91.

(1977) 'Hume's critique of Locke and the "Original Contract"', *Il Pensiero Politico*, 10, 189–201.

Trevor-Roper, H. (1958) *Historical Essays*, London: Macmillan.

(1963) 'The historical philosophy of the Enlightenment', *Studies in Voltaire*, 37, 1667–87.

(1967) 'The Scottish Enlightenment', *Studies in Voltaire*, 58 , 1635–58.

(1977) 'The Scottish Enlightenment', *Blackwood's Magazine*, 322, 371–88.

Tuck, R. (1979) *Natural Rights Theory*, Cambridge: Cambridge University Press.

(1993) *Philosophy and Government, 1572–1651*, Cambridge: Cambridge University Press.

Tully, J. (ed.) (1988) *Meaning and Context: Quentin Skinner and his Critics*, Cambridge: Polity Press.

Ulman, L. (1990) *The Minutes of the Aberdeen Philosophical Society 1758–1773*, Aberdeen: Aberdeen University Press.

Vartanian, A. (1952) *Diderot and Descartes: A Study in Scientific Naturalism in the Enlightenment*, Princeton: Princeton University Press.

Venturi, F. (1971) *Utopia and Reform in the Enlightenment*, Cambridge: Cambridge University Press.

Vereker, C. (1967) *Eighteenth Century Optimism*, Liverpool: Liverpool University Press.

Vlachos, G. (1955) *Essai sur la politique de Hume*, Paris: Institut Français Athènes.

Voges, F. (1986) 'Moderate and evangelical thinking in the later eighteenth century: differences and shared attitudes', *Scottish Church History Society Records*, 22, 141–57.

Walsh, W. (1975) 'The constancy of human nature' in H. Lewis (ed.), *Contemporary British Philosophy*, London: G. Allen & Unwin, pp. 181–98.

Walton, C. (1990) 'Hume's *England* as a natural history of morals' in N. Capaldi & D. Livingston (eds.), *Liberty in Hume's History of England*, pp. 25–52.

Waring, E. (1967) *Deism and Natural Religion: A Source Book*, New York: Ungar.

Webster, C. (1975) *The Great Instauration: Science, Medicine and Reform 1626–1660*, London: Duckworth.

Werhane, P. (1991) *Adam Smith and his Legacy for Modern Capitalism*, New York: Oxford University Press.

Wertz, S. (1975) 'Hume, history and human nature', *Journal of the History of Ideas*, 36, 481–96.

West, E. G. (1969) 'The political economy of alienation: Karl Marx and Adam Smith', *Oxford Economic Papers*, 21, 1–23.

(1975) 'Adam Smith and Alienation' in A. Skinner & T. Wilson (eds.), *Essays on Adam Smith*, pp. 540–52.

Whelan, F. (1985) *Order and Artifice in Hume's Political Philosophy*, Princeton: Princeton University Press.

White, H. (1973) *Metahistory: The Historical Imagination of Nineteenth Century Europe*, Baltimore: Johns Hopkins University Press.

Whitney, L. (1924) 'English primitivistic theories of epic origins', *Modern Philology*, 21, 337–78.

Wilson, A. (1972) *Diderot*, New York: Oxford University Press.

Winch, D. (1978) *Adam Smith's Politics*, Cambridge: Cambridge University Press.

(1983) 'Adam Smith's "enduring particular result"' in I. Hont & M. Ignatieff (eds.), *Wealth and Virtue*, pp. 253–69.

(1988) 'Adam Smith and the Liberal Tradition' in K. Haakonssen (ed.), *Traditions of Liberalism*, St Leonards NSW: Centre for Independent Studies, pp. 83–104.

Winch, P. (1958) *The Idea of a Social Science*, London: Routledge & Kegan Paul.

(1971) 'Understanding a primitive society' in B. Wilson (ed.), *Rationality*, New York: Harper Row, pp. 78–111.

Winkler, K. (1985) 'Hutcheson's alleged realism', *Journal of the History of Philosophy*, 23, 179–94.

Withrington, D. (1987) 'What was distinctive about the Scottish Enlightenment' in J. Carter & J. Pittock (eds.), *Aberdeen and the Enlightenment*, pp. 9–19.

Wokler, R. (1976) 'Tyson and Buffon on the Orang-utan', *Studies in Voltaire*, 155, 1–19.

(1988) 'Apes and races in the Scottish Enlightenment' in P. Jones (ed.), *Philosophy and Science in the Scottish Enlightenment*, pp. 145–68.

Wood, N. (1972) 'The value of asocial sociability' in M. Fleisher (ed.), *Machiavelli and the Nature of Political Thought*, New York: Atheneum, pp. 282–307.

Wood, P. (1989) 'The natural history of man in the Scottish Enlightenment', *History of Science*, 27, 89–123.

(1993) *The Aberdeen Enlightenment: The Arts Curricula in the Eighteenth Century*, Aberdeen: Aberdeen University Press.

Wootton, D. (1993) 'David Hume "the historian"' in D. Norton (ed.), *The Cambridge Companion to Hume*, pp. 281–312.

(ed.) (1994) *Republicanism, Liberty and Commercial Society 1649–1776*, Stanford: Stanford University Press.

Wright, J. (1983) *The Sceptical Realism of David Hume*, Manchester: Manchester University Press.

(1990) 'Metaphysics and physiology: mind, body and the animal economy in eighteenth century Scotland' in M. Stewart (ed.), *Studies in the Philosophy of the Scottish Enlightenment*, pp. 251–301.

Young, J. (1979) *The Rousing of the Scottish Working Class*, London: Croom Helm.

Youngson, A. (1972) *After the Forty-Five: The Economic Impact on the Scottish Highlands*, Edinburgh: Edinburgh University Press.

Zachs, W. (1992) *Without Regard to Good Manners: A Biography of Gilbert Stuart*, Edinburgh, Edinburgh University Press.

Index